Multiple Perspectives on Mathematics Teaching and Learning

Edited by Jo Boaler

International Perspectives on Mathematics Education
Leone Burton, *Series Editor*

ABLEX PUBLISHING
Westport, CT • London

Library of Congress Cataloging-in-Publication Data

Multiple perspectives on mathematics teaching and learning / edited by Jo Boaler.
    p. cm.—(International perspectives on mathematics education, ISSN 1530–3993 ;
    v. 1)
    Includes bibliographical references and indexes.
    ISBN 1–56750–534–1 (cloth)—ISBN 1–56750–535–X (pbk.)
    1. Mathematics—Study and teaching. I. Boaler, Jo, 1964- II. Series.
    QA11 .M79 2000
    510′.71—dc21   00–035567

British Library Cataloguing in Publication Data is available.

Library of Congress Catalog Card Number: 00–035567
ISBN: 1–56750–534–1
    1–56750–535–X (pbk.)
ISSN: 1530–3993

First published in 2000

Ablex Publishing, 88 Post Road West, Westport, CT 06881
An imprint of Greenwood Publishing Group, Inc.
www.greenwood.com

Printed in the United States of America

The paper used in this book complies with the
Permanent Paper Standard issued by the National
Information Standards Organization (Z39.48–1984).

10 9 8 7 6 5 4 3 2 1

Contents

Series Editor's Preface

Leone Burton

With this book, *Multiple Perspective on Mathematics Teaching and Learning*, we begin a new venture in the publishing of mathematics education literature. It is very appropriate that this, the first book in the series *International Perspectives on Mathematics Education*, should appear in the year 2000 and also in the year of the Ninth International Congress of Mathematical Education, a gathering that is only held every 4 years. I hope this series will accomplish a number of things for the current and potential community of mathematics educators. One is to offer a book, per year, that will be thematized to an issue of current concern, siting and justifying that issue with respect to the field of mathematics education as a whole. Another is to build a library of books that, through the themes which are their foci, provide a valuable resource. A third is to celebrate the internationality of the field and, through this, build connections between researchers and practitioners in very different contexts, underlining their similarities *and* their differences. I also hope the books will open and project a future perspective rather than simply reflecting a past, even if that past has been creative. Finally, it is my hope that the books in this series will, themselves, act as mechanisms for communicating an approach to mathematics education that is eclectic and embracing, respectful and engaging, reflective and, ultimately, educational.

Each book contains an opening chapter that synthesizes and summarizes its theme in order to provide an entry point for new researchers as well as concise overview for anyone already interested. The focus is forward looking. The first chapter should make available useful material to support those undertaking courses in research in mathematics education prior to starting some personal research.

The chapters contained in each book have been gathered by its editor(s) from an international search and reflect the globality of the field. In my view, too many previously published mathematics education collections have been rooted in a single, or limited number of, country's experiences and I hoped that this series will break that pattern. Not only is this an undertaking that should be of benefit to readers by making available the complexity of the theme when viewed from very different national perspectives, but also, I hope, it will provide publishing opportunities for authors who, in the past, have found it difficult to make their voices heard. As series editor, I would like to make clear my personal commitment to this endeavour. I hope to be able to pair colleagues from rich countries advantaged by resources and research writing know-how with those in poorer countries where research is difficult and often unsupported so that, jointly, they can achieve a publication rooted in the data collection of one, contextualized and supported into the rich range of resources available to the other. I call upon anyone who is interested in being part of this new and challenging publishing endeavour to contact me, indicating their interests (as editor of a proposed volume, as first author with a research question to pursue, as second author interested in a question and in working collaboratively, or as a pair or team proposing a joint piece of research or writing).

We are often told that we live in interesting times. I suspect that some colleagues might replace the word "interesting" with other words that are less positive. However, in the field of mathematics education, I think we can observe an expansion and a deepening of approaches to what is a most complex area of enquiry. Such an effect is certainly provocative and consequently stimulating. Looking back to the work that was done in the 1970s and 1980s is informative for appreciating the impact of this process. Indeed, as new foci within mathematics education open, we sometimes see similar pathways being trodden as the content of mathematics becomes the primary interest, then the interactions between that content and the learner or the teacher, or both, expand that interest until, eventually, the mathematics is seen as being one part of a leaning environment that is both multicontextual and multiperspectival, both sociocultural *and* personal. This book is an excellent example of this latter position. It makes very clear that its purpose is to surface a social perspective on mathematics education but, at no time, does it suggest a single approach. Indeed, Jo Boaler, the editor, points out that learning must be viewed as situated in, and of, the world and that it is the flow out and back that both defines and affects the complexity of the learning and the consequent difficulties facing the learner and the teacher. She does not need to apologize, therefore, for including chapters that have a "world" orientation from which the mathematics educator can move into more specific problematic questions, as well as chapters that begin in a particular mathematics classroom in order to frame an approach outwards to the world. But the authors in this book are oriented toward a better future for learners of mathematics rather than incremental changes that may or may not influence the discipline of mathematics, of mathematics education, or the classrooms in which learning is meant to happen.

To current or prospective teachers of mathematics, research has important and sometimes profound things to say. As researchers, teachers of mathematics can offer revelations on classroom practices, which are ignored at the peril of learning.

However, tensions exist between the communities of mathematicians, mathematics educators, and practitioners. I very much hope that this series will help to build a necessary bridge between these communities so that we can move toward a world where the learning of mathematics is no longer seen as boring or difficult, but as necessary to effective citizenry as the learning of any other discursive tool.

Acknowledgments

I would like to thank the different authors that appear in this book, for helping create this shared production and for making the process so collaborative. I would also like to thank the series editor, Leone Burton, for supporting the book idea and helping out in many aspects of the decision-making. The following were all willing and insightful chapter reviewers, to whom I am extremely grateful:

Deborah Loewenberg Ball

Leone Burton

Paul Cobb

Peter Gates

James G. Greeno

Colin Haysman

Ralph Putnam

Alan Schoenfeld

Reed Stevens

Dylan Wiliam

Robyn Zevenbergen

Special thanks go to Colin Haysman and Jim Greeno for their varied help and support throughout the book editing process.

—Jo Boaler

Introduction: Intricacies of Knowledge, Practice, and Theory

Jo Boaler

It is interesting to reflect upon the origins of edited collections. Usually they have a common subject—such as teacher education (Darling-Hammond & Sykes, 1999) or social justice within mathematics education (Keitel, 1998)—and frequently they emerge from conferences (Chaiklin & Lave, 1993; Greeno & Goldman, 1998). The chapters in this book have neither a common focus nor a common origin, but they share something that is important. The book was prompted by a general invitation from the series editor, Leone Burton, sent out to an electronic listing. It asked for proposals for edited collections that would appear as part of an annual, international series on mathematics education. This book is the first of that series. At the time I read the invitation in 1998, it seemed that mathematics education had reached a turning point and I wanted to capture a range of ideas that illustrated the shift that was taking place. Stephen Lerman's chapter, "The Social Turn in Mathematics Education," reflects on and describes in its title, the significant change that was—and is—occurring. But now, some months on, I am struck by a diversification of ideas in mathematics education, that extends further than the social turn to which Lerman refers. I offer a brief analysis here of this intriguing and important phenomenon, and what it may mean for mathematics education, as the introduction to this book.

"It is an exciting time to be an educational researcher" is a statement I have heard on numerous occasions over the past few years, particularly from those who have been important players in recent decades of educational research. The source of this excitement is the recognition that knowledge, once regarded as the property of individuals and the bastion of psychologists, may not simply be used in different settings, but emerge as a function of the settings, people, activities, and goals. The implications of this apparently subtle difference are profound and they are only gradually being realized in the educational academy. One of the consequences of the idea that knowledge is socially situated is an expansion and combination of the disciplines that are brought to bear on educational problems. For if knowledge is regarded as distributed among people, systems, and environments, then analyses of teaching and learning should no longer rely solely on psychological representations of the mind at work. They need also to recognize that learners function as part of broader worlds that are socially and culturally constituted; that they have affiliations as learners that intersect with ethnic, gendered, and other identities (Butler, 1993); that they are located within classrooms, schools, and communities; and that the practices in these settings co-determine their knowledge. It is no surprise then that anthropological, sociological, philosophical, political, and other disciplines that have been only minimally represented in mathematics education research in the past, are now being employed to produce broad and powerful analyses of mathematics teaching and learning. Any understanding of learning as participation in different communities of practice will be deeply enriched by the use of multiple perspectives. This book does not attempt to draw from all the disciplines that are gaining currency in the field of mathematics education, but the authors variously employ sociological, psychological, anthropological, political, sociocultural, and mathematical perspectives to produce new knowledge in the field.

Although the idea that knowledge is socially shared and that learning may be represented as participation in social practice has brought new vigor to the educational community; it has also brought tensions, confusions, and dilemmas. I will expand on these as they raise issues of some considerable importance to the theories and practices of teaching and learning. In describing my understanding of the tensions and misconceptions that surround situated theory, I must acknowledge a huge debt to my colleague Jim Greeno. His comprehensive analysis of these, which appeared in *Educational Researcher* in the early months of 1997, has greatly informed my thinking, along with many of our conversations. But I shall attempt to rephrase some of his ideas rather than simply reference his work, as both tensions and misconceptions prevail some years after Greeno's examination of these.

Evidence of the conflict that surrounds the situative challenge to previous models of cognition is provided by the dedication of two consecutive issues of *Educational Researcher* to the debate. Anecdotally, many of us who are interested in the ideas can probably also attest to frosty receptions, claims that situated theories are faddish, and concern from colleagues that situated perspectives are far too extreme. A major and recent publication within mathematics education—"Mathematics Education as a Research Domain: A Search for Identity"—reported the results of a study group of the International Commission on Mathematical Instruction (ICMI), that included some of the most significant researchers in mathematics education from around the world (Sierpinska & Kilpatrick, 1998). Situated perspectives are raised and promptly dismissed in the introduction to the book (although they recur in later chapters). The reason for their dismissal as a significant contributor to our field is attributed to a particular member of the study group who argued that "the idea of situated cognition is trivial: All knowledge is, of course, situated, contextual. But, he said, it is not always situated in real-life situations: There is an important part of mathematics that has to be learned not in authentic but in artificial situations" (Sierpinska & Kilpatrick, 1998, p. 12). This idea communicates a central misconception about situated theory. Others include the equivalence that is drawn between situated perspectives and certain teaching approaches, group and project work being the most common, and the confusion between constructivist and situated theories. These latter two combine when inquirers ask, how is situated teaching significantly different from constructivist teaching? Greeno (1997) demonstrated that Anderson, Reder, and Simon's (1996) challenges to the situated perspective were all based on misconceptions about situated ideas, and I would put these different questions in the same category. But if situated perspectives are to extend knowledge and enhance opportunities for learning, it is important that we move beyond such misconceptions to appreciate the additional insights that situated perspectives may bring.

Anderson, Reder, and Simon raised the following (paraphrased) objections to situated theories—statements with which many would undoubtedly concur: Not all action is situationally grounded; some knowledge does transfer between tasks; training by abstraction is valid; and instruction need not take place in complex, social environments (1996). As Greeno stated in his response (1997), situated theories do not imply that knowledge is not transferable, nor that all teaching should take place in "complex, social environments." What is fundamental to the situated perspective is an idea that knowledge is co-produced in settings, and is not the preserve of individual minds. Situated perspectives suggest that when people develop and use knowledge, they do so through their interactions with broader social systems. This may mean they are learning from a book (written by others) or teacher, or engaging in individual reflection of some socially produced ideas. But the different activities in which learners engage co-produce their knowledge, so that when students learn algorithms through the manipulation of abstract procedures, they do not only learn the algorithms, they learn a particular set of practices and associated beliefs. Students often find it difficult to use school-learned methods in out-of-school situations because the situations and the practices they require have changed. Situated perspectives turn attention away from individual minds and cognitive schemata, so that success is not focused on individual attributes, but on the ways in which those attributes play out in interaction with the world. This is not to say that knowledge cannot be transferred to new situations, only that it is inadequate to focus on knowledge alone, outside of the practices of its production and use.

To give a practical illustration of the distinction that should be drawn between situated perspectives and particular teaching approaches, I will refer back to a study I conducted of students learning mathematics through very different teaching methods (Boaler, 1997, 1998, 1999). One of the two schools in the study taught mathematics through abstract procedure repetition; the other through mathematical project work. The students in the project-based school were more able to use school-learned mathematics in different settings, than the students who had learned in a more procedural way. Some people have suggested that the learning of the "procedural" students was *more* situated, as it appeared to be tied to the situations in which it was learned. This is not the case—all learning is situated, and greater or lesser degrees are unavailable—but the project-based students engaged in particular practices, of discussion and procedure adaptation and application, for example, that were represented in nonschool situations. This does not mean that project-based approaches are more consistent with situated theory. What may be concluded is that project-based approaches are more effective *if* practices of procedure adaptation and others in which students regularly engage as part of project work are valued goals of mathematics education. Those who support abstract procedure repetition as the most efficient way to learn mathematics (Becker & Jacob, 2000) overlook the fact that students are not only learning an efficient set of procedures, but an esoteric set of practices that are not well represented outside of mathematics classrooms (Boaler, 2000).

The arguments in the preceding paragraphs do not imply that abstract procedure repetition should not play a part in learning mathematics. One of the concerns of Anderson et al., as well as those in the ICMI study group, was that situated perspectives render such approaches obsolete. They do not, and Greeno deals with this point well:

> In the situative perspective, use of abstract representations is an aspect of social practice, and abstract representations can contribute to meaningful learning only if their meanings are understood. To the extent that instruction presents abstract representations in isolation from their meanings, the outcome can be that students learn a set of mechanical rules that can support their successful performance on tests requiring only manipulation of the notations, not meaningful use of the representations. On the other hand, it is perfectly consistent with the situative perspective that abstract representations can facilitate learning when students share the interpretive conventions that are intended in their use. (1997, p. 13).

In my own study, some of the students who had learned through the repetition of abstract procedures developed an understanding of the procedures as they engaged in practices of mathematical reflection, but many did not, although they learned to manipulate the procedures in class. More work is needed to understand the potential of abstract and procedural approaches for the encouragement of mathematical knowledge and practice that is generalizable.

I hope to have demonstrated that there is no direct link between situated perspectives and teaching approaches, and that situated ideas do not deny that knowledge is transferred, only that practices of knowledge production are irrelevant to the process. In 1999, Cobb also addressed the problem of translating constructs of general theoretical perspectives into instructional prescriptions, referring to such processes as category errors (Cobb and Bowers, 1999). But what of the differences between situated and constructivist theories? Are they just different versions of the same idea? Or are the differences between the two more fundamental and profound? The central tenet of constructivism is that individuals actively construct their own knowledge, rather than passively absorbing it from others (Phillips, 1995). Although most followers of constructivist theory acknowledge that individuals do so in interaction with the social world, a division is maintained between the individual and the world. This creates what Lave has described as a "boundary between the individual (and thus the 'cognitive') and some version of the World 'out there'" (1993b, p. 64). By contrast, situated perspectives recommend:

> a decentered view of the locus and meaning of learning, in which learning is recognized as a social phenomenon constituted in the experienced, lived-in world, through legitimate peripheral participation in ongoing social practice; the process of changing knowledgeable skill is subsumed in processes of changing identity in and through membership in a community of practitioners; and mastery is an organizational, relational characteristic of communities of practice. (Lave, 1993b, p. 64).

Constructivist and situated perspectives are theoretically and practically distinct by virtue of the fact that situated theories treat relations among people, activities, and settings "as they are *given* in social practice, which is itself viewed as a single theoretical entity" (Lave, 1993a, p. 7, original italics). In theoretical terms, constructivism posits a view of learning as the individual mind being influenced by the social world, whereas situated theories propose that learning is a social phenomenon constituted in the world. In practical terms, a student may be given the opportunity to "construct" their own understanding in a mathematics class, by, for example, thinking about a procedure or using it to solve a problem. But if they are not engaging in practices of discussion, procedure adaptation or modeling, over time, they will only be moving along a trajectory of procedure use and they will construct their identities in relation to that. They will not "develop mastery" of practices of procedure discussion or adaptation, nor will they develop identities as people who adapt and discuss mathematical procedures. The differences between the identities and sets of practices that are developed for students in these two scenarios may or may not matter, depending on their future uses of mathematics, but they exist. Situated perspectives add insights into student competency and knowing, that relate to the identities students develop as learners and their practices of participation. Constructivist theories do not address these aspects of learning.

Perhaps the most important discussion of situated theory concerns the dilemmas faced by researchers who take it seriously. In Alan Schoenfeld's presidential address to the American Educational Research Association (1999), he described a schism "between 'fundamentally cognitive' and 'fundamentally social' studies of human thought and action" (p. 5) and talked about the crucial need for frameworks, perspectives, and methods that acknowledge both the social and individual aspects of learning. This is clearly going to be an important task for educational researchers over the next few years, particularly those of us in mathematics education who recognize the importance of both the social and individual dimensions of learning. For although representations of learning as trajectories of participation within communities of practice may give different insights from previous representations of learning that are solely cognitive, they leave unexplained the subjectivity and regulation of individuals within those practices. This was part of the reason that I chose the title *"Multiple Perspectives* on Mathematics Teaching and Learning" for this book, rather than "Social Perspectives," as the realization that learning is at any one time both individual and social requires that previously developed perspectives that give primacy to one or the other need to be adapted or combined (Rogoff, 1995).

Many of the authors represented in this book are doing important work in this area, producing accounts of teaching and learning that are complexly nuanced to represent educational practices as events that are simultaneously individual and interactional. In Chapter 2, Stephen Lerman considers the developments that have led up to the current interest in social theories of learning within mathematics education, taking us on a journey of the work that has been formative in this process. In doing so he identifies a similar challenge to that raised by Schoenfeld: how may researchers understand learning as a socially constituted endeavor while simultaneously recognizing that individual differences matter? Lerman engages this tension directly, reviewing a number of theories that provide accounts of individual differences in social practices. But acknowledgment of the different ways in which practices of participation have an impact on different people also raises the issue of power relations that are differentially distributed across learners. In an interesting analytical move he raises the importance of sociological theories to account for these—thus acknowledging the individual differences within social accounts of learning and employing sociological analyses to account for broader patterns of difference across individuals.

Lave and Wenger's theories have been widely adopted in education, despite the fact that the authors never claimed to offer such applicability. Indeed Lave has rarely addressed schooling in her many analyses of learning. But the fact that her reflections have been so hugely liberating and generative may rest on the direction of her work, which does not look outward from institutions of education and the culture of the United States, but rather inward from other cultures in the world and other situations for learning. Through studies of tailors in Vai and Gola, Lave found apprenticeship to be an extremely powerful form of learning and set out to consider why. The representations that resulted from her work have helped educational researchers view and understand aspects of learning that other perspectives did not. But there are, as might be expected, limitations to her models when they are moved between contexts, which Lerman describes. As part of his review of the field he offers adaptations of Lave's ideas to help increase the fit with formal institutions of education and acknowledge the diversity of individuals or groups of learners, when the unit of analysis is *one* community of practice. He also offers a comparative analysis of the theories of Lave, Piaget, and Vygotsky and draws out components of each to provide what he proposes as a more complete representation of learning, as "mind-in-society-in-mind." Stephen Lerman's chapter serves as an introduction to many of the theoretical and practical issues that play out in the remainder of the book.

In Chapter 3, Paul Cobb describes the ways in which he and his colleagues are designing research and instruction to understand and account for the social and individual nature of learning. This is a highly important piece of writing that examines the impact of situated accounts of learning for theory, practice, and research. The work of Cobb and his colleagues, through Purdue and Vanderbuilt Universities, is well known throughout the United States and beyond, particularly for the ways in which they have understood and acted on constructivist theories in the design of mathematics teaching environments. In this chapter, Cobb describes their gradual adoption "of an increasingly strong situated perspective" and the significant impact this is having on their work. This change was not driven by theory, but by the practicalities of classrooms; in particular, the need for an analytical framework that considered the classroom as a whole, with all its complexly related factors. Rather than focusing on instructional materials, as has been the tradition in educational research, Cobb describes their attention to classroom norms—mathematical and social—and the nature of students' *activity with* classroom materials. He combines a social perspective that gives insights into the norms of the classroom with a psychological perspective on individual student reasoning and participation. This is achieved through integrated cycles of design and analysis. Cobb's description of his and his colleagues work, and the ways in which classrooms may be understood as places of learning that are both social and individual, will be generative for other researchers attempting to understand the multidimensional nature of learning. Cobb also provides a clear illustration of the ways in which learning is situated for students and recommends ways in which this realization should change educational practices.

Situated and other social accounts of learning are not the only significant developments to be influencing the theory and practice of (mathematics) education at this time. Other changes in the way researchers are thinking about research and theory are having a profound impact on the field. These changes share the characteristic of challenging long-held dualisms (Bredo, 1994), not only between the social and psychological—and between mind and world—but between theory and research, research and practice, and researchers and practitioners. In the past there were clear, assumed directions between theory and research and between research and practice. It was assumed that theory would be examined, from which hypotheses would arise, which would be tested in the field. Results would then be communicated to practitioners who would apply them to their practice. This conception of the educational research enterprise is changing in multiple ways in the face of increasing evidence that it is neither functional nor effective. One of the assumed directions that is being challenged is that from theory to research. Increasingly researchers are recognizing that classrooms are multifaceted environments that do not lend themselves to examination from single or predetermined theoretical perspectives. Different methods are therefore being employed in an attempt to represent what Stephen Ball (1995) has termed the "mobile, complex, ad hoc, messy and fleeting qualities of lived experience" (p. 6). Stephen Ball (1995) and Miles (1982) both warn of the danger of reducing the complexity of experience and striving toward a theory that it "all makes sense" (Miles, 1982, p. 126). As an alternative, researchers are choosing to immerse themselves in educational settings to try to understand the issues that are important to the settings before choosing an analytical lens. This does not mean that previously developed theories are not important; they are still taken into educational settings and considered—theories are an intrinsic part of any researcher's history, so things could not be any other way. But researchers are developing increasing sensitivity to the people and settings in which they work, enabling theories to emerge from these different settings that have more ecological validity. In the new generation of mathematics education research, practice is driving research and ultimately theory, as illustrated by a number of chapters in this book.

Deborah Ball's work exemplifies the shift toward analytical examinations that are grounded in practice and that are productive of theory (Ball & Cohen, 1999). She and Hyman Bass collectively demonstrate in Chapter 4 that a perspective that takes seriously the fact that mathematics teaching and learning is at once socially constructed and *mathematical* has considerable analytical potential for understanding the distance between traditional programs of teacher preparation and the demands of mathematics teaching. Ball and Bass illustrate the use of a perspective that differs from more generic theories of learning, such as constructivism or situated cognition, as it takes the discipline and practice of mathematics as an analytical lens. This subject-specific focus builds on theories about teaching and learning, as they describe in a separate publication (Ball & Bass, 2000), when they set out the following three commitments:

1. To treat the discipline of mathematics with integrity
2. To give serious respect to children's mathematical ideas
3. To see mathematics as a collective intellectual endeavor situated within community

The authors analyze mathematics teaching and learning, as it occurs in classrooms, in order to describe, define, and characterize aspects of teacher knowing that support sophisticated mathematical reasoning. In so doing, Ball and Bass, like Cobb in the preceding chapter, prioritize the activity system of the classroom over individual aspects of the system, such as curricular materials or predefined lists of teacher knowledge. Whereas Cobb examines the system to understand and support student learning, Ball and Bass focus their analysis on the nature of teacher knowledge that is required by practice. One of their central assumptions in doing so is consonant with situated theory—tests of teacher knowledge as demonstrated outside of classroom interactions cannot tell us what situated analyses of practice can. Ball and Bass also challenge the assumption that examinations of curriculum may lead to sufficient understanding of the mathematics knowledge that teachers require. They show through their work that examinations of practice, and of curriculum being enacted in classrooms, give greater insights into the extent and *nature* of knowledge that teachers require.

A simple consideration of the capabilities required by effective mathematics teachers may suggest constructing a list of mathematics content knowledge on which to test teachers (characterizing the latest initiative of the teacher training agency in the United Kingdom; *The Guardian,* January 21, 2000); a more sophisticated and educationally sensitive consideration may produce an additional list of pedagogical content knowledge (Shulman, 1986). Ball and Bass's analysis of practice suggests another kind of knowledge that is simultaneously mathematical *and* social and that may prove to be critical in the design of teacher education programs. That this form of knowledge has not previously been identified or incorporated into programs of teacher education, but emerges with clarity from their analysis, is credit to the analytical power of practice and the sophisticated theorizing that Ball and Bass derive from it.

The chapters by Lerman, Cobb, and Ball and Bass all engage with questions of knowledge—and all produce critical insights into the social nature of student and teacher knowledge as it emerges in practice. In describing their research studies, Cobb, and Ball and Bass, illustrate that important intuitions may be gained by studying classroom systems and identifying influential components of the system, such as teacher interactions or student discussions. The researchers employ different analytical lenses to make sense of these, but they do not go into the different settings with particular hypotheses that they expect to test out. Instead, they go into settings with conjectures about the means of supporting teaching and learning and ways to analyze these, that are viewed as malleable, interpretive intentions. As Cobb has written (personal communication), "the alternative to the standard paradigm is not completely free emergence. One has a starting point for one's own learning trajectory, but it is nothing more than this. A starting point, rather than something to be proven true or false." Analyses emerge from the practices of different settings and are defined by the issues that pertain there.

In highlighting the importance of practice and reflection, I do not wish to downplay the importance of theory in educational research. I agree with Stephen Ball's concern for the deintellectualization of educational research (1995). Theory, for him, is not "simply critical. In order to go beyond the accidents and contingencies which enfold us, it is necessary to start from another position and begin from what is normally excluded. Theory provides this possibility, the possibility of disidentification—the effect of working 'on and against' prevailing practices of ideological subjection" (1995, p. 267). If theory is predetermined at the outset of research, its relevance to the events that take place in educational settings must surely be questionable. Alternatively, if it is adopted as a means of understanding the multiple aspects of classrooms, as Cobb describes, or the salient aspects of discourse, as Ball and Bass describe, then it may indeed be a tool of exploration.

In the subsequent three chapters the focus turns to classroom studies of students, in particular student trajectories of participation and the roles and identities they develop as they engage in the practice of school mathematics. Students in the three studies variously describe themselves as "dumb" (Stevens) "mates" (Barnes) and "creative people" (Boaler and Greeno) and the authors explore the ways that these identities intersect with the students' developing knowledge of mathematics. Stevens and Barnes, in Chapters 5 and 6 respectively, continue the use of grounded analyses of practice, through complex representations of learning within groups.

Both authors captured the work of students on videotape and combined analyses of these with other forms of evidence, producing stark illustrations of the relationship between social interactions and mathematics knowledge. Stevens and Barnes both offer the group as their unit of analysis, rather than individuals or classes, adding a great deal to the field of mathematics education. We have few examples (Barron, in press) of analyses of the way knowledge develops in what is increasingly a pervasive form of mathematics instruction.

In Chapter 5, Reed Stevens reports on an ethnographic study of a group of students working on an architecture design project. He uses an interactional perspective to explore the group relations as students work on emergent and assigned mathematics problems. The study gives a clear illustration of an important fact: classroom conversations about mathematics are simultaneous reflections of social relationships *and* mathematics knowledge. Although we may regard that fact as self-evident, we have few examples to draw on that document the *ways* in which student interactions and mathematics knowledge co-develop. Stevens took personal relationships seriously, and his knowledge of these proved to be key to understanding the mathematical learning of the students. Stevens produces a detailed analysis of a particular practice that enables him to analyze:

- The types of interactions that occur in groups
- The types of mathematical work that constitute problem solving
- The positioning of students in relation to emergent and assigned problems
- The potential role that teachers may play in maximizing understanding as students work in groups

These theoretical and practical insights extend well beyond the particular problems on which the students were working or the particular interactions of the teacher and students Stevens studied. This is testament to the detail of his work and the "social and epistemological complexity" that he captures.

In Chapter 6, Mary Barnes reports on a study that is complementary in its analysis, despite the fact she also takes the group as the main focal point. Barnes also employed videotape to capture the interactions that took place during collaborative group work in a mathematics class, but her aim was to understand the ways in which gender relations influence the emergence of mathematics knowledge. Barnes therefore focuses on the subgroups within the class and the common structure they shared. Like Stevens's work, the complexity of Barnes's analysis of interactions within the class enables her to focus within and outside the group, communicating insights into the role of individuals as well as the broader context of the classroom.

It is interesting to note that there are at least three levels of analysis evident within this and other chapters: that which derives from raw data, that which derives from theory, and that which is more contemplative, deriving from Barnes's time on the project and the filter of many years' experience of theory and practice, within and outside mathematics education. These different levels of analysis are critical in Barnes's report, as she uncovers the hegemonic relations that are a product of and produce small group interactions. Gendered relations have a pervasive impact on mathematics discourse; they are frequently enacted in opposition to teachers' intentions, and they position students in ways that are often unproductive. Despite their influence, the gendered relations that contribute toward knowledge production are not well understood by teachers or researchers of mathematics education. Barnes, like Stevens, concludes the chapter with a number of recommendations for teachers. These are attainable and highly convincing owing to the detail of the analysis and the ecological validity of the account. Both Stevens and Barnes produce significant findings and both acknowledge that their insights derived from the privileged position of being able to study small groups, as teachers engaged with the mathematical work of the whole class.

In Chapter 7, Jim Greeno and I explore students' positioning in the different "figured worlds" (Holland, Lachicotte, Skinner, & Cain, 1998, p. 49) of didactic and collaborative mathematics environments, as revealed by their reports in interviews. We employ both anthropological and psychological lenses to consider the forms of knowing and participation to which students gained access in mathematics classrooms and the ways that these intersected with their developing identities. Notions of identity have traditionally been regarded as individual and relatively stable, but they have recently been presented as a product of individual understanding and community participation (Wenger, 1998). Such a construct brings together sociological and psychological theories of learning, capturing the relationship between individual knowledge and beliefs and the broader communities in which knowledge and beliefs are developed and used. As Wenger (1998) proposes, "learning transforms who we are and what we can do, it is an experience of identity. It is not just an accumulation of skills and information, but a process of becoming—to become a certain person or, conversely, to avoid becoming a certain person" (p. 215). Such theories attempt to provide for the cultural systems, structures, and rules that shape existence, as well as the agency of individuals who are active participants in such systems.

The students we interviewed suggested that success and participation in mathematics classrooms rests less on cognitive "ability" than on identification with particular pedagogical practices. It was unsurprising, but salient, that students in interviews did not describe themselves in cognitive terms, but in terms of their different identities as people. Steele (1997) has proposed that students need to identify with academic success and with mathematics, as a subject, in order to be successful mathematics students, but the interviews we conducted suggested that students negotiated their identification with the pedagogical practices of the mathematics classroom and these practices could not be separated from their notions of "mathematics." Many of the students valued opportunities to be thinking, creative agents, which they regarded as inconsistent with didactic pedagogical practices. In conclusion, we relate the students' reports of their experiences in class to the work of mathematicians. We argue that traditional practices limit students' understanding and perception of mathematics to the elements of mathematical thinking in which the human agent is relatively passive. By relating pedagogy to the students' conceptions of self, we hope to extend the debates that occur around teaching methods. Opponents of collaborative teaching methods frequently argue that they are ineffective because they take the focus away from standard algorithms (Wu, 1999). In such arguments, teaching *methods* are compared to mathematics *knowledge* as though the two are alternative outcomes. But knowledge and methods are neither alternatives nor separate entities. They are both deeply embedded in practice and algorithms cannot be considered as independent entities that somehow stand apart from the practices of their production. Analyses of classroom methods need to take account, not only of *what* students know, but of how they know it, and how they position themselves in relation to that knowing.

Mathematics education is practiced within a social and political domain, and egalitarian achievement practices may depend on greater acknowledgement of that fact. The last three chapters of the book take a sociological focus, recognizing that there is an urgent need for mathematics educators to extend our gaze outside of the mathematics classroom to the framing politics and practices that shape what goes on there. In Chapter 8, Robyn Zevenbergen explores the different ways in which classrooms legitimate certain forms of language, thought, and behavior above others. This makes the degree of continuity in practices between home and school extremely important. Such an area is a relatively new, unexplored, and uncomfortable domain for mathematics educators, partly because we see the practices of homes as out of our sphere of influence. But Zevenbergen makes an important point on this issue—understanding the importance of home-school discontinuities should contribute not toward a discourse of deficit, but instead, toward increased awareness of ways in which classrooms can be made more conducive for learning for wider groups of students. Zevenbergen uses theories developed in the domains of sociology and sociolinguistics to consider the events of mathematics classrooms and the content of mathematics assessments and the ways that these position students differently. In evaluating the importance of language, and exploring the importance of vocabulary, semantics and lexical density, Zevenbergen also parallels the arguments of other authors in this book in their focus on pedagogy and practice. Language, like pedagogy, is not just a medium for the delivery of content, it is central to what is learned.

In addition to analysis of the language demands of mathematics assessments, and the impact of these on the achievement of indigenous students, Zevenbergen provides analysis of classroom interactions. She shows the ways in which working-class students are excluded from learning through their noncompliance with the preferred norms of classroom participation—norms that are largely implicit and unspoken. In documenting and analyzing the processes that produce and reproduce social inequalities in mathematics classrooms, Zevenbergen addresses one of the most important issues for our field. By representing teaching as a cultural event, she shows the subtle ways in which aspects of curriculum, pedagogy, and assessment exclude groups of students, and she helps us understand how practices may be changed in order that they become more equitable.

In Chapter 9, Candia Morgan maintains a focus on assessment, asking a broad and generative question: how could things be different? She does not attend to the detail of different assessments that are produced, questioning their validity or reliability. Instead, she embarks on a bigger, more unusual enterprise—to problematize the notion of assessment and its place within mathematics education. To do this, she questions the assumptions that underpin the research and practices of assessment. For example, do individuals possess knowledge that is sufficiently stable and intransigent to be measurable? Does education need a process, the primary purpose of which is to differentiate between students? And do good assessments improve possibilities for teaching? Morgan deconstructs the foundation on which the discourse of assessment rests, before describing the ways in which a "social" agenda for assessment may be different. Morgan's analysis is both important and controversial. She posits that a social perspective on assessment must question "who benefits and who is disadvantaged" and how "assessment processes and systems act to benefit or disadvantage individuals and groups." Zevenbergen's analysis in the previous chapter would clearly play a useful role in such an endeavor. Morgan correctly recognizes that the majority of research in mathematics education has been driven by an aim to produce *better* assessments, and highlights the need for discussions and questions that are fundamentally different.

Part of the reason that the "math wars" have been so devastating for mathematics educators in the United States, and that traditionalists have been able to hijack reforms with such apparent ease, is our ignorance of the broader stage on which mathematics is played out. Michael Apple's chapter takes us there, in a consideration of the social agendas that have an impact on policy. His chapter does not focus upon mathematics education per se, but the political insights he provides are extremely important for our community. The arbitrary division between mathematics education and the broader sociopolitical context that is maintained in our field was epitomized for me by a recent incident at a conference. At the annual international meeting of the Pyschology of Mathematics Education (PME) group, held in Stellanbosch, South Africa, a few of us gathered together to discuss the "social aspects of mathematics education" as part of a working group of that name. Inevitably perhaps, in such a setting (post-Apartheid South Africa) discussions turned to the broader political agenda, and the ways in which mathematics education, as well as the practices of academics, may contribute toward inequality. After some minutes of increasing frustration, one participant jumped up and said that he had had enough—he had come here to discuss mathematics education, not politics—and left the room. I had some understanding of his perspective, at the same time recognizing that such single-mindedness is no longer tenable, if it ever was.

As mathematics educators, we are generally fascinated by events in classrooms, and we are drawn into debates about the most effective way to introduce Pythagoras's theorem or the variety of activities that generate sums of squares. This is where our interest lies, but also where we feel we can have an influence. Broader social and political movements, such as modernization, may appear too far out of reach to be the site of our interest or work. But the traditional focus of mathematics educators on issues of pedagogy and mathematics has resulted in an insularity and particularism that has left us wide open to the agenda of the conservatives. This is particularly dangerous at the present time as conservative politics have gained a powerful hold on most nations across the world. Indeed, we would be well served to pay attention to research that has considered the relationship between the form and content of curriculum and the distribution of power (see, for example, Bernstein, 1975; Apple, 1979, 1993, 1996; Whitty, 1985). Conservative lobby groups are often organized and wealthy, and they extend their financial support to those who oppose reform based mathematics teaching. When a group of research mathematicians in the United States wanted to protest about the Department of Education's support of reform-based teaching programs, they were supported by a wealthy conservative who funded full-page advertisements in the *Washington Post* and *Los Angeles Times*. The advertisements denigrated the recommendations of educators, and demonstrated a blatant disregard for communication or relationship building, as well as the financial resources on which traditionalists may draw. But these events should not be viewed in isolation. In the same way that we strive to consider learning in its broader context when we work as researchers, so must we consider the movements of traditionalists and other anti-reformers in their wider context. Many political commentators have argued that conservative groups have been able to gain power through the highjacking of other lobby groups' agendas and through the appopriation of their discourse. By understanding the broader social and political movements that are affecting change in mathematics education, we may understand the fears and strategies of anti-reform parents and politicians and find more appropriate ways to address them.

In Chapter 10, Michael Apple enables us to construct such an understanding, through his analysis of "conservative modernization" at work in education. He achieves many things in this chapter, one of them being to locate the current reform movement in its political context, which, he argues, is structured by neoliberal and neoconservative movements. Apple describes an alliance of conservative modernization that has a particular set of ideological commitments—within which education is firmly placed. This includes a commitment to "that eloquent fiction," the free market. Apple illustrates what this does and could mean, through his analysis of events in England, where a new market structure is determining educational practices in multiple and profound ways (Gewirtz, Ball, & Bowe, 1995). The issues that Apple raises in relation to the U.K. context have import beyond the United Kingdom as they can be seen in most Western countries in the world. Apple provides a careful documentation and analysis of such movements, which must surely be a first step in achieving an educational vision that is more democratic. He considers the dominant view that progressive school practices are widespread and that they have eradicated the practices of an idealized past. Research results have not played a large part in this public debate, which is a clear and sensible strategy for those trying to achieve a particular agenda that runs counter to research evidence. Nor have anti-reformers needed to refer to research, as Apple notes—they have merely presented their arguments as commonsense or "basic." Such ideas have flooded the discourse of mathematics education with nontraditional teaching methods being described as the converse. The "mathematically correct" website, which is the source of inspiration and organization for many anti-reformers in the United States, provides an ideal illustration of this linguistic move. Their ideas are defined as "correct" while nontraditional teaching methods are defined as "fuzzy," "trendy," or "mushy." Such linguistic moves are simple and effective in capturing public opinion and are part of the practices that require greater understanding by mathematics educators.

In considering the hidden effects of neoliberal reform recommendations through a detailed consideration of various events that have transpired in the name of educational reform in England, Michael Apple documents an important and subtle shift in emphasis. My own experience in England would concur with his observation that the focus of education has moved—from what schools can do for students, to what students can do for schools. As schools are put under increasing pressure to perform and accountability measures are applied, students become seen as commodities—with equity implications too obvious to be stated here. Apple, like other authors in this book, documents the subtle ways in which children of less affluent parents are disadvantaged in England and other education markets, with the education system serving to reproduce, rather than ameliorate, financial privilege.

Michael Apple reflects on the complexity of the world of education and, like other authors in the book, does not produce a simple analysis of discrimination, but describes the "complex interplay of forces and influences." He ends his chapter with an important warning—by conducting research and scholarly analyses on the conservative agenda, including studying, for example, assessments, markets, and national curricula, we frame educational issues in *their* terms. This reduces the space for thinking about alternatives, and the way things *could be.* I placed this chapter at the end of the book because its focus is broadest and if changes do not take place at the level Apple describes, then the practices and intentions of mathematics educators may amount to very little.

I hope that the collection of chapters in this book provides a lively and interesting addition to our field. In composing this edited volume, I deliberately avoided the more typical array of short chapters, choosing instead to let the authors deal with complex issues in substantive ways. In bringing this introduction to a close, I would simply note that the different chapters in this book do not share a single focus; indeed, they span a wide range of issues that are important for mathematics education—including teaching, learning, language, assessment, groupwork, and policy. But what they do share is a commitment to complex, multidisciplinary representations of the phenomena they seek to understand and explain, producing analyses of practice that have significant importance for the theories and practices of mathematics education.

REFERENCES

Anderson, J., Reder, L., & Simon, H. (1996). Situative versus cognitive perspectives: Form versus substance. *Educational Researcher, 26*(1), 18–21.

Apple, M. (1979). *Ideology and curriculum.* London: Routledge.

Apple, M. W. (1993). *Official knowledge: Democratic education in a conservative age.* London: Routledge.

Apple, M. W. (1996). *Cultural politics and education (the John Dewey lecture).* New York: Teacher's College Press.

Ball, D. L., & Cohen, D. (1999). Developing practice, developing practitioners. In L. Darling-Hammond & H. Sykes (Eds.), *Teaching as the learning profession: Handbook on policy and practice* . San Francisco: Jossey-Bass.

Ball, D. L., & Bass, H. (2000). Making believe: The collective construction of public mathematical knowledge in the elementary classroom. In D. Phillips (Ed.), *Yearbook of the National Society for the Study of Education: Constructivism in education* . Chicago: Chicago University Press.

Ball, S. J. (1995). Intellectuals or technicians? The urgent role of theory in educational studies. *British Journal of Educational Studies, 43*(3), 255–271.

Barron, B. (in press). Problem solving in video-based microworlds: Collaborative and individual outcomes of high achieving sixth grade students. *Journal of Educational Psychology.*

Becker, J., & Jacob, B. (2000). California school mathematics politics: The anti-reform of 1997–1999. *Phi Delta Kappan*, March, 529–537.

Bernstein, B. (1975). *Class, codes and control. Volume 3: Towards a theory of educational transmissions.* London: Routledge.

Boaler, J. (1997). *Experiencing school mathematics: Teaching styles, sex and setting.* Buckingham, UK: Open University Press.

Boaler, J. (1998). Open and closed mathematics: Student experiences and understandings. *Journal for Research in Mathematics Education, 29*(1), 41–62.

Boaler, J. (1999). Participation, knowledge and beliefs: A community perspective on mathematics learning. *Educational Studies in Mathematics, 40,* 259–281.

Boaler, J. (2000). Mathematics from another world: Traditional communities and the alienation of learners. *Journal of Mathematical Behavior, 18*(4).

Bredo, E. (1994). Reconstructing educational psychology: Situated cognition and deweyian pragmatism. *Educational Psychologist, 29*(1), 23–35.

Butler, J. (1993). *Bodies that matter: On the discursive limits of "sex."* London: Routledge.

Chaiklin, S., & Lave, J. (Eds.). (1993). *Understanding practice: Perspectives on activity and context.* Cambridge, UK: Cambridge University Press.

Cobb, P. (1994). Where is the mind? Constructivist and sociocultural perspectives on mathematical development,. *Educational Researcher, 23*(7), 13–20.

Cobb, P., & Bowers. J. (1999). Cognitive and situated learning perspectives in theory and practice. *Educational Researcher, 28*(2), 4–15.

Darling-Hammond, L., & Sykes, H. (Eds.). (1999). *Teaching as the learning profession: Handbook on policy and practice.* San Francisco: Jossey-Bass.

Gewirtz, S., Ball, S., & Bowe, R. (1995). *Markets, choice and equity in education.* Buckingham, UK: Open University Press.

Greeno, J. G. (1997). On claims that answer the wrong questions. *Educational Researcher, 25*(1), 5–17.

Greeno, J. G., & Goldman, S.V. (Eds). (1998). *Thinking practices in mathematics and science learning.* Mahwah, NJ: Lawrence Erlbaum.

Holland, D., Lachicotte, W., Skinner, D., & Cain, C. (1998). *Identity and agency in cultural worlds.* Cambridge, MA: Harvard University Press.

Keitel, C. (Ed) (1998). *Social justice and mathematics education: Gender, class, ethnicity and the politics of schooling.* Berlin: Freie Universitat Berlin.

Lave, J. (1993a). The practice of learning. In S. C. J. Lave (Ed.), *Understanding practice: Perspectives on activity and context.* (pp. 3–34). Cambridge, UK: Cambridge University Press.

Lave, J. (1993b). Situating learning in communities of practice. In L. Resnick, J. Levine, & T. Teasley (Eds.), *Perspectives on socially shared cognition* (pp. 63–85). Washington, DC: American Psychological Association.

Miles, M. B. (1982). A mini cross site analysis (commentary on other studies). *American Behavioural Scientist, 26*(1), 121–132.

Phillips, D. (1995). The good, the bad and the ugly: The many faces of constructivism. *Educational Researcher, 24*(7), 5–12.

Resnick, L. B. (1993). Shared cognition: Thinking as social practice. In L. B. Resnick, J. M. Levine, & S. D. Teasley (Eds.), *Perspectives on socially shared cognition* (pp. 1–22). Washington, DC: American Psychological Association.

Rogoff, B. (1995). Observing sociocultural activity on three planes: Participatory appropriation, guided participation, and apprenticeship. In J. V. Wertsch, P. del Rio, & A. Alvarez (Eds.), *Sociocultural studies of mind.* Cambridge, UK: Cambridge University Press.

Schoenfeld, A. (1999). Looking toward the 21st century: Challenges of educational theory and practice. *Educational Researcher, 28*(7), 4–14.

Shulman, L. (1986). Those who understand: Knowledge growth in teaching. *Educational Researcher*(Feb), 4–14.

Sierpinska, A., & Kilpatrick, J. (Eds.). (1998). *Mathematics education as a research domain: A search for identity. An ICMI study.* Dordrecht, The Netherlands: Kluwer.

Steele, C. (1997). A threat in the air: How stereotypes shape intellectual identity and performance. *American Psychologist, 52*(6), 613–629.

Wenger, E. (1998). *Communities of practice: Learning, meaning and identity.* Cambridge, UK: Cambridge University Press.

Whitty, G. (1985). *Sociology and school knowledge: Curriculum theory, research and politics.* London: Methuen.

Wu, H. (1999). Basic skills versus conceptual understanding: A bogus dichotomy in mathematics education. *American Educator,* Fall, 1999.

2

The Social Turn in Mathematics Education Research

Stephen Lerman

INTRODUCTION

In this introductory chapter, my task is to give an account of the growth of interest in social elements involved in teaching and learning mathematics over recent years, to account for that growth, and to give an overview of the main areas of research that make up the current intellectual climate in the "academy" of mathematics education, from the perspective of the social. The first task involves looking at the relationship between mathematics education and its surrounding disciplines. The second task, accounting for the growth of social theories, is partly an archaeology and partly a personal view of how and why the concerns of researchers and many teachers have moved from largely cognitive explanatory theories to a greater interest in social theories. The third task, giving an overview of current ideas, occupies the major part of this chapter. In that overview, I do not pretend that I have managed to incorporate all the work that is going on currently that positions itself in the "social." That would require much more space and time than is available. Instead, I try to identify what I see as the main directions, their common perspectives, and their differences, and propose a synthesis.

KNOWLEDGE PRODUCTION IN MATHEMATICS EDUCATION

The field of knowledge production in the community of mathematics education research, as with other curriculum domains, gazes for the most part on the mathematics classroom as its empirical field, although also on other sites of learning and social practices defined as mathematical by observers (Hoyles, Noss, & Pozzi, 1999). Researchers in mathematics education draw on a range of disciplines for explanations, analyses, and curriculum designs. The process of adopting theoretical frameworks into a field has been defined by Bernstein (1996) as *recontextualization,* as different theories become adapted and applied, allowing space for the play of ideologies in the process. Prescribing teaching strategies and the ordering of curriculum content on the basis of Piaget's psychological studies is a prime example of recontextualization. Psychologists, sociologists, mathematicians, and others might therefore look at work in mathematics education and at educational studies, in general, as derivative. At the same time, however, we should also look on the process as *knowledge production,* in that new formulations and frameworks emerge in dialectical interaction with the empirical field (Brown & Dowling, 1998) and are therefore *produced* in the educational context. The development of radical constructivism as a field in mathematics education research on the basis of Piaget's work is an example of what is more appropriately seen as knowledge production. The adaptation of the ideas of radical constructivism, or any other theoretical framework, into pedagogy, however, is a process of recontextualization where the play of ideologies is often quite overt.

I propose that there are three levels of knowledge. At the first level are the surrounding (sometimes called foundation) disciplines of psychology, sociology, philosophy, anthropology, (in our case) mathematics, and perhaps others. At the second level are mathematics education and other curriculum areas of educational research. At the third level are curriculum and classroom practice. The process of recontextualization takes place in the movement and adaptation of ideas from one level to the next. One could use this framework to examine changes in practice that are prompted by research findings. In the late 1970s in the United Kingdom, a major study of concept hierarchies in school mathematics influenced the content of both textbooks and government curriculum documents (Hart, 1981). This would be a case of recontextualization from the second to the third level. It is not useful, however, to examine changes in the field of mathematics education as a consequence of changes in, say, mainstream psychology or mathematics. For this reason one should call work at the second level knowledge production, not recontextualization (Bernstein, 1996). Educational research has more of a horizontal relationship to the domains I have described as being at the first level, rather than a hierarchical relationship to them. This chapter is concerned mainly with knowledge production in the field of mathematics education, not with recontextualization into pedagogy. I suggest that there has been a turn to social theories in the field of mathematics education and examine the reasons why.

The range of disciplines on which we draw, which should be seen as *resources* for knowledge production, is wide and one might ask why this is so. I do not mean to imply that mathematics education is different to other fields of knowledge production in educational research: all fields have their similarities and overlapping ideas and each field has its unique features.

> Educational research is located in a knowledge-producing *community.* . . . Of course, communities will display a great deal of variation in their cohesiveness, the strength of their "disciplinary matrix," and the flexibility of the procedures by which they vali-

date knowledge claims. Education as a field of research and theorizing is not firmly rooted in any single disciplinary matrix and therefore probably lies at the weak end of the spectrum, although I think this need not in itself be seen as a weakness. (Scott & Usher, 1996, p. 34)

Few areas of educational research are "home grown" (curriculum studies may be one of the few), and it is typical for all communities in educational thought to draw on other disciplines. The mathematics education research community seems particularly cohesive and active, as evidenced for instance by the fact that the mathematics education group is now the largest division in the American Educational Research Association. The procedures for validating knowledge claims that have emerged in recent decades, including peer review of journal articles, conference papers, research grant applications, and doctoral thesis examinations, are becoming more flexible and the criteria more varied. The numbers of journals and conferences are increasing, and one can expect that the development of on-line journals, and perhaps videoconferencing too, will accelerate the increasing flexibility. A framework for a systematic analysis of the productions of the mathematics education community has been sketched as the first stage in a program to map the elaboration of pedagogical modes over time (Lerman & Tsatsaroni, 1998).

The mathematics education research community appears to be particularly open to drawing on other disciplines, for at least four reasons. First, mathematics as a body of knowledge and as a set of social practices has been and remains of particular interest to other disciplines such as psychology, sociology, and anthropology as it presents particularly interesting challenges to their work. It is not surprising that one of the major challenges for Piaget was to account for the development of logical reasoning, nor that Piaget's account of knowledge schemata used group theory as its fundamental structure. Similarly, it is not surprising that Scribner, Cole, Lave, Saxe, Pinxten, and others found the study of mathematical practices of great interest in their anthropological and cross-cultural studies. Second, mathematics has stood as exemplar of truth and rationality since ancient times, giving it a unique status in most world cultures and in intellectual communities. That status may account for mathematics being seen as a marker of general intellectual capacity rather than simply aptitude at mathematics. Its symbolic power certainly lays mathematics open to criticisms of its gendered and Eurocentric character, creating through its discursive practices the reasoning logical norm (Walkerdine, 1988). Third, mathematics has played a large part in diverse cultural practices (Joseph, 1991), including religious life, music, pattern, design, and decoration. It appears all around when one chooses to apply a mathematical gaze (Lerman, 1998b). Finally, there is the apparent power of mathematics such that its use can enable the building of skyscrapers, bridges, space exploration, economic theories, "smart" bombs, and so on; I should stop as the list descends into ignominy.

Until about 15 years ago, mathematics education tended to draw on mathematics itself, or psychology, as disciplines for the production of knowledge in the field (Kilpatrick, 1992). Analyses of mathematical concepts provided a framework for curriculum design and enabled the study of the development of children's understanding as the building of higher order concepts from their analysis into more basic building blocks. Behaviorism supplied the psychological rationale both for the building blocks metaphor for the acquisition of mathematical knowledge and for the pedagogical strategies of drill and practice, and positive and negative reinforcement. Piagetian psychology called for historical analyses of mathematical (and other) concepts, based on the assumption that the individual's development replays that of the species (ontogeny replicates phylogeny). It was argued that identifying historical and epistemological obstacles would reveal pedagogical obstacles (Piaget & Garcia, 1989; for a critique see Lerman, 1999; Radford, 1997; Rogers, in press). This again emphasized the importance of mathematical concepts for education. In terms of psychology, the influences of Piaget and the neo-Piagetian radical constructivists are too well known to require documentation here, and I would refer in particular to the detailed studies of children's thinking (e.g., Steffe, von Glasersfeld, Richards, & Cobb 1983; Sowder, J., Armstrong, Lamon, Simon, Sowder, L., & Thompson, 1998). Both the disciplines of mathematics and psychology have high status in universities, and locating mathematics education within either group is seen as vital in some countries in terms of its status and therefore funding and respectability. Psychology has well-established research methodologies and procedures on which mathematics education has fruitfully drawn. Evidence can be seen, for instance, in the proceedings of the International Group for the Psychology of Mathematics Education (PME) over the past 22 years and in the *Journal for Research in Mathematics Education (JRME)*.

Interest in the implications of the philosophy of mathematics, for mathematics education research was given impetus by Lakatos's *Proofs and Refutations* (1976), partly, I suspect, because of the style of the book, which is a classroom conversation between teacher and students. More important, though, is the humanistic image of mathematics it presents, as a quasiempiricist enterprise of the community of mathematicians over time rather than a monotonically increasing body of certain knowledge. The book by Davis and Hersh (1981) which was inspired by Lakatos has become a classic in the community, but others (Kitcher, 1983; Restivo, van Bendegem, & Fischer, 1993; Tymoczko, 1986) have become equally influential. A number of researchers (Confrey, 1981; Dawson, 1969; Ernest, 1985, 1991; Lerman, 1983; Nickson, 1981; Rogers, 1978) have studied aspects of teaching and learning mathematics from the humanistic, quasiempirical point of view. That mathematical certainty has been questioned in the absolutism/fallibilism dichotomy is not due directly to Lakatos as he never subscribed to that view. With Popper, Lakatos considered knowledge to be advancing toward greater verisimilitude, but identifying the process of knowledge growth as taking place through refutation, not indubitable deduction, raised the theoretical possibility that all knowledge might be challenged by a future counterexample. In mathematics education the absolutist/fallibilist dichotomy has been used as a rationale for teaching through problem solving and as a challenge to the traditional mathematical pedagogy of transmission of facts. Fallibilism's potential challenge to mathematical certainty has led to mathematical activity being identified by its heuristics, but to a much greater extent in the mathematics education community than among mathematicians (Burton, 1999b; Hanna, 1996). This is another illustration of the recontextualizing process from the field of production of mathematics education knowledge, driven perhaps by democratic tendencies for pedagogy among some schoolteachers.

Although there is a substantial body of literature in social studies of scientific knowledge, there has been much less written about mathematical knowledge, although Bloor (e.g., 1976) is an early exception and Rotman's (1988) and Restivo's (1992) work more recent. Science education research draws heavily on social studies of scientific knowledge: in mathematics education, that resource is still in an early stage.

THEORIES OF THE "SOCIAL"

Studies in epistemology, ontology, knowledge, and knowledge acquisition tend to focus on how the *individual* acquires knowledge and on the status of that knowledge in relation to reality. Theoretical frameworks for interpreting the *social* origins of knowledge and consciousness began to appear in the mathematics education literature toward the end of the 1980s. Shifts in perspectives or the development of new paradigms in academic communities are the result of a concatenation of factors within and around the community. In the title to this chapter, I have called these developments the *social turn* in mathematics education research. This is not to imply that other theories, mathematical, Piagetian, radical constructivist, or philosophical have ignored social factors (Lerman, 2000; Steffe & Thompson, 2000). Indeed, in the preceding discussion I have suggested that the philosophical orientation was coincident with a humanistic, democratic concern by teachers and researchers at that time. Elsewhere (Lerman, 1998d, p. 335), I have discussed Piaget's and von Glasersfeld's emphasis on social interactions as providing a major source of disequilibrium. The *social turn* is intended to signal something different; namely, the emergence into the mathematics education research community of theories that see meaning, thinking, and reasoning as products of social activity. This goes beyond the idea that social interactions provide a spark that generates or stimulates an individual's internal meaning-making activity. A major challenge for theories from the social turn is to account for individual cognition and difference, and to incorporate the substantial body of research on mathematical cognition, as products of social activity.

In making the *social turn* the focus of this chapter, I have created my object of study. It becomes tempting, then, to pin down the emergence of that object in time, although in a "playful" sense. The year 1988 saw the appearance of several texts that have become significant in the social turn in mathematics education research. Jean Lave's book, *Cognition in Practice* (1988), challenged cognitivism and transfer theory in mathematics learning. In that book she described studies of the "mathematical" practices of grocery shoppers and dieters, which raised fundamental questions about mathematical practices in out-of-school practices being seen as merely the application of school techniques. The strategies and decision-making procedures that people used in those situations had to be seen as situated within, and as products of, those social situations. Further, the process of learning the strategies and decision-making procedures in the community of dieters, for example, should be seen as part of who one is "becoming" in that practice. Terezinha Nunes (Carraher, 1988) gave a plenary address at PME in Hungary, reporting on the work of her group, in which she identified differences between street mathematics and school mathematics. For example, she demonstrated that the former is oral, the latter written, and that street mathematics "is a tool for solving problems in meaningful situations" (p. 18). That students who traditionally fail in school mathematics were seen to be successful in street situations made the challenge to knowledge as decontextualized schemata more powerful. Valerie Walkerdine's *Mastery of Reason* (1988) located meanings in practices, not as independent of them, and demonstrated that the notion of a "child" is a product of a discursive practice, which is produced in language and particular social practices. Her Foucauldian analysis of classroom mathematics placed issues of power and the social construction of identity and meanings on the agenda. Alan Bishop's *Mathematical Enculturation* (1988b) gave a cross-cultural view of mathematical practices and attempted to give some universal parameters for their analysis. In the same year Bishop was editor of a special issue of *Educational Studies in Mathematics* on cultural aspects of mathematics education. These writers, and others, had published some of their work before 1988, but the coincidence of these major publications leads me to emphasize that year. It is clear that the community had to be receptive to these ideas for them to gain purchase. In that same year, one day of the Sixth International Congress on Mathematical Education in Hungary, called "Day 5," was devoted to Mathematics, Education, and Society, the result of the efforts of Alan Bishop and colleagues to bring social and cultural issues to the attention of the international mathematics education community. In 1986, a research group had been set up in the United Kingdom by Marilyn Nickson and myself called the group for "Research into Social Perspectives of Mathematics Education" (Nickson & Lerman, 1992). These are just two indicators of the receptivity of the mainstream community. It has to be said, though, that the receptivity of the mathematics education community to social theories was due more to political concerns that inequalities in society were reinforced and reproduced by differential success in school mathematics, than social theories of learning. Ethnomathematics, which was introduced as a new direction by Ubiritan D'Ambrosio at the Fifth International Congress on Mathematical Education in Adelaide in 1984 (D'Ambrosio, 1984), was a key element in the papers presented on Day 5 four years later, and can also be said to have played a large part in creating an environment that was receptive to the social turn.

The other key element in current sociocultural theories in mathematics education is the work of Vygotsky and his colleagues, but it is a little harder to trace the beginnings of Vygotskian influences in mathematics education. Forman (in press) reminds us that Vygotsky's work only became available to the world community with destalinization in the Soviet Union at the end of the 1950s and only slowly and gradually were translations made available. The impact of his revolutionary ideas took time to emerge, Bruner and Wertsch being particularly important figures in that process (see Bruner, 1986; Wertsch, 1981). The significant differences between Vygotsky's theories, and those of Piaget which were, and still are, dominant, took even longer to reach recognition. People working in the field of education for children and adults with special needs (e.g., Donaldson, 1978; Feuerstein, 1980), in studies of self-regulation, and in language development took to Vygotsky's theories at an early stage. Cole, Engeström, and others, including Lave, influenced by activity theory (Cole, 1996; Cole, Engeström, & Vasquez, 1997), drew partly on studies of mathematical practices. However, the significance of Vygotsky's work only came to be appreciated by the mainstream mathematics education community much more recently.

The evidence I have found of Vygotsky's work becoming known within mathematics education suggests, again, that the late 1980s may be seen as something of a marker. From a search without the aid of electronic means, it appears that the first mention of Vygotsky in references:

1. In PME proceedings was Crawford (1988)
2. In *Educational Studies in Mathematics* in a review of Wertsch (1981) by Crawford (1985), but the first mention in an article was Bishop (1988b)
3. In the journal *For the Learning of Mathematics* was Cobb (1989)
4. In the *Journal for Research in Mathematics Education* was English (1993)
5. In the *Journal of Mathematical Behavior* was Schmittau (1993)

The social turn in mathematics education has developed from, I suggest, three main disciplines or resources: anthropology (from, e.g., Lave); sociology (from, e.g., Walkerdine); and cultural psychology (from, e.g., Nunes; Crawford). Each contains a number of streams, of course, and each has a number of influences. I have proposed (Lerman, 1998d) that there are some common themes and I will try to indicate later how these can be brought together into a fruitful and coherent research direction by a consideration of the unit of analysis for research in mathematics education. For now it suffices to consider the person-acting-in-social-practice, not person or their knowing on their own. I frame this discussion by looking at aspects of situated theory, with critiques opening spaces for elaborations from sociology and from cultural or discursive psychology.

SITUATED KNOWING

Situated theories have generated great interest and received much critical attention in recent years (e.g., Andersen, Reder, & Simon, 1997; Greeno, 1997; Kirshner & Whitson, 1997; Watson, 1998). Lave and Wenger (also Lave, 1988; Lave, 1997; Lave & Wenger, 1991; Wenger, 1998) have given radically different meanings to knowledge, learning, transfer, and identity. Lave's studies of the acquisition of mathematical competence within tailoring apprenticeships in West Africa led her to argue that knowledge is located in particular forms of situated experience, not simply in mental contents. Knowledge has to be understood relationally, between people and settings: it is about competence in life settings. One of the consequences of this argument is that the notion of transfer of knowledge, present as decontextualized mental objects in the minds of individuals, from one situation to another, becomes perhaps untenable but at the very least requires reformulation. That argument seems to create special problems for mathematics education. Perceptions of mathematics as a discipline are predicated on increasing abstraction and generality across applications, and mathematical modeling is precisely the application of apparently decontextualized knowledge to almost any situation. Widely held perceptions of child development and of the acquisition of mathematical knowledge also are predicated on a move from the concrete to the abstract, whereby decontextualized mental schemata are constructed and can be used formally, at the appropriate stage of intellectual development. But these are not serious challenges to situated theory. The various subfields of the professional practice of mathematicians can be seen as particular social practices. To apply a mathematical gaze onto a situation and to identify and extract factors and features to mathematics is the practice of mathematical modeling. It has its masters and images of mastery, its apprenticeship procedures, its language, and its goals, just like any other social practice. Learning to "transfer" mathematics across practices is the practice. The belief that the mathematics found in practices by the gaze of the mathematical modeller is an ontologically real feature of those practices is perhaps an extra block to seeing modeling as a social practice (see Restivo, 1992, for examples of sociological, practice-based accounts of the development of abstract mathematical structures).

The practices of the school mathematics classroom are certainly very different to the practices of mathematicians, or those who use "mathematics" in the workplace, at least because school mathematics is not the *chosen* practice of students in classrooms. We can say, however, that learning to read mathematical tasks in classroom problems, which gives the appearance of decontextualized thinking, is again a particular feature of the practice of school mathematics for the "successful" students (Dowling, 1998). It is effected by an apprenticeship into the practices of classroom mathematics that carry cultural capital (Bourdieu, 1979). The agents of the apprenticeship are the teacher and the texts, but also the acceptance or acquiescence of those students who become apprenticed.

In the next three sections I examine aspects of situated theory: the need for a consideration of how subjectivities are produced in practices, as argued by Walkerdine and others; the particular nature of the practices of the mathematics classroom and the implications it has for notions of apprenticeship; and the problem of a suitable mechanism in Lave's theory of learning (1996, p. 156). In the concluding section, I discuss the unit of analysis for the study of individuals in social practices, in an attempt to bring the critiques together into a synthesis of the social turn.

Subjectivity—Regulation in Practices

A community of practice is an intrinsic condition for the existence of knowledge, not least because it provides the interpretive support necessary for making sense of its heritage. Thus, participation in the cultural practice in which any knowledge exists is an epistemological principle of learning. The social structure of this practice, its power relations, and its conditions for legitimacy define possibilities for learning (i.e., for legitimate peripheral participation). (Lave & Wenger, 1991, p. 98)

Walkerdine (1997) suggests that what is missing in Lave's analysis of the subject in practices is subjectivity, the regulation of individuals within practices. In the move away from the notion of an individual transferring decontextualized knowledge from one practice to another, to the notion of knowledge and identity being situated in specific practices, Lave's work might seem to suggest that all individuals are subjected to those practices in the same way. There appears to be a goal for the learning which is characteristic of the practice, and apprenticeship into it is monolithic in its application. However, Walkerdine shows how the notion of "child" is produced in the practices of educational psychology (1988; see also Burman, 1994), differentially positioning those who conform—white boisterous males, and those who do not—nonwhite people, girls, quiet boys, and so on. Significations matter, they are not neutral meanings: situating meanings in practices must also take into account how those significations matter differently to different people. Practices should be seen, therefore, as discursive formations within which what counts as valid knowledge is produced and within which what constitutes successful participation is also produced. Nonconformity is consequently not just a feature of the way that an individual might react as a consequence of her or his goals in a practice or previous network of experiences. The practice itself produces the insiders and outsiders. Analysis of apprenticeship in particular workplace settings might appear not to reveal differing subjectivities produced in the practice. Women and people of ethnicities other than the majority might not choose to become tailors, and those becoming excluded may be forced to leave or may choose to see themselves as not suited to that job or identity. In fact, in recent decades the entrance of women and people of color into high-powered workplace situations that were all-white male domains has highlighted the subtle and not so subtle ways in which those situations have excluded others by virtue of the manner in which those workplaces and their practices are constituted.

The classroom, being a site of a complex of practices, requires a careful consideration of subjectivities. One kind of analysis has been offered by Evans (1993), in which he argues that Foucault's work on the architecture of knowledge captures the way in which individuals are constructed by and within those practices. Evans suggests that discursive practices are not clearly bounded, they are continually changing, and one moves from one discursive practice to another through chains of signification. In a series of interviews, he asked mathematical questions set in different social contexts and identified the discursive practice that was called up by the question in its context, for a particular person. He criticizes the simplistic notion that giving real-world contexts for mathematical concepts provides "meaning" for students—a "meaning" that supposedly exists in some absolute sense and is illustrated by or modeled in that real world context. He identifies school mathematics practice as one of a range of practices that might be called up for an individual.

When that happens, if the interviewee was successful at school, she or he might focus on the mathematical calculation required and answer correctly; more frequently the identity called up would be one of low confidence and lack of success. In another analysis of the production of subjectivities through the discursive practices of the mathematics classroom, Morgan (1998) analyzed the written productions of school students in their mathematics lessons according to the ways in which the teachers framed the task through their use of official discourse (what is expected by examiners), practical discourse (whether it can be understood by nonmathematicians), or professional discourse (what mathematicians might expect).

Much sociology of education presents macro-theories about social movements and the reproduction of disadvantage in schools. Walkerdine's and Evans's accounts draw on sociological theories of poststructuralism, which describe the emergence of discursive practices, the production and maintenance of elites in and through those practices, and the techniques and technologies whereby power and knowledge are produced. Their work enables the use of Foucault's theory to look into specific practices at the micro-level of the mathematics classroom. Dowling's (1998) sociology of mathematics education owes its origins to Bernstein (e.g., 1996), who offers a language for the description of the pedagogical mechanism through which education reproduces social inequality as positionings in the classroom. Dowling carried out a study of a series of four parallel school mathematics texts that are written according to the authors' assumptions of the potentialities of different abilities. He demonstrates how the texts are in fact productive of those differing potentialities, and how the assumptions of ability coincide with the different modes of thinking produced in the stratification of society according to social class, identified through different forms of language. Cooper and Dunne (1998) also use Bernstein's theory to demonstrate how questions set in everyday contexts in national mathematics tests in the United Kingdom disadvantage working-class children. In another use of sociological theories in mathematics education, Brown (1997) draws on the work of Habermas to develop a theory in which individual learners reconcile their constructions with the framing of the socially determined code of the mathematics teacher.

In general, sociology provides resources for identifying the macro-social issues that bear on schooling but not always for making links between them and the micro-social issues that concern us in relation to the classroom. I have argued elsewhere (Lerman, 1998c) that studying individual children or groups of children can be seen as moments in the zoom of a lens in which the other, temporarily out of focus, images must also be part of the analysis. Specifically, Walkerdine brings subjectivity into the study of subject-in-social-practice and I go along with her (and Agre, 1997) in seeing it as a necessary element. Individual trajectories in the development of identities in social practices arise as a consequence of our identities in the overlapping practices in which each of us functions but also emerge from the different positions in which practices constitute the participants. We can capture the regulation of discursive practices by talking of the practice-in-person as the unit of identity, as well as the person-in-practice. I return to the question of the unit of analysis later in this discussion.

The Practices of the Mathematics Classroom

A community of practice is a set of relations among persons, activity, and the world, over time and in relation with other tangential and overlapping communities of practices. (Lave & Wenger, 1991, p. 98)

The classroom is clearly a site of many overlapping practices. Whereas the mathematics teacher's goal may be to initiate learners into (what she or he interprets as) mathematical ways of thinking and acting, learners' goals are likely to be quite different. We must therefore ask how we can extend the notion of apprenticeship to incorporate the mismatch of goals. If we are to extend the valuable insights of the notion of communities of practice into the field of knowledge production in mathematics education, the nature of those goals and of the classroom practices must be analyzed, and I turn to this task here. First, the way in which what constitutes "school mathematics" is produced requires some examination, in terms of the play of values and ideology. Second, the range of goals of the participants, both those present (teacher and students) and those physically absent (state, community, media, school) must be elaborated. At the very least we must ask, who or where are the masters in these multiple practices?

School Mathematics

Bernstein's work over a number of decades has focused on how power and control are manifested in pedagogical relations. In particular, he has looked at how the boundaries between discourses, such as those of the secondary school curriculum, are defined—what he calls the classification rules—and how control is effected within each discourse—the framing rules. As a principle, pedagogical discourse is the process of moving a practice from its original site, where it is effective in one sense, to the pedagogical site where it is used for other reasons; this is the principle of recontextualization. In relation to work practices, he offers the example of carpentry which was transformed into woodwork (in U.K. schools), and now forms an element of design and technology. School woodwork is not carpentry as it is inevitably separated from all the social elements, needs, goals, and so on, which are part of the work practice of carpentry and cannot be part of the school practice of woodwork. Similarly, school physics is not physics, and school mathematics is not mathematics. Bernstein argues that recontextualization or transformation opens a space in which ideology always plays. In the transformation to pedagogy, values are always inherent, in selection, ordering, and pacing.

In relation to mathematics, those values may include preparation for specific workplaces, but this is likely to be at the later stages of school for a small minority of students, at least in the United Kingdom. Other European countries have very different attitudes to vocational education. The school mathematics curriculum may include specific mathematics for everyday life—shopping, paying taxes, investing savings, bank accounts, and pensions—but again these issues will become meaningful to students at the later stages of schooling. The content of a mathematics curriculum which is to provide the skills necessary for either or both of these contexts would be very limited. In any case, the problems of transfer and contextualization of knowledge suggest that the teaching of these skills in the classroom for use elsewhere would be highly problematic. For the most part, curriculum is driven by a view of education that may be (1) an authoritarian view (Ball, 1993), the inculcation of an agreed selection of culturally valued knowledge and a set of moral values and ways of behaving; (2) a neoliberal view (Apple, 1998), producing citizens prepared for useful, wealth-producing lives in a democratic society; (3) a more old-liberal agenda (Hirst, 1974) of enabling children to become educated people able to fulfil their lives to the best of their abilities; or (4) a more radical agenda (Freire, 1985) of preparing people to critique and change the society in which they engage. It may also be driven merely by inertia. Schools as institutions are there, they occupy children all day while some parents and guardians work, and the mathematics curriculum, in terms of topic content, remains very similar to that of 50 years ago. Whatever the ideological and value-laden intentions for teaching on the part of the school, community, or state, the teacher has her or his goals too, which may or may not align with the institutional intentions. Initiatives such as the National Council of Teachers of Mathematics (NCTM) standards in the United States or the National Numeracy Strategy in the United Kingdom (to take two examples with very different orientations) provide yet other sets of values that regulate the teacher's behavior.

The mathematical practices within a class or school, the way in which they are classified and framed, the state/community/school values that are represented and reproduced, and the teacher's own goals and motives, form the complex background to be taken into account by the research community (see Boaler, 1997, for an exemplary study of different school practices). According to Lave, mathematics itself should be seen not as an abstract mathematical task but as something deeply bound up in socially organized activities and systems of meaning within a community. Nor, for that matter, should it be seen as a single practice. Burton (1999b) has found that mathematicians identify themselves by their subfield, as statistician, applied mathematician, mathematical modeller, or topologist. In relation to school mathematics one must be aware of the particular nature of the identities produced. Boaler (1997) has shown how different approaches to school mathematics produce different identities as school mathematicians. She suggests also that the identities produced in one of the two schools in her study, Phoenix Park school, which used a mathematics curriculum built around problem solving, overlap with students' mathematical practices outside of school, but there is less evidence for this as Boaler relies on students' accounts, given in school, of such overlap. Boaler uses both Bernstein's analysis in terms of classification and framing and Lave's communities of practice as resources to explain her findings. Recently Boaler (1999) has talked of the particular practices of the two schools as offering constraints and affordances (Greeno & MMAP, 1998) as a way of interpreting the students' behaviors, which resulted in them working to succeed, in the distinct terms of each school.

In summary, as researchers we need to examine the background that frames the mathematical practices in the classroom, irrespective of their allegiances (reform, authoritarian, or other), and draw on the resources offered by Lave, Walkerdine, Greeno, and others to study the ways that school mathematical identities are produced. In the next part I examine accounts that incorporate individual trajectories through those social practices (Confrey, 1995).

Participants' Goals

Lemke and others point to the paths of particular people's learning by referring to individual trajectories (Lemke, 1997). People come to participate in social practices from an individual set of sociocultural experiences. Individuality, in this sense, "is the uniqueness of each person's collection of multiple subjectivities, through the many overlapping and separate identities of gender, ethnicity, class, size, age, etc., to say nothing of the 'unknowable' elements of the unconscious" (Lerman, 1998c, p. 77). Lemke (1997) refers to the ecosocial system in which people function, and Engeström and Cole (1997) refer to the under-researched resistance of some actors in activities. More important to students than learning what the teacher has to offer are aspects of their peer interactions such as gender roles, ethnic stereotypes, body shape and size, abilities valued by peers, relationship to school life, and others (McLaughlin, 1994). The ways in which individuals want to see themselves developing, perhaps as the classroom fool, perhaps as attractive to someone else in the classroom, perhaps as gaining praise and attention from the teacher or indirectly from their parents, leads to particular goals in the classroom and therefore particular ways of behaving and to different things being learned, certainly different from what the teacher may wish for the learners (Boaler, 2000). Winbourne (1999; see also Winbourne & Watson, 1998) has given an account of individual children's mathematical (and other) activities that set the children in the context of the multiple social and cultural practices in which they are positioned and that influence who they are at different times in the mathematics (and every other) classroom. Santos and Matos (1998) analyze the knowledge development of students in terms that take account of their social relations. Brodie (1995) and Lerman (in press a) offer similar analyses from different perspectives.

All these accounts give social origins to the individual trajectories that clearly manifest in the classroom (Wenger, 1998). The origins of individual meanings being located in sociocultural tools roots individuality or voice in its proper framework. It is not the individualism of private worldviews, which has dominated the debate around subjectivity and voice in recent decades, but power/knowledge as constituted in discourses. Discourses that dominate in the classroom, and everywhere else for that matter, distribute powerlessness and powerfulness through positioning subjects (Evans, in press). Walkerdine's (1989, p. 143) report of a classroom incident in which the emergence of a sexist discourse bestows power on

5–year-old boys, over their experienced teacher, dramatically illustrates the significance of a focus on discourse, not on individuals. In some research on children's interpretations of bigger and smaller, Redmond (1992) found some similar evidence of meanings being located in practices.

> These two were happy to compare two objects put in front of them and tell me why they had chosen the one they had. However when I allocated the multilinks to them (the girl had 8 the boy had 5) to make a tower . . . and I asked them who had the taller one, the girl answered correctly but the boy insisted that he did. Up to this point the boy had been putting the objects together and comparing them. He would not do so on this occasion and when I asked him how we could find out whose tower was the taller he became very angry. I asked him why he thought that his tower was taller and he just replied "Because IT IS." He would go no further than this and seemed to be almost on the verge of tears. (p. 24)

Many teachers struggle to find ways to enable individual expression in the classroom, including expressing mathematical ideas, confronting the paradox of teachers giving emancipation to students from their authoritative position. But this can fruitfully be seen as a dialectic, whereby all participants in an activity manifest powerfulness and powerlessness at different times, including the teacher. When those articulations are given expression, and not denied as in some interpretations of critical pedagogy (Lerman, 1998a), shifts in relations between participants, and crucially between participants and learning, can occur (Ellsworth, 1989; Walcott, 1994).

Learning is predicated on one person learning from another, more knowledgeable, or desired, person, in Lave's terms the master. As Lave has pointed out, there are many overlapping practices in any one practice. This is particularly the case in the classroom as not many students' goals are aligned with the teacher's and very few wish to become teachers of mathematics.

Models of Mastery

Lave and Wenger's (1991) notion of mastery was not focused on school classrooms (see also Wenger, 1998) but clearly offers valuable insights that require development if we wish to use them in the formation of appropriate theoretical frameworks. Learning seen as increasing participation in practices, the gradual attainment of mastery, is a rich description of identity development, which has been shown to be appropriate to at least some aspects of the classroom (Lave, 1996).

Classroom practices include those overlapping identities produced in relation to the mathematics, such as abilities, as in Walkerdine's and Dowling's analyses, and purposes for mathematics. For instance, purposes may include minimum certification for continuing study, a key to careers and further education and training courses, or markers of recognition of general intellectual potential. Classroom mathematics practices also produce the more specific identities as, for example, good at number but not algebra, competitive or collaborative in performance, and so on. The complex of classroom practices also covers those outside of the intention of the teacher, as discussed earlier, particularly in relation to peers, and most importantly the differential regulation of different students within those practices. The teacher may perform the role of "master" for some students in relation to some aspects of what we might call the mathematical identities produced, most often specifically the mastery leading to further study of mathematics, although we are referring here to mastery in terms of school mathematics. But the teacher will not stand as the master for most of the students for most of the classroom social practices that are important for them. How, then, might we extend Lave and Wenger's notion?

I suggest that it may be fruitful to refer to *multiple models of mastery* offered in the complex of classroom practices. Expertise/mastery may be represented in a person or not, hence *models,* and those masters may be present in the classroom or not. In terms of what can be called role models, other students might perform many of the roles that students may desire to emulate. The teacher's personal style is often reported as having been a significant factor in people's identification with, or rejection of, aspects of schooling, including mathematics. In relation to people absent from the classroom, parents' stories of, for instance, their ability or lack in relation to mathematics, can function as models for a student and a sibling or valued other similarly. So, too, images of who students want to become can act as models, perhaps including media personalities. This identifies the need for more complex studies of individual trajectories in the classroom, perhaps through narrative accounts (Burton, 1999a; Santos & Matos, 1998; Winbourne, 1999), examining who are the models and what are the practices that are important to individual students.

A Mechanism for Learning

Lave argues that learning may be represented as increasing participation in communities of practice (Lave, 1996). She writes that she finds the following three features of a theory of learning to be "a liberating analytical tool" (1996, p. 156) for discussing learning as social practice:

1. *Telos:* that is, a direction of movement or change of learning (*not* the same as goal directed activity),
2. *Subject-world relation:* a general specification of relations between subjects and the social world (not necessarily to be construed as learners and things to-be-learned),
3. *Learning mechanisms:* ways by which learning comes about. (p. 156)

She argues that the *telos* of her two case studies, the tailors' apprentices and legal learning in Egypt in the 19th century, is to become masters of tailoring or law and to become respected participants of the everyday life of their communities. The preceding discussions, concerning recontextualization, the multiple practices at play in the mathematics classroom, regulation, and the need for an analysis that offers multiple models of mastery, suggests that we might need to refer to *teloi,* and the plural *subjects-worlds relations* as well as *regulative processes.* Here I wish to address Lave's third feature, that of learning mechanisms. Whatever mechanism is used, whether it is used as an explanatory framework or as an ontological statement, it must take account of the differences between workplace apprenticeships and the classroom, as well as be able to account for both. In the classroom, the teacher intends to teach: this is her or his function, however it is interpreted and realized. The difference to the situation of the master tailor is quite dramatic.

In many places in her writing Lave (e.g., 1997) proposes that one should focus on learning and make a separation of it from teaching. Lave is referring here to school teaching as the culture of acquisition, offering compartmentalized knowledge, and learning at a distance, drawing, that is, on the notion of transfer (pp. 27–28). I suspect many teachers and certainly most, if not all, in the mathematics education research community would subscribe to a move away from that view of teaching. In looking at a (sociocultural) mechanism for learning, however, the teacher has to be placed firmly into the picture. Here I will turn to Vygotsky's work, as his mechanism for learning captures at least some of the features called for by Lave and others.

Vygotsky provided a mechanism for learning with four key elements: the priority of the intersubjective; internalization; mediation; and the zone of proximal development.

- "Every function in the child's cultural development appears twice: first, on the social level, and later, on the individual level; first, *between* people (*interpsychological*), and then *inside* (*intrapsychological*). . . . All the higher functions originate as actual relations between human individuals" (Vygotsky, 1978, p. 57).

- "The process of internalization is not the transferal of an external to a pre-existing, internal 'plane of consciousness'; it is the process in which this plane is formed" (Leont'ev, 1981, p. 57).

- "Human action typically employs 'mediational means' such as tools and language, and that these mediational means shape the actions in essential ways . . . the relationship between action and mediational means is so fundamental that it is more appropriate, when referring to the agent involved, to speak of 'individual(s)-acting with mediational means' than to speak simply of 'individual(s)'" (Wertsch, 1991, p. 12).

- "We propose that an essential feature of learning is that it creates the zone of proximal development; that is, learning awakens a variety of developmental processes that are able to interact only when the child is interacting with people in his environment and in collaboration with his peers" (Vygotsky, 1978, p. 90).

Central to all these features of Vygotsky's mechanism for learning is the role of the teacher, although in various guises. It may be a more informed peer; a parent who has no explicit intention to teach; a master creating, together with the apprentice, a zone of proximal development; a text, a production of the culture from which one can learn; or indeed a teacher whose explicit intention is to enable the student to do something, be someone, or know something that he or she could not do, could not be, or did not know. All human development is led by learning *from others,* from the culture that precedes us.

Vygotsky's theories have been a huge stimulus to research in all kinds of domains of education (e.g., Cole, 1996; Cole & Wertsch, 1996; Forman, Minick, & Stone, 1993; Wertsch, 1997, to name just a few recent works) and this includes mathematics education (for a review that relates to reform-related research, see Forman, in press; see also Lerman, 1998c, 1998d) and some, hopefully productive controversy (Lerman, 1996; Lerman, 2000; Steffe & Thompson, 2000). Recent work on discourse studies (Forman, in press; Forman & Larreamendy-Joerns, in press; Krummheuer, 1995), dynamic assessment (Brown & Ferrara, 1985;) and learning in the zpd (Lerman, in press a; Meira & Lerman, 1999) are just some illustrations of the continuing interest in developing Vygotskian theories.

To what extent, though, does Vygotsky's perspective provide the mechanism to which Lave refers? Where Piaget offers equilibration as the mechanism for learning, Vygotsky proposes the zone of proximal development. For Lave, learning is transformation through increasing participation in social practices, and a mechanism for learning would need to take account of the goals of the individual in joining, or being coerced into joining, the social practice, and the specificities of the practice in terms of situated meanings and situated ways of being. The mechanism would need to take account of the factors that contribute to the individual trajectory through the practice, including what an individual brings to a practice in terms of their prior network of experiences, and the regulating effects of the practice. Vygotsky was not directly concerned with social practices. At the time of the Russian revolution the singular discourse of dialectical materialism, and the drive for progress from a feudal society to communism did not allow for the availability of other theoretical resources. His early death in 1934, at the age of 38, precluded any engagement with more relativistic social theories. However, Vygotsky's psychology is a cultural psychology (Cole, 1996; Daniels, 1993) and it opens up spaces for different analyses than those that appeared during Vygotsky's life.

Vygotsky's work is generally taken to be about the *individual learning* in a *social context,* but I have suggested in this section that his theories make it clear that the zpd offers more than that. First, in that consciousness is a product of communication, which always takes place in a historically, culturally and geographically specific location, *individuality* has to be seen as emerging in social practice(s). Vygotsky's personal history as a member of a discriminated-against minority, the Jews, whose culture is carried in specific languages (Hebrew and Yiddish) and practices, which is obviously about identity, was a key factor in forming his thinking about development (Kozulin, 1990; Van der Veer & Valsiner, 1991). Second, I have argued that all *learning* is from others, and as a consequence meanings signify, they describe the world as it is seen through the eyes of those sociocultural practices. In his discussion of inner speech, Vygotsky makes it clear that it is the process of the development of internal controls, metacognition, that is, the internalization of the adult. Again, these are mechanisms that are located in *social contexts.* Finally, the zpd is a product of the learning activity (Davydov, 1988), not a fixed "field" that the child brings with her or him to a learning situation. The zpd is therefore a product of the previous network of experiences of the individuals, including the teacher, the goals of teacher and learners, and the specificity of the learning itself. Individual trajectories are therefore key elements in the emergence (or not) of zpds (Meira & Lerman, 1999).

In fact, Lave suggests that the need for learning mechanisms "disappear(s) into practice. Mainly, people are becoming kinds of persons" (1996, p. 157). The process of accounting for "becoming kinds of persons" still calls for a mechanism, however, and I am proposing here that internalization through semiotic mediation in the zpd is a suitable candidate.

CONCLUSION: UNIT OF ANALYSIS

Perhaps the greatest challenge for research in mathematics education (and education or social sciences in general) from perspectives that can be described as being within the social turn is to develop accounts that bring together agency, individual trajectories (Apple, 1991), and the cultural, historical, and social origins of the ways people think, behave, reason, and understand the world. Any such analysis must not ignore either: it should not reduce individual functioning to social and cultural determinism nor place the source of meaning making in the individual. In order to develop such accounts, researchers can choose to begin from the development of the individual and explain the influences of culture, or from the cultural and explain individuality and agency (Gone, Miller, & Rappaport, 1999). I have argued here for the latter. In my review I have used Lave and Wenger's situated theories as a foundation and attempted to open spaces, through critique, for the development of their theories for our needs in mathematics education research. I have argued for consideration of the regulating effects of discursive practices. I have discussed the multiple practices at play in the mathematics classroom, most of which are not the intention of the teacher. As a result, the notions of mastery and legitimate peripheral participation need careful analysis in order to extend them to the classroom, and I have suggested that narrative methods of research are proving to be most fruitful in research. I have suggested that Vygotsky's notion of the zone of proximal development, when set within a discursive and cultural psychology that was not fully available to him, in terms of intellectual resources, during his lifetime, can perhaps provide the mechanism of learning to study the process of people "becoming kinds of persons."

> The study of the mind is a way of understanding the phenomena that arise when different sociocultural discourses are integrated within an identifiable human individual situated in relation to those discourses. (Harré & Gillett, 1994, p. 22)

Individuality and agency, then, emerge as the product of each person's prior network of social and cultural experiences, and their goals and needs, in relation to the social practices in which they function. I proposed the metaphor of a zoom lens for research, whereby what one chooses as the object of study becomes:

> A moment in socio-cultural studies, as a particular focusing of a lens, as a gaze which is as much aware of what is not being looked at, as of what is. . . . Draw back in the zoom, and the researcher looks at education in a particular society, at whole schools, or whole classrooms; zoom back in and one focuses on some children, or some inter-actions. The point is that research must find a way to take account of the other elements which come into focus throughout the zoom, wherever one chooses to stop." (Lerman, 1998c, p. 67)

But the object of study itself needs to take account of all the dimensions of human life, not a fragment such as cognition, or emotion. Vygotsky searched for a unit of analysis that could unify culture, cognition, affect, goals, and needs (Zinchenko, 1985). According to Minick (1987), Vygotsky moved from "the 'instrumental act' and the 'higher mental functions' . . . to the emergence of 'psychological systems'" (p. 24) and then to his third and final formulation, that "the analysis of the development of word meaning must be carried out in connection with the analysis of word in communication" (p. 26). Further on, Minick said "In 1933 and 1934 Vygotsky began to reemphasize the central function of word meaning as a means of communication, as a critical component of social practice" (p. 26). Minick pointed out (p. 18) that there is a continuity among these three stages and that they should be seen as developments, each stage incorporating the other and extending it. In the second stage, Vygotsky and Luria had carried out their seminal study (Luria, 1976) on the effects of language development on the higher mental functions, a classic piece of research (Brown & Dowling, 1998) and characteristic of Vygotsky's approach in that stage. What was missing was "the child's practical activity" (Minick, 1987, p. 26), and in the third stage he argued for the importance of incorporating goals and needs into the unit of analysis.

> Of course, by "relationship" Vygotsky meant here not a passive relationship of perceiving or processing incoming stimuli, but a relationship defined by the child's needs and goals, a relationship defined by the forms of social practice that "relate" the child to an objective environment and define what the environment means for the child. (p. 32)

The defining and prior element is the social practice, that the child's goals and needs are a crucial factor in the learning process, and that what the environment signifies is also defined by the social practice, not by the child. Minick stated that by this formulation:

> Vygotsky was making some significant strides toward the realization of the goal that he had established in 1924 and 1925, the goal of a theoretical perspective that would allow a unified analysis of behavior and consciousness while recognizing the unique socio-historical nature of the human mind. (p. 33)

The first part of a unit of analysis is provided by Lave's work and incorporates Vygotsky's goal, that of person-in-activity. Vygotsky's book title, *Mind in Society* (1978), is of the same essence. I have argued in this chapter for a theory of teaching and learning mathematics that incorporates Lave and Wenger's communities of practice notion with the regulative features of discursive practices and the consequences of the multiple practices that manifest in the classroom. I want, therefore, to extend the unit of person-in-activity to incorporate these bodies of work. When a person steps into a practice, she or he has already changed. The person has an orientation toward the practice, or has goals that have led the person to the practice, even if she or he leaves the practice after a short time. One can express that change by noting that the practice has become in the person. In order to incorporate these developments, I want to suggest that the unit of analysis be extended to person-in-practice-in-person or, to give credit to Vygotsky, mind-in-society-in-mind (Slonimsky, personal communication, September 1999).

Finally, I want to propose a task for the reader, first suggested by Slonimsky (personal communication, September 1999), to search for a suitable metaphor for mind-in-society-in-mind. The search is a productive activity, in that proposing metaphors and working with them to locate meanings in the two domains linked by the metaphor develops the potentialities of the meaning and use of, in this case, the notion mind-in-society-in-mind. By way of a first attempt, I offer the image of a shoot on the side of a growing plant. What is required for a suitable metaphor is, at least, that the metaphorical referent has a history (development of the plant to that point, genetic material), that it allows for an individual trajectory (one cannot predict its growth), and that it allows for experiences of overlapping practices (other plants taking nutrients, perhaps a wall or fences that alter the growth).

Research that works with person-in-practice, or mind-in-society, as a unit of analysis, such as activity theory (Cole et al., 1997) and some of the work on development in the zone of proximal development, would need to hold a focus on agency and the regulating effects of the practice(s). The notion of mind-in-society-in-mind is yet further indication of the extent of the contextualization of human activity.

REFERENCES

Agre, P. E. (1997). Living math: Lave and Walkerdine on the meaning of everyday arithmetic. In D. Kirshner & J. A. Whitson (Eds.), *Situated cognition: Social, semiotic and psychological perspectives* (pp. 71–82). Mahwah, NJ: Erlbaum.

Andersen, J. R., Reder, L. M., & Simon, H. A. (1997). Situative versus cognitive perspectives: Form versus substance. *Educational Researcher 26*(1), 18–21.

Apple, M. (1991). The culture and commerce of the textbook. In M. Apple & L. Christian-Smith (Eds.), *The politics of the textbook* (pp. 22–39). London: Routledge.

Apple, M. (1998). Markets and standards: The politics of education in a conservative age. In A. Olivier & K. Newstead (Eds.), *Proceedings of the twenty-second annual meeting of the International Group for the Psychology of Mathematics Education* (Vol. 1, 19–32). Stellenbosch, South Africa: Faculty of Education, The University of Stellenbosch.

Ball, S. J. (1993). Education, majorism and the "curriculum of the dead." *Curriculum Studies, 1*(2), 195–214.

Bernstein, B. (1996). *Pedagogy, symbolic control and identity: Theory, research, critique.* London: Taylor & Francis.

Bishop, A. J. (1988a). *Mathematical enculturation.* Dordrecht, The Netherlands: Kluwer.

Bloor, D. (1976). *Knowledge and social imagery.* London: Routledge.

Bishop, A. J. (1988b). Mathematics education in its cultural context. *Educational Studies in Mathematics 19*(2), 179–191.

Boaler, J. (1997). *Experiencing school mathematics: Teaching styles, sex and setting.* Buckingham, UK: Open University Press.

Boaler, J. (1999). Participation, knowledge and beliefs: A community perspective on mathematics learning. *Educational Studies in Mathematics 40,* 259–281.

Boaler, J. (2000). Mathematics from another world: Traditional communities and the alienation of learners. *Journal of Mathematical Behavior 18*(4), 1–19.

Bourdieu, P. (1979). *An outline of a theory of practice.* Cambridge, UK: Cambridge University Press.

Brodie, K. (1995). Peer interaction and the development of mathematical knowledge. In D. Carraher & L. Meira (Eds.), *Proceedings of the nineteenth annual meeting of the International Group for the Psychology of Mathematics Education,* (Vol. 3, 216–223). Recife, Brazil: Universidade Federal de Pernambuco.

Brown, A., & Dowling, P. (1998). *Doing research/reading research: A mode of interrogation for education.* London: Falmer.

Brown, A., & Ferrara, R. (1985). Diagnosing zones of proximal development. In J. Wertsch (Ed.), *Culture, communication and cognition: Vygotskian perspectives* (pp. 273–305). Cambridge, MA: Harvard University Press.

Brown, T. (1997). *Mathematics education and language: interpreting hermeneutics and post-structuralism.* Dordrecht, The Netherlands: Kluwer.

Bruner, J. (1986). *Actual minds, possible worlds.* Cambridge, MA: Harvard University Press.

Burman, E. (1994). *Deconstructing developmental psychology.* London: Routledge.

Burton, L. (1999a). The implicatons of a narrative approach to the learning of mathematics. In L. Burton (Ed.), *Learning mathematics: From hierarchies to networks* (pp. 21–35). London: Falmer.

Burton, L. (1999b). The practices of mathematicians: What do they tell us about coming to know mathematics? *Educational Studies in Mathematics, 37,* 121–143.

Carraher, T. (1988). Street mathematics and school mathematics. In A. Borbás (Ed.). *Proceedings of the twelfth annual meeting of the International Group for the Psychology of Mathematics Education* (Vol. 1, pp. 1–23). Veszprém, Hungary: OOK.

Cobb, P. (1989). Experiential, cognitive, and anthropological perspectives in mathematics education. *For the Learning of Mathematics 9*(2), 32–43.

Cole, M. (1996). *Cultural psychology: A once and future discipline.* Cambridge, MA: Harvard University Press.

Cole, M., Engeström, Y., & Vasquez, O. (1997). *Mind, culture and activity.* Cambridge, MA: Harvard University Press.

Cole, M., & Wertsch, J. V. (1996). *Contemporary implications of Vygotsky and Luria.* Worcester, MA: Clark University Press.

Confrey, J. (1981). *Using the clinical interview to explore students' mathematical understanding.* East Lansing, MI: Institute for Research on Teaching, Science-Mathematics Teaching Center, Michigan State University.

Confrey, J. (1995). Student voice in examining "splitting" as an approach to ratio, proportions and fractions. In L. Meira & D. Carraher (Eds.), *Proceedings of the nine-*

teenth annual meeting of the International Group for the Psychology of Mathematics Education (Vol. 1, p. 3–29). Recife, Brazil: Universidade Federal de Pernambuco.

Cooper, B., & Dunne, M. (1998). Anyone for tennis? Social class differences in children's responses to national curriculum mathematics testing. *The Sociological Review, 46*(1), 115–148.

Crawford, K. (1985). Review of Wertsch (1981). *Educational Studies in Mathematics 16*(4), 431–433.

Crawford, K. (1988). New contexts for learning in mathematics. In A. Borbás (Ed.), *Proceedings of the twelfth annual meeting of the International Group for the Psychology of Mathematics Education* (Vol. 1, pp. 239–246). Veszprém, Hungary: OOK.

D'Ambrosio, U. (1984). Socio-cultural bases for mathematical education. In *Proceedings of the fifth international congress on mathematical education* (pp. 1–6). Boston: Birkhäuser.

Daniels, H. (Ed.) (1993). *Charting the agenda: Educational activity after Vygotsky.* London: Routledge.

Davis, P. J., & Hersh, R. (1981). *The mathematical experience.* Brighton: Harvester.

Davydov, V. V. (1988). Problems of developmental teaching. *Soviet Education, 30,* 6–97.

Dawson, A. J. (1969). *The implications of the work of Popper, Polya and Lakatos for a model of mathematics instruction.* Unpublished doctoral dissertation, University of Alberta.

Donaldson, M. (1978). *Children's minds.* London: Fontana.

Dowling, P. (1998). *The sociology of mathematics education.* London: Falmer.

Ellsworth, E. (1989). Why doesn't this feel empowering? Working through the repressive myths of critical pedagogy. *Harvard Educational Review, 59*(3), 297–324.

Engeström, Y., & Cole, M. (1997). Situated cognition is search of an agenda. In D. Kirshner & J. A. Whitson (Eds.), *Situated cognition: Social, semiotic and psychological perspectives* (pp. 301–309). Mahwah, NJ: Erlbaum.

English, L. D. (1993). Children's strategies for solving two- and three-dimensional combinatorial problems. *Journal for Research in Mathematics Education, 24*(3), 255–273.

Ernest, P. (1985). The philosophy of mathematics and mathematics education. *International Journal of Mathematical Education In Science and Technology, 16*(5), 603–612.

Ernest, P. (1991). *The philosophy of mathematics education.* London: Falmer.

Evans, J. (1993). *Adults and numeracy.* Unpublished PhD Thesis, University of London Institute of Education.

Evans, J. T. (in press). *Mathematical thinking and emotions: A study of adults' numerate practices.* London: Falmer.

Feuerstein, R. (1980). *Instrumental enrichment: An intervention program for cognitive modifiability.* Baltimore: University Park Press.

Forman, E. (in press). A sociocultural approach to mathematics reform: Speaking, inscribing, and doing mathematics within communities of practice. In J. Kilpatrick, G. Martin, & D. Schifter (Eds.), *A research companion to the NCTM Standards.* Reston, VA: National Council of Teachers of Mathematics.

Forman, E. A., & Larreamendy-Joerns, J. (in press). Making explicit the implicit: Classroom explanations and conversational implicatures. *Mind, Culture, and Activity.*

Forman, E. A., Minick, N., & Stone, C. A. (Eds.) (1993). *Contexts for learning: Sociocultural dynamics in children's development* (pp. 213–229). New York: Oxford University Press.

Freire, P. (1985). *The politics of education.* Basingstoke, UK: MacMillan.

Gone, J. P., Miller, P. J., & Rappaport, J. (1999). Conceptual narrative as normatively oriented: The suitability of past personal narrative for the study of cultural identity. *Culture & Psychology, 5*(4), 371–398.

Greeno, J. G. (1997). On claims that answer the wrong question. *Educational Researcher, 26*(1), 5–17.

Greeno, J. G. & MMAP (1998). The situativity of knowing, learning and research. *American Psychologist,* 5–26.

Hanna, G. (1996). The ongoing value of proof. In L. Puig & A. Gutiérrez (Eds.), *Proceedings of the twentieth conference of the International Group for the Psychology of Mathematics Education* (Vol. 1, pp. 21–34). Dept. de Didàctica de la Matemàtica, Universitat de València.

Harré, R. & Gillett, G. (1994). *The discursive mind.* London: Sage.

Hart, K. (Ed.) (1981). *Children's understanding of mathematics: 11–16.* London: Murray.

Hirst, P. H. (1974). *Knowledge and the curriculum.* London: Routledge.

Hoyles, C., Noss, R., & Pozzi, S. (1999). Mathematizing in practice. In C. Hoyles, C. Morgan, & G. Woodhouse (Eds.), *Rethinking the mathematics curriculum* (pp. 48–62). London: Falmer.

Joseph, G. G. (1991). *The crest of the peacock.* London: Taurus.

Kilpatrick, J. (1992). A history of research in mathematics education. In D. A. Grouws (Ed.), *Handbook of research on mathematics teaching and learning* (pp. 3–38). New York: MacMillan.

Kirshner, D., & Whitson, J. A. (1997). *Situated cognition: Social, semiotic and psychological perspectives.* Mahwah, NJ: Erlbaum.

Kitcher, P. (1983). *The nature of mathematical knowledge.* New York: Oxford University Press.

Kozulin, A. (1990). *Vygotsky's psychology: A biography of ideas.* Hemel Hempstead, UK: Harvester Wheatsheaf.

Krummheuer, G. (1995). The ethnography of argumentation. In P. Cobb & H. Bauersfeld (Eds.), *The emergence of mathematical meaning: Interaction in classroom cultures* (pp. 229–269). Hillsdale, NJ: Erlbaum.

Lakatos, I. (1976). *Proofs and refutations* Cambridge, UK: Cambridge University Press.

Lave, J. (1988). *Cognition in practice: Mind, mathematics and culture in everyday life* Cambridge, UK: Cambridge University Press.

Lave, J. (1996). Teaching, as learning, in practice. *Mind, Culture & Activity, 3,* 149–164.

Lave, J. (1997). The culture of acquisition and the practice of understanding. In D. Kirshner & J. A. Whitson (Eds.), *Situated cognition: Social, semiotic and psychological perspectives* (pp. 17–35). Mahwah, NJ: Erlbaum.

Lave, J., & Wenger, E. (1991). *Situated learning: Legitimate peripheral participation.* New York: Cambridge University Press.

Lemke, J. L. (1997). Cognition, context and learning: A social semiotic perspective. In D. Kirshner & J. A. Whitson (Eds.), *Situated cognition: Social, semiotic and psychological perspectives* (pp. 37–55). Mahwah, NJ: Lawrence Erlbaum.

Leont'ev, A. N. (1981). The problem of activity in psychology. In J. V. Wertsch (Ed.), *The concept of activity in soviet psychology* (pp. 37–71). Armonk, NY: Sharpe.

Lerman, S. (1983). Problem-solving or knowledge-centred: The influence of philosophy on mathematics teaching. *International Journal of Mathematical Education in Science and Technology, 14*(1), 59–66.

Lerman, S. (1996). Intersubjectivity in mathematics learning: A challenge to the radical constructivist paradigm? *Journal for research in mathematics education 27,* 133–150.

Lerman, S. (1998a). The intension/intention of teaching mathematics. In C. Kanes (Ed.), *Proceedings of Mathematics Education Research Group of Australasia* (Vol. 1, pp. 29–44). Griffith University at the Gold Coast, Australia: Mathematics Education Research Group of Australasia Inc.

Lerman, S. (1998b). Learning as social practice: an appreciative critique. In A. Watson (Ed), *Situated cognition and the learning of mathematics* (pp. 33–42). Oxford, UK: Centre for Mathematics Education Research, University of Oxford Department of Educational Studies.

Lerman, S. (1998c). A moment in the zoom of a lens: Towards a discursive psychology of mathematics teaching and learning. In A. Olivier & K. Newstead (Eds.), *Proceedings of the twenty-second annual meeting of the International Group for the Psychology of Mathematics Education* (Vol. 1, 66–81). Stellenbosch, South Africa: Faculty of Education, The University of Stellenbosch.

Lerman, S. (1998d). Research on socio-cultural perspectives of mathematics teaching and learning. In J. Kilpatrick & A. Sierpinska (Eds.), *Mathematics education as a research domain: A search for identity* (Vol. 1, pp. 333–350). Dordrecht, The Netherlands: Kluwer.

Lerman, S. (1999). Doing research in mathematics education in time of paradigm wars. In O. Zaslavsky (Ed.), *Proceedings of the twenty-third annual meeting of the International Group for the Psychology of Mathematics Education* (Vol. 1, pp 85–87). Haifa, Israel: Technion-Israel Institute of Technology.

Lerman, S. (2000). A case of interpretations of social: A response to Steffe and Thompson. *Journal for Research in Mathematics Education, 31*(2), 210–227.

Lerman, S. (in press). Accounting for accounts of learning mathematics: Reading the ZPD in videos and transcripts. In D. Clarke (Ed.), *Perspectives on meaning in mathematics and science classrooms.* Dordrecht, The Netherlands: Kluwer.

Lerman, S., & Tsatsaroni, A. (1998). *Why children fail and what mathematics education studies can do about it: The role of sociology.* Paper presented at First International Conference on Mathematics, Education and Society (MEAS1), University of Nottingham. Available at: http://www.nottingham.ac.uk/csme/meas/plenaries/lerman.html

Luria, A. R. (1976). *Cognitive development: Its cultural and social foundations.* Cambridge, MA: Harvard University Press.

McLaughlin, M. (1994). Somebody knows my name. *Issues in Restructuring Schools, Fall*(7), 9–11.

Meira, L., & Lerman, S. (1999). *The zone of proximal development as a symbolic space.* Manuscript submitted for publication.

Minick, N. (1987). The development of Vygotsky's thought: An introduction. In R. W. Rieber & A. S. Carton (Eds.), *The collected works of L. S. Vygotsky. Volume 1: Problems of general psychology* (pp. 17–36). New York: Plenum.

Morgan, C. (1998). *Writing mathematically: The discourse of investigation.* London: Falmer.

Nickson, M. (1981). *Social foundations of the mathematics curriculum.* Unpublished doctoral dissertation, University of London Institute of Education.

Nickson, M., & Lerman, S. (Eds.) (1992). *The social context of mathematics education: Theory and practice.* London: South Bank Press.

Piaget, J., & Garcia, R. (1989). *Psychogenesis and the history of science.* New York: Columbia University Press.

Radford, L. (1997). On psychology, historical epistemology, and the teaching of mathematics: Towards a socio-cultural history of mathematics. *For the Learning of Mathematics, 17*(1), 26–32.

Redmond, J. (1992). *Are 4–7 year-old children influenced by discursive practices when asked to make comparisons using quantities?* Unpublished manuscript, South Bank University, London.

Restivo, S. (1992). *Mathematics in society and history.* Dordrecht, The Netherlands: Kluwer.

Restivo, S., van Bendegem, J. P., & Fischer, R. (Eds.) (1993). *Math worlds: Philosophical and social studies of mathematics and mathematics education.* Albany, NY: State University Of New York Press.

Rogers, L. (1978). The philosophy of mathematics and the methodology of teaching mathematics *Analysen, 2,* 63–67.

Rogers, L. (in press). The biogenetic law and its influence on theories of learning mathematics. In T. Rowland (Ed.), *Proceedings of British Society for Research into Learning Mathematics, Vol. 2.* Spring 2000.

Rotman, B. (1988). Towards a semiotics of mathematics. *Semiotica, 72*(1–2), 1–35.

Santos, M. dos, & Matos, J.-F. (1998) School mathematics learning: Participation through appropriation of mathematical artefacts. In A. Watson (Ed.), *Situated cognition and the learning of mathematics.* Oxford, UK: Centre for Mathematics Education Research, University of Oxford Department of Educational Studies.

Schmittau, J. (1993). Connecting mathematical knowledge: A dialectical perspective. *Journal of Mathematical Behavior, 12*(2), 179–201.

Scott, D., & Usher, R. (Eds.) (1996). *Understanding educational research.* London: Routledge.

Sowder, J., Armstrong, B., Lamon, S., Simon, M., Sowder, L., & Thompson, A. (1998). Educating teachers to teach multiplicative structures in the middle grades. *Journal of Mathematics Teacher Education, 1*(2), 127–155.

Steffe, L. P., & Thompson, P. W. (2000). Interaction or intersubjectivity? A reply to Lerman. *Journal for Research in Mathematics Education 31*,(2), 191–209.

Steffe, L. P., von Glasersfeld, E., Richards, J., & Cobb, P. (1983). *Children's counting types: Philosophy, theory and application.* New York: Praeger Scientific.

Tymoczko, T. (Ed.) (1986). *New directions in the philosophy of mathematics.* Boston: Birkhaüser.

Van der Veer, J., & Valsiner, J. (1991). *Understanding Vygotsky: A quest for synthesis.* Oxford, UK: Oxford University Press.

Vygotsky, L. (1978). *Mind in society.* Cambridge, MA: Harvard University Press.

Vygotsky, L. (1986). *Thought and language* (trans. and ed. A. Kozulin). Cambridge, MA: MIT Press.

Walcott, R. (1994). Pedagogical desire and the crisis of knowledge. *Discourse, 15*(1), 64–74.

Walkerdine, V. (1988). *The mastery of reason.* London: Routledge.

Walkerdine, V. (1997). Redefining the subject in situated cognition theory. In D. Kirshner & J. A. Whitson (Eds.), *Situated cognition: Social, semiotic and psychological perspectives* (pp. 57–70). Mahwah, NJ: Erlbaum.

Walkerdine, V., & Girls and Maths Unit. (1989), *Counting girls out.* London: Virago.

Watson, A. (Ed.) (1998). *Situated cognition and the learning of mathematics.* Oxford, UK: Centre for Mathematics Education Research, University of Oxford Department of Educational Studies.

Wenger, E. (1998). *Communities of practice: Learning, meaning and identity.* Cambridge, UK: Cambridge University Press.

Wertsch, J. V. (Ed.) (1981). *The concept of activity in Soviet psychology.* Armonk, NY: Sharpe.

Wertsch, J. V. (1991). *Voices of the mind: A sociocultural approach to mediated action.* Cambridge, MA: Harvard University Press.

Wertsch, J. V. (1997). *Mind as action.* Oxford, UK: Oxford University Press.

Winbourne, P. (1999). Mathematical becoming: The place of mathematics in the unfolding stories of learners' identities. In A. Olivier & K. Newstead (Eds.), *Proceedings of the twenty-second annual meeting of the International Group for the Psychology of Mathematics Education* (Vol. 1, p. 329). Stellenbosch, South Africa: Faculty of Education, The University of Stellenbosch.

Winbourne, P., & Watson, A. (1998). Learning mathematics in local communities of practice. In A. Olivier & K. Newstead (Eds.), *Proceedings of the twenty-second annual meeting of the International Group for the Psychology of Mathematics Education* (Vol. 4, pp. 177–184). Stellenbosch, South Africa: Faculty of Education, The University of Stellenbosch.

Zinchenko, V. P. (1985). Vygotsky's ideas about units for the analysis of mind. In J. V. Wertsch (Ed.), *Culture, communication, and cognition: Vygotskian perspectives* (pp. 94–118). Cambridge, UK: Cambridge University Press.

3

The Importance of a Situated View of Learning to the Design of Research and Instruction

Paul Cobb

INTRODUCTION

My purpose in this chapter is to illustrate the situated approach that I and my colleagues[1] take in our work as mathematics educators and instructional designers. The type of research that we conduct involves classroom teaching or design experiments of up to a year in duration. In these experiments, the teacher is a full member of the research team that collectively assumes responsibility for supporting the students' mathematical learning. One of our primary motivations when conducting a design experiment is to explore the prospects for reform at the classroom level by investigating what might be possible for students' learning in particular mathematical domains. To this end, we develop, test, and revise sequences of instructional activities and associated resources, such as computer-based tools, while the experiment is in progress. These ongoing modifications are informed by the analyses of classroom events that we discuss in debriefing meetings held after every classroom session. As it transpires, this daily cycle of planning, instruction, and analysis is highly consistent with the practices of skilled teachers whose overriding goal is to nurture their students' development of relatively deep mathematical understandings (cf. Ball, 1993; Franke et al., 1998; Lampert, 1990; Simon, 1995; Stigler & Hiebert, 1999). As a consequence, the implications of this type of research are usually realized relatively quickly because the findings are grounded in the reality of learning and teaching in school classrooms.

When we began conducting design experiments 13 years ago, we initially followed a constructivist psychological approach that involved focusing almost exclusively on individual students' mathematical activity and reasoning. However, we have gradually adopted an increasingly strong situated perspective as we have addressed the concrete questions and issues that have arisen in the course of our classroom-based work. It is important to stress that we did not consciously decide to take a situated approach to the problems of mathematics learning and teaching in what might be termed a top-down manner. Instead, our shift in theoretical orientation has been highly pragmatic. I take a similarly pragmatic approach in the first of the four major sections of this chapter by framing a recent design experiment as a paradigm case in which to illustrate how I and my colleagues view students' mathematical learning as situated with respect to the means by which it is supported in the classroom. In doing so, I also argue that the classroom in which we conducted this experiment can be viewed as a classroom activity system that was specifically designed to produce mathematical learning. In the second part of the chapter, I highlight the central features of the design experiment methodology to illustrate that it is well suited to the task of testing and improving classroom activity systems, and thus the mathematical learning of the participating students. Given our goals as mathematics educators and instructional designers, a thoroughgoing situated perspective that highlights systems as well as individuals can therefore be viewed as a strength rather than a weakness. My focus shifts in the third major section of the chapter to the interpretive approach that we use when making sense of classroom events. To provide direction for this discussion, I begin by outlining three criteria that an approach appropriate for our purposes should satisfy. I then describe in some detail the general theoretical orientation that has emerged in the course of our work in classrooms. My intent in doing so is to clarify how we have drawn on ideas from a range of different paradigms by adapting them to our purposes. This theoretical overview then serves as a backdrop against which to outline the specific framework that we use to organize classroom analyses. Finally, in the last section of the chapter, I step back to consider the usefulness of interpretive approaches of this type. In doing so, I consider their pragmatic value and then focus on their explanatory power, contrasting them with more traditional interpretive schemes that involve the manipulation and control of independent variables.

SUPPORTING STUDENTS' MATHEMATICAL LEARNING

The design experiment that I use to illustrate the sense in which I and my colleagues view students' mathematical learning as situated was conducted in an American seventh-grade classroom and focused on statistical data analysis. I first give an overview of the experiment and then discuss four aspects of the classroom learning environment that proved critical in supporting the students' mathematical development:

- The instructional tasks
- The structure of classroom activities
- The computer-based tools the students used
- The classroom discourse

Background to the Design Experiment

In preparing for the 10–week experiment, the researchers conducted interviews and whole-class performance assessments with a group of seventh graders from the same school in which we planned to work. These assessments indicated that data analysis for most of these students involved "doing something with the numbers" (McGatha, Cobb, & McClain, 1999). In other words, they did not view data as measures of aspects or features of a situation that had been generated in order to understand a phenomenon or make a judgment (e.g., the points that a player scores in a series of basketball games as a measure of her skill at the game). In a very real sense, rather than analyzing data, the students were simply manipulating numbers in a relatively procedural manner. Further, when the students compared two data sets (e.g., the points scored by two basketball players in a series of games), they typically calculated the means without considering whether this was useful given the question or issue at hand. In the case of the points scored by the two basketball players, for example, the approach of simply calculating the means would not necessarily be a good way to select a player for an important game because it ignores possible differences in the range and variability of the players' scores (e.g., the player with a slightly lower mean might be much more consistent). I should stress that in interpreting these findings, we did not view ourselves as documenting a psychological stage in seventh graders' reasoning about data. Instead, we were documenting the consequences of the students' prior instruction in statistics. They had, for example, previously studied measures of center (i.e., mean, mode, and median) as well as several types of statistical graphs (e.g., bar graphs, histograms, and pie charts). Our assessments therefore told us something about not just the content but the quality of that prior instruction. They indicate, for example, that classroom activities had emphasized calculational procedures and conventions for drawing graphs rather than the creation and manipulation of graphs to detect trends and patterns in the data. This view of the students' reasoning as situated with respect to prior instruction proved useful in that it enabled us to clarify the starting points for the design experiment. For example, we concluded from the assessments that our immediate goal was not one of merely remediating certain competencies and skills. Instead, the challenge was to influence the students' beliefs about what it means to do statistics in school. In doing so, it would be essential that they actually begin to analyze data in order to address a significant question rather than simply manipulate numbers and draw specific types of graphs.

The students' reasoning in these initial assessments contrasts sharply with the ways in which they analyzed data at the end of the 10–week experiment. As an illustration, in one instructional activity, the students compared two treatment protocols for patients with acquired immunodeficiency syndrome (AIDS) by analyzing the T-cell counts of people who had enrolled in one of the two protocols. Their task was to assess whether a new experimental protocol in which 46 people had enrolled was more successful in raising T-cell counts than a standard protocol in which 186 people had enrolled. The data the students analyzed is shown in Figure 1 as it was displayed in the second of the two computer-based minitools that they used.

Figure 1.
The AIDS protocol data partitioned at T-cell counts of 525.

Experimental treatment

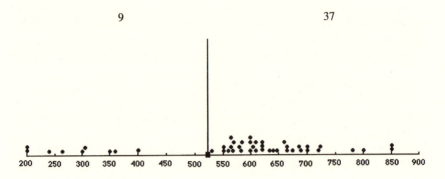

Traditional treatment

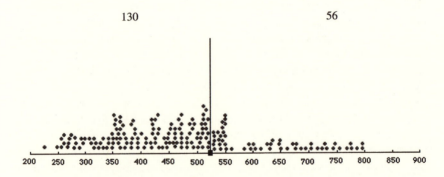

All 29 students in the class concluded from their analyses that the experimental treatment protocol was more effective. Nonetheless, the subsequent whole-class discussion lasted for over an hour and focused on both the adequacy of the reports the students had written for a chief medical officer and the soundness of their arguments. For example, one group of students had partitioned the two data sets at T-cell counts of 525 by using one of the options on the minitool as shown in Figure 1. In the course of the discussion, it became clear that the choice of 525 was not arbitrary. Instead, they had observed that what they referred to as the "hill" in the experimental treatment data was above 525 whereas the "hill" in the standard treatment data was below 525. It was also apparent from the discussion that both they and the other students who contributed to the discussion reasoned about the display shown in Figure 1 in terms of relative rather than absolute frequencies (i.e., they focused on the *proportion* rather than the absolute number of the patients in each treatment protocol whose T-cell counts were above and below 525). This was indicated by explanations in which students argued that the majority of the T-cell counts in the experimental treatment were above 525 but the majority of the T-cell counts in the traditional treatment were below 525.

This analysis was one of the most elementary that the students produced on this task. As a point of comparison, another group of students had hidden the individual data points and had used a second option on the computer minitool to partition the two data sets into four groups, each of which contained one-fourth of the data points (see Figure 2). In this option, 25 percent of the data in each data set are located in each of the four intervals bounded by the vertical bars (similar to a box-and-whiskers graph). As one student explained, these graphs show that the experimental treatment is more effective because the T-cell counts of 75 percent of the patients in this treatment were above 550 whereas the T-cell counts of only 25 percent of the patients who had enrolled in the standard treatment were above 550. This student's argument was representative in that he, like the other students who contributed to the discussion, was actually reasoning about data rather than attempting to recall procedures for manipulating numerical values.

As we have reported elsewhere, we also conducted individual interviews with the students at the end of the experiment (Cobb, 1999; McClain, Cobb, &

Figure 2.

Experimental Treatment

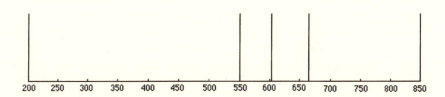

Traditional Treatment

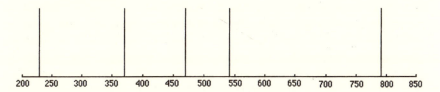

Gravemeijer, in press). The analysis of these interviews corroborates our class-room observations and indicates that a significant majority of the students came to reason about data in relatively sophisticated ways. In this regard, Konold, Pollatsek, Well, and Gagnon (1996) argue that a focus on the rate of occurrence (i.e., the proportion) of data within a range of values (e.g., above or below T-cell counts of 525) is at the heart of what they term a statistical perspective. As discussions in the latter part of the experiment involved a concern for the proportion of data within various ranges of values, the students appeared to be developing this statistical perspective. It is also worth noting that the following school year we conducted a second design experiment with some of the same students that focused on statistical covariation. Our observations during the first part of this experiment indicate that there had been no regression in the students' reasoning about data during the 9–month gap between the two experiments (Cobb, McClain, & Gravemeijer, 2000).

This brief overview of the experiment gives some indication of how the students' reasoning about data changed during the 10–week experiment. To illustrate how their development was situated with respect to the classroom learning environment, I focus next on the process of change and the means by which it was supported and organized.

Instructional Tasks

In preparing for the design experiment, we took account of the profound changes in the discipline of statistics that have been fueled by the development of computer-based data analysis tools. The statistics that most of us studied in college emphasized the formulation and testing of hypotheses (e.g., performing a t-test to investigate whether the difference between the means of experimental and control groups is due to chance variation or whether it might reflect more general differences in the treatments). In this approach, the way in which the data are to be analyzed has to be stated *before* they are even inspected. In contrast, statisticians now use computer-based tools to search for trends and patterns in data in a previously forbidden post hoc manner (Cobb, 1997). This process of "data snooping," which is called exploratory data analysis (EDA), complements traditional computational methods with new techniques that involve creating and manipulating graphical representations of data (Moore, 1996). Biehler and Steinbring (1991) use the metaphor of detective work to characterize EDA in that the purpose is to search for evidence whereas traditional methods of statistical inference play the role of the jury that decides on the basis of evidence. As they make clear, this exploratory orientation is central to data analysis and constitutes an important instructional goal in its own right. From this, my colleagues and I concluded that it would be essential for students' activity in the design experiment classroom to be imbued with the spirit of genuine data analysis from the outset. This in turn implied that the instructional tasks should all involve analyzing realistic data sets for a purpose that the students considered reasonable. As a consequence, the tasks we developed involved analyzing either (1) a single data set to understand a phenomenon, or (2) comparing two data sets to make a decision or judgment. The example of the two AIDS treatment protocols illustrates the second of the two types of instructional tasks.

In terminology consistent with a situated perspective, our concern that the students' activity should involve the genuine spirit of data analysis highlights the importance of considering the overall goal or motive of their activity in the classroom (cf. Leont'ev, 1978). Our view that the motive for doing statistics should be to search for trends and patterns in data had concrete implications for our instructional design. Their learning was therefore situated with respect to this general motive which served to orient the way in which they approached specific instructional activities (cf. Saxe, 1991). It is also worth observing that the changes I have noted in statistics as a discipline illustrate a contention that is central to all situated viewpoints, namely, that the use of new tools does not merely amplify an activity by making it more efficient but can change the very nature of the activity (cf. Dörfler, 1993; Pea, 1993; Wertsch, del Rio, & Alvarez, 1995). It was only as desktop computers became commonplace that the general approach of EDA originally proposed by Tukey (1977) became feasible, and this in turn led to the further development of data analysis methods. In this case, the changes were in the activities of an entire disciplinary community. As we will see, this core assumption of situated approaches to mathematical learning also has implications for instructional design in which the goal is to support and organize changes in the activities of classroom communities.

The Structure of Classroom Activities

A second major design decision that we made when preparing for the teaching experiment stemmed from our concern that statistics should actually involve analyzing data rather than merely manipulating numbers. To this end, we developed an approach in which the teacher talked through the data generation process with the students. These conversations often involved protracted discussions during which the teacher and students together framed the particular phenomenon under investigation (e.g., AIDS), clarified its significance (e.g., the importance of developing more effective treatments), delineated relevant aspects of the situation that should be measured (e.g., T-cell counts), and considered how they might be measured (e.g., taking blood samples). The teacher then introduced the data the students were to analyze as being produced by this process. The resulting structure of classroom activities, which often spanned two or more class sessions, was therefore (1) a whole-class discussion of the data creation process, (2) individual or small-group activity in which the students worked at computers to analyze data, and (3) a whole-class discussion of the students' analyses.

In outlining this activity structure, we conjectured that as a consequence of participating in discussions of the data creation process, the data would come to have a history for the students such that it reflected the interests and purposes for which it was generated (cf. Latour, 1987; Lehrer & Romberg, 1996; Roth, 1997). As it transpired, this conjecture proved to be well founded. For example, we have clear indications that within a week of the beginning of the design experiment, doing statistics in the project classroom actually involved analyzing data (Cobb, 1999; McClain, et al., in press). In addition, changes in the way that the students contributed to discussions of the data creation process as the experiment progressed indicate that there was a gradual handover of responsibility from the teacher to the students (Tzou, 2000). Initially, the teacher had to take an extremely proactive role. However, later in the experiment, the students increasingly initiated shifts in these discussions in the course of which they raised concerns about the need to control extraneous variables and about sampling methods. These contributions suggest that most if not all the students had developed some awareness that the legitimacy of the conclusions drawn from data depends crucially on the data generation process (cf. Cobb & Moore, 1997). We should stress that the teacher did not attempt to teach the students how to generate sound data directly. Instead, she subtly guided the emergence of a classroom culture in which a premium was placed on the development of data-based arguments. It was against this background that the students gradually became able to anticipate the implications of the data generation process for the conclusions that they would be able to draw from data. Thus, the students' learning appeared to be situated with respect to their participation in the conversations that the teacher orchestrated about the data generation process.

Tool Use

As I have noted, the use of computer-based tools to create and manipulate graphical representations of data is central to EDA. In the design experiment, the students used two computer minitools that were explicitly designed as means of supporting the development of their reasoning. We conjectured that as the students used these minitools, they would come to reason about data in increasingly sophisticated ways. I described the second of these tools when I discussed students' analyses of the AIDS treatment data. The interface for the first minitool is shown in Figure 3. This minitool enabled the students to order, partition, and otherwise organize sets of up to 40 data points in a relatively immediate way. When data are entered, each individual data point is inscribed as a horizontal bar. The students could select the color of each bar to be either pink or green, thus enabling them to enter and compare two data sets. In addition, they could sort the data both by size and by color. Our choice of this relatively elementary way of inscribing individual data values reflected our goal of ensuring the students were actually analyzing data. To this end, the initial data sets the students analyzed were also selected so that the measurements made when generating the data had a sense of linearity and thus lent themselves to being inscribed as horizontal bars. For example, Figure 3 shows data that were generated to compare how long two different brands of batteries last. Each bar shows a single case. In this instance, the case is the life span of one of the 10 batteries of each brand that was tested. The students' task was to assess the relative merits of the two brands. As I have indicated, the choice of this inscription together with the approach of talking through the data creation process proved to be effective in that the students began to actually reason about data shortly after this minitool was introduced.

In addition to the options I have described thus far, the students could use a value tool to find the value of any data point by dragging a vertical red bar along the horizontal axis as shown in Figure 3. Further, they could find the number of data points in any horizontal interval by using a range tool (see Figure 3). Our intent in developing the value tool was to provide the students with a way of "eyeballing" the center or balance point of a set of data points. However, the students used it to partition data sets and to find the value of specific data points. In the case of the range tool, our intent was to provide the students with a means of investigating the "spreadoutness" of data sets. Although the students used the range tool in this way to some extent, they also used it to isolate the data points within a particular interval. As the students used these two options, they began to reason about (1) the range, and maximum and minimum values of data sets, (2) the number of data points above or below a particular value or within a specified interval, and (3) the median and its relation to the mean. Against this background, the teacher introduced the second minitool in which data points were inscribed as dots in an axis plot (see Figure 1).

Our intention in designing the second minitool was to build on the ways of reasoning about data that the students had developed as they used the first minitool. For example, the dots at the end of the bars in the first minitool have, in effect, been

Figure 3.
The first computer minitool.

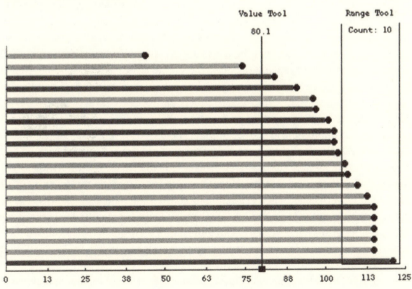

collapsed down onto the axis in the second minitool. The teacher, in fact, introduced this new way of inscribing data by first showing a data set inscribed as horizontal bars, then removing the bars to leave only the dots, and finally transposing the dots onto the horizontal axis. As we had hoped, the students were able to use the second minitool to analyze data almost immediately and it was apparent that the axis plot inscription signified a set of data values rather than merely a collection of dots spaced along a line. In our view, it was not possible to explain this development solely in terms of the teacher's careful introduction of the new minitool. Instead, we had to consider what the students learned as they *used* the first minitool. I can tease out this learning by focusing on the students' reasoning as they compared data sets in terms of the number of data points either within a particular interval or above or below a particular value. In the case of the battery data, for example, the first student who explained her reasoning said that she had focused on the 10 highest data values (i.e., those bounded by the range tool as shown in Figure 3). She went on to note that 7 of the 10 longest-lasting batteries were of one brand and concluded that this brand was better. Assisted by the teacher, another student challenged her argument by observing that the next four longest lasting batteries were of the other brand and that if they were included, there would be seven batteries of each brand in the highest 14. Against this background, the next student said that he had partitioned the data at 80 hours as shown by the value tool in Figure 3. He then argued that some of the batteries of one brand were below 80 hours whereas all those of the other brand lasted more than 80 hours. He judged this latter brand to be superior because, as he put it, he wanted a consistent battery.

The crucial point to note is that in making these arguments, the students were focusing on the location of the dots at the end of the bars with respect to the axis. In other words, a subtle but important shift occurred as the students used the first minitool (cf. Meira, 1998). Originally, the individual data values were represented by the lengths of the bars. However, in the very process of using the minitool, these values came to be signified by the endpoints of the bars. As a consequence, the students could readily understand the teacher's explanation when she introduced the second minitool by collapsing dots down onto the axis. Further, as the options in this new minitool involved partitioning data sets in various ways, students could use it immediately because they had routinely partitioned data sets when they used range and value options of the first minitool.

It is almost impossible to deduce this significant step in the students' learning by inspecting the physical characteristics of the first minitool. As a basic design principle, we do not, in fact, attempt to build the mathematics we want students to learn into tools and then hope that they might come to see it in some mysterious and unexplained way. Instead, when designing tools, we focus squarely on how students might actually use the tools and what they might learn as they do so. This emphasis on the nature of students' activity with tools rather than on the tools in and of themselves illustrates a further way in which their learning was viewed as situated. More generally, the contention that the tools students use profoundly influence not only the process of their learning but also its products, the types of mathematical reasoning that they develop, is not merely a theoretical commitment for us. Instead, it is a basic feature of the world in which we work as we attempt to support students' mathematical learning in classrooms. Students' use of the tools we develop serves as a primary means of supporting their development along learning trajectories that aim at significant mathematical ideas. In the case of the statistics design experiment, the significant idea that emerged as the students used the second minitool was that of data sets as wholistic distributions which had shape and structure rather than as amorphous collections of individual data points (Cobb, 1999; McClain et al., in press). Had the design of the two minitools been significantly different, it is doubtful that this idea would have become routine in the project classroom.

Classroom Discourse

The most important feature of the classroom environment that I have overlooked to this point is that of the classroom discourse—the ways in which the teacher and students talked about data. As the situatedness of students' learning with respect to classroom discourse has been discussed by a number of researchers in some detail (e.g., Dörfler, in press; Ernest, 1994; Forman, 1996; Lampert & Cobb, in press; O' Connor, 1998; Sfard, in press; Walkerdine, 1988; Wertsch & Toma, 1995), I will restrict my focus to two characteristics that relate specifically to mathematical learning. The first of these concerns the norms or standards for what counts as an acceptable mathematical explanation whereas the second deals more directly with what might colloquially be termed the content of whole-class discussions.

Earlier, I noted that the overall motive for doing statistics in the project classroom was to identify trends and patterns in data. However, explanations in which students indicated such a pattern were not necessarily treated as legitimate. I can illustrate this point by returning to the students' analyses of the battery data. Recall that the first student who explained her reasoning argued that one of the brands was better because 7 of the 10 longest-lasting batteries were of that brand. During the ensuing discussion, it became apparent that her decision to focus on the 10 rather than, say, the 14 longest-lasting batteries was relatively arbitrary. In contrast, the next student who presented an analysis explained that he had partitioned the data at 80 hours because he wanted a consistent battery that lasted at least 80 hours. In doing so, he clarified why the way in which he had organized the data was relevant with respect to the question at hand, that of deciding which of the two brands was superior.

As the classroom discussion continued, the obligation to give a justification of this type became increasingly explicit. For example, a third student compared the two analyses by commenting that although 7 of the 10 longest-lasting batteries were of one brand, the two lowest batteries were also of that brand and "if you were using the batteries for something important, you could end up with one of those bad batteries." As a consequence of exchanges such as this, the teacher and students established relatively early in the design experiment that to be acceptable, an argument had to justify why the way in which the data had been structured was relevant to the question under investigation. The students' learning was situated with respect to this norm in that their participation in its continual regeneration served to constrain the way in which they approached data. It is also worth noting that, in the process, the students were inducted into an important disciplinary norm, namely that the appropriateness of the statistics used when conducting an analysis has to be justified with respect to the question at hand.

In switching the focus now from the general characteristics of mathematical explanations to the substance of what the teacher and students talked about, it is helpful if I outline the approach we took when planning for the whole-class discussions. Typically, while the students were analyzing data at the computers, the teacher and a second member of the research team circulated around the classroom to gain a sense of the various ways in which the students were organizing and reasoning about the data. Toward the end of the small-group work, they then conferred briefly to develop conjectures about mathematically significant issues that might emerge as topics of conversation in the subsequent whole-class discussion. Their intent was to capitalize on the students' reasoning by identifying data analyses that, when compared and contrasted, might give rise to substantive mathematical conversations. In the discussion of the battery data, for example, the issue of justifying the way in which the data had been structured emerged from the contrast between the two analyses. In the case of the AIDS data, a sequence of four analyses was selected so that the issue of reasoning proportionally about data came to the fore.

This opportunistic approach to instructional planning clearly takes account of the diversity in students' reasoning. However, it should also be apparent that our intent in including whole-class discussions in the classroom activity structure was not simply to provide the students with an occasion to share their reasoning. Instead, our overriding concern was with the quality of discussions as social events in which the students participated. In our view, the value of such discussion is suspect unless mathematically significant issues that advance the instructional agenda become explicit topics of conversation. Conversely, students' participation in substantive discussions can serve as a primary means of supporting their induction into the values, beliefs, and ways of knowing of the discipline. It is in this sense that I and my colleagues view students' mathematical learning as situated with respect to the culture in which it takes place. In our work as instructional designers, our immediate focus is on the culture of the classroom, which encompasses general norms of participation, such as those for argumentation, as well as the specific mathematical issues that are judged to be worthy of serious discussion.

The Classroom Activity System

I began the discussion of the statistics teaching experiment by demonstrating that the students' learning was reasonably impressive and then went on to tease out the various means by which that learning was supported and organized. In doing so, I clarified that both the process and the products of that learning can be viewed as situated with respect to these means of support. However, as I have described these various means in separate paragraphs, they might at first glance appear to be a largely independent collection of factors that influence learning. It is therefore important to emphasize that they are, in fact, highly interrelated. For example, the instructional tasks as they were actually realized in the classroom depended on:

- The overall motive for doing statistics (i.e., to identify patterns in data that are relevant to the question or issue at hand)

- The structure of classroom activities (e.g., talking through the data creation process)

- The computer minitools that the students used to conduct their analyses

- The nature of the of the classroom discourse (e.g., engaging in discussion in which mathematically significant issues emerged as topics of conversation)

It is easy to imagine how the instructional tasks would be realized very differently in a classroom where the overall motive is to apply prescribed methods to data, or where there are no whole-class discussions and the teacher simply grades students' analyses. Given these interdependencies, it is reasonable to view the various means of support I have discussed as constituting a single *classroom activity system*. The students' learning in the design experiment classroom can therefore be viewed as situated with respect to this entire system. Pragmatically, the comprehensiveness of this system implies that an approach to instructional design that takes the situated nature of students' mathematical reasoning seriously must necessarily extend beyond the traditional focus on curricular materials. The intent is instead to design classroom activity systems such that students develop significant mathematical ideas as they participate in them and contribute to their evolution. This in turn indicates the need for methodologies that are well suited to the task of testing and improving activity systems that are designed to produce such learning. It will become clear when I discuss such a methodology in the following pages that part of its strength derives from its treatment of design as a site for the development of instructional theory.

DESIGN RESEARCH

The example of the statistics experiment provides a useful introduction to the design experiment methodology. It clarifies, for example, that our goal when conducting an experiment of this type is both to develop sequences of instructional activities and associated tools, and to conduct analyses of the process of the students' learning and the means by which that learning is supported and organized. Research of this type falls under the general heading of design research in that it involves both instructional design and classroom-based research (see also Brown, 1992; Cobb, in press; Confrey & Lachance, in press; Simon, in press). Gravemeijer (1994a) has written extensively about the first aspect of the design research cycle shown in Figure 4, instructional design, and clarifies that the research team conducts an anticipatory thought experiment when preparing for a design experiment. In doing so, the team formulates a hypothetical learning trajectory that involves conjectures about both (1) a possible learning route or trajectory that aims at significant mathematical ideas, and (2) the specific means that might be used to support and organize learning along the envisioned trajectory (i.e., aspects of the classroom activity system). As I illustrated when discussing the statistics experiment, these means of support are construed broadly and extend beyond the resources typically considered by materials developers. Although instructional planning that considers the various aspects of the classroom activity system in a comprehensive manner is unusual in the United States, there are several notable exceptions (e.g., Confrey & Smith, 1995; Lehrer, Schauble, Carpenter, & Penner, in press; Simon, 1995). In addition, an encompassing approach of this type is the norm in Japan where members of professional teaching communities often spend several years teaching and revising the hypothesized learning trajectories that underpin a sequence of mathematics lessons (Stigler & Hiebert, 1999).

It is important to stress that the conjectures inherent in a hypothetical learning trajectory are just that; they are tentative, provisional, eminently revisable conjectures that are tested and revised on a daily basis once the experiment begins. Our goal when experimenting in a classroom is therefore not to try and demonstrate that the instructional design formulated at the outset works. Instead, it is to improve the design by testing and modifying conjectures as informed by ongoing analyses of both students' reasoning and the classroom activity system in which it is situated. As a consequence, although we formulate a hypothetical learning trajectory in advance and also outline possible types of instructional activities, we develop the specific instructional activities used in the classroom only a day or two before they are needed. I mention this to clarify that the methodology is relatively labor-intensive. Formal design experiments should therefore not be confused with informal explorations in which research assistants are delegated to work in a classroom in a less principled way.

Figure 4.
The design research cycle.

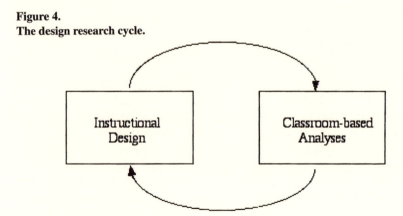

My immediate purpose in outlining the methodology that I and my colleagues use is to highlight what I take to be a defining characteristic of design research, the tightly integrated cycles of design and analysis. Given our goals as mathematics educators, we require a methodology that results in analyses that inform the ongoing design effort. Gravemeijer (1998) differentiates what he refers to as daily minicycles from macrocycles that span an entire teaching experiment. This latter, longer-term cycle involves a retrospective analysis that is conducted once the design experiment is completed and that can feed forward to guide the formulation of a revised learning trajectory for follow-up teaching experiments.

My larger purpose in discussing design experiments is to illustrate the value of a methodological approach in which the process of designing in classrooms serves as a primary setting for the development of instructional theory. The resulting theory can therefore be thought of as situated with respect to the activity of supporting students' learning in classrooms. This characteristic of design experiments becomes apparent once I clarify that the questions and concerns that arise while an experiment is in progress are typically pragmatic and relate directly to the goal of supporting the participating students' learning. In contrast, the intent when conducting a retrospective analysis of an experiment is to contribute to the development of a domain-specific instructional theory (see Figure 5). This theory emerges over the course of several macrocycles and consists of (1) a demonstrated learning route that culminates with the emergence of significant mathematical ideas, and (2) substantiated means of supporting and organizing learning along that trajectory. As Steffe and Thompson (in press) clarify, it is this theory that makes the results of a series of design experiments potentially generalizable even though they are empirically grounded in analyses of only a small number of classrooms. In their terms, this is generalization by means of an explanatory framework rather than by means of a representative sample in that the insights and understandings developed and tested during a series of experiments can inform the interpretation of events and thus pedagogical planning and decision making in other classrooms.

Design experiments in which the development of theory and the improvement of an instructional design co-emerge can be contrasted with an alternative approach to design that involves the following sequence of steps:

1. The development of psychological theory
2. The derivation of principles for design from the psychological theory
3. The translation of the principles into concrete designs
4. The assessment of the designs to test whether they work as anticipated

It is, of course, debatable whether this putative sequence is ever strictly adhered to in practice. Nonetheless, mathematics educators have traditionally looked to cognitive psychology for guidance and have based designs on theories that specify developmental routes that apparently unfold independently of the means by which that development is supported. This is reflected in research reports that are written so as to imply that the development of an instructional design involves a one-way

Figure 5.
Design minicycles and macrocycles. (Adapted from K. Gravemeijer, 1998.)

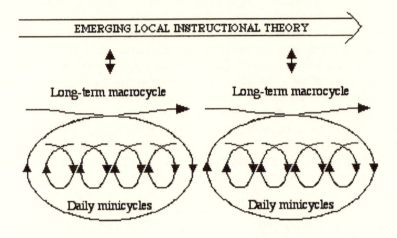

chain of reasoning from cognitive theory to instructional practice. The general approach is therefore alive in the discourse of mathematics education research, where it is frequently assumed to be the ideal.

As an initial observation, it is worth noting that the feedback loop from the concluding assessment step to the design principles and cognitive theory is relatively weak. It is not clear, for example, that these principles and the underlying theory are open to the results of an unfavorable assessment of a specific design. This is disconcerting if one takes the view that educational reform should be an ongoing, continual process of iterative improvement characterized by what Lampert (1990) terms a zigzag between conjectures and refutations. Beyond this general observation, the practical feasibility of employing this idealized approach to design in specific mathematical domains is open to question. In preparing for the statistics design experiment; for example, I and my colleagues conducted a reasonably extensive review of the literature but found only a small number of studies that could guide our formulation of a hypothetical learning trajectory. There did not even appear to be a consensus on the overarching statistical ideas that should constitute the potential endpoints of a learning trajectory. However, rather than waiting for development of cognitive theory, we drew on the available literature to formulate initial conjectures about major shifts in students' statistical reasoning and the means by which these shifts might be supported. Not surprisingly, a number of these conjectures proved to be unviable when we began experimenting in the classroom. We therefore began the process of revising conjectures on line and eventually formulated a new learning trajectory that was empirically grounded in our work in the classroom. We contend that what we learned about the design of classroom activity systems and the learning of the students who participate in them by proceeding in this way can contribute to an emerging instructional theory that aims at a significant statistical idea, that of distribution.

It is important to note that the lack of an adequate research base is not unique to statistical data analysis. The same observation applies to areas such as algebra and geometry which are also undergoing relatively profound changes (Cobb, 1997; Kaput, 1994; Lehrer, Jacobson, Kemney, & Strom, 1999). In domains such as these, the idealized top-down approach to instructional design in which psychological theory trickles down to instructional practice appears to be untenable. Instead, the bootstrapping approach integral to design research in which theory and instructional designs evolve together appears to be more feasible. Some years ago, educator Freudenthal (1973) argued that psychology should follow instructional design rather than the reverse. If one heeds Freudenthal's advice, the limitations of the traditional type of psychological theory that he had in mind in which a series of developmental levels or stages are delineated also become apparent. Freudenthal was pointing to the need for accounts of learning in particular mathematical domains that are tied to the means by which that learning can be supported. To be sure, he thought of these means of support primarily in terms of the instructional tasks that students were to solve. However, if we follow his lead while broadening our view of the means of support that can be used to organize students' learning, we arrive at the view of mathematical learning as situated with respect to the classroom activity system. I will return to this issue of the usefulness of a situated perspective on students' mathematical activity once I have discussed the interpretive approach that I and my colleagues use to make sense of classroom events.

INTERPRETIVE APPROACH

To this point, I have been primarily concerned with the process of design as it occurs both while preparing for an experiment and when actually working in a classroom. My focus in the remainder of this chapter is on the process by which we make sense of what is happening in these classrooms. I first discuss three criteria that an interpretive approach appropriate for our purposes should satisfy and then describe both our general theoretical orientation and the specific interpretive framework that we use.

Learning and Teaching Mathematics in Social Context

As we know all too well, classrooms are messy, complex, and sometimes confusing places. One of the concerns that I and my colleagues have struggled with as we have worked in classrooms is that of developing an analytical framework that enables us to come to terms with this complexity so that we can begin to see some pattern and order in what appear at first glance to be ill-structured events. Our concerns and interests give rise to several criteria that an analytical approach should satisfy if we are to contribute to reform in mathematics education as an ongoing, iterative process of improvement. These criteria include that:

1. It should result in analyses that feed back to inform the improvement of instructional designs.

2. It should enable us to document the collective mathematical learning of the classroom community over the extended periods of time spanned by design experiments.

3. It should enable us to document the developing mathematical reasoning of individual students as they participate in the practices of the classroom community.

The rationale for the first criterion follows directly from the tightly integrated cycles of design and analysis that I have discussed at both the micro- and macro-levels (see Figures 4 and 5). The second criterion, which emphasizes the importance of focusing on the mathematical learning of the classroom community, stems from the approach we take to instructional design. As I have noted, the designer develops conjectures about an anticipated learning trajectory when preparing for a design experiment. However, these conjectures cannot be about the trajectory of each and every student's learning for the straightforward reason that there are significant qualitative differences in their mathematical thinking at any point in time. In my experience, descriptions of planned instructional approaches written so as to imply that all students will reorganize their thinking in particular ways at particular points in an instructional sequence involve, at best, questionable idealizations. For similar reasons, I also find analyses that speak of changes in *the students'* reasoning potentially misleading in that they imply that the students have all reorganized their activity in the same way. In this regard, I should acknowledge that I did, in fact, speak in these terms when I described the statistics teaching experiment in the first section of this chapter. Although this might be adequate when providing a broad overview, it does not provide us with the precision we need to improve our designs. An issue that has arisen for me and my colleagues is therefore that of clarifying what the envisioned learning trajectories that are central to our (and others') work as instructional designers might be about. The resolution we propose involves viewing a hypothetical learning trajectory as consisting of conjectures about the collective mathematical development of the classroom community. This proposal, in turn, indicates the need for a theoretical notion or construct that enables us to talk explicitly about collective mathematical learning and it is for this reason that we have developed the notion of a classroom mathematical practice. Cast in these terms, an hypothetical learning trajectory then consists of an envisioned sequence of mathematical practices together with the means of supporting and organizing the emergence of each practice from prior practices.

The last of the three criteria that an interpretive approach should satisfy focuses on the qualitative differences in individual students' mathematical reasoning. The rationale for this criterion is again deeply rooted in our work in classrooms. In particular, the classroom sessions we conduct during a design experiment are frequently organized so that students initially work either individually or in small groups before convening for a whole-class discussion of their solutions. During the discussion of the statistics teaching experiment, I illustrated a strategy for planning for these discussions that we have found productive in which the teacher and one or more of the project staff circulate around the classroom to gain a sense of the diverse ways in which students are interpreting and solving instructional activities.

Toward the end of the individual or small-group work, the teacher and project staff members then confer briefly to prepare for the whole-class discussion. In doing so, they routinely focus on the qualitative differences in students' reasoning in order to develop conjectures about mathematically significant issues that might, with the teacher's proactive guidance, emerge as topics of conversation. Given this pragmatic focus on individual students' reasoning, we require an analytical approach that takes account of the diverse ways in which students participate in communal classroom practices. In the hands of a skillful teacher, this diversity can be a primary motor of the collective mathematical learning of the classroom community.

In addition to providing a rationale for the three criteria, this discussion clarifies that I and my colleagues view theoretical constructs as conceptual tools whose development reflects particular interests and concerns. From this point of view, the relevant concern when assessing the value of theoretical constructs is that of whether they enable us to be more effective in supporting students' mathematical learning. It should also be apparent that an interpretive approach that satisfies the three criteria will characterize students' mathematical learning in highly situated terms. However, in doing so, it will take a different cut on the classroom activity system. The aspects of this system that I discussed when giving an overview of the statistics experiment dealt with resources (tasks, tools) and with characteristics of collective activity (the structure of classroom activities, classroom discourse). What is missing from this picture is an analysis of the process by which increasingly sophisticated mathematical ways of reasoning emerged as the students participated in these collective activities by using the tools to complete instructional tasks. The specific analytical approach that I and my colleagues follow is designed to address this shortcoming.

General Theoretical Orientation

The interpretive framework that has emerged as we have addressed concrete problems and issues that have arisen while working in classrooms over the past 13 years involves the coordination of two distinct perspective on classroom activity. One is a social perspective that is concerned with ways of acting, reasoning, and arguing that are normative in a classroom community. From this perspective, an individual student's reasoning is framed as an act of participation in these normative activities. The other is a psychological perspective that focuses squarely on the nature of individual students' reasoning or, in other words, on their particular ways of participating in communal activities. Thus, whereas the social perspective brings to the fore normative, taken-as-shared[2] ways of talking and reasoning, the psychological perspective brings to the fore the diversity in students' ways of participating in these taken-as-shared activities. Together, these two perspectives therefore address the second and third of the three criteria that an analytical approach should satisfy if it is to be appropriate for our purposes.

Although we have written extensively about the coordination of these perspectives in the past, we have sometimes been interpreted as advocating the pasting together of two epistemologically incompatible theoretical orientations in a relatively superficial manner (e.g., Lerman, 1996; Waschescio, 1998). It is therefore important to clarify that we take the relation between the social and psychological perspectives to be one of reflexivity. This is an extremely strong relationship that does not merely mean that the two perspectives are interdependent. Instead, it implies that neither perspective exists without the other in that each perspective constitutes the background against which mathematical activity is interpreted from the other perspective (cf. Mehan & Wood, 1975). For example, normative activities of the classroom community (social perspective) emerge and are continually regenerated by the teacher and students as they interpret and respond to each other's actions (psychological perspective). Conversely, the teacher's and students' interpretations and actions in the classroom (psychological perspective) do not exist except as acts of participation in communal classroom practices.

We have described and illustrated the specific method we use to analyze the data generated during a classroom design experiment in some detail elsewhere (Cobb, Stephan, McClain, & Gravemeijer, in press). It is, however, worth clarifying that when we view classroom video recordings, we do not see the classroom community as the discrete, concrete entity in the same way that we see the teacher and students as distinct physical beings. As a consequence, we cannot observe normative, taken-as-shared meanings directly any more than we can directly observe the meanings that individual students' mathematical activity has for them. Instead, we develop and test conjectures about both communal mathematical activities (social perspective) and individual students' reasoning (psychological perspective) as we analyze what the teacher and individual students say and do in the classroom. The distinction between the two interpretative perspectives resides in what might be termed the grain size with reference to which we characterize what they are doing. In the case of the psychological perspective, we view the teacher and students as a group of individuals who engage in acts of reasoning as they interpret and respond to each other's actions. In contrast, when we take the social perspective, we view the teacher and students as members of a local community who jointly establish communal norms and practices. As a consequence, the coordination is not between individual students and the classroom community viewed as separate, sharply defined entities. Instead, the coordination is between two alternative ways of looking at and making sense of what is going on in classrooms. The resulting analytical approach brings the diversity in students' mathematical reasoning to the fore while situating that diversity in the social context of their participation in the classroom activity system. Engestrom (1999), in different terms, describes what is involved in pursuing an analytical approach of this type.

> The analyst constructs the activity system as if looking at it from above [social perspective]. At the same time, the analyst must select a subject, a member (or better yet, multiple different members) of the local activity [system], through whose eyes and interpretations the activity [system] is constructed [psychological perspective]. (p. 10)

In terms of intellectual lineage, the social perspective draws inspiration from sociocultural theory (e.g., Cole, 1996; Lave, 1988; Rogoff, in press) and from ethnomethodology and symbolic interactionism (Blumer, 1969) as they have been adapted to problems and issues in mathematics education (cf. Bauersfeld, Krummheuer, &Voigt, 1988). The lineage of the psychological perspective can be traced to both constructivism (Piaget, 1970; Steffe & Kieren, 1994; Thompson, 1991) and to distributed accounts of intelligence (e.g., Hutchins, 1995; Pea, 1993). Given this relatively comprehensive list of intellectual sources, I should clarify that our goal has not been not to achieve some grand theoretical synthesis. Instead, our focus has been pragmatic and has centered on supporting and organizing students' mathematical learning. As a consequence, in drawing on the theoretical sources I have listed, we have appropriated and modified ideas to suit our purposes. The process by which we have developed our theoretical orientation therefore parallels that of instructional design as characterized by Gravemeijer (1994b).

> [Design] resembles the thinking process that Lawler (1985) characterizes by the French word *bricolage,* a metaphor taken from Claude Levi—Strauss. A *bricoleur* is a handy man who invents pragmatic solutions in practical situations. . . . [T]he bricoleur has become adapt at using whatever is available. The bricoleur's tools and materials are very heterogeneous: Some remain from earlier jobs, others have been collected with a certain project in mind. (p. 447)

Similarly, we acted as bricoleurs when developing our theoretical orientation by adapting ideas from a range of theoretical sources for pragmatic ends. Casting our work in these down-to-earth terms serves to differentiate it from more ambitious efforts that aim to fashion theoretical cosmologies (cf. Shotter, 1995).

As an example of the way in which we have appropriated ideas to our purposes, consider one of the key theoretical constructs that we use when we take a social perspective, that of a classroom mathematical practice. We developed this construct by adapting sociocultural theorists' notion of a cultural practice (cf. Axel, 1992; Minick, 1989). In sociocultural theory, this notion typically refers to normative ways of acting that have emerged during extended periods of human history. We found this idea attractive in that it makes it possible to characterize mathematics as a complex human activity rather than as disembodied subject matter (van Oers, 1996). Further, it provides a useful way of framing instructional issues in broad terms. In particular, the task facing both the teacher and the instructional designer can be seen as that of supporting and organizing students' induction into the practices that have emerged during the discipline's intellectual history (Dörfler, in press; Forman, 1996).

Despite these advantages, sociocultural theorists' notion of a cultural practice is not a completely adequate conceptual tool given our interest in changes in the normative activities of classroom communities. For example, in sociocultural theory, the historically developed practices of the discipline are seen to exist prior to and independently of teachers and their students. In contrast to these disciplinary practices, the normative practices of a local classroom community do not exist independently of the teacher and his or her students, but are instead constituted by them in the course of their ongoing interactions (cf. Beach; 1999; Boaler, 1999). Thus, when we take a local classroom community rather than the discipline as our point of reference, a practice is seen to be an emergent phenomenon rather than an already-established way of reasoning and communicating into which students are to be inducted. Further, although the practices of the discipline can be seen as primary when one adopts a sociocultural point of view, the relation between local classroom mathematical practices and the reasoning of the students who participate in them is better characterized as reflexive.

We made similar modifications when fashioning a psychological perspective that is appropriate for our purposes, in this case by drawing on constructivism and distributed theories of intelligence. For example, we take from constructivism the basic notion that learning is a process of reorganizing activity. However, influenced by distributed theories of intelligence, we have found it important to broaden our view of activity so that it is not restricted solely to internal mental activity but instead reaches out into the world and includes the use of tools and symbols (Bateson, 1973). The rationale for this modification is at least in part pragmatic in that our work as instructional designers involves developing notation systems, physical tools, and computer-based tools for students to use. We therefore need an analytical approach that can take account both of the diverse ways in which students reason with tools and symbols, and of how those ways of reasoning evolve over time. An approach of this type is fundamentally nonduelist in that learning involves the reorganization of the world acted in as well as ways of acting in the world (cf. Roth & McGinn, 1998).

This debt to distributed accounts of intelligence acknowledged, we could not accept this theoretical orientation ready-made given its rejection of analytical approaches that focus explicitly on the nature of individual students' reasoning (see the third of the three criteria). Pea (1993), for example, has been outspoken in delegitimizing analyses that involve such a focus. The modification we have made is to redefine the individual as it is characterized in distributed accounts rather than to dismiss this analytical focus entirely. On our reading, distributed theories of intelligence have been developed in reaction to mainstream American psychology's focus on internal cognitive processes that intervene between an external stimulus environment and observed output activity (Greeno, 1997). In developing their approach, Pea and other distributed intelligence theorists do not directly challenge mainstream psychology's portrayal of the individual as a disembodied creator of internal representations and a processor of information. Instead, they question the legitimacy of taking this mainstream character as a unit of analysis. Their proposal is to equip the individual conjured up within the discourse of mainstream psychology with cultural tools and place it in social context. In their view, the functional system consisting of the individual, tools, and social contexts constitutes the appropriate unit of analysis. A key point that is often overlooked is that the individual in this theoretical scheme is that of mainstream discourse (cf. Cobb, 1998). Distributed intelligence theorists therefore appear to have accepted the mainstream psychological view of the individual at face value rather than as a theoretically loaded characterization. When this point is lost sight of, their arguments for the rejection of the individual of mainstream psychology as a unit of analysis are presented as implying that all approaches that focus on the quality of individuals' reasoning should be rejected regardless of how the individual is conceptualized. It is this subtle shift that results in the claim that all methodologies that involve a concern for individual interpretation and meaning should be abandoned.

In contrast to distributed accounts, the psychological perspective that we favor has not evolved from mainstream American psychology, but instead draws on an alternative European constructivist tradition that can trace its roots to aspects of Piaget's genetic epistemology (Piaget, 1970). In this tradition, there is no talk of processing information or creating internal representations. Instead, intelligence is seen to be embodied, or to be located in activity (Johnson, 1987; Winograd & Flores, 1986). Further, rather than representing a world, people are portrayed as individually and collectively enacting a taken-as-shared world of signification (Varela, Thompson, & Rosch, 1991). The goal of analyses conducted from this psychological perspective is therefore not to specify cognitive mechanisms located inside students' heads. Instead, it is to infer the quality of individual students' reasoning in, with, and about the world, and to account for developments in their reasoning in terms of the reorganization of activity and the world acted in.

Once the mainstream characterization of the individual is challenged and a shift is made from internal cognitive behaviors to activity-in-the-world, it no longer makes sense to talk of intelligence being stretched over individuals, tools, and social contexts. In the psychological perspective that we take, the tools and symbols that students use are not considered to stand apart from or outside the individual, but are instead viewed as constituent parts of their activity (cf. Dewey, 1981). Consequently, what is viewed as a student-tool system from the perspective of distributed intelligence is, from the psychological perspective we have outlined, an individual student engaging in mathematical activity that involves *reasoning with* tools and symbols. Thus, although the focus of this psychological viewpoint is explicitly on the quality of individual students' reasoning, its emphasis on tools is generally consistent with the notion of mediated action as discussed by sociocultural theorists (cf. Kozulin, 1990; van der Veer & Valsiner, 1991; Wertsch, 1994). Further, as I have indicated, the remaining component of the functional system posited by distributed theories of intelligence, social context, becomes an explicit focus of attention when this psychological perspective is coordinated with the social perspective.[3]

Interpretive Framework

The specific interpretative framework that we use to organize our analyses of individual and collective mathematical learning is shown in Figure 6. The column headings "Social Perspective" and "Psychological Perspective" refer to the two distinct viewpoints that constitute our overall theoretical position. The entries in the column under social perspective indicate three aspects of the classroom microculture that we have found it useful to differentiate, and the entries in the column under psychological perspective indicate three related aspects of individual students' activity in the classroom. The classroom microculture encompasses the normative or taken-as-shared ways of acting, reasoning, and arguing that emerge as the teacher and students use available resources (e.g., instructional tasks and tools) to jointly enact classroom activities (e.g., classroom activity structure and discourse). Thus, whereas the classroom activity system specifies what the teacher and students do together, the classroom microculture is concerned with the normative meanings that emerge in the course of this collective activity. In Lemke's (1997) terms, an analysis of the classroom microculture therefore describes an ecosocial system whose ecology is semiotic; its ecology is one of meaning making in which one thing is taken as a sign for another. As Lemke observes, such systems are self-organizing systems that continually set up the conditions for their own future development. Over time, they therefore enact trajectories of learning. Our goal when analyzing a data corpus such as that generated during the seventh-grade statistics experiment is to document the mathematical learning trajectories of both the classroom community as a whole and of individual participating students.

In describing the three aspects of the classroom microculture shown in Figure 6, I draw on whole-class discussions conducted during the statistics design experiment to provide illustrations. The first of the three aspects, *classroom social norms,*

Figure 6.
An interpretive framework for analyzing classroom mathematical activity and learning.

Social Perspective	Psychological Perspective
Classroom social norms	Beliefs about own role, others' roles, and the general nature of mathematical activity in school
Sociomathematical norms	Mathematical beliefs and values
Classroom mathematical practices	Mathematical interpretations and reasoning

enable us to document what Erickson (1986) and Lampert (1990) call the classroom participation structure. The social norms for whole-class discussion that became established relatively early in the statistics design experiment included that students were obliged to explain and justify solutions, to make sense of explanations given by others, to indicate agreement or disagreement, and to question alternatives when conflicts in interpretations had become apparent. As these examples make clear, the participation structure of a particular activity such as a whole-class discussion should not be confused with the overarching structure of classroom activities. The latter describes the general flow of classroom activities (e.g., talking through the data creation process, analyzing data individually or in small groups, discussing the resulting analyses as a class). In contrast, the participation structure documents both the expectations that the teacher and students had for each other's actions and the obligations that were established for their own actions in each phase of the classroom activity structure. In the statistics experiment, for example, the norms of participation differed for the first and third phases even though both were whole-class activities.

It is important to emphasize that classroom social norms are established jointly by the teacher and students. We would therefore question accounts framed in individualistic terms in which the teacher is said to establish or specify social norms for students. To be sure, the teacher is (and should be) an institutionalized authority in the classroom (Bishop, 1985). He or she expresses that authority in action by initiating, guiding, and organizing the renegotiation of classroom social norms. However, the students also play their part in contributing to the evolution of social norms. One of our primary conjectures is in fact that in making these contributions (social perspective), students reorganize their individual beliefs about their own role, others' roles, and the general nature of mathematical activity (psychological perspective). As a consequence, we take these beliefs to be, for want of a better term, the psychological correlates of classroom social norms (see Figure 6). We therefore contend that in guiding the establishment of classroom norms for whole-class discussions, the teacher in the statistics design experiment was simultaneously supporting her students' reorganization of these beliefs. I should also clarify that consistent with the reflexive relation between the social and psychological perspectives, we give primacy to neither the social norms nor individual students' beliefs. This implies that it is neither a case of a change in social norms causing a change in students' beliefs, nor a case of students first reorganizing their beliefs and then contributing to the evolution of social norms. Instead, social norms and the beliefs of the participating students co-evolve in that neither is seen to exist independently of the other.

It is readily apparent from this brief discussion that classroom social norms are not specific to mathematics, but apply to any subject matter area. For example, one might hope that students would explain and justify their reasoning in science or history classes as well as in mathematics. In contrast, the second aspect of the classroom microculture shown in Figure 6, *sociomathematical norms,* deals with normative aspects of classroom action and interaction that are specific to mathematics (Lampert, 1990; Simon & Blume, 1996; Voigt, 1995; Yackel & Cobb, 1996). Examples of sociomathematical norms include what counts as a different mathematical solution, a sophisticated mathematical solution, an efficient mathematical solution, and an acceptable mathematical explanation. The last of these norms proved to be particularly crucial in the statistics design experiment. Recall, for example, the episode in which the teacher and students discussed analyses of the battery data near the beginning of the experiment (see Figure 3). I noted that the first student to give an explanation argued that one of the two brands of batteries was better because 7 of the 10 longest-lasting batteries were of that brand. She was immediately challenged even though she had explained how she had structured and interpreted the data sets and was obliged to justify why she had focused on the 10 longest-lasting batteries. In the ensuing discussion, her elaboration that she had focused on these batteries because 10 was half of 20, the total number of batteries, was delegitimized. Crucially, she did not explain why focusing on the 10 longest-lasting batteries was an appropriate way of comparing the two brands. In contrast, the next student who presented an analysis explained that he had partitioned the data at 80 hours because he wanted a consistent battery that lasted at least 80 hours. The teacher and other students accepted his argument as legitimate because he explained why the way in which he had organized the data was relevant with respect to the question at hand, that of determining which of the brands was superior. In the course of this and similar exchanges, it became established that to be acceptable, an argument had to involve an explanation of why the way in which the data had been structured was relevant to the issue under investigation. The emergence of this sociomathematical norm for what counted as an acceptable mathematical explanation occurred within the first few classroom sessions and it remained relatively stable throughout the remainder of the experiment.

Pragmatically, the analysis of sociomathematical norms has proven useful in helping us understand the process by which the teachers in this and other design experiments were able to foster their students' development of intellectual autonomy. This issue is particularly significant to us given that the development of student autonomy was an explicitly stated goal of our work in classrooms from the outset. However, we originally characterized intellectual autonomy in individualistic terms and spoke of students' awareness of and willingness to draw on their own intellectual capabilities when making mathematical decisions and judgements (Kamii, 1985; Piaget, 1973). As part of the process of supporting the growth of autonomy, the teachers with whom we have collaborated initiated and guided the development of a community of validators in their classrooms such that claims were established by means of mathematical argumentation rather than by appealing directly to the authority of the teacher or textbook. For this to occur, it was not sufficient for the students to merely learn that they should make a wide range of mathematical contributions. It was also essential that they became able to judge both when it is appropriate to make a mathematical contribution and what constitutes an acceptable contribution. This required, among other things, that the students could judge what counted as a different mathematical solution, an insightful mathematical solution, an efficient mathematical solution, and an acceptable mathematical explanation. However, these are precisely the types of judgments that are negotiated when establishing sociomathematical norms. We therefore contend that students develop specifically mathematical beliefs and values that enable them to act as increasingly autonomous members of the classroom mathematical community as they participate in the negotiation of sociomathematical norms (Yackel & Cobb, 1996). Further, we take these specifically mathematical beliefs and values to be the psychological correlates of the sociomathematical norms (see Figure 6). In doing so, we conjecture that in guiding the establishment of particular sociomathematical norms, teachers are simultaneously supporting their students' reorganization of the beliefs and values that constitute what might be called their mathematical dispositions.

It is apparent from this discussion of sociomathematical norms that we have revised our conception of intellectual autonomy over the years as we worked in classrooms. At the outset, we defined autonomy in purely individualistic terms as a characteristic that students possessed. However, as the notion of sociomathematical norms emerged, we came to view autonomy as a characteristic of an individual's way of participating in the practices of a community. In particular, the development of autonomy can be equated with a gradual movement from relatively peripheral participation in classroom activities to more substantial participation in which students increasingly rely on their own judgments rather than on those of the teacher (cf. Forman, 1996; Lave & Wenger, 1991). The example of autonomy is paradigmatic in this regard in that it illustrates the general shift we have made in our theoretical orientation during the 13 years that we have worked in classrooms away from an initially individualistic position toward one that involves coordinating social and psychological perspectives.

The third aspect of the classroom microculture shown in Figure 6, *classroom mathematical practices,* deals with the normative ways of reasoning mathematically that emerge as students use particular tools to complete specific instructional tasks. I have already noted that, in contrast to classroom social norms, sociomathematical norms are specific to mathematical activity. However, they are still relatively broad. For example, the sociomathematical norm for argumentation that emerged relatively early in the statistics design experiment is quite general and applies to the analysis of bivariate as well as univariate data. The challenge when delineating the mathematical practices that became established during the experiment was to specify what might be termed the normative or taken-as-shared mathematical content of these arguments. This required us to tease out the taken-as-shared interpretations of data that became established as the students used the two computer minitools.

As an illustration, again consider the discussion of the battery data. Thus far, I have concentrated on the differences between the two data-based arguments that I have described. It is therefore important to note that there was also an underlying commonality, namely that both students compared sets of data that they had structured in additive part-whole terms. For example, the first student who gave an explanation partitioned the two data sets when she isolated the 10 longest-lasting batteries and focused on how many of these batteries were of each brand. This argument can be contrasted with an alternative that focuses on the proportion of each data set that is among the 10 highest values. An argument of this type would involve comparing two data sets that have been structured multiplicatively. Crucially, such an argument is concerned with the relative amount of the data in each set that is above a certain value and thus with how each data set is distributed. Although additive reasoning is sufficient when comparing data sets with equal numbers of data points, the students failed to make arguments that involved reasoning about data proportionally when they encountered difficulties while using the first of the two minitools to compare unequal data sets. This indicates that data sets were constituted in public classroom discourse during the first part of the design experiment as collections of data points rather than as distributions. The classroom mathematical practice that emerged as the students used the first minitool might therefore be described as that of *exploring trends and patterns in collections of data points.*

This taken-as-shared way of reasoning about data can be contrasted with that which became established in the latter part of the design experiment. Recall, for example, the relatively elementary analysis of the AIDS treatment data in which a group of students partitioned the two data sets at the T-cell count of 525 (see Figure 1). Both they and the other students who contributed to the discussion focused on the proportion rather than the absolute number of patients in each treatment protocol whose T-cell counts were above and below 525. Similarly, the group of students who produced a relatively sophisticated analysis by partitioning the two data sets into four equal groups, each of which contained one fourth of the data points (see Figure 2), also reasoned multiplicatively about the data. We did not realize until midway through the design experiment that a concern with patterns in the way that data are distributed within a space of possible values in fact assumes that the data have been structured multiplicatively (Cobb, 1999; McClain et al., in press). There was every indication that data sets were constituted in public classroom discourse as distributions rather than merely as collections of data points during the latter part of the teaching experiment. The classroom mathematical practice that emerged as the students used the second minitool can therefore be described as that *of exploring trends and patterns in data distributions.*

It is also worth noting that in addition to involving a shift from structuring data sets additively to structuring them multiplicatively, the transition from the first to the second mathematical practice involved a change in the nature of the whole-class discussions. Initially, the focus was on the practical decision or judgment that needed to be made. For example, during the discussion of the battery data, the students developed data-based arguments in order to justify their claim that one of the two brands was superior. In contrast, the students agreed that the new treatment for AIDS patients was better than the standard treatment at the beginning of the discussion. The focus was now on different ways of describing patterns in the two data distributions rather than on the practical decision or judgment per se. It might therefore be said that participation in the second mathematical practice involved analyzing data from a mathematical point of view.

The two examples of classroom mathematical practices that I have given provide snapshots of the starting and ending points of the classroom community's actual learning trajectory. A complete analysis of this trajectory would specify a sequence of practices that led from the starting to ending points together with an account of how each was constituted as a reorganization of previously established practices. One of the strengths of an analytical approach of this type is that it takes what are traditionally called issues of mathematical content seriously. However, this approach also calls into question the metaphor of mathematics as *content*. The content metaphor entails the notion that mathematics is placed in the container of the curriculum, which then serves as the primary vehicle for making it accessible to students. In contrast, the approach I have illustrated characterizes what is traditionally called mathematical content in emergent terms. For example, the mathematical idea of distribution emerged as the collective practices of the classroom community evolved. This theoretical orientation clearly involves a significant paradigm shift in how we think about both mathematics and the means by which we might support students' learning. I would, however, note that it is consistent with the view of mathematics as a socially and culturally situated activity (cf: Bauersfeld, 1992; John-Steiner, 1995; Lave, 1993; Sfard, in press).

It is also important to clarify that analyses of this type bear directly on the issue of situating students' mathematical learning with respect to the classroom microculture. Viewed against the background of classroom social and sociomathematical norms, the mathematical practices established by a classroom community can be seen to constitute the immediate, local situations of the students' development. Consequently, in delineating sequences of such practices, the analysis documents the evolving social situations in which students participate and learn. I and my colleagues therefore take individual students' mathematical interpretations and actions to be the psychological correlates of these practices and view the two as reflexively related (see Figure 6). What is seen from one perspective as an act of individual learning in which a student reorganizes his or her mathematical reasoning is seen from the other perspective as an act of participation in the evolution of communal mathematical practices. In coordinating social and psychological perspectives, the approach that we propose therefore seeks to analyze the development of students' mathematical reasoning in relation to the local social situations in which they participate and to whose emergence they contribute.

USEFULNESS

I have argued that the approach of coordinating psychological and social perspectives on mathematical activity addresses two of the three criteria that an analytical approach which is appropriate for purposes of design research should satisfy. However, I have thus far said little about the remaining criterion; namely, that analyses should feed back to inform the ongoing improvement of instructional designs.

This criterion requires that accounts of students' mathematical learning be tied to analysis of what happened in the classrooms where that learning occurred. In this regard, I contend that analyses cast in terms of classroom mathematical practices satisfy this criterion because, when they are coordinated with psychological analyses of individual students' reasoning, they provide situated accounts of students' learning in which the process of learning is directly related to the means by which it was supported. As a consequence, a difficulty that often arises when more individualistic approaches are followed, that of figuring out what the results of an analysis might imply for instruction, simply fails to materialize. Instead, we are in a position to develop testable conjectures about how we might be able to improve the means of supporting students' learning. For our purposes as instructional designers, the situated nature of this analytical approach is a strength when compared with alternative approaches that aim to produce context-free descriptions of cognitive development that apparently unfold independently of situation and purpose. Wertsch (1991) makes a similar point when he observes that

> much contemporary research in psychology does not in fact have the practical implications claimed for it. In my view, a major reason is the tendency of psychological research, especially in the United States, to examine human mental functioning as if it exists in a cultural, institutional, and historical vacuum. (p. 2)

The all-to-familiar gulf between theoretical analyses and instructional practice is sidestepped in an approach of the type that I have described, because theoretical insights about the means of supporting students' learning in a particular domain are rooted in the practice of attempting to support that learning. Such approaches are therefore well suited to the task of supporting educational innovation as a process of continual, iterative improvement.

In addition to having practical utility in the context of design research, situated approaches that link students' mathematical learning to the social situations in which it occurs have considerable explanatory power. This becomes apparent when we focus on the issue of replicability. As we know only too well, the history of educational research in general, and in mathematics education in particular, is replete with more than its share of disparate and irreconcilable findings. Often, different patterns of learning are documented when instructional sequences that had previously proven effective are enacted in other classrooms. In my view, a primary source of difficulty is that the independent variables of traditional psychological experimental research are often relatively superficial and have little to do with either context or meaning (Forman, 1998). The conceptualization of the classroom as a matrix of environmental variables is at odds with the approach I have taken in which the classroom microculture is viewed as a semiotic ecology that has meaning making at its core. In the standard psychological paradigm, the relationship between the developing mind and the environment is analogous to that between jello and a mold. From this it follows that just as we should study the mold if we want to understand the shape of the jello, so we should analyze the pre-given environment if we want to understand the contours of the mind. In contrast, in the situated approach that I have outlined, the analogue of the mold, the classroom microculture, is not viewed as independent of the teacher's and students' activity. Instead, students are seen to actively contribute to the evolution of the microculture that both enables and constrains the development of their reasoning. It is this sense of participation in an evolving community of practice that typically falls beyond the purview of traditional experimental research.

In my view, the central issue is not so much that findings are often disparate, but that they are typically irreconcilable—it has not been possible to account for differences in findings when different groups of students have received supposedly the same instructional treatment. In contrast to traditional experimental research, the challenge as I see it is not that of replicating instructional treatments by ensuring that instructional sequences are enacted in exactly the same way in different classrooms. The conception of teachers as professionals who continually adjust their plans on the basis of ongoing assessments of their students' reasoning would, in fact, suggest that complete replicability is neither desirable nor, perhaps, possible (Ball, 1993; Franke et al.; 1998, Gravemeijer, 1994b). The challenge is instead to develop ways of analyzing treatments so that their realizations in different classrooms can be made commensurable. I contend that situated approach of the type that I have illustrated offers this possibility. This is because an analysis of the mathematical practices that are established when an instructional sequence is enacted in a particular classroom documents the evolving social situation in which the students' mathematical learning occurs. Consequently, an analysis of two different enactments of the same instructional sequence enables us to relate the differing patterns of what are traditionally called learning outcomes to the differing situations of learning that were actually constituted in the two classrooms. In such an analysis, the focus on the practices in which the students actually participate as they reorganize their mathematical reasoning brings context and meaning to the fore. This in turn makes it possible to compare and contrast critical aspects of different enactments of a treatment, thereby making them commensurable. I therefore claim that an analytical approach of this type can lead to greater precision and control by facilitating disciplined, systematic inquiry into instructional innovation and change that embraces the messiness and complexity of the classroom.

CONCLUSION

Throughout this article, I have stressed that I and my colleagues' overall goal is to be increasingly effective in developing instructional designs that support student mathematical learning. I reiterate this point to emphasize that our commitment to a situated viewpoint on mathematical activity is not ideological in the pejorative sense of the term. When I described our general theoretical orientation, I clarified that the approach we take focuses squarely on the diversity of individual students' reasoning. Our reasons for doing so are pragmatic and relate directly to the purposes of design research. As I indicated, we find it essential to take account of the particular ways in which individual students are reasoning when we make instructional decisions in the classroom. In addition to acknowledging this emphasis, I also explained why we have come to reject purely individualistic approaches and, instead, find it useful to view students' mathematical reasoning as acts of participation in communal practices that they and the teacher establish in the course of their ongoing interactions. The reasons I gave were again pragmatic and relate to the process of planning a design experiment. In particular, I discussed why we need theoretical constructs that make it possible for us to develop conjectures about the envisioned learning of the classroom community. I also illustrated that this approach has the benefit of enabling us to develop analyses that relate individual students' mathematical learning to the evolving social situations in which that learning occurs.

In light of these considerations, the situated approach that I have described might be best viewed as having the status of a report from the field. For us, the approach is nothing more than a potentially revisable solution to the concrete problems and issues that we have encountered while experimenting in classrooms. Further, the various constructs that I have discussed are, for us, conceptual tools that are appropriate for certain purposes but not others. As a consequence of this pragmatic orientation, we can readily accept that alternative approaches might be more appropriate when investigations are motivated by other concerns. I therefore leave it to the reader to assess whether aspects of the analytical approach that I have presented are relevant to the problems of interest to them.

ACKNOWLEDGMENT

The analysis reported in this chapter was supported by the National Science Foundation under grant No. REC9814898 and by the Office of Educational Research and Improvement under grant number R305A60007. The opinions expressed do not necessarily reflect the views of the Foundation or OERI.

NOTES

1. My colleagues in classroom design experiments conducted since 1992 have been Kay McClain and Koeno Gravemeijer. My colleagues in prior design experiments were Erna Yachel and Terry Wood.

2. We speak of normative activities being taken-as-shared rather than shared to leave room for the diversity in individual students' ways of participating in these activities. The assertion that a particular activity is taken-as-shared makes no deterministic claims about the reasoning of the participating students, least of all that their reasoning is identical.

3. This approach of coordinating psychological and social analyses is closely related to serveral other proposals. These include Hatano's (1993) call to synthesize constructivism and Vygotskian perspective, Saxe's (1991) discussion of the intertwining of cultural forms and cognitive functions, and Rogoff's (1995) distinction between three planes of analysis that correspond to personal, interpersonal, and community processes.

REFERENCES

Axel, E. (1992). One developmental line in European Activity Theory. *Quarterly Newsletter of the Laboratory of Comparative Human Cognition, 14*(1), 8—17.

Ball, D. (1993). With an eye on the mathematical horizon: Dilemmas of teaching elementary school mathematics. *Elementary School Journal, 93,* 373–397.

Bateson, G. (1973). *Steps to an ecology of mind.* London: Paladin

Bauersfeld, H. (1992). Intergrating theories for mathematics education. *For the Learning of Mathematics, 12,* 19–28.

Bauersfeld, H., Krummheuer, G., & Voigt, J. (1988). Interactional theory of learning and teaching mathematics and related microethnographical studies. In H.- G. Steiner & A. Vermandel (Eds.), *Foundations and methodology of the discipline of mathematics education* (pp. 174–188). Antwerp: Proceedings of the TME Conference.

Beach, K. (1999). Consequential transitions: A sociocultural expedition begond transfer in education. *Review of Research in Education, 24,* 103–141.

Biehler, R., & Steinbring, H. (1991). Entdeckende Statistik, Stenget-und-Blatter, Boxplots: Konzepte, Begrundungen and Enfahrungen eines Unterrichtsversuch es [Explorations in statistics, stem-and-leaf, boxplots: Concepts, justifications, and experience in a teaching experiment]. *Der Mathematikunterricht, 37*(6), 5–32.

Bishop, A. (1985). The social construction of meaning—a significant development for mathematics education? *For the Learning of Mathematics, 5*(1), 24–28.

Blumer, H. (1969). *Symbolic interactionism: Perspectives and method.* Englewood Cliffs, NJ: Prentice-Hall.

Boaler, J. (1999). Participation, knowledge and beliefs: A community perspective on mathematics learning. *Educational Studies in Mathematics, 40,* 259–281.

Brown, A. L. (1992). Design experiments: Theoretical and methodological challenges in creating complex interventions in classrooms. *Journal of the Learning Sciences, 2,* 141–178

Cobb, G.W. (1997.) More literacy is not enough. In L.A. Steen (Ed.), *Why numbers count: Quantitative literacy for tomorrow's America* (pp. 75–90). New York: College Entrance Examination Board.

Cobb, G. W., & Moore, D. S. (1997). Mathematics, statistics, and teaching. *American Mathematical Monthly, 104,* 801–823.

Cobb, P. (1998). Learning from distributed theories of intelligence. *Mind, Culture, and Activity, 5,* 187–204.

Cobb, P. (1999). Individual and collective mathematical development: The case of statistical data analysis. *Mathematical Thinking and Learning, 1,* 5–44.

Cobb, P. (in press). Conducting classroom teaching experiments in collaboration with teachers. In R. Lesh & E. Kelly (Eds.), *New methodologies in mathematics and science education.* Dordrecht, Netherlands: Kluwer.

Cobb, P., McClain, K., & Gravemeijer, K. (2000). *Learning about statistical covariation.* Paper presented at the annual meeting of the American Educational Research Association, New Orleans.

Cobb, P., Stephan, M., McClain, K., & Gravemeijer, K. (in press). Participating in classroom mathematical practices. *Journal of the Learning Sciences.*

Cole M. (1996). *Cultural psychology.* Cambridge, MA: Belknap Press of Harvard University Press.

Confrey, J., & Lachance, A. (in press). A research design model for conjecture-driven teaching experiments. In R. Lesh & E. Kelly (Eds.), *New methodologies in mathematics and science education.* Dordrecht, Netherlands: Kluwer.

Confrey, J., & Smith, E. (1995). Splitting, covariation, and their role in the development of exponential functions. *Journal for Research in Mathematics Education, 26,* 66–86.

Dewey, J. (1981). Experience and nature. In J. A. Boydston (Ed.), *John Dewey: The later works, 1925–1953,* Vol. 1. Carbondale: Southern Illinois University Press (Originally published 1925).

Dörfler, W. (1993). Computer use and views of the mind. In C. Keitel & K. Ruthven (Eds.), *Learning from computers: Mathematics education and technology* (pp. 159–186). Berlin: Springer-Verlag.

Dörfler, W. (in press). Means for meaning. In P. Cobb, E. Yackel, & K. McClain (Eds.), *Symbolizing and communicating in mathematics classrooms: Perspectives on discourse, tools, and instructional design.* Mahwah, NJ: Erlbaum.

Engestrom, Y. (1999). Activity theory and individual and social transformation. In Y. Engestrom, R. Miettinen, & R.-L. Punamaki (Eds.), *Perspectives on activity theory* (pp 19–38). New York: Cambridge University Press.

Erickson, F. (1986). Qualitative methods in research on teaching. In M.C. Wittrock (Ed.), *The handbook of research on teaching* (3rd. ed., pp. 119–161). New York: Macmillan.

Ernest, P. (1994). The dialogical nature of mathematics. In P. Ernest (Ed.), *Mathematics, education, and philosophy: An international perspective* (pp. 33–48). London: Falmer.

Forman, E. (1996). Forms of participation in classroom practice: Implications for learning mathematics. In P. Nesher, L. Steffe, P. Cobb, G. Goldin, & B. Greer (Eds.), *Theories of mathematical learning* (pp. 115–130). Hillsdale, NJ: Erlbaum.

Forman, E. A. (1998, March). *A sociocultural approach to mathematics reform: Speaking, inscribing, and doing mathematics within communities of practice.* Paper presented at the conference on the Foundations of School Mathematics, Atlanta.

Franke, M. L., Carpenter, T. P., Levi, L., & Fennema, E. (1998, April). *Capturing teachers' generative change: A follow-up study of teachers' professional development in mathematics.* Paper presented at the annual meeting of the American Educational Research Association, San Diego.

Freudenthal, H. (1973). *Mathematics as an educational task.* Dordrecht, Netherlands: Kluwer.

Gravemeijer, K. E. P. (1994a). *Developing realistic mathematics education.* Utrecht, Netherlands: CD-B Press.

Gravemeijer, K. (1994b). Educational development and developmental research. *Journal for Research in Mathematics Education, 25,* 443–471.

Gravemeijer, K. (1998, April). Development research: Fostering a dialectic relation between theory and practice. Paper presented at the Research pre-session of the annual meeting of the National Council of Teachers of Mathematics, Washington, D.C.

Greeno, J.G. (1997). On claims that answer the wrong questions. *Educational Researcher, 26*(1), 5–17.

Hatano, G. (1993). Time to merge Vygotskian and constructivist conceptions of knowledge acquisition. In E. A. Forman, N. Minick, & C. A. Stone (Eds.), *Contexts for learning: Sociocultural dynamics in children's development* (pp. 153–166). New York: Oxford University Press.

Hutchins, E. (1995). *Cognition in the wild.* Cambridge, MA: MIT Press.

Johnson, M. (1987). *The body in the mind: The bodily basis of reason and imagination.* Chicago: University of Chicago Press.

John-Steiner, V. (1995). Spontaneous and scientific concepts in mathematics: A Vygotskian approach. In L. Meira & D. Carraher (Eds.), *Proceedings of the 19th International Conference for the Psychology of Mathematics Education* (Vol. 1, pp. 30–44). Recite, Brazil: Program Committee of 10th PME Conference.

Kamii, C. K. (1985). *Young children reinvent arithmetic: Implications of Piaget's theory.* Columbia, NY: Teacher College Press.

Kaput, J. J. (1994). The representational roles of technology in connecting mathematics with authentic experience. In R. Biehler, R. W. Scholz, R. Strasser, & B. Winkelmann (Eds.), *Didactics of mathematics as a scientific discipline* (pp. 379–397). Dordrecht, Netherlands: Kluwer.

Konold, C., Pollatsek, A., Well, A., & Gagnon, A. (1996, July). *Students' analyzing data: Research of critical barriers.* Paper presented at the Roundtable Conference of the International Association for Statistics Education, Granada, Spain.

Kozulin, A. (1990). *Vygotsky's psychology.* Cambridge, MA: Harvard University Press.

Lampert, M. (1990). When the problem is not the question and the solution is not the answer: Mathematical knowing and teaching. *American Educational Research Journal, 27*(1), 29—63.

Lampert, M., & Cobb, P. (in press). White paper on communication and language. In J. Kilpatrick, D. Shifter, & G. Martin (Eds.), *Principles and practices of school mathematics: Research companion volume.* Reston, VA: National Council of Teachers of Mathematics.

Latour, B. (1987). *Science in action.* Cambridge, MA: Harvard University Press.

Lave, J. (1988). *Cognition in practice: Mind, mathematics and culture in everyday life.* Cambridge, MA: Harvard University Press.

Lave, J. (1993). Word problems: A microcosm of theories of learning. In P. Light & G. Butterworth (Eds.), *Context and cognition: Ways of learning and knowing* (pp. 74–92). Hillsdale, NJ: Erlbaum.

Lave, J., & Wenger, E. (1991). *Situated learning: Legitimate peripheral participation.* Cambridge, MA: Harvard University Press.

Lawler, R. W. (1985). *Computer experience and cognitive development: A child's learning in a computer culture.* New York: Wiley.

Lehrer, R., Jacobson, C., Kemney, V., & Strom, D. A. (1999). Building upon children's intuitions to develop mathematical understanding of space. In E. Fennema & T. R. Romberg (Eds.), *Mathematics classrooms that promote understanding* (pp. 63–87). Mahwah, NJ: Erlbaum.

Lehrer, R., & Romberg, T. (1996). Exploring children's data modeling. *Cognition and Instruction, 14,* 69–108.

Lehrer, R., Schauble, L. Carpenter, S., & Penner, D. (in press). The inter-related development of inscriptons and conceptual understanding. In P. Cobb, E. Yackel, & K. McClain (Eds.), *Symbolizing, mathematizing, and communicating: Perspectives on discourse, tools, and instructional design.* Mahwah, NJ: Erlbaum.

Lemke, J. L. (1997). Cognition, context, and learning: A social semiotic perspective. In D. Kirshner & J. A. Whitson (Eds.), *Situated cognition theory: Social, semiotic, and neurological perspectives* (pp. 37–56). Hillsdale, NJ: Erlbaum.

Leont'ev, A. N. (1978). *Activity, consciousness, and personality.* Englewood Cliffs, NJ: Prentice-Hall.

Lerman, S. (1996.) Intersubjectivity in mathematics learning: A challenge to the radical constructivist paradigm? *Journal for Research in Mathematics Education, 27,* 133–150.

McClain, K., Cobb,P., & Gravemeijer, K. (in press). Supporting students' ways of reasoning about data. In M. Burke (Ed.), *Learning mathematics for a new century* (2001 Yearbook of the National Council of Teachers of Mathematics). Reston, VA: NCTM.

McGatha, M., Cobb, P., & McClain, K. (1999, April). *An analysis of students' initial statistical understanding.* Paper presented at the annual meeting of the American Educational Research Association, Montreal.

Mehan, H., & Wood, H. (1975). *The reality of ethnomethodology.* New York: Wiley.

Meira, L. (1998). Making sense of instructional devices: The emergence of transparency in mathematical activity. *Journal for Research in Mathematics Education, 29,* 121–142.

Minick, N. (1989).. Literacy's I *L. S. Vygotsky and Soviet activity theory: Perspectives on the relationship between mind and society.* Literacy's Institute, Special Monograph Series No. 1. Newton, MA: Educational Development Center.

Moore, D. S. (1996). New pedagogy and new content: The case of statistics. In B. Phillips (Ed.), *Papers on statistics education.* Hawthorn, Australia: Swinburne.

O'Connor, M. C. (1998). Language socialization in the mathematics classroom: Discourse practices and mathematical thinking. In M. Lampert & M. L. Blunk (Eds.), *Talking mathematics in school* (pp. 17–55). New York: Cambridge University Press.

Pea, R. D. (1993). Practices of distributed intelligence and designs for education. In G. Solomon (Ed.), *Distributed cognitions* (pp. 47–87). New York: Cambridge University Press.

Piaget, J. (1970). *Genetic epistemology.* New York: Columbia University Press.

Piaget, J. (1973). *To understand is to invent.* New York: Grossman.

Rogoff, B. (1995). Observing sociocultural activity on three planes: Participating appropriation, guided participation, and apprenticeship. In J. V. Wersch, P. del Rio, & A. Alvarez (Eds.), *Sociocultural studies of mind* (pp. 139–164). New York: Cambridge University Press.

Rogoff, B. (in press). Evaluating development in the process of perticipation: Theory, methods, and practice building on each other. In E. Amsel & A. Renninger (Eds.), *Change and development: Issues of theory, application and method.* Mahwah; NJ: Erlbaum.

Roth, W-M. (1997). Where is the context in contextual word problems? Mathematical practices and products in grade 8 students' answers to story problems. *Cognition and Instruction, 14,* 487–527.

Roth, W-M., & McGinn, M. K. (1998). Inscriptions: Towards a theory of representing as social practice. *Review of Educational Research, 68,* 35–59.

Saxe, G. B. (1991). *Culture and cognitive development: Studies in mathematical understanding.* Hillsdale, NJ: Erlbaum.

Sfard, A. (in press). Symbolizing mathematical reality into being. In P. Cobb, E. Yackel, & K. McClain (Eds.), *Symbolizing, communicating, and mathematizing in reform classrooms: Perspectives on discourse, tools, and instructional design.* Mahwah, NJ: Erlbaum.

Shotter, J. (1995). In dialogue: Social constructionism and radical constructivism. In L. P. Steffe & J. Gale (Eds.), *Constructivism in education* (pp. 41–56). Hillsdale, NJ: Erlbaum.

Simon, M. A. (1995). Reconstructing mathematics pedagogy from a constructivist perspective. *Journal for Research in Mathematics Education, 26,* 114–145.

Simon, M.A. (in press). Research on mathematics teacher development: The teacher development experiment. In R. Lesh & E. Kelly (Eds.), *New methodologies in mathematics and science education.* Dordrecht, Netherlands: Kluwer.

Simon, M. S., & Blume, G. W. (1996). Justification in the mathematics classroom: A study of prospective elementary teachers. *Journal of Mathematical Behavior, 15,* 3–31.

Steffe, L.P., & Kieren, T. (1994). Radical constructivism and mathematics education. *Journal for Research in Mathematics Education, 25,* 711–733.

Steffe, L. P. & Thompson, P. W. (in press). Teaching experiment methodology: Underlying principles and essential elements. In R. Lesh & E. Kelly (Eds.), *New methodologies in mathematics and science education.* Mahwah, NJ: Erlbaum.

Stigler, J. W., & Hiebert, J. (1999). *The teaching gap.* New York: Free Press.

Thompson, P. W. (1991). To experience is to conceptualize: A discussion of epistemology and mathematical experience. In L. P. Steffe (Ed.), *Epistemological foundations of mathematical experience* (pp. 260–281). New York: Springer-Verlag.

Tukey, J. W. (1977). *Exploratory data analysis.* Reading, MA: Addison-Wesley.

Tzou, C. (2000). *Learning about data creation.* Paper presented at the annual meeting of the American Educational Research Association, New Orleans.

van der Veer, R., & Valsiner, J. (1991). *Understanding Vygotsky: A quest for synthesis.* Cambridge, MA: Blackwell.

van Oers, B. (1996). Learning mathematics as meaningful activity. In P. Nesher, L. Steffe, P. Cobb, G. Goldin, & B. Greer (Eds.), *Theories of mathematical learning* (pp. 91–114). Hillsdale, NJ: Erlbaum.

Varela, F. J., Thompson, E., & Rosch, E. (1991). *The embodied mind: Cognitive science and human experience.* Cambridge, MA: MIT Press.

Voigt, J. (1995). Thematic patterns of interaction and sociomathematical norms. In P. Cobb & H. Bauersfeld (Eds.), *Emergence of mathematical meaning: Interaction in classroom cultures* (pp. 163–201). Hillsdale, NJ: Erlbaum.

Walkerdine, V. (1988). *The mastery of reason: Cognitive development and the production of rationality.* London: Routledge.

Waschescio, U. (1998). The missing link: Social and cultural aspects in social constructivist theories. In F. Seeger, J. Voigt, & U. Waschescio (Eds.), *The culture of the mathematics classroom* (pp. 221–241). New York: Cambridge University Press.

Wertsch, J. V. (1991). *Voices of the mind: A sociocultural approach to mediated action.* Cambridge: Harvard University Press.

Wertsch, J.V. (1994). The primacy of mediated action in sociocultural studies. *Mind, Culture, and Activity, 1,* 202–208.

Wertsch, J., del Rio, P., & Alvarez, A. (1995). Sociocultural studies: History, action, and mediation. In J. V. Wertsch, P. del Rio, & A. Alvarez (Eds.), *Sociocultural studies of mind* (pp. 1–34). New York: Cambridge University Press.

Wertsch, J., & Toma, C. (1995). Discourse and learning in the classroom: A sociocultural approach. In L. P. Steffe & J. Gale (Eds.), *Constructivism in education* (pp. 159–174). Hillsdale, NJ: Lawrence Erlbaum Associates.

Winograd, T. & Flores, F. (1986). *Understanding computers and cognition: A new foundation for design*. Norwood, NJ: Ablex Publishing Corporation.

Yackel, E., & Cobb, P. (1996). Sociomath ematical norms, argumentation, and autonomy in mathematics. *Journal for Research in Mathematics Education, 27,* 458–477.

4

Interweaving Content and Pedagogy in Teaching and Learning to Teach: Knowing and Using Mathematics

Deborah Loewenberg Ball and Hyman Bass

INTRODUCTION[1]

Suppose you posed four numbers—7, 38, 63, and 90—to a class and asked the students to identify which of the numbers were even. And suppose, further, that you got this paper back from one of the students, with none of the numbers circled:

7   38   63   90

What would you make of this? Is this answer surprising or predictable? What might this student actually know? What number or numbers would you pose next to find out with more precision what the student thinks? Why would that selection be useful?

Thinking about this and figuring out what to do next this is one of many examples of the kind of mathematical problem solving in which teachers regularly engage. Although no teacher we have ever met could not correctly identify which numbers are even in the preceding list, understanding what there is to know about even numbers goes beyond being able to do this oneself and is critical to teaching well.

Identifying any even number entails knowing a definition for even numbers and being able to use that definition for any number. Viable definitions include:

> *Fair share:* A number N is even if it can be divided into two (equal) parts with nothing left over (algebraically, $N = 2 \times k$; i.e., $k + k$).
>
> *Pair:* A number N is even if it can be divided into twos (pairs) with nothing left over (algebraically, $N = k \times 2$; i.e., $2 + 2 + 2 + \ldots + 2$ [k terms]).
>
> *Alternating:* The even and odd numbers alternate on the number line.

Units digit: A number is even if its units digit is even (e.g., 712 is even because 2 is even).

But these definitions are not enough in themselves. One would need to know, first of all, how to use them to consider and determine the status of specific numbers. This is particularly salient with the units digit definition. This criterion can be easy to use, for, because one does not have to worry about any digit other than the units, one can deploy it routinely. However, it is more subtle to explain. Justifying it requires understanding place value, for this definition is based on understanding the decomposition of a number represented in decimal form—that is, that $712 = 7 \times 10^2 + 1 \times 10^1 + 2 \times 10^0 = 700 + 10 + 2$. If one does not understand that this is the basis on which the definition is founded, one may get confused if one forgets the algorithm; 712 can look ambiguous, for the 7 and the 1 are both odd.

Another important understanding is to know the domain to which these definitions are usefully and conventionally applied. (Even the appreciation that this is a fundamental mathematical question about a definition is an important sensibility.) For example, are fractions typically categorized as even or odd? Is zero?

Third, one should have good sense of when each definition might be useful. For example, the units digit definition is useful for large numbers; the alternating definition is cumbersome for any but very narrow intervals in which one already has an established referent (e.g., with small numbers, or with large numbers where some neighboring number is already known to be even).[2]

Finally, one would want to understand how the four definitions compare: Why do they each work to identify the same set of numbers? How might one explain these correspondences *mathematically?*

Knowing and being sensitive to all these things, and being able to use them in the context of the student's response, can equip one to consider plausible reasons why a child might not mark any of the numbers. Seven is not even, and, like the even/odd status of each of the digits, can be simply memorized as such. Thirty-eight includes an odd digit as well as an even one, and one might consider it "mixed." Sixty-three is not even, and a child might consider it mixed (as 38) or might use one of the other definitions to establish it as odd. Ninety packs a double mathematical issue: 9 is odd, and for the same reason as 38, might present difficulties. Moreover, 0 might be considered odd, or neither even nor odd.

Knowing and being sensitive to all these kinds of things and being able to use them is also critical to be able to manage other kinds of situations that might arise. A child might ask why the units digit definition works. Another might ask whether 1/2 (or 2/3) is even. Children often wonder about the status of zero. Managing these real situations demands a kind of deeply detailed knowledge of mathematics and the ability to use it in these very real contexts of practice. This chapter draws from work we have been doing to understand the mathematical knowledge entailed by teaching (e.g., Ball, 1999; Ball & Bass, 2000). We begin by looking backward, acknowledging that this question is far from new and that our work builds on substantial recent progress to address it.

CHASMS IN KNOWING AND LEARNING PRACTICE

At the turn of the 20th century, John Dewey (1904/1964) articulated a fundamental tension in the preparation of teachers—that of the "proper relationship" of subject matter and method. At the turn of the 21st century, this tension endures. In fact, many of the same questions persist. On the one hand, to what extent does teaching—and hence, learning to teach—depend on the development of knowledge of subject matter? On the other, to what extent does it rely on the development of pedagogical method?

Clearly the answer must be, "it depends on both." Yet, across the century, this tension has continued to simmer, with strong views on both sides of what is unfortunately often seen as a dichotomy. Policymakers debate whether teachers should major in education or in a discipline. Others argue that what matters is caring for students as well as skills at working effectively with diverse learners. Dewey's (1904/1964) conception of the relationship of subject matter knowledge and method was sophisticated and subtle—so much so that 100 years later, his idea is still elusive. He wrote:

> Scholastic knowledge is sometimes regarded as if it were something quite irrelevant to method. When this attitude is even unconsciously assumed, method becomes an external attachment to knowledge of subject matter. (p. 160)

This separation of substance from method, he argued, fundamentally distorted knowledge. How an idea is represented is part of the idea, not merely its conveyance.

Dewey also believed that good teachers were those who could recognize and create "genuine intellectual activity" in students, and he argued that methods of such activity were intimately tied into disciplines. Subject matter, he believed, was the embodiment of the mind, the product of human curiosity, inquiry, and the search for truth. Teachers who were accustomed to viewing subject matter from the perspective of its growth and development would be prepared to notice nascent intellectual activity in learners. Such individuals would know subject matter in ways that prepared them to hear and extend students' thinking. To do this, he argued, teachers would need to be able to study subject matter in ways that took it back to it "psychical roots" (p. 162).

Despite these prescient ideas that intimately interweave knowledge and learning, teacher education across the 20th century has consistently been severed by a persistent divide between subject matter and pedagogy. This divide has many traces. Sometimes it appears in institutional structures as the chasm between the arts and sciences and schools of education, or as the gulf between universities and schools (Lagemann, 1996). Sometimes the divide appears as fissures in the prevailing curriculum of teacher education, separated into domains of knowledge, complemented by "experience"—supervised practica, student teaching, practice itself. In all of these, the gap between subject matter and pedagogy fragments teacher education by fragmenting teaching.

In recent years, in yet another peculiar fragmentation, commitments to equity and concerns for diversity have often been seen as in tension with a focus on content in teacher education. Courses in multiculturalism contend with subject matter courses for space in the professional curriculum. Yet subject matter understanding is essential in listening flexibly to others and hearing what they are saying or where they might be heading. Knowing content is also crucial to being inventive in creating worthwhile opportunities for learning that take learners' experiences, interests, and needs into account. Contending effectively with the resources and challenges of a diverse classroom requires a kind of responsibility to subject matter without which efforts to be responsive may distort students' opportunities to learn (Ball, 1995). Moreover, the creativity entailed in designing instruction in ways that are attentive to difference requires substantial proficiency with the material.

The overarching problem across these many examples is that the prevalent conceptualization and organization of teachers' learning tends to splinter practice, and leave to individual teachers the challenge of integrating subject matter knowledge and pedagogy in the contexts of their work. We assume that the integration required to teach is simple and happens in the course of experience. In fact, however, this does not happen easily, and often does not happen at all.

QUESTS TO BRIDGE THE CHASM

These chasms in our ways of thinking about content and pedagogy have plagued researchers, teacher educators, and policymakers. And although perhaps not in these forms, these issues have plagued teachers as well, for our incomplete understanding of how content matters in practice has often left practitioners under-prepared for their work, challenged by the problems and mysteries that arise with distressing regularity.

That teachers' own knowledge of the subject affects what they teach and how they teach seems so obvious as to be trivial. However, the empirical support for this "obvious" fact has been surprisingly elusive.[3] And although conceptions of what is meant by "subject matter knowledge," as well as valid measures thereof, have been developing, we lack an adequate understanding of what and how mathematical knowledge is used in practice.

What are the weaknesses in current widely shared ideas about teacher content knowledge? First, subject matter knowledge for teaching is often defined simply by the subject matter knowledge that students are to learn—that is, by the curricular goals for students. Put simply, most people assume that what teachers need to know is what they teach. Many would also add to the list, arguing that teachers must know more in order to have a broad perspective on where their students are heading. Nothing is inherently wrong with this perspective. However, to assume that this suffices is to assume that the enactment of the curriculum relies on no other mathematical understanding or perspective.

Furthermore, the use of mathematical knowledge in teaching is often taken for granted. The mathematical problems teachers confront in their daily work—such as the simple case at the beginning of this chapter—are left unexplored, the occasions that require mathematical sensitivity and insight unprobed. Hence, the content and nature of the mathematical knowledge needed in practice is insufficiently understood. Moreover, the role played by such knowledge is also left unexamined.

In 1986, Lee Shulman, Suzanne Wilson, Pamela Grossman, and Anna Richert introduced "pedagogical content knowledge" to the lexicon of research on teaching and teacher education (Shulman, 1986). The term called attention to a special kind of teacher knowledge that links content and pedagogy. In addition to general pedagogical knowledge and knowledge of the content, argued Shulman and his colleagues, teachers needed to know things like what topics children find interesting or difficult or the representations most useful for teaching a specific content idea. These scholars identified and named a unique kind of knowledge that intertwines aspects of teaching and learning with content.

The introduction of pedagogical content knowledge brought to the fore questions about the content and nature of teachers' special subject matter understanding. Consider the following example. As an experienced classroom teacher, Ball knows that figuring out what her fifth graders know about decimals depends in part on her knowledge of number systems and in part on her understanding of the kinds of errors that 10–year-olds typically make. For example, she knows that they will often confuse .5 with .05 and that they draw this confusion, in part, from their prior conviction that 5 and 05 *are* the same number. This means that a fifth-grade teacher needs to understand a lot about the base 10 number system and about positional notation. When a fifth grader asks, "Where is the 'oneths' place?," a teacher needs to be able to hear that this likely emanates from a 10–year-old's reasonable expectation that if there is a ones place to the left of the decimal point, and a tens place to the left of that, there should be a symmetry to the right of the decimal. In other words, why is the place immediately to the right the tenths place, and not a "oneths" place? But being able to hear this student is not enough. Why *isn't* there a "oneths" place? Answering this for oneself requires a certain explicit understanding of place value and of the multiplicative structure of the base 10 system that goes beyond being able to name the places (ones, tens, hundreds, etc.) or read numbers. And then, beyond being clear about the mathematics, helping a fifth grader understand the missing "oneths" requires an intertwining of content and pedagogy, or pedagogical content knowledge.

This kind of understanding is not something a mathematician would have, but neither would it be part of a high school social studies teacher's knowledge. It is special to the teaching of elementary mathematics. Pedagogical content knowledge—representations of particular topics and how students tend to interpret and use them, for example, or ideas or procedures with which students often have difficulty—describes a unique subject-specific body of pedagogical knowledge that highlights the close interweaving of subject matter and pedagogy in teaching. Bundles of such knowledge are built up by teachers over time as they teach the same topics to children of certain ages, or by researchers as they investigate the teaching and learning of specific mathematical ideas.

Liping Ma (1999) describes the "knowledge packages" that are part of the knowledge of the 72 Chinese elementary teachers whom she interviewed. These packages constituted a refined sense of the organization and development of a set of related ideas in an arithmetic domain. The teachers in her study had clearly articulated ideas about "the longitudinal process of opening up and cultivating such a field in students' minds" (Ma, 1999, p. 114). Their knowledge packages consisted of key ideas that "weigh more" than other ideas in the package, sequences for developing the ideas, and "concept knots" that link crucially related ideas. Ma's notion of "knowledge packages" represents a particularly generative form of and structure for pedagogical content knowledge.

Our work builds on pedagogical content knowledge by complementing what it offers for practice. Pedagogical content knowledge is a special form of knowledge that bundles mathematical knowledge with knowledge of learners, learning, and pedagogy. These bundles offer a crucial resource for teaching mathematics, for they can help the teacher anticipate what students might have trouble learning, and have ready alternative models or explanations to mediate those difficulties. Because one big challenge of teaching is to integrate across many kinds of knowledge in the context of particular situations, the fact that there are patterns in and predictability to what students might think, and that there are well-tried approaches to develop certain mathematical ideas, can help manage this challenge. However, a body of such bundled knowledge may not always equip the teacher with the flexibility needed to manage the complexity of practice. Teachers also need to puzzle about the mathematics in a student's idea, analyze a textbook presentation, consider the relative value of two different representations in the face of a particular mathematical issue. To do this, we argue, requires a kind of mathematical understanding that is pedagogically useful and ready, not bundled in advance with other considerations of students or learning or pedagogy.

Although pedagogical content knowledge provides a certain anticipatory resource for teachers, it sometimes falls short in the dynamic interplay of content with pedagogy in teachers' real-time problem solving. No repertoire of pedagogical content knowledge, no matter how extensive, can adequately anticipate what it is that students may think, how some topic may evolve in a class, the need for a new representation or explanation for a familiar topic. Moreover, more than one mathematical issue or goal may be at play at once, requiring simultaneous consideration of different content within the pedagogical context. That is, as they meet novel situations in teaching, teachers must bring to bear considerations of content, students, learning, and pedagogy. They must reason, and often cannot simply reach into a repertoire of strategies and answers. When teachers look at student work, choose a text to read, design a task, or moderate a discussion, they must attend, interpret, decide, and make moves. Their thinking depends on their capacity to call into play different kinds of knowledge, from different domains. An endless barrage of situations—of what we are beginning to understand as mathematical problems to be solved in practice—entails an ongoing use of mathematical knowledge. It is what it takes *mathematically* to manage these routine and nonroutine problems that has preoccupied our interest as we seek to build on the groundbreaking research on pedagogical content knowledge.[4] It is to this kind of *pedagogically useful mathematical* understanding that we attend in our work.

This chapter draws on work that we—Bass, a professional mathematician, and Ball, an educational researcher and elementary school teacher—began in 1996. We have been using our distinct disciplinary perspectives to probe the interplay of mathematics and pedagogy in practice.[5] The problem on which we have been working is one that is central to both professional education and instructional improvement: What mathematical knowledge is needed to teach elementary school mathematics well? How must it be understood and held so that it is available for use? Working with primary records of teaching and learning—videotapes, student work, curriculum materials, teacher notes[6]—we have been trying to analyze and articulate ways in which mathematical insight, sensibilities, and knowledge are entailed by the practice of teaching mathematics.[7]

Our research turns the usual approach to this problem on its head. Rather than identifying the mathematical knowledge needed for teaching by examining the curriculum, or by interviewing teachers, we begin instead with an examination of practice itself. Examining the curriculum, although useful, is incomplete for it fails to anticipate the mathematical demands of its enactment in classrooms. Interviewing teachers, though also valuable, is incomplete because it infers teaching's mathematical demands from teachers' accounts of what they think or would do. Without knowing whether the teachers interviewed are actually able to help all students learn mathematics well, what they report remains in some significant ways unwarranted. In any case, neither of these approaches bridges the gap between knowledge and practice, except indirectly through inference or report.

We seek to complement the examination of curriculum and of what experienced teachers know with a mathematical analysis of core activities of mathematics teaching. We intend with the phrase "core activities" to include such things as figuring out what students know; choosing and managing representations of mathematical ideas; appraising, selecting, and modifying textbooks; deciding among alternative courses of action; steering a productive discussion—and we seek to identify the mathematical resources entailed by these teacher activities.

In this work, we see teaching as a practice embedded with both regularities and endemic uncertainties. For example, some topics—such as arithmetic with integers, probability, and fractions—are quite often difficult for students. Certain ways of approaching these topics—particular representations and methods of development—can help mediate these difficulties. Oft-used mathematical tasks can be mapped by the range of typical approaches used by students of a given age (Stigler & Hiebert, 1999). Being prepared for these regularities of practice is enabled by what we think of as "pedagogical content knowledge," clusters that embed knowledge of mathematics, of students, and of pedagogy. However, no amount of pedagogical content knowledge can prepare a teacher for all of practice, for a significant proportion of teaching is uncertain. Many others have written about the uncertainties of teaching (Ball, 1996; Cohen, in preparation; Lampert, 1985; Lampert &

Ball, 1999; Lortie, 1975; McDonald, 1992), citing numerous sources of uncertainty and providing analyses of the consequences for teachers and their work. Sources of uncertainty in teaching derive in part from its foundations: the impossibility of knowing definitely what students know, and the necessarily incomplete nature of knowledge of teaching, and even the inherent indeterminacy of mathematical knowledge itself that is germane to a given instructional context (Ball, 1996). Because teaching practice is constructed in the interplay of mathematics, students, and pedagogy, considerable parts of teachers' work are embedded with uncertainties. Acknowledging the uncertainty of teaching does not mean that teachers cannot be prepared to know in practice. Quite the contrary: Knowing mathematics for teaching must take account of both the regularities and the uncertainties of practice, and must equip teachers to know in the contexts of the real problems they have to solve.

Because we are interested in the mathematical entailments of practice, we are interested not only in what teachers must know, but also how they must be able to use that knowledge (Cohen & Ball, 1999). "Knowing teaching is more than applying prior understandings. It also depends fundamentally on being able to know things *in the situation*" (Lampert & Ball, 1999, p. 38).

Our approach, a kind of "job analysis" of classroom teaching focused on the actual work, is rooted in these premises about practice and seeks to locate and analyze mathematics as it is used in practice. Such a mathematical perspective on the work of teaching can extend what we currently understand about the mathematical resources needed for teaching, the role of such resources in practice, and, by implication, what opportunities for teachers and prospective teachers need to be developed for them to be prepared to teach mathematics well.

KNOWLEDGE IN PRACTICE

We begin with two examples, each offering a closer look at a sliver of the work of teaching. Consider, first, the work of examining and preparing to teach a mathematics problem (Gelfand & Shen, 1993):

> Write down a string of 8's. Insert some plus signs at various places so that the resulting sum is 1,000.

At first glance, this problem may look trivial and uninteresting—one way of solving it entails simply adding 125 8's together. A closer look reveals that if several 8's are written together—888 or 88—many more solutions are possible. And working on the problem a little further reveals interesting and provocative patterns in the solution set. Figuring out how to organize the solutions is itself an interesting component of the work, and depending on how they are organized, different elements of the problem and its solutions are visible.

A teacher preparing to use this task must contemplate: Would this be a good problem for my students? What would it take to figure out the patterns and nuances? Is it worthwhile in terms of what students might learn? At least, it would be important to know what the problem is asking, whether it has one or many solutions, how the solutions might be found. How is it (or could it be) related to other parts of the curriculum? It seems obvious that the task entails some computation—for example, verifying any one solution—but what is the mathematical potential of the task? Are there important ideas or processes involved in the problem? What would it take to use this task well with students? It would help to know what might make the problem hard, and how students might get stuck, and anticipate what the teacher might do if they did. Would students find this interesting? What might it take to hook them on it?

Perhaps, on looking at this problem, a teacher would decide that it is interesting but a bit too difficult for her students. What would it take to make a mathematically similar problem that is a bit easier? At what grade levels would some mathematically equivalent but simpler version of this problem be accessible? How might one rescale the problem, for example, for third graders? For first graders—Could a similar problem structure be set up with Cuisenaire rods? Suppose, in contrast, the teacher worries that this problem is too easy. What would it take to make a more challenging, but again, mathematically similar task? What happens to the problem if one replaces 1,000 with other numbers, or 8 with some other digit? How might one modify the problem so that there are no solutions? Infinitely many solutions? This sort of analysis and preparation of a single math problem begins to reveal how much significant mathematical reasoning is entailed within the work of teaching.

We turn now to a second example. Unlike the preceding example, which provides a glimpse of the work of preparing to use a task with students, this example shows the work of using a task during class. In each example, we seek to remind the reader that the work of teaching, too often thought to be generic, is embedded with significant mathematical analysis and problem solving. Moreover, we seek to show that the mathematical resources entailed in such analysis and problem solving may not in fact be evident on the surface of the school curriculum. Simply looking at the math problem or considering the content on which students are working does not lead to a sufficient appreciation of the specific mathematical knowledge or sensibility that it takes to teach that problem or that content.

The following example, drawn from Ball's third-grade class, centers on the children's work on subtraction of multidigit numbers, learning the conventional place value algorithm, and also using other procedures. We drop in near the beginning of class. The students are discussing solutions to the simple problem:

Joshua ate 16 peas on Monday and 32 peas on Tuesday.
How many more peas did he eat on Tuesday than he did on Monday?

Several solutions are offered. Sean goes to the board and, counting up from 16 to 32 on the number line, explains,

I went sixteen . . . , 1, 2, 3, 4, 5, 6, 7, 8, 9, 10, 11, 12, 13, 14, 15, 16 and I ended up on 32.

Lucy agrees with him, saying that she "got the same answer and did it the same way." Riba concurs, and offers to "prove that his answer is right." She explains:

Riba: Because a half of . . . a half of 32 would be 16.

Ball: Uh huh. And how does that prove that his answer is right?

Riba: I . . . because . . . it's . . . it's a half of 32. Sixteen is a half of 32. That proves his answer.

Ball, not sure what to do with Riba's idea, continues on. Betsy, speaking mostly to Sean, says that she used beansticks[8] to solve the problem and that she has gotten 15. She goes up to the overhead projector and lays out representations of 16 and 32:

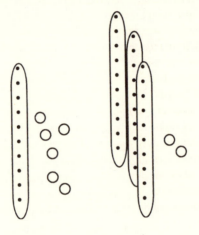

She begins matching individual beans, and then trades a beanstick for 10 loose beans. She continues matching individual beans with others and then one beanstick from each group. Mei objects to Betsy's method of representing both 16 and 32 beans on the overhead:

If you do that you'll . . . if you want to do 32 take away 16 or something like that, you'll need to take away only 16 and . . . and you shouldn't be putting on 32 *and* 16 up there.

Betsy tries to explain. She counts out her beans and sticks, saying that the 16 "what he ate on Monday" and the 32 was what he ate on Tuesday. Then she tries to justify her method:

So, what I'm doing is I'm seeing how much more he ate by putting them together. And when you put them together, you're matching it up just like . . . just about the same way Sean would. But, see instead of adding them together, I'm putting them together like this. And then, since it has a match, I'm putting it down here. So that means you don't count these ones because those are the one that have a match. So, I keep . . . I did this and then see I can't take 4 away from 10. So, what I do is take this in for 10 beans and then I match these together. Then, I counted how many I had.

Mei seems unconvinced. Betsy goes through her solution again. With the teacher's help, she narrates the placement of beansticks and what they represent. She explains the processes she is using to compare the two amounts:

See, I'm taking these two beans and matching them with these two beans. I'm taking these two beans and matching them with these two beans. These two beans and matching them with them.

After doing it, slowly, with explanations, Betsy arrives at the correct answer, 16, which she recognizes is inconsistent with her original answer, 15. Experiencing, in front of the class, as well as in her own mind, the disequilibrium of this contradiction, she proceeds, with the invitation of her teacher and indulgence of her classmates, to reenact carefully the matching of the 16 beans with part of the 32 beans, and, once again, finds that 16 beans remain unmatched. At this point she places (a still slightly tentative) confidence in the answer, 16. Moreover she retracts her earlier notion that her solution is like the method of "counting up" on the number line used by Sean. The class goes on to see yet another solution, presented by Cassandra, hers using the conventional subtraction algorithm. This prompts Sean to offer

$$\begin{array}{r} {}^{1}16 \\ +16 \\ \hline 32 \end{array}$$

for another approach.

By the end of class, the children have seen six different methods, and worked back and forth between the symbolic representations and the concrete forms. They have discussed why some children used subtraction while others added, and they have tried to identify similarities and differences across the methods. This apparently simple word problem has taken the teacher and the children deep into some significant mathematical territory, invisible on the surface of the problem. How are subtraction and addition related, in both symbolic and concrete models? How are the comparison and "take-away" interpretations of subtraction related? How do the beanstick representations map onto the symbolic forms, and how do the processes used by each child map onto each of these? How, for example, does Betsy's method of matching compare with Sean's "counting up" method? Was Mei's objection that Betsy should not represent both the 32 and the 16 legitimate? What is Betsy doing, and how can one reconcile it with Mei's objection? What is Riba thinking when she seeks to "prove" Sean's answer by talking about 16 being "half of" 32?

When teachers hold class discussions, they make decisions about which (and whose) ideas to pick up and pursue and which (and whose) to suspend or let drop. The teacher formulates probes, pushes students, offers hints, and provides explanations. Students get stuck: What does one do to help them remobilize? None of these tasks of teaching can be carried out generically. No matter how committed one is to caring for students, to taking students' ideas seriously, to helping students develop robust understandings, none of these tasks of teaching is possible without making use in context of mathematical understanding and insight.

Herein lies a fundamental difficulty in learning to teach, for despite its centrality, usable mathematical knowledge is not something teacher education, in the main, provides effectively. Although some teachers have important understandings of the content, they often do not know it in ways that help them hear students, select good tasks, and help all their students learn. No prospective or practicing teacher we know is unable to solve the problem of Joshua and the peas. But the mathematical issues embedded in the enactment of this task in class are not trivial. Being able to help Riba develop her idea, for example, would require that a teacher be sensitive to the nature of mathematical reasoning and the need for the steps in an argument to be developed, at a level of granularity appropriate for the context (Ball & Bass, 2000). Riba's claim—that 16 is half of 32—is correct; the issue is not this, but rather how this can support a proof of Sean's claim. The teacher would need to "hear" (and guess) the unspoken elements of her proof and be able to think of what to ask or say that might help Riba develop her idea enough so that the other children could consider what she is saying.[9]

Thus, teachers need mathematical knowledge in ways that equip them to navigate these complex mathematical transactions flexibly and sensitively with diverse students in real lessons. Not providing this undermines and makes hollow efforts to prepare high-quality teachers who can reach all students, teach in multicultural settings, and work in environments that make teaching and learning difficult. Despite frequently heard exhortations to teach all students, many teachers are unable to hear students flexibly, represent ideas in multiple ways, connect content to contexts effectively, and think about things in ways other than their own. For example, in their study of a middle school teacher's attempt to teach the concept of rate, Thompson and Thompson (1994) highlight the crucial role played by language. They describe, vividly, the situation of one teacher who, although he understood the concept of rate himself, was restricted in his capacity to express or discuss the ideas in everyday language. Satisfied with computational language for his own purposes, when these did not help students understand, he was not able to find other means of expressing key ideas. In addition, teachers may not be able to size up their textbooks and adapt them effectively; they may omit topics central to students' futures or make modifications that distort key ideas. They may substitute student interest for content integrity in making subject matter choices.

A recent analysis provides a glimpse of the importance of the distinction between knowing how to do math and knowing it in ways that enable use in practice. This distinction is key to understanding how mathematics knowledge matters in good teaching. In general, astonishingly little empirical evidence exists to link teachers' content knowledge to their students' learning. One hypothesis has been that what is being measured as "content knowledge" (often teachers' course attainment) is a poor proxy for pedagogically usable subject matter understanding. However, in their 1997 *Sociology of Education* article describing their analysis of data from the National Education Longitudinal Study of 1988, Rowan and his colleagues report strong positive correlations between teachers' responses to items designed to measure the use of mathematical knowledge in teaching and their students' performance (Rowan, Chang, & Miller, 1997).[10] This analysis provides some confirmation that understanding the use of mathematics in the work of teaching is a critical area ripe for further examination. It is not just what mathematics teachers know, but how they know it and what they are able to mobilize mathematically in the course of teaching.[11] Though less easily quantified than other indices, such as courses taken, it is this pedagogically functional mathematical knowledge that seems to be central to effective teaching.

An important challenge for teacher education at the beginning of the 21st century is to bridge the chasm identified by John Dewey almost 100 years ago. Our schools are more diverse than ever and we ask more of both teachers and students. What would it take to bring the study of content closer to practice and prepare teachers to know and be able to use subject matter knowledge effectively in their work as teachers?

CLOSING THE GAP: DEVELOPING AND USING KNOWLEDGE IN PRACTICE

Three problems stand out; problems that we must solve if we are to meet this challenge to prepare teachers who not only know content but can make use of it to help all students learn. One problem concerns identifying the content knowledge that matters for teaching, a second regards understanding ways in which such knowledge needs to be held and a third centers on what it takes to learn to use such knowledge in practice.

What Mathematics Is Entailed by Teaching?

First, we would need to reexamine what content knowledge matters for good teaching. Subject matter knowledge for teaching has too often been defined by the subject matter knowledge that students are to learn. Put simply, many assume that what teachers need to know is what they teach—plus a broad perspective on where their students came from and are heading. Nothing is inherently wrong with this perspective. However, the lists of what teachers should know that are produced by analyzing the school curriculum are long and largely arbitrary. Little is known about how "knowing" the topics on these lists affects teachers' capabilities. The unexamined conviction that possessing such knowledge is all that teachers need to know has blocked the inquiry needed to bring together subject matter and practice in ways that would enable teacher education to be more effective.

Instead of beginning solely with the curriculum, our understanding of the content knowledge needed in teaching must start also with practice. We must understand better the work that teachers do, and analyze the role played by content knowledge in that work.

Consider, on one hand, the subtraction problem. We have what looks like a simple calculation, 32 – 16, embedded in a simple story problem. Viewed purely from the point of view of curriculum, this lesson entails some rudimentary knowledge of place value, and of how the algorithm for subtraction with borrowing works.

Consider, on the other hand, the mathematical themes and events encountered as the problem unfolded in the children's work. Sean counted the distance up from 16 to 32 on the number line, finding 16. Riba observed that 16 is half of 32, proposing that this "proved" the correctness of Sean's answer. Betsy used base 10 bean sticks to construct a physical matching between a collection of 16 beans with a part of a separate collection of 32 beans, and then counted the unmatched beans, which involved trading in a 10–stick for 10 individual beans. The result of this, 16, contradicted Betsy's original answer of 15, which she then tried to reconcile. Mei protested that Betsy should not have displayed a separate collection of 16 beans, but only the collection of 32 beans. The physical presence of the 16 beans looked to Mei as though they were being added, not taken away. Sean used the symbolic addition, 16 + 16 = 32, as the basis for another derivation of the answer 16. In the end, the students produced six mathematically distinct approaches to the problem.

What mathematical demands are created by this lesson, beyond knowledge of the symbolic algorithm for subtraction with borrowing, and of the underlying place value system? First are the several models or representations of the problem. Symbolically, the subtraction, 32 – 16 = ?, is equivalent to the missing addend problem, 16 + ? = 32. There are the two interpretations of subtraction, "take away" (if you take 16 away from 32, how many are left?) and "compare" (how many more is 32 than 16?). Second are the many representations of these. One is on the number line, counting 16 down from 32, or counting the distance up from 16 to 32 (as done by Sean). Other representations use bean sticks, either removing 16 from 32 beans (which entails trading a 10–stick for 10 individual beans) or matching 16 beans with some of the 32 beans, and counting what remains (as done by Betsy; which also entails trading a 10–stick for 10 individual beans). Finally, given the multiple approaches produced by the students, there is a profound mathematical imperative to inspect, analyze, and reconcile them.

Permeating this lesson is also a set of class norms for how to justify mathematical claims. This is another large domain of mathematical knowledge on which the teacher must draw, for example in assessing, by both teacher and students, the different student responses, and in evaluating and processing claims such as Riba's pretended "proof" of Sean's answer. What kind of functional knowledge of proof, of mathematical justification, is germane to elementary instruction?[12]

This kind of direct examination of practice seeks to uncover what teachers need to know and be sensitive to about content in order to teach well. This kind of analysis may bring some surprises. For example, in our research, we expected to see that concepts such as place value and decimal notation, the arithmetic of fractions, and so on, would be central—and they have been, as have operations and informal methods of reasoning. But beyond that, we have been struck by the unanticipated but recurrent prominence of certain mathematical notions. For instance, we have found that ideas about similarity, equivalence, mapping among representations, and even isomorphism emerge across many instances of ordinary and extraordinary teaching and learning. We have also uncovered salient issues involving mathematical language—symbolic notation and definitions of terms, their formation and expansion to larger mathematical domains (Ball & Bass, 2000). Similarly new notions are emerging from parallel work in the teaching and learning of history and science (Rose, 2000; Wilson, in press). Inquiries that begin with practice are revealing subject matter entailments of teachers' work that are not seen when we begin with lists of content to be taught that are derived from the school curriculum. These content demands emerge from analyzing the sorts of challenges with which teachers must contend in the course of practice, as they mediate students' ideas, make choices about representations of content, modify curriculum materials, and the like.

What Makes Mathematical Knowledge *Usable* for Teaching?

A second problem concerns *how* subject matter must be understood in order to be usable in teaching. We need to probe not just *what* teachers need to know, but to learn how that knowledge needs to be held and used in the course of teaching. Working on this problem requires examining the assumption that mathematically proficient people know the content sufficiently well to solve the mathematically implicated problems that arise in the course of teaching elementary students. We do not examine here the other sorts of knowledge they would need—of students, of teaching methods, of the contexts, of curriculum. We mean to refer here to how one must be able to understand mathematics in order to manage the deeply content-related issues that can arise.

Ma (1999) describes what she calls "profound understanding of fundamental mathematics" in terms of the depth, breadth, and thoroughness of the knowledge teachers need. "Depth," according to Ma, refers to the ability to connect ideas to the large and powerful ideas of the domain, whereas "breadth" has to do with connections among ideas of similar conceptual power. Thoroughness is essential in order to weave ideas into a coherent whole. In addition to the premium she places on connections, Ma also emphasizes flexibility as held in a multiplicity of representations and approaches. Drawing on Bruner's (1960) ideas about the "structure" of a discipline, Ma stresses the importance of teachers knowing and attending to the "simple but powerful basic concepts and principles of mathematics" (p. 122), and developing "basic attitudes" (p. 122)—for example, to seek to justify claims, to seek consistency in an idea across contexts, to know how as well as why. How such profound understanding of fundamental mathematics (PUFM) is used in practice is both dynamic and situated in contexts. Ma argues that teachers' knowledge of mathematics for teaching must be like an experienced taxi driver's knowledge of a city, whereby one can get to significant places in a wide variety of ways, flexibly and adaptively (p. 123).

It is to the question of use that we have been drawn. Looking at knowledge from the perspective of practice, and the actual work of teaching, we have been increasingly intrigued by the many moments in teaching when mathematical insight, knowledge, and sensibility matters. In the wide variety of mathematical issues, problems, and tasks that arise, we are struck with the variety of ways in which mathematics is entailed by practice.

Flexibility and adaptiveness are clear requirements of teaching. As Ma (1999) argues, teachers must be able to reorganize what they know in response to a particular context. To do this, one needs to be able to deconstruct one's own mathematical knowledge into less polished and final form, where elemental components are accessible and visible. We refer to this as *decompression*. Paradoxically, most personal knowledge of subject matter, which is desirably and usefully compressed, can be ironically inadequate for teaching. In fact, mathematics is a discipline in which compression is central. Indeed, its polished, compressed form can obscure one's ability to discern how learners are thinking at the roots of that knowledge. Knowing flexibly in and for teaching requires a transcendence of the tacit understanding that characterizes much personal knowledge (Polanyi, 1958). Because teachers must be able to work with content for students in its growing, not finished, state, they must be able to do something perverse: work backward from mature and compressed understanding of the content to unpack its constituent elements (Cohen, in preparation).

For example, they must be ready to hear students' ideas, and to hypothesize about their origin, status, and direction. And, in order to ascertain the opportunities for learning embedded in the examples and work that they assign, teachers must be able to decompose a mathematics task, considering its diverse possible trajectories of enactment and engagement. Teaching mathematics entails work with microscopic elements of mathematical knowledge, elements invisible that were, for someone with mature mathematical fluency, long ago covered up—or perhaps never even known. Speculating on why a six-year-old might write "1005" for "one hundred five," and not reading it as a mistaken count—"one thousand five"—requires the capacity to appreciate the elegance of the compressed notation system that adults use readily for numbers but that is not automatic for learners. After all, Roman numerals follow precisely the same structure as the young child's inclination, each element with its own notation—CV for "one hundred five"—without the "place value" core of our system. Being able to see and hear from someone else's perspective, to make sense of a student's apparent error or appreciate a student's unconventionally expressed insight requires this special capacity to unpack one's own highly compressed understandings that are the hallmark of expert knowledge. Even producing a comprehensible explanation depends on this capacity to unpack one's own knowledge, for an explanation works only if it is at a sufficient level of granularity—that is, if its logical steps are small enough to make sense for a particular learner or a whole class, based on what they currently know or do not know (Ball & Bass, 2000).

Being able to use mathematical knowledge involves using mathematical understanding and sensibility to reason about subtle pedagogical questions. What are the advantages and disadvantages of particular metaphors or analogies? Where might they distort the subject matter? For example, both "take away" and "borrowing" create problems for students' understanding of subtraction. These problems cannot be discerned generically, for they require a careful mapping of the metaphor against critical aspects of the concept being learned and against how learners interpret the metaphor. And knowing that subtraction is a particularly difficult idea for students to master is not something that can be seen from knowing the "big ideas" of the discipline. This kind of knowledge is quite clearly mathematical, yet formulated around the need to make ideas accessible to others.

These aspects of content knowledge help to illuminate the territory to which Dewey called attention almost a century ago, bridging the divide between content and pedagogy. However, teaching is a practice. It is, in Lampert's terms, "a thinking practice"—that is, it integrates reasoning and knowing with action (Lampert, 1998). Our tendency to focus either on its cognitive demands (teachers' knowledge, reasoning, decision making, reflection) or on its actions (teacher behavior, classroom management) is yet one more recent form of fragmentation in teacher education, and in particular in our efforts to help teachers acquire usable content knowledge.

How Might Teachers Develop Usable Mathematical Understanding?

Hence, a third problem we would have to solve is how to create opportunities for learning subject matter that would enable teachers not only to know, but to learn to use what they know in the varied contexts of practice (Ball & Cohen, 1999). Even with more grounded analyses of what there is to know and a more finely tuned conception of the nature of the understanding needed to teach, simply teaching such content may not solve the problems of use. How do teachers use content understanding in the context of practice to carry out the core activities of their work? How can opportunities for learning be designed that are aimed at helping teachers learn to use subject matter knowledge to figure out what their students know, to pose questions, to evaluate and modify their textbooks wisely, to design instructional tasks, to manage class discussions, to explain the curriculum to parents?

Some such work along these lines is already underway. One promising possibility is to design and explore opportunities to learn content that either simulate or are situated in the contexts in which subject matter is used—core activities of teaching.

Consider, for example, what is entailed in preparing and using academic tasks. As teachers construct or select a task, they analyze the nature and territory of the task and consider the curricular learning goals its engagement might support. They appraise its accessibility and challenge: For example, they examine whether it has multiple entry and exit points, whether it admits multiple solution strategies, and multiple solutions or levels of solution. They also size up whether it supports collective class work or is better suited to individual (home) work. At times, they seek ways of scaling the problem up or down in difficulty, linking the problem to other domains of the class work, and so on. In either teacher education or professional development settings, these deliberate opportunities for analysis and design could be used as sites for an integral part of the teacher's learning of mathematical content.

For example, with the 8's problem discussed earlier, mathematical analysis might start with construction of a solution, inspecting the methods used, then looking for other solutions, and further trying to find them all (seeing that there are only finitely many), trying to organize (or give structure to) the solution set, and contemplating ways of proving that one has all solutions. How many terms (addends) or how many digits does each solution involve? What are the patterns of these numbers? Further analyses could probe how these features are affected when various terms of the problem are varied, such as replacing 1,000 by another number, or 8 by another digit, or allowing other operations than +. These variations might produce versions that would challenge college students. On the other hand, one could try to model a "mathematically similar" version of this problem accessible to first graders. In each instance one could consider the design of enactment of the task with a given level of students, anticipating the likely results of student engagement, possible readings or misreadings of different formulations of the problem, and so on. Each of these analyses embeds crucial mathematical work, and as such, could be wielded to be critical points for teachers to learn mathematics.

As another example, some teacher educators use student work as a site to analyze and interpret what students know and are learning and, in so doing, to work on the content itself.[13] Another example lies in the use of videotape of classroom lessons or cases of classroom episodes (Lampert & Ball, 1998; Stein, Smith, Henningsen, & Silver, in press). Here the moves made by the teacher could be analyzed to consider the impact on the course of the lesson, the trajectory of the class's work, and the opportunities for learning for particular students and for the group. In both instances (using student work, using videotapes or cases of classroom lessons) teachers or prospective teachers might engage in content-based design work—developing a possible next assignment in response to their analysis of students' work, or planning a next instructional segment based on analysis of the classroom episode. Each of these activities takes a task of teaching that entails content knowledge and creates a possible site for teachers' learning of and using that content in authentic contexts.

But much more work is needed to contend with this endemic problem of use. Working in specific contexts might run the risk of limiting the generality of teachers' learning of content and their capacity to use it in a variety of contexts. How can teachers be prepared to know content sufficiently flexibly such that they are able to make use of content knowledge with a wide variety of students, across a wide range of environments? How could teachers develop a sense of the trajectory of a topic over time, how to develop its intellectual core in students' minds and capacities, so that they eventually reach mature and compressed understandings and skills?

Solving these three problems—what teachers need to know, how they have to know it, and helping them learn to use it—by grounding the problem of teachers' content preparation in problems and sites of practice, could help to close the gaps that have plagued progress in teacher education. But we should realize the challenges that doing this would pose. After all, Dewey thought his vision at the turn of the 20th century was imminently realizable. He thought that what he was describing was "nothing utopian." He suggested that, "the present movement . . . for the improvement of range and quality of subject matter is steady and irresistible" (Dewey, 1904/1964, p. 170). One hundred years later, as we stare at university and college catalogs that divide "methods" courses from disciplinary studies from practica, or at professional development offerings that are devoid of content or chock full of activities for kids, we should understand that bridging these strangely divided practices will be no small feat.

ACKNOWLEDGMENT

This work is supported, in part, by the Spencer Foundation for the project, "Crossing Boundaries: Probing the Interplay of Mathematics and Pedagogy in Elementary Teaching," (MG #199800202).

NOTES

1.The ideas in this chapter about subject matter knowledge in teaching—its nature, uses, and how it might be acquired—have benefited from and drawn on Ball's work and discussions with colleagues David Cohen, Magdalene Lampert, Suzanne Wilson, and Joan Ferrini-Mundy. Members of the Mathematics Teaching and Learning to Teach Group have also contributed significantly to the development of our ideas: Mark Hoover, Jennifer Lewis, Ed Wall, Raven Wallace, Merrie Blunk, Deidre LeFevre, Geoffrey Phelps, Katherine Morris, Heather Lindsay.

2. This definition helps also for general claims, such as the fact that any product, N $(N + 1)$, (N a whole number) is even, which is one explanation of why the binomial coefficient, N $(N + 1) / 2$, is an integer.

3. See, for example, Ball (1999) and Ball, Lubienski, and Mewborn (in press).

4. See, for example, Shulman (1986, 1987); Wilson, Shulman, and Richert (1987); Wilson (1988); Grossman (1990); and Ma (1999).

5. Ball (1999).

6. These main data comprise a year's worth of primary records of teaching and learning gathered in Ball's third-grade class during 1989—1990, under a grant from the National Science Foundation to Magdalene Lampert and Deborah Ball. In addition, we study records from other elementary classrooms, as a means to compare the mathematical entailments across classrooms.

7. See, for example, Ball (1999); Ball and Bass (2000).

8. Beansticks are a base 10 model, constructed with 10 dried beans glued to a popsicle stick to represent tens, and loose beans to represent units. Ten 10–sticks can be glued side

by side on a cardboard square to represent hundreds. The children were working only with tens and ones in this lesson.

9. One plausible line of reasoning might go as follows: Sixteen is half of 32. So Joshua ate half as many peas on Monday as he ate on Tuesday. So the other half was how many more peas he ate on Tuesday than on Monday. In other words, half of 32, or 16, is how many more peas he ate on Tuesday than on Monday.

10. These items were developed at the National Center for Research on Teacher Learning, Michigan State University. See Kennedy, Ball, and McDiarmid (1993).

11. These ideas about the use of mathematics knowledge in teaching draw on Ball's work with David K. Cohen. See, for example, Cohen and Ball (1999).

12. We explore this in Ball and Bass (in press).

13. Several professional development curricula in mathematics are built on this idea. See, for example, Schifter; Barnett; and Stein, Smith, Henningsen, and Silver (in press).

REFERENCES

Ball, D. L. (1995). Transforming pedagogy: Classrooms as mathematical communities. A response to Timothy Lensmire and John Pryor. *Harvard Educational Review, 65,* 670–677.

Ball, D. L. (1996). Teacher learning and the mathematics reforms: What do we think we know and what do we need to learn? *Phi Delta Kappan, 77*(7), 500– 508.

Ball, D. L. (1999). Crossing boundaries to examine the mathematics entailed in elementary teaching. In T. Lam (Ed.), *Contemporary mathematics.* Providence, RI: American Mathematical Society.

Ball, D. L. & Bass, H. (2000). Making believe: The collective construction of public mathematical knowledge in the elementary classroom. In D. Phillips (Ed.), *Yearbook of the National Society for the Study of Education, Constructivism in Education.* Chicago: University of Chicago Press.

Ball, D. L. & Cohen, D. K. (1999). Developing practice, developing practitioners: Toward a practice-based theory of professional education. In G. Sykes and L. Darling-Hammond (Eds.), *Teaching as the learning profession: Handbook of policy and practice* (pp. 3–32). San Francisco: Jossey Bass.

Ball, D., Lubienski, S., & Mewborn, D. (in press). Research on mathematics teaching. In V. Richardson (Ed.), *Handbook for research on teaching* (4th ed.). New York: Macmillan.

Barnett, C. (1998). Mathematics case methods project. *Journal of Mathematics Teacher Education* 1(3), 349–356.

Bruner, J. (1960). *The process of education.* Cambridge, MA: Harvard University Press.

Cohen, D. K. (in preparation). *Teaching practice and its predicaments.* Unpublished manuscript, University of Michigan, Ann Arbor.

Cohen, D. K., & Ball, D. L. (1999). *Instruction, capacity, and improvement* (CPRE Research Report No. RR-043). Philadelphia: University of Pennsylvania, Consortium for Policy Research in Education.

Dewey, J. (1964). The relation of theory to practice in education. In R. Archambault (Ed.), *John Dewey on education* (pp. 313–338). Chicago: University of Chicago Press. (Original work published 1904.)

Gelfand, I. M., & Shen, A. (1993). *Algebra.* Boston: Birkhäuser.

Grossman, P.L. (1990). *The making of a teacher: Teacher knowledge and teacher education*. New York: Teachers College Press.

Kennedy, M. M., Ball, D. L., & McDiarmid, G. W. (1993). *A study package for examining and tracking changes in teachers' knowledge* (Technical Series 93–1). East Lansing, MI: The National Center for Research on Teacher Education.

Lagemann, E. (1996). *Contested terrain: A history of education research in the United States, 1890—1990*. Commissioned paper, Spencer Foundation, Chicago, IL.

Lampert, M. (1985). How do teachers manage to teach? Perspectives on problems in practice. *Harvard Educational Review, 55*(2), 178–194.

Lampert, M. (1998). Studying teaching as a thinking practice. In J. Greeno & S.G. Goldman (Eds.), *Thinking practices* (pp. 53–78). Hillsdale, NJ: Erlbaum.

Lampert, M., & Ball, D. L. (1998). *Teaching, multimedia, and mathematics: Investigations of real practice*. New York: Teachers College Press.

Lampert, M., & Ball, D. L. (1999). Aligning teacher education with contemporary K-12 reform visions. In G. Sykes & L. Darling-Hammond (Eds.), *Teaching as the learning profession: Handbook of policy and practice* (pp. 33–53). San Francisco: Jossey Bass.

Lortie, D. C. (1975). *Schoolteacher: A sociological study*. Chicago: University of Chicago Press.

Ma, L. (1999). *Knowing and teaching elementary mathematics*. Mahwah, NJ: Erlbaum.

McDonald, J. (1992). *Teaching: Making sense of an uncertain craft*. New York: Teachers College Press.

Polanyi, M. (1958). *Personal knowledge: Towards a post-critical philosophy*. Chicago: University of Chicago Press.

Rose, S. L. (1999). *Understanding children's historical sense-making: A view from the classroom*. Unpublished doctoral dissertation, Michigan State University, East Lansing.

Rowan, B., Chiang, F., &Miller, R. (1997). Using research on employees' performance to study the effects of teachers on students' achievement. *Sociology of Education, 70*(4), 256–284.

Schifter, D. (1998). Learning mathematics for teaching: From the teacher's seminar to the classroom. *Journal for Mathematics Teacher Education, 1*(1), 55–87.

Shulman, L. S. (1986) Those who understand: Knowledge growth in teaching. *Educational Researcher, 15,* 4–14.

Shulman, L. S. (1987). Knowledge and teaching: Foundations of the new reform. *Harvard Educational Review, 57,* 1–22.

Stein, M. K., Smith, M., Henningsen, M., & Silver, E. A. (2000). *Exploring cognitively challenging mathematical tasks: A casebook for teacher professional development*. New York: Teachers College Press.

Thompson, P., & Thompson, A. (1994). Talking about rates conceptually, Part I: A teacher's struggle. *Journal for Research in Mathematics Education, 25,* 279–303.

Wilson, S. M. (1998). *Understanding historical understanding*. Unpublished doctoral dissertation. Stanford, CA: Stanford University.

Wilson, S. M. (in press). Research on history teaching. In V. Richardson (Ed.), *Handbook of research on teaching* (4th ed.). New York: Macmillan.

Wilson, S. M., Shulman, L. S., & Richert, A. (1987). "150 different ways of knowing": Representations of knowledge in teaching. In J. Calderhead (Ed.), *Exploring teacher thinking* (pp. 104–124). Sussex, UK: Holt, Rinehart & Winston.

5

Who Counts What As Math? Emergent and Assigned Mathematics Problems in a Project-Based Classroom

Reed Stevens

INTRODUCTION

This chapter presents a case study of a type of mathematics education that continues to stir controversy in America: project-based mathematics (PBM). PBM classrooms are variable in their enactments but share the following basic structure: students work on projects guided by the teacher, usually in groups, that are extended over weeks or months and are organized around fields of inquiry other than disciplinary mathematics. These other fields of inquiry—such as architectural design or science—are intended to give shape and meaning to student uses and learning of mathematics.

PBM education is controversial (Battista, 1999) in part because it violates widespread assumptions about what counts as mathematics. For parents, administrators, politicians, and sometimes students themselves, PBM does in fact present a very different image of mathematics from that found in the mass-marketed mathematics textbooks they encountered in their own K-12 schooling experiences. With no other significant images of mathematics than those generated in these experiences and with the default measure of student success being performance on standardized tests, project-based classrooms can easily appear lacking. Another set of stakeholders—professional mathematicians—seem to hold PBM in particular disdain (Wu, 1997) because of how project-based efforts misrepresent "real mathematics," which is what, by definition, they do.[1] Some prominent mathematicians have been near the center of the "Math Wars" (Jackson, 1997a; Jackson, 1997b), a battle that unfortunately has pitted mathematicians and parents concerned mainly about test scores on one side against mathematics education reformers on the other.

One of the shared features of the positions held by many professional mathematicians and these other educational stakeholders (some parents, politicians, etc.) is that both evaluate PBM efforts in terms of absences not presences. By this I mean PBM efforts are criticized on the basis of what they *are not* (i.e., not like research mathematics, not like the textbooks) rather than what they *are*. However, as has been argued from diverse points in the social sciences, analyses organized around absences are intellectually problematic (Cole & Scribner, 1974; Garfinkel, 1967; Lave, 1988; Smith, diSessa, & Roschelle, 1994). In light of this, I offer here an analysis organized mostly around what was present in a project-based classroom. My data are field notes and video recordings made in this classroom over a school year. The goal of this analysis is not to fight a battle in the Math Wars, though my sympathies and participation in education reform will be clear enough. From a personal perspective on this research, I was a former mathematics student who was diverted from pursuing a Ph.D. in the discipline by questions about learning and student experience that arose when I was a mathematics teacher. I have an enduring respect for the *discipline* (in both senses of the word) of mathematics; however, as my experiences as a teacher and a researcher (cf. Hall & Stevens, 1995; Stevens & Hall, 1998; Stevens, 1999) and other research suggests (e.g., Boaler, 1997), traditional mathematics education remains problematic. It seems neither to teach people to use mathematics as a generative resource in their out-of-school lives nor to enlist enthusiasts or apprentices to the discipline of mathematics except from among a highly privileged minority. And the sequence of mathematics courses remains a remarkably effective social filter that helps to ensure our society's continued disproportionate allocation of knowledge-making rights. Add these deficiencies to the fact that almost everyone who was ever a student dreaded or feared math class (just ask them) and we have a strong justification for considering carefully and empirically the alternative of PBM education. It is important to note that an analysis of actual events does not entail an affirmation of project-based curricula; rather it provides validity for an evaluation of the opportunities and dilemmas this form of classroom experiment presents for student learning and school experience. In fact, I later propose some generalizations that point to dilemmas involved in PBM, rooted in the organizational structure of schools and the familiar cultural practices of school mathematics.

Another outcome of this sort of analysis can be proposals for future educational design (cf. Brown, 1992). Project-based classroom experiments, at least in their current instantiation, are still relative yearlings in the span of educational time. As such they should be considered not as fixed entities but as revisable. It is argued at the end of the chapter that these analyses of classroom events provide specific revising resources both for educational designers and for teachers for whom the project-based classroom is still unfamiliar territory.

METHODS OF ANALYSIS

This analysis is built around analytical descriptions of four interactional events involving middle school students and a teacher. These descriptions are then used to ground further ethnographic descriptions of patterns of classroom activity. The interactional analyses are detailed and built up from audio-video recordings of naturally occurring classroom events, thus preserving the ecological validity (Cole, Hood, & McDermott, 1997) of the events described. Talk, being the primary communicative medium for these events, is focal and has been transcribed according to simplified conventions from conversation analysis (Goodwin & Heritage, 1990; Sacks, Schegloff, & Jefferson, 1974). Because talk here is concurrent with relevant representational action of other kinds (e.g., drawing, gesturing, and tool-mediated action), action descriptions are incorporated within the transcript. Although the larger studies from which this case study is drawn (Hall, 1995; Stevens, 1999) involved systematic interviews with participating students and the teacher, no interview material is drawn upon for this analysis. As Marjorie Goodwin describes in her explanation of similar methodological choices for her analysis of childrens' out-of-school activities:

> Treating language as a "mode of social action rather than a mere reflection of thought" (Malinowski 1959, pp. 312–313) necessitates investigation of how competent members of a society use language to deal with each other. This requires first, methods of data collection that maintain the sequential structure of indigenous interactive events (i.e., ones that exclude the ethnographer's intervention through elicitation) and make visible the process that these events are both embedded within and constitute; and second, a mode of analysis that, rather than treating talk as either a means for obtaining information *about* other phenomena or a special type of verbal performance, focuses on how competent members use talk socially to act out the ordinary scenes of everyday life. (Goodwin, 1990, p. 286)

The question of what to count as mathematical (cf. McDermott & Webber, 1998) looms over this analysis as it does, I believe, over the entire field of mathematics education. No definitive (or definitional) answer to this question is offered here but as my earlier remarks suggest, the vernacular definitions of mathematicians and former textbook users are insufficient (but not irrelevant) for an analysis of PBM classrooms.[2] One corrective to working from a normative and stable definition of what counts as mathematical is ethnomethodological whereby the orientations of the students or the teacher, or both, toward events, representations, or actions as mathematical provide the analytical basis for selecting and analyzing them as such. This replaces an external definition of the mathematical, possibly irrelevant to locals, with one defined and maintained locally.

For the most part, an ethnomethodological perspective is taken here. My analysis diverges from this perspective when I, as a mathematics educator not just a disinterested analyst, want to point to particular events as mathematical that are not seen or valued as such by students or teachers themselves or when I want to point to lost opportunities that accord with what mathematicians might more readily recognize as mathematical. In other words, my analysis is designed to represent, as its first order of business, the presences in the data; but the analysis also takes account of some absences of educational relevance. By relating the presences to the absences, I hope to provide a balanced representation from which appropriately weighted evaluations may be made.

Although what counts as mathematics is a central concern in this chapter, my criterion for selecting particular events for analysis from the recorded data corpus was a bit wider. Events that students or teachers counted as *problems* (i.e., not just math problems) have been selected for this analysis. Because problems in PBM classrooms *emerge* in the process of pursuing nonmathematical objectives (like designing a livable building), mathematics is not always in the foreground; other criteria such as designability, aesthetics, or projected inhabitant functionality often take precedence in project work just as they do in professional architecture firms (Stevens, 1999). However, once problems emerge, it is a central question for this analysis how or if mathematical practices are relevant to their resolution by students and if the students count these practices as mathematical. It is my strong position that if our analyses do not take seriously the framing projects (e.g., architectural design) that are meant to give shape to mathematical work, then we are implicitly and hypocritically treating these frames as little more than elaborate cover stories for traditional mathematics, as are algebra story problems. Likewise, if our analyses are to be of use in following students outside of school, we need analytical tools that can recognize and analyze mathematics *in* an activity not only *as* the activity.[3]

As an example, consider one of the instances discussed in depth later in this analysis. Two student designers decided to include a "bavarium" in the middle of the Antarctic research station they were designing for hypothetical scientists. A bavarium is not, as readers might think, a German beer garden but instead a glass enclosure filled with plant life used for research purposes, in other words, a vivarium, misheard by the initiating student. In considering where to place the bavarium the student designers sought to place it in the middle of the already established dimensions of the research station. This was their problem: placing the bavarium "in the middle of everything." What this problem created was a subsidiary math problem of evenly spacing the rectangular bavarium within the perimeter of an existing rectangular design structure. How this happened, what it meant for the evolving design, and for the students' working relationship are the elements that constitute my analysis.

As in this example, problems emerged in this project-based classroom as students designed together. However, mathematics problems appeared in this classroom in more traditional ways as well. Probably like many project-based classrooms, a necessary compromise was struck that made this classroom a hybrid of traditional and reform practices. Students were allowed to find, formulate, and solve their own problems, mathematical and otherwise, in the course of designing together. However, as a mathematics classroom held accountable to standards at many levels, students were also *assigned* mathematics problems that looked a good deal more traditional. In the curricular package used in this classroom (MMAP, 1995), work sheet-like "math activities" were assigned to students that thematized topics that were recognizably aligned with National Council of Teachers of Mathematics (NCTM) standards, such as the general relationship between the geometric concepts of area and perimeter. These assigned problems were designed to be integrated within the project, but as my analysis seeks to show, the contrast was often stark between the social and epistemological impact of these assigned problems and those that emerged.

The analytical units around which this case study is organized are a *team* of students working together on a *project*. Although my examples are drawn from a single student team, a methodological choice warranted by the goal of assembling a detailed developmental history of a team and a project, my broader fieldwork activities and collaboration with colleagues in the Math @ Work project suggest that there are important generalizable features of this analysis. Because the issue of generalizability is always at issue with case studies (Ragin & Becker, 1992), I will seek to clearly identify the features of this analysis that appear generalizable and those that are specific to this team's activities. My position on this issue returns me to the basic ideas of grounded theory (Charmaz, 1983; Glaser & Strauss, 1967; Strauss & Corbin, 1990) and the collective nature of the research enterprise across our field. The processes, dilemmas, and opportunities I identify in this chapter may turn out to be local to this school, this class, and this curriculum, but this awaits comparative analysis with other instantiations of PBM.

Another important caveat about this analysis, given the worn-out but time-honored opposition in our field between the individual and the social, is that differences between individuals need not be and are not here erased even though the leading unit of analysis is a collective—a student team. As my previous work has sought to show (Stevens, 1997; Stevens, in press) and as I describe here, differences between students within the team are critical, and in this case I will demonstrate differences in the impact of assigned and emergent problems on different students. The notion that people enter new collectives with personal inclinations, habits, and ideas based in their own histories is an essential claim of constructivism, but just as essential is the notion drawn from interactionist research that participation in collectives organizes which of these personal traits are displayed, valued, and developed. Interactionist research also argues against analyses that begin with a reduction of a relationally organized system to its commonsense components (e.g., individuals and their intentions). In light of these constructivist and interactionist perspectives, the analytical approach I take to these data is to follow the contributions by individuals *within* the collectively defined and developed events of problem finding, formulating, and solving.

For more than a decade, one of the main goals of mathematics education reform has been to organize instruction so that mathematics is experienced as a sense-making resource for students rather than a rote activity (Schoenfeld, 1992). In focusing on how mathematical practices emerge as people design, this chapter clearly stands within this research tradition. This chapter diverges from this tradition in that much of the research on sense-making has been on the relation between individuals and already mathematized situations (cf. DeCorte, Greer, & Verschaffel, 1996). Much less empirical attention has been paid to how people use mathematical practices *to make sense together* or to *when and how people mathematize situations* (see, however, Cobb, 1995). Toward this purpose, I identify the data exemplars in two different ways. In the first two data exemplars, I describe how emergent problems functioned in *cooperative sense-making* situations. By cooperative sense-making, I am referring to situations in which interactants work together to pursue a shared objective. In the third data exemplar, I analyze a *competitive sense-making* situation in which different participants argue for alternative versions of a situation.

ETHNOGRAPHIC BACKGROUND

The classroom setting where I conducted the fieldwork for this study was a public middle school classroom at Pine Middle School in a middle-class neighborhood in Alameda, California. The teacher, Ms. Leoni,[4] was at the time in her first year of teaching at Pine, having recently moved from another middle school in Alameda. She described this change as less than favorable as she found many of the features of the new school restrictive and counterproductive to her reform teaching goals. In fact, Ms. Leoni left Pine at the end of the school year, moving to another school that she regarded as being a more conducive environment. Ms. Leoni was a practiced user of the particular curriculum (MMAP) at her former school, and she had even participated in its development.

The neighborhood in which the school was located was modest, consisting of small, single-family homes and apartments. The ethnic makeup of the class was roughly 40 percent Caucasian-American, 40 percent Asian-American, and 20 percent African-American. Ms. Leoni was of Caucasian-American descent. The student team that I followed over the course of the project included two girls and two boys. Both girls were Chinese-American (Marsha and Cathy), one boy was of Polynesian descent (Henry), and one boy was Caucasian (Ted).

These students began the design project (in which they were assembled as a team) with some prior school-based experiences of each other that I did not systematically explore but came to understand through the stories they told to and about each other over the course of the school year. Ted and Marsha had known each other from their earliest schooling experiences and had a relationship that could be characterized as semihostile familiarity not uncommon between boys and girls at this age. The relationship between Cathy and Ted was more recent but was significantly more hostile, with Cathy indicating from the outset that sitting next to Ted was a source of displeasure. Early on she explained to Marsha, when Ted was not present, that she had recently secured a seat away from Ted in another class. There was no clear sense of why Ted faced this hostility other than the fact that he was perceived as "annoying" by these students and also to some degree by the wider community of students. Cathy and Marsha shared a partially overlapping out-of-school network owing to their participation in Chinese cultural activities, such as after-school Chinese language classes that both currently attended. In school, however, Marsha and Cathy appeared not to be part of the same friendship network, with Marsha being clearly a popular girl whereas Cathy was not. Throughout the project, I often felt that both Cathy and Ted were orienting to Marsha's popularity. Henry was the quietest and was the most disconnected member of the group. The primary reason for this is that Henry's best friend, Dinesh, was also in the class, and Henry spent as much time as possible away from the team table with him.

The MMAP curriculum unit was designed at the Institute for Research on Learning (MMAP, 1995). It was designed to frame a series of activities for students that resemble the activities of professional adults, in this case the activities of professional architects. Architectural design projects are considered a vehicle for the learning and using of mathematics, as an "anchoring event," as Bransford and colleagues call it (Van Haneghan, Barron, Young, Williams, Vye, & Bransfield, 1992), an idea described in an overview document from the developer of these curricular materials.

> The Antarctica Project, and the units that follow it, are based on a new way of thinking about mathematical applications. Traditionally, in math classrooms, applications were something that came at the end of the chapter, in the form of a few of those dreaded word problems, and exercised students' abilities to use the algorithm they just learned to do. . . . Our applications are simulations of some part of the real world that become the context for complex, open-ended design and analysis problems with many different solutions and paths to solutions. We believe that greater conceptual understanding of mathematics can be attained when children are given opportunities to participate in activities similar to those of people who use math in their work. (MMAP, 1995, pp. 1–2)

In the Antarctica unit students were asked to imagine themselves as members of architectural teams hired to build a research station for scientists who would "winter over" in Antarctica. The students were provided with information about their hypothetical clients, paper design materials, and relatively frequent access to computer software with which to draft their station in floor plan view. With this software, students could also set various features of the interior and exterior environments (e.g., temperature, insulation values) and then see the result of automatic calculations performed by the software's underlying (but inaccessible) mathematical model. For example, with a drafted station, students could have the software quickly calculate and display heating costs or overall buildings costs based on the model. Progress through the project unit was regulated by a set of "memos" distributed by the teacher to the students, moving them through research, design, analysis, and presentation phases of activity. In addition to this design project framework as a "context for complex open-ended design and analysis" problems, mathematical activities were, as I have described, assigned to students in a manner more recognizable as school mathematics: as numbered work sheet-like "math activities" selected from the curricular package. The expressed intent of these activities was to present students with exposure to easily recognizable and valued mathematical concepts and tools that the curricular designers "expect[ed] to come up as students work through the design problems in the Antarctica Project Unit" (MMAP, 1995).

Because of its particular relevance to this case, the grading practices in this classroom deserve special mention. Grading was complicated, because although the school was typical and the teacher was required to grade and rank individual class members, she was ambivalent about grading. Her ambivalence, from my perspective, could be most closely tied to her affiliation with reform practices that problematize the relation of grading to learning. What this led to in practice was a very complex system of grading that changed over the course of the project. At first, Ms. Leoni gave few grades and focussed her energies on helping the students move along with their projects. However, as time passed she faced a deadline—midterm and eventually semester grades—that led her to try to generate more grades. The fact is that she had no consistent policy on grading; sometimes she assigned grades to individuals based on assignments every student completed, and sometimes she assigned grades to teams based on what a subset of team members accomplished as representative of their teams. At the end of the project, she assigned grades to students on the basis of reports they generated individually about their participation in the project and assigned grades to each team member based on an assessment of a shared final product. My analyses suggest that these practices, against the background of the simpler system to be found in more traditional individual focussed classrooms, was confusing for the students and challenging for the teacher to maintain. In retrospect, all of us involved in enacting this project probably wish we had organized a different assessment system at the outset, but such are the virtues of hindsight.

DATA COLLECTION AND SELECTION OF DATA EXEMPLARS

The data analyzed in this chapter is drawn from fieldwork and recordings made at Pine Middle School between October 1996 and February 1997. My field notes reflect a broad perspective on classroom events, but the video recordings I made focussed on a single student team. With the exception of 3 days I missed due to illness, I made audio-video records of the activities of this team during every class period from the beginning of the project to its end. One of the characteristics of this data collection is that because my camera captured events local to the student team, I had access to events that were largely unknown to the teacher unless I described them to her. In total, nearly 60 hours of videotape were watched, logged, and analyzed. From these analyses the four extended exemplars represented in this chapter were drawn. I also collected most of the paper materials produced by this team during the unit, including copies of their journal writing, design sketches, and work on assigned problems. At the beginning and end of the project, I did collective interviews with the members of the student team, though I do not report on this interview material here for the reasons described earlier.

The four segments analyzed in depth in this chapter were chosen for two reasons: (1) to explore the complexities of the category of problems I have called emergent, and (2) to draw a contrast between emergent problems and ones that were assigned. Three of the exemplars are drawn from the corpus of emergent problems and one from those assigned. I have chosen here to give more attention to the emergent problems under the assumption that they are less well understood by our research community. There are now many careful studies of student (and teacher) work on assigned problems (for a review, see DeCorte et al., 1996) but few that focus on emergent problems (see, however, Saxe & Guberman, 1998). The first three exemplars involve emergent math problems—those that come up in the course of student design—and the fourth involves a math problem, drawn from the curriculum, assigned to students by the teacher.

DATA ANALYSIS

Data Exemplar 1: "Putting the Bavarium Right in the Middle of Everything"

This collection of episodes I present and analyze are drawn from the first day that students were allowed to design. This was not the first day of the project, as the first 2 weeks had been occupied with other preliminary activities. These preliminaries included a sequence of assignments from the teacher drawn from the curriculum, including journal writing exercises (e.g., asking individual students about their expectations for team membership), a choice and design of a team name and logo (e.g., this team became LIFE, standing for Life In Frigid Environments), brainstorming exercises asking the students to list the features they wanted to include in their research station, and an assigned math problem, completed by individuals, about converting Fahrenheit temperatures to a Celsius scale. This assigned math problem required that the students first do tutorials on the use of a spreadsheet and graphing program that was intended as a tool for solving the conversion problem. My analyses in this chapter focus on the team's activities that followed this initial sequence of activities once the design project was tangibly under way. It is during this phase that problems emerged, that the design gained a durable life of its own within the team, and that students had to juggle accountabilities to this work and the math problems they were periodically assigned.

As in any institutional setting where actions are not fully prescribed, the student team faced the challenge of organizing a beginning for their project work together. Up until this point, roles and activities had more or less been prescribed as is common in middle school, but at this point the students were implicitly granted a significant degree of discretion to organize themselves. The resources the students had for assembling this beginning were as follows: a blank piece of graph paper, a list of features to possibly include in the station, and a very tenuous social relationship among the participants. Another initial constraint was that Ted began with the piece of graph paper on which the initial design was to be inscribed. Ted held this initial position based on a random assignment by the teacher, picking one student from each team without regard for their specific identity to have first control of the paper. (A similar random assignment was used to rotate control of the paper among the eight teams' members.)

A factor that I described earlier, but that bears repeating because of its ethnographic relevance, was the relationship between Ted and the two girls which was strained from the outset. Because I was in a position to overhear many of the conversations within the group, I was able to learn that Cathy, in particular, disliked Ted, based on experiences in another class. For example, she had told Marsha, when Ted was away from the table, that she had even sought to be moved apart from Ted in this other class. Marsha's regard for Ted was more ambivalent, though she resisted association with him and occasionally used him as a vehicle for her sharp wit during the first 2 weeks. Ted's perspective on Marsha and Cathy was harder to establish because he did not have a conversational partner in the group to whom he made his feelings known. However, there was no interactional evidence that he bore either any particular animus.

Evidence for this social relationship and its bearing on the beginning of the working relationship is offered in the first transcript segment I present. In this segment, the LIFE team was gathered at their table. With the blank paper before him, Ted tried to enlist his teammates into a design conversation about the research station.

Segment 1.1

1 Ted: Should it have two stories Marsha?

2 Marsha: Don't ask me. I'm not the only person in this group.

3 Ted: What about you Cathy? I think two stories would be better, because of our limited space.

4 Ted: (Pause, Ted pays attention to the plan for 30 seconds.) Alright do you all think its alright to have a two-story building? Do you like it Marsha?

5 Marsha: Why are you asking me?

6 Ted: Do you like it Henry?

7 Henry: (inaudible with an ambiguous shrug)

8 Cathy: (to Marsha) I want it (inaudible, followed by laughter).

9 Marsha: (laughter)

10 Ted: (turns to Cathy) Do you want it two story?

11 Cathy: (looking forward, not to Ted) No. (laughter)

In the interactional analyses of transcript segments in the chapter, I have adapted a set of framing terms from Toulmin (1958) for naturally occurring argumentation. The remainder of the analytical language is drawn from a diverse body of interaction analysis studies (Duranti & Goodwin, 1992; Goodwin & Heritage, 1990; Goodwin, 1990). Based on Toulmin's framework, when a participant represents a possible design feature in talk or visual representation, I will refer to this as a *design proposal*. I will call those design proposals that are recognized by someone else in talk or action *recognized design proposals*. Those proposals that are also accompanied by grounds are called *grounded design proposals*. In this segment, Ted produced a grounded design proposal (Turn 3) that combines a possible feature of the station ("two stories") with a ground for that feature ("limited space"). Although Ted did not further specify what he meant by "limited space," he likely was referring to the only area constraint the teams were required to satisfy: that the station fit within a region 17 by 30 meters. In soliciting feedback to the grounded proposal, Ted clearly tried to begin a collaborative design conversation (Turns 1, 3, and 6). However, Ted was resisted in this attempt. Evidence for this resistance includes: Cathy's nonresponse to his question in Turn 3, her bald negation in Turn 11, and Marsha's redirections in Turns 2 and 5. These are forms of response that in everyday interaction are conventionally heard as disaffiliative (Goodwin & Heritage, 1990) or, in other words, are ways of interacting that erode rather than build up an interaction. In addition, Turns 8 through 11, although not audible enough to be transcribed accurately, quite clearly involve a joke at Ted's expense, an inference I base on the bodily orientation of Marsha and Cathy with respect to Ted and on their laughter that followed their remarks to each other. In summary, this segment shows how Ted made an initial move to establish a design conversation and how his attempt failed.

With this example, the team appears to be some distance from encountering emergent math problems as they design together. However, they were not so far. Shortly thereafter Ted reintroduced a design idea he had been talking about during the prior week: the bavarium. Unlike in the prior segment when Ted was rebuked, this segment (Segment 1.2, following) illustrates a beginning to a collaborative design conversation between Ted and Marsha, thus setting the stage for emergent mathematical problems.

Segment 1.2

1 Ted: (an inaudible sentence about the bavarium) And we all agree it should be on the first floor right? (looking at Marsha, who nods begrudgingly)

2 Marsha: (Following a facial exclamation of excitement, her hands come forward over a sheet of paper in her open binder and she leans in to speak to Ted.) I think (hands come together to form an enclosed volume in the middle of the paper) it should be right in the middle of everything. (She gestures a perimeter with fingers from both hands.)

3 Ted: Oh, yeah, yeah, yeah. (His hands come together to make an enclosed volume as Henry hands something to Cathy in the line of vision between Marsha and Ted. *Marsha leans under Henry's arm to see what Ted is doing.* Inaudible.)

4 Marsha: (Henry pulls back.) And it's like central heating (accompanying gestures) you know. (audibly excited) And so like you have like glass screen doors to observe the presence of the living environment.

5 Ted: That's a good idea.

In this segment, Marsha and Ted did two important things together that reshaped their working relations and the space where these were enacted. First, unlike Ted's prior attempt to begin a design conversation (Segment 1.1), this attempt is not rebuked; instead, Marsha built on Ted's initial proposal for the bavarium by tacitly accepting "it" (i.e., the bavarium) as one of the station's design features and proposing its location: "right in the middle of everything" (Turn 2). The second important feature of their interaction involved how they oriented their bodies in such a way to show each other that they were designing together. Following Ted's enthusiastic affirmation of Marsha's proposal (Turn 3), he produced a gestural animation that Marsha bent her body to see (description italicized in transcript) beneath Henry who happened at the moment to be reaching in front of her for some materials on the table, thereby recognizing his design proposal. What is clear in this segment is what I have called elsewhere an *intersubjective media space* (Stevens, 1999) was developing for the new participation structure of collaborative design.

Because Ted still controlled the paper and he had affirmed Marsha's idea as "good," it fell to him to solve the emergent mathematics problem she had posed of putting the bavarium "right in the middle of everything." "Everything" at this point was not much, as Ted had only drawn the perimeter of their building to the maximal allowable dimensions of 17 by 29 meters.[5] This problem, and Ted's solution, were relatively simple and straightforward, drawing on what was clearly an existing mathematical resource, counting. Because the representational space was prestructured as a grid (i.e., graph paper), it afforded counting. To place the bavarium, Ted repeated the same strategy to locate the two sets of parallel sides of a rectangular bavarium. Counting in an equal distance from the edges of the station's perimeter, Ted drew the two sets of sides and joined them to form a rectangle. In so doing, he had realized Marsha's idea of putting the bavarium right in the middle of everything.

Were this example offered as evidence of mathematical sophistication by Ted, it could easily affirm the image of PBM as intellectually trivial. With a narrow focus on the content of the mathematics alone and the demands the problem placed on the student, the intellectual challenge Ted faced was small. However, a wider view shows the central importance of this problem and challenges the singular narrow focus on content alone. Although some problems are worthy of solution because they challenge students to learn new and powerful mathematical ideas, others are worthy because they move along collective endeavors. In this case, Ted solidified the fragile working relationship with Marsha, the team member who also was actively pursuing an interest in the design, by solving *her* problem. Recall that she had done something similar just before with *his* design idea, the bavarium, by implicitly accepting "it" as a feature and proposing its location. By this analysis, it is the recognized design proposals that were the connective tissue that set the stage for the designers to act as each other's agents in these early moments of the projects. In turn, these acts established a working relationship between Ted and Marsha as collaborative designers and set the stage for subsequent mathematical activity to emerge. So despite being ostensibly mathematically trivial, this first emergent math problem had enormous social significance and was developmentally essential for later mathematical activity.

Data Exemplar 2: "Can You Make It Circlelike?"

An enduring question about PBM education concerns the role of the teacher. As is now widely acknowledged, when students are meant to find, formulate, and solve mathematical problems that emerge in their inquiries, the stereotypical didactic image of the math teacher is of limited use. But what is her or his role? Is it to stay out of the students' way? To help them structure problems? To offer tailored hints or techniques for solving problems? To offer general information to the whole class? To synthesize ideas across a classroom of distinct teams and distinct projects? In my ethnographic observations, all of these modes are appropriate at different moments in the span of a project of this kind. In this example, I consider an instance of how the teacher, Ms. Leoni, participated in an emergent mathematics problem generated by the LIFE design team. From my perspective, this episode exemplifies some of the promise that this sort of classroom holds for teaching and learning mathematics in a project-based way, while at the same time exemplifying one of the primary challenges.

A few days after the LIFE designers placed the bavarium "right in the middle of everything" and had been designing station features around it, they reopened a conversation about the bavarium and sought to further specify its features.

Segment 2.1

1 Ted: Marsha I was thinking, maybe the bavarium could go up all the way. Both stories, instead of staying on the bottom—

2 Marsha:—Ooo, that'd be pretty cool it's like the airport (inaudible).

3 Ted: Do you know what I mean? Do you like that idea? And the roof of the bavarium can be attached to the roof of the thing. So you can draw, so you can like plant taller stuff, and plus you can have it also two stories in the bavarium, kinda like a walkway—

4 Marsha: You know what would be cool if it was round. (Gestures a circle on the plan.)

5 Ted: Whoa, ho, ho, ho. (She smiles widely at his assessment.)

6 Marsha: Then how do we draw that? And we need stairs too.

7 Ted: Na, hey, if it's going to be round, have those round stairs (gestures a spiral up) going up like this.

8 Marsha: Oh my gosssh (hearable as an evaluation of how hard this will be).

9 Ted: That'd be cool. It'd like match.

Over the course of this brief segment, Marsha and Ted jointly produce the "cool" idea of making a two-story, round bavarium with circular stairs to "match." In making this proposal, they proposed two possible emergent mathematical problems: (1)

replacing the nearly square bavarium with a circular one, and (2) designing and representing stairs that spiral around the circular bavarium. Before further formulating the problem, Ted and Marsha called on Ms. Leoni with a question as she was circulating in the classroom.

Segment 2.2a

1 Ted: (to LL) Can we make it be round? (gestures)

2 Ms. Leoni: Why not? (As she answers him, Marsha who was looking at LL looks at Ted.)

3 Ted: Well how would we do that? Would we like have a compass in there (pointing to the plan and gestures a radial motion) and,

4 Ms. Leoni: You know what will be difficult is when you try to put it on to the computer (pointing at the computer)

5 Ted: Yeah, that's what I was thinking.

6 Ms. Leoni: Yeah, but there is a way, you could make it more circular-LIKE. How would you do that? To be more circlelike?

There are a number of points to be made about this segment. First, in bringing this emergent mathematical problem to the teacher, we are offered an image of how differently a teacher can participate in this role compared to a traditionally didactic one. In this case, she helps them to formulate a doable problem (cf. Fujimura, 1987) that had emerged in their own design project work. One basis for her reformulation of circular to "circlelike" is an upstream expectation the students were aware of but have apparently forgotten; they would have to put the hand-drawn design plan into the computer design program and curved shapes could not be represented in this software program. Artfully she used this do-ability constraint that Ted recognized (Turn 5) to pose an important mathematical question about circlelike shapes composed of linear segments. For those familiar with the calculus, approximating curvilinear shapes with rectilinear segments is a foundational idea. Ted answered Ms. Leoni's question this way:

Segment 2.2b

7 Ted: You could have it go, ching, ching. (These sounds go with gestures around his head that indicate linear segments of an enclosing structure.) Kind of like an octagon. (Ms. Leoni and Marsha nod in affirmation.) Cuz the glass isn't round, so whether we like it or not, it's not going to be perfect.

Ted provided the key insight that both Ms. Leoni and Marsha affirmed: a regular n-gon approximates a circle.[6] In addition to articulating a key mathematical idea, equally important across this collaboratively produced reformulation (Turns 1 to 7) is how many realms of meaning it connects. At the same time as an important mathematical idea is expressed (i.e., n-gons are circlelike), concerns are addressed about both what is represented (i.e., "glass isn't round") and how it is represented (i.e., "how do we draw that" and "difficult to put on the computer"). In uniting practical, representational, and mathematical considerations, this episode is an exemplar of the clear promise of a PBM classroom. But the story continues.

Following their collective reformulation of the problem, Ms. Leoni left the LIFE designers to try to solve it. At this point, Marsha had control of the paper design. She started by erasing the existing bavarium on the floor plan and drawing (using a ruler) three contiguous equal-length segments as possible sides of a polygon, further evidence that regularity was part of their intent. At this point, Ted made an observation that this approach would produce "excess space," or what Marsha would shortly thereafter call "wasted space." The region of wasted space to which they referred is represented in Figure 1.

The recognition of the wasted space was a recognition of an *unintended consequence* (Schon, 1990) of another design objective. As a result, the designers abandoned the attempt to place a polygon and sought to place a square. A square, while a regular polygon, is a rather poor approximation of a circle and was relatively easy for Marsha to re-place. In this light an interpretation of this event is that an opportunity for the more complex mathematical work of constructing a regular n-gon was lost. This interpretation of events is an important one (which I will consider shortly), but it oversimplifies the situation.

Mathematics problems that emerge are not always solved (in the conventional sense). Sometimes they are *resolved* by making a conventional solution unnecessary through a consideration of different accountabilities that bear upon it or because a different socio-logic (Coulter, 1989) is operative than an academic

Figure 1.
Students identified the triangular region as "wasted space" and abandoned the contruction of the n-gon on this basis.

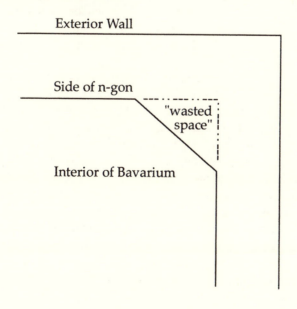

mathematical one (cf. de la Rocha, 1986; Lave, 1988; Stevens & Hall, 1998; Stevens, 1999). Such resolutions are a feature of professional engineering design competence (Hall & Stevens, 1995; Stevens & Hall, 1998), and Schon's analyses have found responsiveness to unintended consequences to be a measure of a good architectural design. In other words, these students' actions can be interpreted as sensible not only within their own framing of events but from an external disciplinary perspective on design competence. In addition, the concept of avoiding "wasted space" became an enduring design heuristic for these designers, one that was affirmed when professional architects visited the classroom and critiqued the student teams' designs. As one of these architects said to half the students in the class, "[In architecture], there's no such thing as leftover space."

What I am seeking to keep in the picture here is the relevance of both the mathematical and the design considerations to these students' self-organized activities. The questionable alternative is to treat the design projects as little more than a cover story for creating math problems. This is problematic analytically because it treats a particular type of mathematics as paramount when it is not for the participants and when something else clearly is (e.g., design functionality). The effect of discarding the carcass of the project to remove the white meat of mathematics is to diminish the authenticity (in any sense of the word) of everything about the project (e.g., designing, collaborating) that is not mathematical. Reflexively, this can diminish the authenticity of the mathematical activities themselves.

Notwithstanding this important analytical point, Data Exemplar 2 does represent a missed opportunity in which an interesting mathematical problem once found by students was subsequently lost, even though it was lost for the good reasons described earlier. As mathematic educators at all levels know, it is extremely difficult to create the conditions for students to pursue genuinely applied mathematics problems. What this example shows is a common tension in PBM between the desire to keep mathematics at or near the center of student activity and the desire to allow projects to be real enough in their organization to allow mathematical problems to emerge *or not*.

One advocate for keeping mathematics near the center of student activity can be, and in this instance was, the teacher. Readers may wonder what happened to Ms. Leoni following her initial participation in the formulation of the interesting and doable math problem. Did she follow up? Did she return to affirm the value of this problem as mathematics or to help formulate solution strategies? After she helped the students begin a redesign of the bavarium as circlelike, Ms. Leoni was thrown back into the hurly-burly of the wider classroom. The period was about half over (i.e., 20 minutes remained), but she never was able to return to this team. Why was this? Her answer is typical and mundane but nonetheless important. Demands from the other seven teams and accountabilities to maintaining the bureaucratic machinery of the classroom took precedence. When I asked her about it during a daily debriefing that followed each class, she simply said, "I didn't have time." And in some sense, the familiarity of these events and this response leave nothing further to say except to consider how and if things should be different. These are central topics of my remarks later in the chapter.

Data Exemplar 3: "That Hallway's Way Too Big"

This example represents an instance of competitive sense-making centered around a disagreement between Marsha and Ted about whether a proposed design feature would be "too big" or not. As in the previous data exemplars, the mathematical practices that are enacted as mathematics are not particularly sophisticated, but they are decisive in settling the students' disagreement through persuasion and altering the course of collaborative action.

In this exemplar, the design was much further along than in the first two first exemplars, and students were considering a revision based on some feedback they had received when professional architects had visited. The architects had questioned the team's decision to locate a laundry room near the front entrance of the station, because a laundry room is not a central function in a research station and therefore should be located in a less prominent part of the station. In this segment, the students are in the midst of deciding where to move the laundry room and what to put in its place.

Segment 3.1

1 Ted: I know but, the laundry room just kinda doesn't fit.

2 Marsha: Well we're moving it, we already decided THAT.

3 Ted: I know but we're trying to figure out what we want to put in.

4 Marsha: NOT a computer room (throws her logbook up for emphasis).

5 Ted: What are some of your suggestions?

6 Marsha: (no response)

Although this segment begins as a cooperative sense-making situation ("we're moving [the bavarium], we already decided THAT" (Turn 2), it quickly turns into a competitive one when Marsha anticipates and rejects a previous proposal of Ted's ("a computer room"). In response, Ted challenges her to produce an alternative (Turn 5). Marsha does not respond with words but draws an alternative. Using trace paper over the top of the existing design, she proposed eliminating the laundry room and expanded the contiguous library and hallway (Figure 2).

When Marsha showed her proposal to Ted, he challenged it.

Segment 3.2

1 Ted: That's one hell of a hallway. (Looks at her trace drawing for a short time.) That would never work. That hallway's just way too big.

2 Marsha: No it's not, you could always put like a (tree?) on it and you can put a bench there.

3 Ted: What the hell (pointing, possibly counting over the trace).

Figure 2.
A composite figure of the base drawing and the trace used by Marsha in making
her proposal. The base drawing is black and the trace lines are gray. Notice that
Marsha has redrawn much of the station, with changes proposed in the lower right
portion of the plan to the entry, the library, and the front door. Her proposal would
eliminate the laundry room and the closet near the front door.

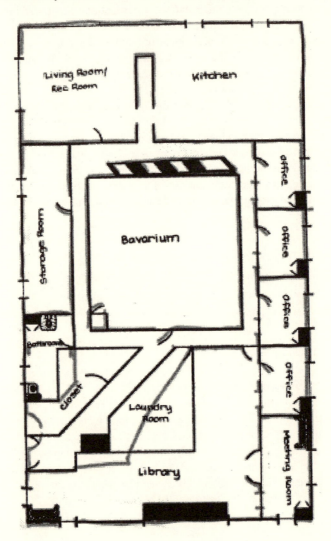

4 Marsha: We're taking out the entire laundry room. I just expanded the library and
just made the entrance bigger.

5 Ted: That is one hell of a big room. (Points to library.) That's like twice the size of the
bavarium and the bavarium's bigger than this whole room.

In this segment, Ted began a mathematically grounded argument against Marsha's new proposal. First, he offered an ungrounded challenge to the proposed hallway as "way too big." Second, he grounded a challenge to the size of the expanded library (Turn 5) with a complex quantitative relation that compared the proposed library's size (i.e., its area) to twice the size of the bavarium. In turn, this quantity was compared to the actual dimensions of the classroom they currently occupied.

Marsha, however, was not persuaded by either of Ted's challenges and called on him (as he had done to her) to materially produce an alternative. With paper and trace in hand, he spent a number of minutes trying to do so but could not produce an alternative that satisfied him. A short time later another team member (Henry), who had been looking on and growing impatient with Ted, held up Marsha's proposal and challenged Ted to tell him "what's wrong with this."[7]

Segment 3.3

1 Henry: What are the changes?

2 Ted: Nothing so far.

3 Henry: (Henry picks up Marsha's proposal.) What's wrong with this?

Because Ted had not produced an alternative and was clearly stymied, he reiterated his challenge to the size of the hallway proposed by Marsha. Though he did not have an alternative, this time he offered grounds for his challenge to her hallway proposal. After positioning the traced revision over the grided floor plan and counting the units on the grid, Ted pursued his argument.

Segment 3.4a

1 Ted:—That hallway will never work though. (Stretches fingers across its length.) It's just—

2 Marsha: Why not?

3 Ted: It's too damn big. It's huge. Here. (Picks up pencil.) How long do you think this is Henry? (Points with pencil to opening.)

4 Marsha: (leaning in) That's a meter (pointing to the width of the previous hallway on the plan).

5 Ted: So we figure, one, two, three, four five, six, seven.

6 Marsha: Now if you look (using the graph paper plan) at the dots ok. I just opened it up like this (gesturing over).

7 Ted: So it'd be about eight.

8 Marsha: And that's a closet now. (Points to a region on the plan.)

9 Henry: (to Reed?) What do you think? Hey Reed (inaudible).

10 Ted: Let's see, where's a meter stick? (Gets up to fetch one.)

11 Marsha: It's going to be a really big nice hallway.

Ted retrieved a meter stick and returns to the table.

Segment 3.4b

12 Ted: Just to say, Marsha. That is a meter (holding it up on the desk momentarily). Eight meters would be (lays it down on the floor) there, from right here. (Now he kneels on the floor with stick laid down.) One. (Slides stick.)

13 Marsha: (reaching for her trace plan) Fine, I could always fix it.

14 Ted: Two. (He moves along the floor one more meter.)

15 Henry: (with pencil poised over paper) We extended the hallway right?

16 Ted: Marsha, this room (has reached an eight count, points from one end to the other) is eight meters. It would never work. (walking back) How can you have a hallway, the length of this room? It's huge.

In this extended segment, Ted's mathematically grounded argument eventually persuaded Marsha that her hallway was too big. Marsha capitulated in Turn 13 with the succinct announcement that "I could always fix it" and the retrieval of her sketch. Ted's argument was, in fact, so well built up for Marsha that she, seeing where his demonstration was leading from almost the moment when he kneeled on the floor and began counting meters across the classroom, conceded the contested point just as he had *begun* the demonstration (Figure 3).

Figure 3.
Ted's argument succeeds when his demonstration leads to Marsha's (begrudging) acknowledgement of his point and the retrieval of the sketch for repair (Turn 12-13).

What had Ted's argument involved? First, he had superimposed an unmeasured space on another with a unitized grid. He used this superimposition to determine the scaled length of the hallway and then had used that number to lay out the actual length in the classroom. By showing Marsha that her proposed hallway was bigger than the long dimension of a "room," he had effectively challenged the proposal for a "hallway." Again, the mathematical depth of this instance may appear minimal. Although true from one perspective, we may wish to value this instance for its type not its degree, as it is an instance of mathematical grounds being offered and accepted as a basis for settling a disagreement. Whereas she was not persuaded by ungrounded challenges, she was convinced by this more mathematically grounded one. Marsha's reception of Ted's argument was therefore just as important as his capacity to make it as it indicates the development of shared practice between them of settling disputes discursively using mathematical resources.

In addition, a broader perspective might certainly recognize here a proto-form of mathematical argumentation in the discipline's conventional sense. By proto-form, I am referring to a form that can be seen as an early version of a recognizable disciplinary practice.[8] To make this proto-form recognizable to the mathematically enculturated, I have abstracted Ted's challenges (to the hallway and to the library) as follows:

Let us assume that y is clearly too big (y is this room's area or its long dimension). If $x > y$ (x is the hallway's length or the library's area), then x must also be too big.

For some, mathematics is seen as continuous with less formal reasoning practices.[9] For mathematics educators and mathematicians of a similar inclination, I offer the (hardly unbiased) suggestion that professional ethnographic and interactional analyses such as this one (see also Boaler, 1997; Cobb, 1995; Hall & Rubin, 1998; O'Connor, Godfrey, & Moses, 1998) have a great deal more validity than amateur blitzkrieg ethnographies (e.g., Wu, 1993) for answering questions about whether project-based classrooms foster the development of mathematical proto-forms and prepare students for a future in the discipline.

Data Exemplar 4: "It's Not Our Problem You're Dumb"

Thus far, my analysis has focussed on mathematics problems that emerged in the course of student design. In this data exemplar, I analyze events involving one of the *assigned* mathematics problems. As my analysis seeks to show, the contrast between events surrounding emergent and assigned problems was fairly stark and is the basis for an ethnographically grounded distinction between the emergent and assigned problems as different contexts for the organization of student activity (Stevens, 1999). In turn, this raises the question of what accounts for the contrast. Following my analysis of this assigned problem, I offer a possible explanation of this difference in terms of the issue of who counts what as math and when.

In the data thus far presented, a focus on emergent problems has meant largely a focus on the collaborative activities of Ted and Marsha, because divisions of labor emerged within the team in which these students became the designers and Cathy and Henry became responsible for other parts of the project (Stevens, 1997; Stevens, in press). In this assigned problem, Cathy plays a much more significant role because, within the overall emergent division of labor, Cathy became the center of responsibility for and production of the assigned problems (Stevens, 1999).

This segment involves the second problem the students had been assigned. The first had been assigned to all the individual students and involved converting a table of Fahrenheit temperature conversions to Celsius. The second problem was assigned to teams, which meant that a single product would be the source of the grade for all the team members. The first problem also was assigned before designing had actually begun, and thus students did not yet face major competing demands on their time. The events described here took place 3 days after the events of Data Exemplar 2 (redesigning the bavarium as a polygon). During these 3 days, Marsha and Ted had continued to design together, and Cathy and Henry had spent most of their time translating the hand-drawn design into the computer.

The first transcribed segment begins just after Ms. Leoni handed out the Area and Perimeter problem (Figure 4) to the teams. When Ms. Leoni handed out the Area and Perimeter problem, she told the students that the problem needed to be turned in for grading at the end of class.

Ms. Leoni set the day's events in motion by pairing students and having one pair continue with ongoing project activities and the other pair begin the assigned problem. She explained to the class that she would call for a switch in the middle of the class period so that both pairs of students would have a chance to work on the assigned area and perimeter problem. She reminded the students repeatedly that the assignment would be collected and graded at the end of the period. As a result of the pairings made by Ms. Leoni, Marsha and Cathy were sent to the computer and the boys remained at the table to work on the assigned problem.

After Ms. Leoni released the students to work, the girls moved to the computer and Ted read the area and perimeter problem. After about a minute, Ted set the problem aside and began working on the floor plan design that he and Marsha had worked on during the 3 prior days. At this point, Henry was for the moment at a friend's table across the room. While Henry was away, Cathy returned to the table to retrieve a paper and saw that Ted was not working on the area and perimeter problem.

Segment 4.1

1 Cathy: (returning to the table) You're supposed to do this. (Shakes the area and perimeter work sheet at Ted.)

2 Ted: We're working on the top floor.

3 Cathy: No, we have to work on that (pushes finger onto the work sheet).

4 Ted: I'm not good at that, but I'll try. (Cathy leaves.) (low) Never have been, never will be.

Figure 4.
The Area and Perimeter problem.

AREA AND PERIMETER

Are area and perimeter related? If so, how? You get a chance to explore and find out.

1 Draw two floor plans that have exactly the same floor area but different wall perimeters.

2 How is it possible that two figures with the same area have different perimeters?

3 Pick a floor area between 4 and 20 square units. Play around with different shapes of buildings that have that area.

4 Make a chart or poster that *shows* the answer to this question:
Assume that you can only make "right angle" buildings with whole number length walls. Then what are ALL the different perimeter measures you can get for your chosen floor area?

5 Have a poster fair. For each group's poster, make a conjecture about a mathematical rule or pattern that you see relating area and perimeter. Your conjecture can be about one poster, or about all I the posters. Here are some examples of conjectures:

The perimeter is always larger than the area.
The perimeter can never be an odd number.

FYI
A conjecture is your best guess, based on evidence. You don't know for sure that it is true, but you have reason to think it might be.

6 In your group, pick a conjecture and make an argument for or against it. Keep doing this until you have 3 conjectures with arguments FOR them.

7 In your log:
• Write out one of your conjectures and the argument that goes with it.
• Write a paragraph explaining how the conjecture could be used to help you make a better ArchiTech design.

5 Ted: (Looks at the work sheet for another minute and then Henry returns to the table.) You do that (hands paper and work sheet to Henry) and I'll work on this (picks up ruler and floor plan paper).

6 Henry: (Henry looks at papers.) What the?

7 Ted: What they said to do.

The preceding segment is a complex instance of the work of dividing labor and attributing responsibility within the team. In Turn 1, Cathy directs Ted to what he ("you") as an individual is supposed to be doing. Ted responds in Turn 2 that he and Henry ("we") are working on the floor plan. In response, Cathy tells him what the team ("we") has to work on. In response to this stated accountability, Ted accepted the task, saying that he ("I") while not good at that would try. When Henry returned, the pronouns continued to shift with Ted passing the work sheet to Henry, instructing him ("you") to "do that." When Henry asks why (Turn 6), Ted refers to what the girls ("they") "said to do."

Whereas the previous data exemplars were more straightforward instances of joint action—representing either cooperative or competitive sense-making—this exemplar is complicated, beginning with Ted pushing the assigned problem away, Cathy pushing it back toward him, and finally Ted pushing it toward Henry. What explains these polarities? My answer to this question is that both Ted and Cathy counted this problem as mathematics but attributed very different meanings to this recognition. My analyses interpret Ted's utterance (Turn 4) as referring to school mathematics. Though only a seventh grader, Ted's school experiences had led him to believe not only that he "never ha[d]" been good at *what he recognized as math* but that he "never w[ould]" be. As a result, Ted resisted working on this problem.[10]

Cathy, like Ted, clearly counted the area and perimeter problem as mathematics. Because she was regarded by herself, her peers, and her teacher as good at math, Cathy was concerned (as the next segment shows) about how Ted's work on the problem would reflect on her standing and her grade. The following segment occurred after Cathy, who had been monitoring the progress of the boys, returned to the table.

Segment 4.2

1 Cathy: You guys have to work on the area and perimeter (inaudible word).

2 Henry: (toward both girls) He's not working with me.

3 Ted: (toward both girls, pointing at the design) I'm working on this story.

4 Marsha: It's due TODAY.

5 Ted: Yea.

6 Cathy: We're being graded and if I get an "F" on it, I'm going to kill you.

7 Ted: Good luck. (He looks down to his floor plan as she turns back to the computer.)

8 Henry: Man, just for-get it. (Puts the area and perimeter papers in the folder.)

As in the previous segment, Cathy offered a moral admonishment (Turn 1). What was different about this admonishment was that Henry now stood accused with Ted ("you guys") of not working on the problem, to which Henry responded by laying blame on Ted for not working with him (Turn 2). This was followed by Marsha stating the urgency (Turn 4) of the deadline, Cathy issuing a more severe threat (Turn 6), Ted resisting further (Turn 7), and Henry displaying frustration (Turn 8). The girls returned to the computer for a short time, but then conflict between Cathy and Ted continued. Cathy again returned to the table and issued a directive to Ted ("you're not working on [the floor plan]"). In response, he reiterated his incompetence, "I'm not good at the other area and perimeter thing." Given the repeated nature of this conflict, the team was clearly at an impasse. The outcome of this conflict was, however, different from the previous instance, with Ted proposing a shift in the division of labor wherein the girls would work on the problem and he and Henry would move to the computer. This interactional move was similar to his attempt to delegate this problem to Henry in that he acted to see that the problem would be completed by someone other than himself.

The girls accepted the proposed change in the division of labor, seemingly based on a shared awareness that otherwise the problem would not be completed by the end of the period. As the boys moved over to the computer, the girls returned to the table, read the work sheet together quickly and announced to each other that they didn't understand how to do it either. Marsha then went to request help from Ms. Leoni but she was busy with other students. Marsha returned to the table and was followed shortly thereafter by Ms. Leoni, who had apparently seen Marsha waiting to ask a question. When Ms. Leoni arrived, she asked the team if they had done the assigned problem.

Segment 4.3

1 Ms. Leoni: Did you guys do your [area and perimeter problem]?

2 Marsha: We just got off the computer and they didn't do anything.

3 Ms. Leoni: Uh-oh. (Henry starts to say something, inaudible.)

4 Marsha: Well he (points to Henry) was doing something and he (points to Ted, who was now waiting for the group's printouts) wasn't doing anything.

Two things Marsha said in response to Ms. Leoni's question were not literally true from my perspective as an observer and subsequent analyst of these events. Ted had done "something," working the entire time on the floor plan, and Henry did no more than Ted on the assigned problem, though Ted had been the audible spokesperson for not doing it. Marsha had been placed in a position by the teacher of accounting for the team's prospective failure to complete the assignment and had blamed Ted. And whereas Marsha's claim that Ted "wasn't doing anything" was not literally true, it was in a sense organizationally true because Ted was spending time on an activity (i.e., designing) that did not count *at that moment* to anyone else in the organization.[11] Ted may have even shared this interpretation, because he did not defend his design work when the teacher—the organization's local authority—was present (Segment 4.3) as he did when he was talking only to his team members (Segment 4.2).

When Ms. Leoni left the team with an injunction to complete the task in the remaining time (13 minutes), further recriminations were directed at Ted as the girls realized the pressure they faced to quickly finish and turn in the assignment.

Segment 4.4

1 Cathy: Ok, now we have to do, we have to do all this [the area and perimeter work sheet] hecka fast, because I don't want to get a, a really bad grade.

2 Marsha: (turning toward Ted at the printer) Uh, look what you did? (Growls and shakes her body.)

3 Cathy: I know. I told you guys to work on it with somebody—

4 Henry:—(pointing at Ted, who's still out of frame) It was him. He didn't help me.

5 Marsha: OK, then we'll blame it on him.

During the next few minutes, the girls struggled to render the problem doable as the grading deadline approached. Henry, perhaps feeling some culpability for the situation the team found themselves in, left the table to solicit help from his friend Dinesh at a nearby table. A moment later, Henry and Dinesh returned together, and Dinesh, prompted by Henry, delivered a piece of succinct direction instruction on how to do the assigned problem.

Segment 4.5

1 Dinesh: (leaning in, speaking quickly) What you do is you take all these shapes, you cut em out, and set em on a piece of paper like this (puts hand over a piece of construction paper).

2 Marsha: That's it? I can do that. (Marsha and Cathy quickly begin cutting shapes.)

What Dinesh had provided was the baldest form of instruction, a form that allowed Marsha and Cathy to complete only a superficial version of the assignment under the severe time constraints they now faced.[12] When Ted returned to the table a moment later after collecting some team printouts he saw his fellow team members at work and proposed to help. It was, however, too late for Ted and Marsha delivered a summation of who Ted had become for her, an identification that would "stick" to Ted with respect to assigned mathematics problems.

Segment 4.6

1 Ted: How do you want me to help you? How?

2 Marsha: See. That's your problem, you don't know what to do and you can't help us. It's not our fault you're dumb.

3 Ted: Yeah.

Ted's final affirmation of being "dumb" was not an ironic response; audibly he shared the identification. For the purposes of my remarks about this complex segment, I will stipulate and hope the reader will agree that the identifications of Ted (by himself and others) throughout the segment are unfortunate. Also unfortunate were the experiences of Cathy and Marsha, who cared about their grade on the assignment but were largely powerless to control its fate. These unfortunate outcomes raise the following questions: (1) what accounts for them? and (2) why does this segment contrast so significantly with those already described around the emergent problems, especially with regard to the relationship between Ted and Marsha?

With respect to the first question, there is surely plenty of blame that could be distributed across the student team and perhaps to the teacher as well for how the assignment was made. In other words, one account of this event might appeal to the contingent details of who participated and how this problem was enacted. This perspective, although in part true, obscures a more general point, because across each of the participants the recognizability of this problem as school mathematics was not in question. It was a piece of work to be completed (or not), turned in, and graded as mathematics. At just 12 years of age, these students were already well enough enculturated into school mathematics to recognize the assigned problem as an instance and to behave accordingly. For Ted, behaving accordingly meant avoiding mathematics because of his own self-identified incompetence. For Cathy and Marsha, behaving accordingly meant saying whatever they felt necessary to and about Ted to assure a good grade on a problem that counted as mathematics. For the teacher, behaving accordingly meant deploying a recognizable instance of mathematics, packaged more or less as a work sheet in the curriculum, to assemble student grades as a midterm grading period approached.

These ways of participating in the cultural practices of school math by students and teachers alike may surprise no one. What may surprise some readers is the contrast between the relationships among students (e.g., Marsha and Ted) across the two types of problems in the same mathematics classroom over just a few days. Whereas Marsha and Ted were antagonistic around this assigned problem, they worked collaboratively around the emergent problems that arose in their design work. And when they disagreed and engaged in what I have called competitive sense-making (as in Data Exemplar 4), they settled their disputes with arguments grounded in mathematical and design considerations rather than in attributions about their respective incompetence as individuals. In other words, and my broader analyses (Stevens, 1999) support this generalization, the differential recognizability of problems as mathematics invoked differential ways of interacting with each other. And, simply put, the ways students interacted around the emergent problems accorded better with educational values for collaboration and sociable discourse (Lampert, Rittenhouse, & Crumbaugh, 1996).

Before proceeding with this analysis, I want to forestall (but not dismiss) two interpretations of the contrast I have drawn between emergent and assigned problems as different contexts for student activity: (1) the area and perimeter problem was just a bad mathematics problem, and (2) the distinction between assigned and emergent can be collapsed into a distinction between graded and not graded. Of interpretation 1, it can be argued that the underlying mathematical content (i.e., the general relationship between area and perimeter) could easily have been relevant to student design work. Because heat loss was one of the considerations students faced (as they were designing a research station for Antarctica), an understanding of this general relationship could have allowed them to maximize floor area and minimize perimeter, thereby minimizing heat loss and thereby minimizing cost. This is precisely the kind of complex, quantitative relation that architects manage (Stevens, 1999) and that we might wish to see among students doing projects like these. In fact, a strong affirmation of this idea's utility was provided when practicing architects visited the classroom and, while critiquing student designs independently, identified this issue of the relation between heat loss and perimeter. What this means is that the problem itself cannot be blamed for the contrast.

Of interpretation 2, grades were surely relevant to the interactional trouble that occurred in the student team around the assigned problem. However, my analyses argue against collapsing the distinction between assigned and emergent problems into the distinction between graded and nongraded work. For example, Ted did care about his grades at times and nearly always he cared about how his work was assessed. This was particularly true when professional architects visited and reviewed their design work. Ted also explicitly identified math, not grading, as the reason for why he resisted working on the area and perimeter problem. He knew that the problem was going to be graded and tried to delegate it because of this; it was math he was avoiding, not grading. With respect to the higher performing students such as Marsha, what counted as math may have been more equivalent with what counted for a grade. However, collapsing emergent into nongraded would fail to explain why Marsha invested so much energy and collaborated so fully with Ted on the emergent design and mathematics problems. If these were only nongraded work to her, she would not have bothered.

It is beyond the scope of this chapter to further analyze the multiple episodes in which Ted positioned himself or was positioned by his team members as incompetent or trustworthy with respect to the assigned math problems. However, I want to avoid freezing the action around this episode lest it produce a caricature of either these students or assigned problems. As the project proceeded, the dynamics of the team and their approach to both the emergent and assigned problems was negotiated, often implicitly, within the team. Ted did not remain identified exclusively as "dumb," though both Cathy and Marsha repeatedly complained that he "did nothing" when it came time to work on these problems.

What the negotiation begot was a division of labor in which Cathy more or less took over the production of all the assigned problems and was trusted to do so by her teammates. At times, this meant that she would volunteer to do work assigned to all the team members as when, later in the project, she told her teammates that "I'll do the chart (a spreadsheet based problem) for you guys." At other times this meant that while the other students worked on other activities, such as designing, Cathy would be the first to complete assigned problems and then "share" her work with her teammates. I place quotes around the word share to index a further complexity: that Cathy, holding the official capital resource of this classroom, would distribute it differentially to the other members. Whereas Marsha could ask to "see [her] numbers" and had this request granted without question on every occasion, similar requests by Ted would often yield a response that he "should do it [himself]." In these instances, Cathy's actions could be construed as unfair but may also be interpreted as pedagogical; my interpretation of many of these moments suggests that Cathy allowed Marsha to see her numbers because she had confidence that Marsha could do the work if she tried. Because she did not have the same confidence in Ted, she wanted him to try to do it himself. In summary, the assigned mathematics in this classroom had a complicated existence. Rather than simply being given by the teacher and taken by the students (a presumption that underlies most evaluations of classrooms of all types), assigned problems were treated differently by different students and were, among other things, ignored, resisted, delegated, shared, copied, commodified, and sometimes solved.[13]

DISCUSSION

Based on the data presented in this chapter, it would be premature to claim that the distinction between emergent and assigned problems as different contexts for student activity is necessarily a general one. However, I do wish to *propose* the distinction as a generalizable one, awaiting comparisons with studies of other classrooms that involve emergent and assigned problems[14] and to argue for some of the potential theoretical and pedagogical entailments of this distinction. These entailments are: (1) a productive way to think about context, (2) the institutional invisibility of emergent mathematics problems, and (3) the tradeoffs involved with emergent mathematics problems.

A Productive Way to Think About Context

One of the potentially distinctive theoretical features of the contrast I have drawn is how it extends the concept of context. In ethnographically grounded educational research, context has been a key term that is usually assigned to *different settings* which, in turn, are argued to organize different social and epistemological outcomes. Such setting-based comparisons of contexts include school and work (Becker, 1986; Hall, 1995; Lave & Wenger, 1991; Scribner & Cole, 1973; Stevens, 1999), types of classrooms (Boaler, 1997; Cobb, Wood, Yackel, & McNeal, 1992), and in versus out-of-school environments (Newman, Griffin, & Cole, 1989). This chapter's analysis is distinctive in showing *different contexts within a single setting*. What this implies is a dynamic sense of context in which the same participants assemble themselves and local materials from a single setting to be and mean very different things (Duranti & Goodwin, 1992; McDermott, 1993; Phillips, 1983). This finer-grained sense of context is, if nothing else, a tool for avoiding premature conclusions about what a setting is based on its name or official primary function. For the setting under consideration here, this "project-based classroom" was too complicated a hybrid of old and new educational practices to serve to finalize an evaluation of educational experiments that go by this name. And perhaps by extension we might suspect that nearly all settings are equally hybrid when examined closely.

As evidence for how emergent and assigned problems were different contexts, the students' comparative participation in each is illustrative. Whereas Ted was an active and enthusiastic participant in the problems, mathematical and otherwise, that emerged in design, Ted resisted those problems that were assigned and thereby clearly recognizable as school mathematics. From this analysis, the contrastive images to keep in mind are, on the one hand, Ted crawling on the floor, measuring stick in hand, to bring an extended mathematical argument to a conclusion and, on the other hand, Ted taking less than a minute to size up and set aside an assigned problem as something he is "not good at . . . never have been, never will be." Emergent and assigned problems provided different contexts for Cathy as well, but in somewhat the opposite manner. As I described earlier, she was fully invested in and responsible for the assigned problems, but took almost no role in designing and emergent problems. For Marsha, these were different contexts not so much in terms of how she participated, but in how her teammates appeared to her. Around the emergent problems of design, Ted was a collaborator. Around the assigned problems, Ted was untrustworthy and Marsha looked to Cathy for help and sharing of work.[15]

Given the selection of the particular assigned problem and my analysis of the trouble it caused, readers might wonder about my assessment of assigned problems in project based classrooms? Am I suggesting they be banished? Not quite. Rather, where I am led to is the idea that the assigned problems, in the form they took—as numbered work sheets highlighting mathematical content distributed to all the students[16]—were too *easy* to treat as *cover stories* for school math as usual. They were easy to see this way by the students and easy to use this way by the teacher. Part of this ease can be accounted for by the institutional arrangements that were already in place at this mostly traditional middle school. Even though Ms. Leoni articulated, in various meetings and informal interviews, a distrust in grading as a vehicle for teaching and learning, she was accountable to grading individuals as one of the main requirements and measures of her job performance. This explains in part the ambivalence and disorganized perspective she displayed about grading that I described at the beginning of the chapter and why she fell back on the assigned problems when she needed to produce grades. For the students, project-based instruction was new and stood out against the background of their otherwise normal schooling experiences involving textbooks, daily assignments, quizzes, and tests. And because of this existing and seemingly durable cultural knowledge about what counts as school math and school in general, it was often hard to trick them into believing that this was something different when they could assemble enough local evidence that it was not. Both of these facts reaffirm for me the idea that consistent, school-wide organizational change is necessary if reform practices are to have a real chance to succeed and endure (Brown & Campione, 1994; Sizer, 1992).

The Institutional Invisibility of Emergent Mathematics Problems: Emergent mathematics problems were invisible and did not count in at least three senses.

1. Emergent mathematical problems did not count outside the team-local events. Except on a few serendipitous occasions when Ms. Leoni's contact with the team

intersected with a "live" emergent problem, most of the mathematics problems that emerged in the course of design work came and went within the confines of the team. And on no occasion did any of the emergent mathematical problems in this team or in any other find their way from the local team to the public arena of the whole-class discussion. Although this practice has been tied to artful teaching (Hall & Rubin, 1998) and its absence here might suggest that Ms. Leoni was less than artful, it is important also to point out that this sort of classroom circulation may have failed to occur because of more systemic features. In this regard, it is important to reiterate that events involving emergent math problems were observable infrequently to Ms. Leoni; they were outside her horizons of observation (Hutchins, 1995). Only from my position as observer, recorder, and analyst of the team were these events observable.

2. Emergent mathematical activities did not count because there were no assessment technologies in the class for recording them. Even if there had been a way for Ms. Leoni to see and then facilitate the circulation of emergent problems to the public sphere as examples of mathematics, no assessment infrastructure existed for counting them. With respect to grading, the work sheet-like "math activities" were preprinted, numbered for scoring, and distributable to all students. As such, they provided a resource for doing what routinely happens in school; giving everyone the same thing to do and using what students do with them as a means to rank order them (Mehan, 1990). No such system existed for the emergent problems, because these were diverse across the teams and, as I described earlier, mostly came and went, within each team. When Ms. Leoni did bump into an emergent problem while making her classroom rounds, she had artful pedagogical strategies for scaffolding mathematical activity (e.g., Data Exemplar 2, the circlelike bavarium). What she did not have were organizational devices for keeping these problems in the foreground; as such it was too easy to get caught up in a welter of classroom management and, as occurred with the circlelike bavarium, never return to the team after initial scaffolding. The sort of organizational device I have in mind might be a document for recording the finding, formulating, and solving of emergent math problems across the different teams. Teachers always have material support for recording comparative individual work on uniform assignments, but nearly nothing beyond their own memories to record diversity, collective achievements, and emergent features of student work.

3. Emergent math problems did not count in that students did not recognize these problems as mathematics. As I have argued, these seventh-grade students had already a relatively well developed notion of what counted as mathematics around traditional forms and social functions—as what appeared on tests, on work sheets, in textbooks, or in standard mathematical orthography.[17] And in large part, because of the two prior senses of invisibility—to the teacher and to the assessment system—the emergent problems did not count as mathematics to the students even though they were central to the progress of the project.

There are two paradoxical implications of these ways in which the emergent problems did not count for local participants as mathematics. The first paradox is that the organizational invisibility, although troubling from one perspective, also can be seen as beneficial. This is because by not counting these problems as mathematics, the teacher and the students did not invoke the less desirable cultural practices of school math. In this case, what was *not* invoked around the emergent problems were such things as easy attributions of personal inability or the political economy of grading and giving credit at the expense of learning (i.e., as in the assigned problem). The second paradox, set against the first, is that student participation in emergent problems may have meant they learned valuable mathematical or proto-mathematical practices such as using mathematics as a vehicle for building a relationship (Exemplar 1), for formulating design problems (Exemplar 2) and for settling intellectual disputes (Exemplar 3) even though these achievements went unremarked as related to mathematics.

The Tradeoffs Involved with Emergent Mathematics Problems

The emergent problems may have fostered mathematical learning and were clearly vehicles to important ends within the team. In fact, this team's design when reviewed by architects at the end of the project was considered the best among not only the teams in this class but also in competition with designs from another class at another middle school. Despite these positive features of the emergent problems, their mathematical content (to use a practical if simplifying construct) was, as I described in my analysis of the emergent problems, often minimal. Students could solve their design problems with simple mathematical techniques that used features of their tools or their environment and could set complex math problems aside because their design ideas took them in other directions. Although people in everyday life often avoid mathematics and get along fine with other resources and practices (de la Rocha, 1986; Lave, 1988), we may not want to make it so easy for students in school. Just as educators in language arts want students to experience the complexity and potential impact on student life of obscure unpopular novels, essays, and poems, we may wish students to be exposed to mathematical ideas and tools they would not otherwise encounter. Such exposure, if done in *a* right way, may allow students themselves to make connections between things mathematical and the rest of their life. What, then, is a right way? Or at least a better one? How might classrooms like this be reorganized to "count" emergent problems as mathematics? Can a classroom be centered around students finding, formulating, and solving their own problems while at the same time nurturing and maintaining the mathematical content of these problems? Are these mutually exclusive goals?

PEDAGOGICAL RECOMMENDATIONS: REVISING RESOURCES FOR EDUCATORS INTERESTED IN PBM

In this section, I propose that these goals are not mutually exclusive. As I stated in the introduction, project-based efforts are still new and invite revision prior to final assessments of their educational viability. With this perspective in mind, the following are some recommendations, based on my analyses of classroom activity, that may mitigate some of the tensions and enhance the environments of PBM. Although the remarks that follow are meant to be general to project-based environments, where appropriate I use the specific case considered here—architectural design projects as a vehicle for learning mathematics—to frame the proposals.

The organizational conditions of classrooms such as these make it difficult for teachers to play the roles they seem to most want to play and those they are asked to play within reform documents: as guides, coaches, and peripheral collaborators. What would assist teachers in doing so with respect to emergent problems would be a documentary infrastructure for keeping track of emergent problems at different stages in their development. Problem-finding, formulating, and solving would be relevant categories to represent in such a document, which would provide the teacher with a synoptic view of how different teams are encountering mathematics problems in the course of their project work. Such documents would support various sorts of whole-class lectures or discussions and would act as an aid to memory so that teachers could remember to follow up with teams that had an interesting problem at some stage of development.[18]

Such documents would help, but they would not be enough, because it is still the case that emergent problems could remain largely invisible. As I have suggested, only infrequently are teachers at the right time and the right place to participate pedagogically in emergent problems. In light of this, students themselves should have a greater role in identifying and circulating those problems that emerge in projects as prospectively mathematically relevant. In other words, the responsibility for the identification and circulation of such events should be distributed across the students and the teacher. A prerequisite for such a set of classroom practices by students would, I believe, be explicit and ongoing discussions about what counts as math and how PBM may differ in form and function from textbook-based mathematics. Such discussions could set up something of a nomination practice, in which students nominate problems to the teacher and her or his classmates to consider as mathematics. These instances could then enable whole-class discussions.

Finally, the classroom practices where revision might have the greatest impact involve how mathematics is assessed. Emergent mathematical problems and their solutions simply need to be *counted* if PBM education is to be anything more than cover stories for math as usual. As cover stories, they unnecessarily complicate an already complicated environment for students and teachers. As something more, they can be environments for mathematics to be found, formulated, and solved and thereby experienced as relevant to students.

How to organize such an assessment system to register emergent practices in a classroom is a larger topic than can be treated adequately here. However, one idea, based on our prior research of the distributed nature of mathematical activities in professional settings (Hall & Stevens, 1995; Hall, Stevens, & Torralba, in press; Stevens, 1999) would be give credit to students on two bases: (1) their success in finding, formulating, and solving emergent math problems, and (2) their success in making and using project-relevant architectural generalizations. With respect to using mathematical generalizations or tools, students might be provided with a sourcebook of possibly relevant mathematical ideas such as the general relationship between area and perimeter. This sourcebook would be compiled to reflect possible mathematical opportunities that might arise in the project, thus matching the intent of the assigned "mathematical activities" in the curriculum but pursuing this intent through different means. In other words, rather than assigning and grading work sheets, students would receive credit when they could *use* and justify the use of one of these generalizations or tools in the course of their project work. Even more credit could be assigned to students to *create* their own tools or generalizations for other's use in the classroom.

With respect to both the circumstances under which students could earn credit, the students themselves would be primarily responsible for *seeking* credit for work they *proposed* as mathematical, proposals that could be decided by the teacher and the students together. With these as the main sources of credit-giving in the classroom, the teacher would likely have more freedom to encourage, shape, and advocate the mathematical qualities of student projects. Students' work could also be "published" (i.e., made public) through posting in classroom space or electronically. And under the assumption that teachers would use a project-based curriculum over a number of years, these publications could be available to students in future years' classes with students receiving due authorship credit. Although there are many routes to desired ends, this is one way by which a classroom of this kind might become more of a genuine community of learners (Brown & Campione, 1994).

The sourcebook of mathematical generalizations and tools I have described is one way these curricula might be revised. Another idea—directed at enhancing the mathematical content in the project-based curriculum without reducing it to a cover story—involves borrowing and adapting some ideas from the professional practice of architecture (or whatever the framing disciplinary practice might be: biology, cartography, digital imaging, etc.). For example, in my research on the forms and functions of mathematics among professional architects, I found that the single most prevalent accountability faced by architects that generated emergent mathematics problems was *code*. This term refers to federal, state, and municipal rules that architects must follow when designing buildings; these legal standards enforce such design features as the maximum slope of a wheelchair ramp or an acceptable range for the ratio of stairway risers and runners. Plans do not receive approval and buildings are not built unless code is met. As such, architects are continuously trying to satisfy code in ways that save money and meet design goals, and this forces them to confront many emergent mathematics problems. In the student projects, variants of code could be requirements for students. For example, students might be required to make their bathrooms accessible to disabled persons. This would involve, among other things, designing 5–foot radial regions in all toilet rooms, a problem that, as I have shown elsewhere, bears similarities but also important differences from the traditional mathematical problem of inscribing a circle within a square (Stevens, 1999). The advantages of giving assignments of this kind, versus more typical assignments such as the area and perimeter problem of Data Exemplar 4, are threefold: (1) code does not specify a single correct answer but allows a range of correct solutions, and (2) code creates different emergent problem for different projects because surrounding constraints differ, and (3) students can learn about authentic concerns in the building process, such as making it possible for a disabled person to be able to use a building. One benefit of this is that assigned problems of this kind could provide an answer to the ubiquitous and hard-to-answer student question, "What are we ever going to use this for?"

CONCLUSION

Despite some caricatures in circulation, PBM (or project-based science) was not born of the whims of politically radical, know-nothing "education people." These educational experiments were born, at least in the versions with which I am familiar, against the background of a recalcitrant system of mathematics education that has worked for a privileged few and failed many. At least at the level of espoused goals, these endeavors, as diverse as they are, represent an attempt to make mathematical tools and ideas available to the many. These experiments also seek to provide students with opportunities to connect mathematics to experience and make mathematics a resource, though only one among many, for making sense of that experience. As I have sought to show in this chapter, these experiments and the emergent mathematical practices they generate are socially and epistemologically complex. In this chapter I also have tried to follow the often-ignored recommendation by Brown (1992) to represent the gold of educational experiments as well as the dross.

I began this chapter with a description of the political storm surrounding PBM education. So much of this storm rages around the issues of standards and test scores. At the eye of this storm, hard to reach and often unexamined, is the question of who counts what as math. This chapter probably will do little to quiet the storm, but I hope it will contribute to making it harder to talk only about the alleged absences of project-based classrooms. In so doing, I also hope that it will contribute to complicating the discussion a bit by bringing other terms into the equation. I see raising standardized test scores as one sort of objective, but I see helping *most* students learn to use mathematical tools and ideas to support arguments, to work together, to make things, and to resolve problematic situations from daily life as very different sorts of objectives. More important ones, I would argue. And while I do not propose that current versions of PBM education will achieve these objectives, I do propose that we consider this a better starting point than the alternatives.

ACKNOWLEDGMENTS

I would like to thank Rogers Hall and Andy diSessa for helpful comments on an earlier version of this chapter and Jo Boaler and Leslie Herrenkohl for helpful comments on the current version. I would also like to thank the Spencer Foundation for a dissertation fellowship that supported this research.

NOTES

1. Recently over 200 research mathematicians and physicists ran a full-page advertisement in the *Washington Post* (November 18, 1999) demanding that the federal government retract its recommendations for a number of well-known reform curriculum packages. Clearly not all research mathematicians share this disdain for the reform movement; exceptions include Steve Monk of the University of Washington and Hyman Bass of the University of Michigan.

2. I have found them even more inadequate for an analysis of mathematics in the workplace (Stevens, 1999).

3. See Hall and Stevens, 1995; Stevens and Hall, 1998; and Stevens, 1999.

4. The names of the school, teacher, and students are pseudonyms.

5. The project constraints actually allowed the longer dimension to be 30 meters, but the graph paper only had 29 units across its long dimension and thus the students took this as their long dimension.

6. Although Ted did not use the word "regular," he represented it nonetheless with vocally animated gestures. Further evidence for regularity as an assumed feature of the students' plan is provided later.

7. The basis for Henry's impatience was rooted in a role he had been assigned by the teacher: to record the changes made by the team during that class period. As yet, he had nothing to record and the end of period was drawing near.

8. M.C. O'Connor (1998) has used this specific term in a study of classroom mathematics. See also, Bruner (1960/1977).

9. See Schoenfeld (1990) for arguments supporting this principle of continuity in mathematics learning and diSessa (1983,1993) for related arguments about the continuity of physics learning.

10. Although Ted resisted work on this problem, it cannot simply be interpreted in terms of what Ted did not do (i.e., as an absence), for the following reasons. First, Ted did visibly try to do the problem if only for about a minute or so (Turn 5, earlier, and prior to the excerpt); second, Ted was legitimately continuing with another line of work that no one in the team or the class has suggested should be shut down (i.e., the design); and third, he did show some accountability to the team by delegating the assigned problem to Henry while he continued with the design.

11. See Garfinkel (1967) on accountability and Star and Strass (in press) on invisible work for relevant treatments of the relations between social phenomena and their organizational recognizability.

12. I call their version superficial because what they turned met neither of the mathematical criteria stipulated in the problem: (1) to make rectangles that held the area constant but varied the perimeter, and (2) to make a conjecture about the general relationship between area and perimeter.

13. Despite the large corpus of studies that focus on assigned mathematics problems, it is worth considering whether these studies provide an analytical vocabulary wide enough to encompass this sort of variety in the ways that students "take" assignments (cf. Lemke, 1990, on differences between the intended and lived curriculum).

14. Because of the demands of this type of data collection and analysis, it is likely that generalizations will be produced across members of our field, through comparative analysis of cases, rather than by single researchers.

15. The fourth member of the team, Henry, because he was quiet and often away from the table, is harder to assess relative to the distinction between assigned and emergent problems.

16. The designers of this curriculum may be disheartened by these perceptions and uses, because the text of the teachers' guide repeatedly warned against them, as in the emphatic: "These are NOT worksheets."

17. This is supported by the pieces of text the students wrote in their journals midway through the project. When asked to describe how they had used mathematics, students referred to basic operations such as measuring, dividing, and adding but did not refer to such activities as using quantitative comparisons to make design decisions or related judgments of scale to make arguments (cf. Boaler, 1997 for a similar finding).

18. These ideas also may have implications for teacher education programs.

REFERENCES

Battista, M. (1999, February). The mathematical miseducation of America's youth. *Phi Delta Kappan*, 425–433.

Becker, H. S. (1986). A school is a lousy place to learn anything. In, *Doing things together: Selected papers*. Evanston, IL: Northwestern University Press.

Boaler, J. (1997). *Experiencing school mathematics*. Buckingham, UK: Open University Press.

Brown, A. (1992). Design experiments: Theoretical and methodological challenges in creating complex interventions in classroom settings. *The Journal of Learning Sciences, 2*(2), 141–178.

Brown, A. L., & Campione, J. C. (1994). Guided discovery in a community of learners. In K. McGilly (Ed.), *Classroom lessons* (pp. 229–270). Cambridge, MA: MIT Press.

Bruner, J. S. (1960/1977). *The Process of education*. Cambridge, MA: Harvard University Press.

Charmaz, K. (1983). The grounded theory method: An explication and interpretation. In R. M. Emerson (Ed.), *Contemporary field research* (pp. 109–126). Boston: Little, Brown.

Cobb, P. (1995). Mathematical learning and small-group interaction: Four case studies. In P. Cobb & H. Bauersfeld (Eds.), *The emergence of mathematical meaning: Interaction in classroom cultures* (pp. 25–129). Hillsdale, NJ: Erlbaum.

Cobb, P., Wood, T., Yackel, E., & McNeal, B. (1992). Characteristics of classroom mathematics traditions: An interactional analysis. *American Educational Research Journal, 29*(3), 573–604.

Cole, M., Hood, L., & McDermott, R. P. (1997). Concepts of ecological validity: Their differing implications for comparative cognitive research. In M. Cole, Y. Engestrom, & O. Vasquez (Eds.), *Mind, culture and activity: Seminal papers from the laboratory of comparative human cognition* (pp. 49–56). Cambridge, UK: Cambridge University Press.

Cole, M., & Scribner, S. (1974). *Culture and thought: A psychological introduction*. New York: Wiley.

Coulter, J. (1989). *Mind in action*. Atlantic Highlands, NJ: Humanities Press.

de la Rocha, O. (1986). *Problems of sense and problems of scale: An ethnograpic study of arithmetic in everyday life*. Unpublished dissertation, University of California, Irvine.

DeCorte, E., Greer, B., & Verschaffel, L. (1996). Mathematics learning and teaching. In D. Berliner & R. Calfee (Eds.), *Handbook of educational psychology* (pp. 491–549). New York: MacMillan.

diSessa, A. (1983). Phenomenology and the evolution of intuition. In D. Gentner & A. L. Stevens (Eds.), *Mental models*. Hillsdale, NJ: Erlbaum.

diSessa, A. A. (1993). Toward an epistemology of physics. *Cognition & Instruction, 10*(2–3), 105–225.

Duranti, A., & Goodwin, C. (Eds.). (1992). *Rethinking context: Language as an interactive phenomena*. Cambridge, UK: Cambridge University Press.

Fujimura, J. (1987). Constructing "do-able" problems in cancer research: Articulating alignment. *Social Studies of Science, 17*, 257–293.

Garfinkel, H. (1967). *Studies in ethnomethodology*. Englewood Cliffs, NJ: Prentice-Hall.

Glaser, B., & Strauss, A. (1967). *The discovery of grounded theory*. Chicago: Aldine.

Goodwin, C., & Heritage, J. (1990). Conversation analysis. *Annual Review of Anthropology, 19*, 283–307.

Goodwin, M. H. (1990). *He-said-she-said: Talk as social organization among black children*. Bloomington, IN: Indiana University Press.

Hall, R., & Rubin, A. (1998). There's five little notches in here: Dilemmas in teaching and learning the conventional structure of rate. In J. Greeno & S. Goldman (Eds.), *Thinking practices in mathematics and science learning* . Mahweh, NJ: Erlbaum.

Hall, R., & Stevens, R. (1995). Making space: A comparison of mathematical work in school and professional design practices. In S. L. Star (Ed.), *The cultures of computing* (pp. 118–145). London: Basil Blackwell.

Hall, R., Stevens, R., & Torralba, A. (In press). Analyses of work across disciplinary boundaries making and using generalizations: Interdisciplinary consulting in entomology versus architecture. In S. Derry (Ed.), *Cognitive perspectives on interdiscipinarity*. Mahweh, NJ: Erlbaum.

Hall, R. P. (1995). Exploring design oriented mathematical practices in school and work settings. *Communications of the ACM, 38*(9), 62.

Hutchins, E. (1995). *Cognition in the wild*. Cambridge, MA: MIT Press.

Jackson, A. (1997a, June/July). The math wars: California battles it out over mathematics education reform (Part I). *Notices of the ACM*, 695–702.

Jackson, A. (1997b, August). The math wars: California battles it out over mathematics education reform (Part II). *Notices of the ACM*, 817–823.

Lampert, M., Rittenhouse, P., & Crumbaugh, C. (1996). Agreeing to disagree: Developing sociable mathematical discourse. In D. R. Olson & N. Torrance (Eds.), *The handbook of education and human development* (pp. 731–764). Cambridge, MA: Blackwell.

Lave, J. (1988). *Cognition in practice: Mind, mathematics, and culture in everyday life*. Cambridge, UK: Cambridge University Press.

Lave, J., & Wenger, E. (1991). *Situated learning: Legitimate peripheral participation*. Cambridge, UK: Cambridge University Press.

Lemke, J. L. (1990). *Talking science: Language, learning, and values*. Norwood, NJ: Ablex.

McDermott, R., & Webber, V. (1998). When is math or science? In J. Greeno & S. Goldman (Eds.), *Thinking practices in mathematics and science learning* . Mahweh, NJ: Erlbaum.

McDermott, R. P. (1993). The acquisition of a child by a learning disability. In S. Chaiklin & J. Lave (Eds.), *Understanding practice: Perspectives on activity and context*. Cambridge, UK: Cambridge University Press.

Mehan, H. (1990). The school's work of sorting students. In D. Boden & D. H. Zimmerman (Eds.), *Talk and social structure*. Cambridge, UK: Polity Press.

MMAP. (1995). *The Antarctica project: A middle-school mathematics unit*. Palo Alto, CA: Institute for Research on Learning.

Newman, D., Griffin, P., & Cole, M. (1989). *The construction zone: Working for cognitive change in school*. New York: Cambridge University Press.

O'Connor, M. C. (1998). Language socialization in the mathematics classroom: Discourse practices and mathematical thinking. In M. Lampert & M. L. Bunk (Eds.), *Talking mathematics in school: Studies of teaching and learning*. New York: Cambridge University Press.

O'Connor, M. C., Godfrey, L., & Moses, R. P. (1998). The missing data point: Negotiating purposes in classroom mathematics and science. In J. Greeno & S. Goldman (Eds.), *Thinking practices in mathematics and science learning* . Mahweh, NJ: Erlbaum.

Phillips, S. U. (1983). *The invisible culture: Communication in classroom community on the Warm Springs Indian Reservation*. Prospect Heights, IL: Waveland Press.

Ragin, C. C., & Becker, H. S. (Eds.). (1992). *What is a case?: Exploring the foundations of social inquiry*. Cambridge, UK: Cambridge University Press.

Sacks, H., Schegloff, E. A., & Jefferson, G. (1974). A simplest systematics for the organization of turn-taking in conversation. *Language, 50*, 696–735.

Saxe, G., & Guberman, S. (1998). Emergent arithmetical environments in the context of distributed problem solving: Analyses of children playing an educational game. In J. Greeno & S. Goldman (Eds.), *Thinking practices in mathematics and science learning* . Mahweh, NJ: Erlbaum.

Schoenfeld, A. H. (1990). On mathematics as sense-making: An informal attack on the unfortunate divorce of formal and informal mathematics. In D. N. Perkins, J. Segal, & J. Voss (Eds.), *Informal reasoning and education*. Hillsdale, NJ: Erlbaum.

Schoenfeld, A. H. (1992). Learning to think mathematically: Problem solving, metacognition, and sense making in mathematics. In D. Grouws (Ed.), *Handbook for research on mathematics teaching and learning* (pp. 334–370). New York: Macmillan.

Schon, D. A. (1990). The design process. In V. A. Howard (Ed.), *Varieties of thinking: Essays from Harvard's philosophy of education research center* (pp. 110–141). New York: Routledge.

Scribner, S., & Cole, M. (1973, November 9). Cognitive consequences of formal and informal education. *Science*.

Sizer, T. R. (1992). *Horace's compromise: The dilemma of the American high school*. Boston: Houghton Mifflin.

Smith, J. P., diSessa, A. A., & Roschelle, J. (1994). Misconceptions reconceived: A constructivist analysis of knowledge in transition. *Journal of the Learning Sciences, 3*(2), 115–163.

Star, S. L., & Strauss, A. (in press). Layers of silence, arenas of voice: The dialogues between visible and invisible work. *Journal of Computer-Supported Cooperative Work.*

Stevens, R. (1997). *Divisions of labor in computer-assisted design: A comparison of cases from work and school.* Paper presented at the proceedings of the Second International Conference on Computer Support for Collaborative Learning, Toronto, CA.

Stevens, R. (in press). Using the division of labor concept to compare computer-supported collaborative work and learning across settings. In T. Koschmann, N. Miyake, & R. Hall (Eds.), *Computer supported collaborative learning: Continuing the conversation.* Mahwah, NJ: Erlbaum.

Stevens, R., & Hall, R. (1998). Disciplined perception: Learning to see in technoscience. In M. Lampert & M. L. Blunk (Eds.), *Talking mathematics in school: Studies of teaching and learning.* New York: Cambridge University Press.

Stevens, R. R. (1999). *Disciplined perception: Comparing the development of embodied mathematical practices at work and in school.* Unpublished dissertation, University of California, Berkeley.

Strauss, A., & Corbin, J. (1990). *Basics of qualitative research: Grounded theory procedures and techniques.* Thousand Oaks, CA: Sage.

Van Haneghan, J., Barron, L., Young, M., Williams, S., Vye, N., & Bransford, J. (1992). The "Jasper" series: An experiment with new ways to enhance mathematical thinking. In D. F. Halpern (Ed.), *Enhancing thinking skills in the sciences and mathematics* (pp. 15–38). Hillsdale, NJ: Erlbaum.

Wu, H. (1993). *Review of interactive mathematics program (IMP) at Berkeley High School* (commissioned report). Berkeley, CA: Berkeley High School.

Wu, H. (1997). The mathematics education reform: Why you should be concerned and what you can do. *American Mathematical Monthly, 104*, 946–954.

6

Effects of Dominant and Subordinate Masculinities on Interactions in a Collaborative Learning Classroom

Mary Barnes

INTRODUCTION

This chapter is based on the first stage of an ethnographic study of students' experiences of collaborative learning in secondary mathematics, which aims to investigate the interaction of student gender, the social construction of mathematical competence, and ways in which mathematics is valued. A class of Year 10 students in an independent coeducational school regularly worked in small groups on challenging mathematics problems, followed by reporting-back and whole-class discussion. One group of boys was observed to exert a disproportionate influence on classroom proceedings. Within the achievement-oriented culture of this school, these boys ("the Mates") came closest to the stereotype of hegemonic masculinity. They were able and ambitious, but restless and attention-seeking and frequently initiated off-task talk and banter. Another identifiable group of boys ("the Technophiles") were rather isolated within the class. They had poorer communication skills and valued obtaining an answer quickly more than justifying it to others. This chapter discusses the possible effects of these students' behavior on their own learning and that of their classmates, and makes some tentative suggestions about implications for teaching.

Why Collaborative Learning?

Collaborative learning—students working together, usually in small groups, on a shared activity and with a common goal—has been widely recommended in recent years as a strategy to enhance mathematics learning for all students (see, for example, Australian Education Council, 1991; National Council of Teachers of Mathematics, 1989). It is argued that social processes involving the negotiation of meaning play a key role in the learning of mathematics (Cobb & Bauersfeld, 1995), and that small-group discussions enable all students to be involved in the co-construction of "common knowledge" (Edwards & Mercer, 1987). However, as Neil Davidson and Diana Kroll observed,

> a relatively small percent of the studies have attempted to study the interactions that take place during cooperative work to determine how various academic, social, or psychological effects are produced. (Davidson & Kroll, 1991, p. 363)

Although more work along these lines has been done since 1991, understanding the effects of interactions within collaborative groups remains a key focus for researchers on collaborative learning.

Working collaboratively has also been seen as especially beneficial for girls. Reasons given are that most girls prefer collaboration to competition; girls generally have good communication skills and benefit from and enjoy discussion; small collaborative groups facilitate "connected" learning and support and encourage risk taking; and collaboration helps to create a more egalitarian environment (Cordeau, 1995; Jacobs, 1994; Morrow & Morrow, 1996; Solar, 1995). In a comparative study of two schools, Jo Boaler (1997a, 1997b, 1997c) found that girls in a school that used an approach based on collaboration and open-ended inquiry reported increased confidence and enjoyment of mathematics. Girls in a school with a similar population that used a traditional textbook-based approach reported widespread disaffection, lack of confidence, and the feeling that they were not being given a chance to understand.

For people concerned with gender equity, another potential benefit of the collaborative approach is that boys may play a less dominant role in small-group discussions than they do in whole-class teaching. Studies of the latter have consistently found that a disproportionate number of teacher-student interactions are with boys (Howe, 1997; Koehler, 1990; Leder, 1990). Collaborative work in small groups may allow more students the opportunity to articulate their ideas than would be possible in whole-class teaching, and so may have the effect of counteracting the tendency for a few males to dominate classroom interactions.

Although many studies of gender and classroom interaction, such as those cited earlier, have looked at the context of whole-class instruction, relatively few have investigated the influence of gender on interaction in a collaborative inquiry context. I am interested in how students interact with one another in such a classroom, and how student gender and the social construction of mathematical competence have an impact on one another.

Masculinities and Femininities As Social Constructs

As many writers have pointed out, neither biologically based theories nor sex-role socialization theories have been found adequate to explain the complex process of the formation of gender identity (see, for example, Connell, 1987; Davies, 1989; Gilbert & Gilbert, 1998; Mac an Ghaill & Haywood, 1998; Weiner, 1994). Feminist poststructuralist theory recognizes the ways in which gender is contested and reconstructed daily through the multiple discursive practices in which individuals participate (see Davies, 1989; Davies, 1994; Johnson, 1997; Jones, 1993; Walkerdine, 1986; Weedon, 1987). As Sally Johnson explains it:

> Masculinity and femininity are not character traits or social roles which are learned during childhood and adolescence, and which are fixed and intransigent in adult life. Instead, they are ongoing social processes dependent upon systematic restatement, a process which is variously referred to as "performing gender" or "doing identity work." (Johnson, 1997, p. 22)

Bronwyn Davies further claims that,

> Who one is is always an open question with a shifting answer depending on the positions made available within one's own and others' discursive practices and within those practices, the stories through which we make sense of our own and others' lives. (Davies, 1989, p. 229)

This theory implies that people's sense of who they are is dependent on the subject positions made possible for them by the available discourses. Although gender construction takes place largely within the discourses and practices of the family, the peer group, and the wider society, the school also plays an important part.

> Schools may be seen as active agents in the making of . . . femininities and masculinities. In this way, the official and hidden curricula do not merely reflect the dominant role models of the wider society, but actively produce a range of femininities and masculinities that are made available in local schooling arenas for pupils collectively to negotiate and inhabit within peer subcultures. (Mac an Ghaill & Haywood, 1998, p. 215).

My main interest is in what happens within the mathematics classroom. As students interact with one another while struggling to make meaning of the mathematical ideas they are encountering, they are at the same time developing ideas about how to learn mathematics, and constructing views of themselves as learners or doers of mathematics. These views, too, are not fixed, but may shift and change depending on the context, the other people with whom the student is interacting, and the discourses and power relations called into play—and in these processes gender plays a significant role.

A number of ethnographic studies of school peer groups, and in particular of boys in school (Beynon, 1989; Eckert, 1989; Mac an Ghaill, 1994; Walker, 1988; Weis, 1989; Willis, 1977) have identified subgroups which, despite inevitable within-group variability, could be observed to share a common subculture. As Rob and Pam Gilbert (1998) point out, different studies have identified groups with considerable degrees of similarity, and although group membership was continually shifting, it tended to stabilize as students grew older.

Maírtín Mac an Ghaill (1994) described a group in an English comprehensive school that he called "the Macho Lads." These represented a stereotype of hegemonic masculinity—tough, dominating, rebellious, and anti-school. Other studies have reported groups with broadly similar characteristics. For example, Jim Walker, in a study of an Australian inner-city school, identified an ascendant group "the footballers," who primarily valued sporting success in the dominant football code. They displayed aggressive competitiveness, liked to engage in jokes, insults, and real or pretend physical violence, and seemed to enjoy roving around in a restless way, dominating the space in the school grounds. In addition, they displayed a disdain for teacher values but, because they recognized the need for credentials, did not reject the school culture outright.

Many of the previously cited studies focused on disaffected students or troublemakers. Robert Connell, Dean Ashenden, Sandra Kessler, and Gary Dowsett (1982), on the other hand, showed that the form taken by hegemonic masculinity is class-dependent. In what they call "the ruling-class schools," they found a somewhat different form of dominant masculinity, "Motivated to compete, strong in the sense of one's own abilities, able to dominate others and to face down opponents in situations of conflict" (Connell et al., 1982, p. 73). Although this shares some of the toughness and dominance of Mac an Ghaill's "Macho Lads," and Walker's "footballers," it differs in important ways. It is not anti-school; indeed, it accepts and adopts the values promoted by the school. And the emphasis on competition and success means that both academic achievement and sporting prowess are valued.

Set in opposition to the dominant group in all these studies were other forms of masculinity and femininity. As one of Robert Connell's informants described it, "the cool guys hang out together, and the cool girls hang out together, and there was the swots and the wimps" (Connell, 1989, p. 295). In one of the "ruling-class schools" studied by Connell and associates, boys who rejected sporting prowess in favor of "study, debating, theatricals and the like" (Connell et al., 1982, p. 96) were scornfully dubbed "the Cyrils." Although relatively lacking in power and subject to derogatory comments, including implications of effeminacy or homosexuality, boys in such marginalized groups still struggled to maintain some status, and in particular to emphasize their superiority to girls. This was made explicit by one of Mac an Ghaill's "Academic Achievers," who explained his interest in literature as being the acquisition of expertise as a critic, which he saw as quite different from the approach taken by girls: "Because even if you're doing the same subjects, men and women have completely different things that they're interested in. I think that men would be more intellectual and women more emotional" (Parminder, quoted in Mac an Ghaill, 1994, p. 61). In the present study, I observed forms of masculinity that bore some similarities to those described earlier, and had an important influence on classroom interactions.

DESCRIPTION OF THE STUDY

Methods

The data reported here are drawn from an ethnographic study of a Year 10 mathematics class (students aged 15 to 16 years) in an independent, coeducational school in an Australian city. This study forms part of a larger study of collaborative learning in mathematics. The class of 22 students (11 males and 11 females) was following an accelerated mathematics program that included mathematical content, such as introductory calculus, normally studied in Year 11. This class had been formed to cater to students who were achieving very high grades in tests and examinations. These students were generally extremely able and ambitious. They were not, however, the highest-achieving mathematics students in their year—a more advanced accelerated class was following the full Year 11 course. The class was selected for the study because of the teacher's interest in, and experience in using, the collaborative inquiry approach described in the following pages.

The usual procedure in the class was for students to work in groups of three or four on challenging mathematical problems. This would be followed by a reporting-back session and whole-class discussion. A series of lessons was observed, and 17 of them were videotaped. Whenever the students were working in small groups, the camera was trained on one of these groups. Transcripts of the videotapes were prepared, including descriptions of actions, gestures, facial expressions, or voice intonations that were judged to be relevant. Interviews were conducted with eight students who had been selected as key informants, as well as the teacher and two senior members of the school executive. There were also separate interviews with groups of six girls and six boys. Data collected also included field notes, work sheets, student work samples, and general information about the school.

The Classroom Context

Although the school was coeducational, it had in other respects much in common with the "ruling-class schools" described by Connell and associates (1982). The predominating culture was competitive, emphasizing high achievement in all areas of the curriculum. There was a strong focus on examination success and, ultimately, on competition for university entrance. Alongside that, there was also an emphasis on the co-curriculum, especially a wide variety of sports, but also outdoor education, creative activities such as music and drama, and exchange visits to other countries. The very broad range of activities meant that students frequently missed classes because of other activities in which they were involved. The school prospectus also stressed opportunities for leadership, character development, and service to the wider community.

In mathematics, a traditional approach to teaching was the norm. The mathematics staff generally placed heavy reliance on the textbook and regular testing. Students came to expect large quantities of practice exercises, and to value only those activities that would contribute to their end-of-year grade. The teacher of the class in the study said she had noticed that if students were not going to be given a grade for a piece of work, or if they thought that a topic would not be tested in an examination, then they judged it to be of lesser importance. Comments from some of the students confirmed this attitude. For example, one student said,

The work that we're doing isn't actually something that we could be assessed on, in terms of having a test, so it kind of takes away a bit from the syllabus, from the curriculum that's been laid out. . . . And it may not sort of help us much for next year. (Jacqui)

In this case the work that they were doing was, in fact, an introduction to calculus, which would help them very much indeed for the following year. But because the introduction had been by means of a series of investigations, and the student could not see where they were leading, she had at that stage decided that it was unimportant and unlikely to be useful.

The teacher of the class in the study had introduced a collaborative inquiry approach, which involved students working together in small groups on substantive mathematical tasks. Although parts of these tasks at times involved familiar material, there were other parts for which the students had no learned routine, and for which they had to use their own resources to find a solution, by combining their knowledge of mathematics and other relevant topics and using a variety of problem-solving skills as well as imagination, intuition, and inspiration. While the groups were working, the teacher circulated and asked questions to help clarify understanding of the task, check progress, and encourage breakthroughs and explanations. From time to time, group members were asked to report their solutions to the rest of the class. This was usually followed by a whole-class discussion during which misunderstandings were cleared up, alternative methods proposed, and, where appropriate, generalizations formulated.

In attempting to make sense of the small-group interactions, I found it necessary to bear in mind the complexity of the classroom context, and the differing values and expectations of the teacher and the students. The students found themselves functioning at the intersection of several powerful but conflicting discourses: notably those of the school, their parents, the mathematics department, the class teacher, and the peer group.

The teacher had taken trouble to establish norms for behavior when students were working in groups. These included listening to other people, valuing what they said, justifying any assertions made, and making sure that everybody in the group understood the group's final solution. Her insistence on collaboration among the students, and on the need to understand and explain their solutions, and her downplaying of competition, rote learning, and mindless practice, meant that the culture this teacher was introducing in her classroom was to some extent in conflict with that predominating in the school, especially in other mathematics classes.

Most students valued and enjoyed the collaborative approach. Typical comments included the following:

I think it's really beneficial. Some people say "Oh, it's a bit of a bludge," but you know you've all got to put in . . . doing the group work we're doing at the moment we're all putting in ideas and getting the end result, which we probably couldn't do by ourselves. It's a good way to learn because you're getting other people's opinions, not just your own. (Jacqui) and,

> I like working in groups. . . . I find that usually if I don't understand something some-
> one else in the group might understand it, and you know because it's not the whole
> class you don't feel really embarrassed about saying, "I don't really get it, so can you
> explain it to me?" (Mandy)

My observations have led me to believe that, in general, the group collaborative
process was extremely effective. The students struggled with difficult ideas such as
limit and derivative, and in the process developed considerable insights, which, as
the previously quoted student claimed, they probably could not have achieved if
working by themselves. These insights were revealed and developed further
through whole-class discussions. For example, a number of very common misunderstandings about limits, which often cause students confusion for many years and
create problems at university level, were brought into the open by the students
themselves, and discussed at some length, until the class had reached a consensus
and everyone was satisfied. The students also began gradually to appreciate the
power of calculus as an analytical tool. As an illustration, when others in his group
explained to Adam how to use the derivative to find turning points, the following
exchange took place:

> Adam: It's a cubic—but we're doing it like a quadratic because of this beautiful deriv-
>   ative!
>
> Con: Yeah because of the derivative.
>
> Adam: It's beautiful! . . . Oh, I love it!

Incidents such as these led me to conclude that the students in this class were developing a far deeper understanding and appreciation of calculus concepts, in particular, of how derivatives are found and how they are used, than is usual at this
introductory stage.

The teacher had established a warm and friendly relationship with the class, and
the atmosphere was generally relaxed and positive. There was broad participation
in class discussions, and most students appeared to feel comfortable about contributing. I believe that it is important to emphasize these points, because the analysis
that follows focuses on factors that tended to disrupt the easy flow of communication, and I want to stress that these were noticeable because they represented a de-
parture from the norm.

On some occasions the collaboration was less effective than the teacher would
have wished. To a large extent, this appeared to result from the behaviors and attitudes of certain groups of boys, and it is on these groups that this chapter focuses.
The class teacher was aware of these groups and their behavior, but it is impossible
for anyone to hear and see everything that happens in a classroom. The researcher
with a camera has the advantage of being able to focus in detail on one group for a
whole lesson, and thus to become aware of the extent and the details of behaviors

far more than could be possible for any teacher, no matter how attentive and sensitive to group dynamics and student behavior in general.

There are also inherent problems arising from the presence of a researcher with a camera in the classroom. Some students obviously "play up" to the camera, whereas others may become more reticent. The teacher may feel constrained in what he or she does by a desire to assist the research, or may be consciously or unconsciously inhibited by the presence of a camera and an observer. As a result the teacher may not interact with the students in quite the same way as under normal circumstances. Thus, some aspects of behavior may be exaggerated, and some may be deemphasized. However, although the observer's presence may introduce some distortion to classroom interactions, it is highly unlikely that it will change the fundamental nature of these interactions.

OBSERVATIONS

The Mates

One group of five boys, Vic, Mike, Steve, Adam, and Con, "the Mates," exercised considerably more influence on class proceedings than the rest of the students. They knew one another well, having been together at the school for several years, and all were highly successful in a variety of sports. Most of them were in the same class for other school subjects, and shared in out-of-class activities, including the school band. Vic held a significant leadership position within the student body. The physical presence of these boys in the classroom was always noticeable. Their behavior was restless and attention-seeking; they tended to take up more space than other students, to move around more, and to make more noise.

My attention was first drawn to this group during a teacher-led whole-class lesson. When they were not working in groups, these boys always sat together in the front row, with the rest of the boys in the row behind, and the girls occupying the two back rows. From their position at the front, the dominant group was able to claim the teacher's attention more easily than other students. Because disaffected students tend to locate themselves away from the teacher's gaze to allow fuller rein to off-task activities, sitting at the front indicates an interest in learning. Nevertheless, the teacher's management of the lesson was made more difficult by frequent interruptions from this group—but they were work-related interruptions. These boys called out answers, asked questions, or made comments, while other students sat with their hands up waiting to be called on. Occasionally, there would be a chorus of answers to a question, and when this happened, the voices of this group, and particularly of Vic their leader, were clearly audible above all the rest.

When the teacher wanted the class to work in small groups, she usually selected the groups herself. She explained the reasons for this to the class in the following way:

I try and mix different thinking styles together, and different personalities. . . . So, in mixing you up, I'm trying to get a nice flow through of ways of thinking about the different tasks. (Sarah James, teacher)

In a subsequent interview she explained to me, "you need to make sure the groups are right or they're not going to work." In general, the Mates were placed in different groups. In spite of this, they maintained intermittent voice and eye contact with one another while they worked. This seemed to be mainly for the purpose of livening up the lesson and bringing in friendly rivalry. They monitored the progress of groups containing other Mates, attended to the teacher's evaluative comments about these groups, and remarked on them. For example:

Teacher's voice in the background [to Steve's group.]: Very good! Well done!

Mike: Well done! What ho, Stevo. (Lesson 2)

Teacher's voice in background: A few of the groups are a bit stuck, so we may need to—

Steve: [in amused voice] Are you stuck, West? [to Mike West, in another group] (Lesson 6)

In this way, they introduced an element of competition to the collaborative tasks. They vied with one another for their group to be finished first, and boasted jokingly about their success. For example, in response to an inaudible question from another group, Mike was heard to reply,

That's basic, look. . . . It's cos we're so good, you know. (Lesson 2)

The Mates were confident in their interactions with other students and quite willing to make use of their expertise. When disagreement about an answer arose within Vic's group, he sought confirmation, first by eavesdropping on another group, and then by asking them directly:

We're on the same track as what they're on. Two point four two. [Turns round and calls out] Sally, I heard two point four two, which is exactly what we've got. Is that right for graphing the thing? [shows calculator to Sally] (Lesson 15)

From time to time, there were brief episodes of banter between groups, or talk about irrelevant off-task topics such as sport or TV programs. Throughout the 17 lessons recorded, I observed frequent instances of students calling out comments from one group to another in this way; in all but one case these exchanges were initiated by one of the Mates. From time to time, two of the Mates in different groups would make eye contact, and then join in softly singing or beating out a rhythm on the desk.

If a group contained only one of the Mates, this boy frequently took on the role of "manager"—calling the group to order, reading out the questions, keeping them on task. Occasionally, this appeared to be a device to avoid having to do too much thinking—the "manager" read out the questions, waited for other group members to suggest answers, and wrote these down. But on many other occasions, the student combined the managerial role with full participation in the problem-solving process. On the other hand, when another student in the group had taken on the role of manager, the Mate was likely to display frequent signs of boredom, intermittently tuning out from the discussion and either resting his head on the desk or leaning back in his seat and looking around the room. When the teacher joined the group, however, the Mate paid full attention and took a major part in the discussion, even if it concerned ideas and results to which he had contributed little. To some extent this can be seen as appropriating other group members' work. An extreme example of claiming ownership of others' work occurred when Vic left two girls in his group to carry out necessary calculations while he joked with students in another group, and then turned back to the girls and asked, "What've we got?"

On the few occasions when circumstances made it necessary for two or more of the Mates to be in the same group, the amount of off-task conversation, banter, singing, and "fooling around" significantly increased. In their talk, these boys hinted at a degree of worldly experience, by discussing such topics as girls, horse racing, and betting. There was, however, no way of knowing how much of this was exaggeration. In talk with other students they often displayed an attitude of not taking work seriously, but when it came to receiving marks for their efforts this was revealed to be a pose—they took this aspect of their work very seriously indeed. When Vic, in particular, received a grade lower than he thought he deserved, he made no attempt to hide his astonishment, said he thought it was unfair, and later argued with the teacher about his mark.

The Mates appeared to enjoy reporting on their group's work to the rest of the class. They were willing to volunteer to do so, and were generally effective reporters. But when other students were reporting they displayed a tendency to interject, make jokes, make faces or laugh, and in a variety of ways to disrupt the reporting process. Sometimes the reporter was distracted by this treatment, but on other occasions laughed it off. When the teacher reprimanded them for interrupting the student at the board, the response was, "It's okay, we're mates" (Lesson 6).

Two of the boys from this group were interviewed and proved to be charming and very happy to talk about themselves. Both revealed that they had been recognized as good at mathematics, and had enjoyed it, in primary and the lower years of secondary school. They had been achieving very high marks before being selected for the accelerated class, but were now finding it more effort, were not always so successful, and so tended to become bored. Both spoke of "tuning out" in mathematics lessons:

I find it too easy to tune out in maths and I do get a bit bored. And when I get behind, I don't know what's going on, don't understand it. (Adam)

There may be times when you may not do much work because you just tune out together, and you sort of talk to the other person a lot. It occasionally happens with me, because I get lapses in concentration. (Vic)

Note that Vic seems to be suggesting that his lapses in concentration just happen—they are not his responsibility.

Responses to a questionnaire completed by all students in the class revealed that all the Mates were planning careers in either business or medicine. On items measuring attitudes to mathematics, they gave broadly similar responses to the rest of the class, with one exception. In spite of the broad range of applications that the teacher had presented, they tended to hold more strongly than others in the class the view that the main importance of mathematics is as a credential, a necessary qualification to gain entry into a career or course of study, rather than something interesting or likely to be useful to them personally. As the two Mates interviewed said,

> Some areas I think, I just think to myself, "Why, why are we doing this, because there will be no way that I will use this later on in life." (Vic)

> I don't have any trouble doing the problems and working out the answers, but I can never understand the point of it. (Adam)

Questionnaire responses also indicated that the Mates also tended to hold less strongly than others a view of mathematics as a cohesive subject, that is, a view that focuses on the connections between mathematical concepts, and between mathematics and other subjects, including real world applications. The latter point was reinforced by Vic's observation,

> I also see it as very mixed, mixed up, that there's so many workings and problems and functions that it's all over the place for me. (Vic)

Both boys claimed that they did not mind challenging tasks, but showed no enthusiasm for them and said they preferred to tackle such tasks in a group. They admitted to a tendency not to persevere very long with something difficult if they were on their own.

> If I get stuck on one thing, or have trouble getting started, I just stop and I just can't do anything else. (Adam)

In an interview with a group including four of the Mates, they claimed that they "muck around" because "it makes it more fun." While admitting that this fooling around might distract others, Vic added confidently and rather selfishly, "as our marks show, not us."

The Technophiles

Three other boys, Robert, John, and Charles, formed a contrast in behavior to the Mates. This group appeared to be somewhat isolated socially from the rest of the class. If given the choice, they sat together and worked together. Although there were considerable individual differences in personality among the three, they all had a keen interest in computers, and expressed the desire to follow careers in science, engineering, or information technology. They were quick to make use of their graphics calculators in exploring and solving mathematics problems, and displayed a facility in their use. I have chosen to characterize them as "the Technophiles."

During small-group discussions, the Technophiles usually stuck to the point. They took little part in irrelevant talk, and when they had completed the set task would sit quietly while others chatted. They were very focused on the problem, and on getting a solution as quickly as possible. In part, this seemed to be because it gave them a sense of superiority:

> It makes me feel glad when my group's worked it out before any other group. I like that when I know that I've got something right and heaps of other people are still struggling. (John)

In their rush to solve a problem, they often made authoritative pronouncements, apparently expecting others to follow their reasoning, or simply to accept what they said. They appeared to be more interested in getting an answer quickly than in exploring possibilities or seeking alternative approaches. Although they agreed that it was helpful to discuss ideas with friends, they preferred to attempt problems by themselves first. As Robert said:

> It's probably best if you can get away, do it your own way, see if you can get it to work, and then get together, see how each of you's done it, see who's right, how you've done it, if there's a consensus. . . . (Robert)

When other students were in a group with only one of the Technophiles, they tended to use him as an expert resource, asking him questions, and persuading him to do the calculations, or work them out on his calculator. On the other hand, when two of the Technophiles worked together, they communicated with one another in brief, rather cryptic remarks, which others found difficult to follow. They seemed to be unaware of the extent to which this excluded other students from the discussion. In whole-class lessons, the Technophiles frequently volunteered answers, but otherwise did not draw attention to themselves.

The teacher reported that written assignments from all three boys were inadequate and did not reflect their understanding. Work was frequently submitted late, was shallow or scrappy, and appeared to indicate lack of effort. John and Robert (the only two interviewed) claimed that they were not good at written explanations and tended to excuse themselves by downplaying the importance of this skill.

> I'm not so good on my writing up. I just get the answer, because I know that's the answer, but then I can't explain it mathematically a lot of the time. . . . I can explain it on the board, I can say why it is, but I just can't write up the sum, and say this is why it is, and [sigh]. (Robert)

> I just prefer the actual solving to the communicating of it. I mean, like, I'm usually not really worried about sort of like—I mean I'm interested in being an engineer . . . other

people will probably be more interested in the answer than how you actually got the answer, unless they're trying to solve things like that themselves. (John)

Because the three Technophiles had very different personalities and did not form such a tightly knit group as the Mates, it may help to understand some of their behavior and attitudes if we briefly consider them separately.

To the extent that the group had a leader, it was John. He was very quick at problem solving and was perceived by the teacher to be the most mathematically able of the three, in fact, one of the two most mathematically able in the class. He claimed to like mathematics because of its logic, and preferred to learn by thinking about it by himself. He explained that he learned mathematics best by:

> having notes put up on the board . . . and then trying to understand them myself, and usually I find that a lot of the time I just need to do a couple of examples and then I understand it. (John)

It is not clear what exactly John meant by "understand." He claimed to be able to pick things up quickly, but observation of his interaction in groups suggests that he may have been more focussed on knowing what to do than on knowing why. After talking about the logic of mathematics, he went on to speak of "going through the various processes, to work out the answer." It is possible that he liked to see why each step followed from the one before, but was less interested in deeper understandings, such as getting a more holistic picture of a topic or making connections with other aspects of mathematics.

He was less enthusiastic about the value of collaboration than most of the other students in the class. He said "they [i.e., other students in the group] just help you understand a bit better, and learn it a bit better, and point out where you're wrong," but then added, "I don't know whether you necessarily learn better in groups." Robert, his friend, described him as uninterested in listening to other students, because his own ideas were usually better. He also claimed that John at times made use of other people's ideas but was reluctant to give them credit for them. John was not very interested in explaining or justifying his statements to others:

> I'm not sort of trying to—when I'm working through the problem I'm not trying to do it so that other people can understand it, it's just so that I can get the answer. (John)

> I don't really feel very concerned with having everybody understanding just what I did, as long as myself and a couple of other people understand it, and we think it's right, then I'm happy. (John)

He was willing to report to the class on his group's solutions but admitted to some reservations about this, because he found explaining his ideas difficult:

> I often feel that perhaps other people might not understand what I'm saying, like when I do go up and have to show how I got it on the board, I find I usually have to be like re-

ally basic, like I suppose I speak a little bit slowly. Perhaps sometimes I'll go through
it slowly, thinking that some people might not understand. (John)

From the way it was said, I interpret this statement as reflecting a sense of superiority to the other students rather than feelings of inadequacy about his own communication skills.

John showed an interest in practical interpretations of the mathematics they
were doing, speculating, for example, about what road or traffic conditions might
have caused a car to travel more slowly for one section of its journey, although this
was not a question that had been asked. He looked for ways to generalize results,
explaining that a generalization would save time by providing a quick method of
solving a large number of problems.

Robert was much more thoughtful than John and showed no signs of John's arro-
gance. He showed more awareness of other students' reactions and sensitivity to
their feelings. Although not as quick at solving problems, his responses to the questionnaire indicated that he derived more enjoyment from mathematics than John
and felt more confident in face of the challenges inherent in problem solving. He,
too, appreciated practical aspects of mathematics, especially applications to science, and did not enjoy repetitive practice.

Robert was also a better oral communicator than John, and discoursed at considerable length in the interviews. He was eager to explain his group's solutions to the
class, believing that he was good at it (an opinion with which the teacher con-
curred), but he had some hesitations about how other students perceived him.

Well, sometimes they don't value what I'm saying. Like, they don't think of me highly
as someone who um, who is good at this. (Robert)

He had observed that, apart from the other Technophiles, students in the class sel-
dom sought his opinion, preferring to ask people like Mike (one of the Mates).

Everyone reckons he's like really good at maths, so they always ask him, you know,
"What's this?" Now I don't usually, I don't usually get asked, at all. (Robert)

Robert admired John, and enjoyed working with him, but sometimes found it
hard to keep up with his thinking:

. . . he does go extremely fast, and it's hard for me to follow. Sometimes I go oh oh oh
slow down, John. Just tell me what you've done, and then he goes, right. You know he
tells me like commando talk. (Robert)

Robert's admiration for and friendship with John may have caused him to under-
value his own real strengths. By adopting John's rather cryptic "commando talk,"
and in part his attitude of superiority, Robert may have isolated himself from the
rest of the class, and so failed to gain as much from the collaborative process as he
might otherwise have done. They may also have encouraged one another in devalu-
ing written explanations.

Robert and John were not exclusively focused on science and technology. Both had a range of other interests, including drama and various sports (though unlike the Mates they did not excel at sport). Charles fitted more closely to the stereotype of "nerd," lacking both social and communication skills. He appeared nervous both in small groups and whole-class discussions. Within a group, he tended to be inarticulate, making suggestions, but often failing to explain them clearly enough for the others to follow his thinking. As a result, his ideas were frequently ignored, and he withdrew into silence. Unfortunately, Charles was not one of the key informants in the study. Without knowing more about him and his background, it is impossible to tell whether his nervousness and inarticulateness may be a consequence of previous disparaging comments or negative interactions with other students. He did, however, make insightful contributions to whole-class discussions, especially when encouraged by the teacher. In this situation, the teacher's authority lent weight to his ideas, and the other students were more prepared to listen to him.

The Rest of the Class

After these detailed descriptions of the behavior and attitudes of two groups of boys, it is natural to wonder about the rest of the class. Were there similar groups of girls with distinct behaviors, attitudes, and values? And what about the remaining boys?

Although there were equal numbers of girls and boys in the class, the girls seemed to operate as a single group, rather than forming cliques or gangs as the boys did. Although it was possible to identify groups of girls with similar characteristics—for example, there were several confident, active, and powerful girls with good leadership skills who spoke out readily in discussions, and a number of quieter, more studious girls—these groups did not keep to themselves but mixed with all the others. On the occasions when the students were free to choose where to sit, the girls all sat in the back two rows, but I could discern no patterns in who sat with whom. Even pairs of close friends did not always sit together.

The small discussion groups generally worked well, but groups consisting entirely or mainly of girls appeared to function particularly effectively, keeping on task and involving everyone in the discussion. As Jacqui explained, referring to an all-female group she had recently been in, "we're all putting in ideas and getting the end result." Although this group was not videotaped, Jacqui's comment was confirmed by the teacher's observation that the group had worked well together.

The Mates tended to try to position girls as helpers or assistants, but the girls often resisted being given orders, as the following exchange illustrates:

Vic: Will it still fold into a box, this sheet of paper? [Raised voice to attract attention]

[Vic takes the sheet of paper from Zoe, gestures with it, then gives it back to her.]

[Zoe smiles and nods.]

Vic: Fold it into a box then.[Challenging tone of voice. Sits back, chin on hands.]

Zoe: To get it into a box, you'll have to cut out the corners. No, you can easily fold it.
[Pushes the paper back towards Vic]

If the Mates showed a tendency to fool around, a girl was likely to take the lead in
managing the group, so that they could get on with the work. As Sally explained:

Let's say I was in a group with three males, there'd be no question, I'd just do it [i.e.,
take the lead] straight away without thinking about it, because, with all due respect
they're sort of, they're really unmotivated and they'd rather discuss the weekend
sporting event or, you know, the latest chick at the disco, or whatever. . . . It tends to be
the really blokey blokes that can't get focused, but . . . if you just get them going, then
it happens. (Sally)

Other girls expressed similar attitudes. From the description she gave, Sally was
presumably referring to the Mates. She made it clear, however, that taking the lead
was largely a matter of self-interest on her part:

I just basically took on the thought that if I don't do it, nobody else is going to do it, and
we're all going to sit here and do absolutely nothing and get nowhere, and then have to
do it for homework, and that's going to be a pain in the neck. (Sally)

Publicly, the girls appeared to tolerate and even excuse the Mates' tendency to
interject and disrupt when another student was reporting. Referring to one incident,
Jacqui said:

Mandy got up to report, and Vic was just, you know, making a bit of a fool of her. . . .
They're pretty good friends, so he's allowed to. He wouldn't do that to anyone he
wasn't really friends with. (Jacqui)

Jacqui admitted that "it can be a bit intimidating sometimes, if you're not really
that sure." The intimidation came from the "louder" (male) half of the class and
made her feel that "you'd rather not make a mistake, yeah, cos it would definitely
get picked up." Some of the other girls, however, did not appear to feel like this.
They were quite capable of keeping the Mates under control, speaking out if one of
the Mates overstepped the line and giving back as good as they got. The shyer boys,
on the other hand, may have been as much intimidated by the Mates' behavior as
any of the girls. During my discussion with the group of girls, they described the
Mates as "the louder ones" and said:

Megan: They've got their own group of friends and they sort of "Yeah I want to work
with them cos they're my mates."

. . .

Jacqui: They're more interested in talking about the latest footy scores, cricket or ra
-cing.

. . .

Zoe: There's a lot of guys in this class who've got—

Megan:—testosterone overload.

Zoe: Yeah, overload! [General laughter, indicating agreement]

This indicates that these girls tended not to take the Mates too seriously. However, the testosterone comment shows that they may have accepted the discourse of biological essentialism as an explanation for the Mates' behavior. They also accepted to some extent the idea that they should able to "take a joke" without revealing weakness.

The Technophiles tended to position other students as less able, and sometimes ignored their attempts to contribute to a discussion. Reporting on her experience of working with Robert and John, Jacqui said:

> They're sort of friends with each other, and it's kind of weird because I don't really associate with them that much, and they're sort of they're like happy to do it all by themselves, and they'll be, they'll want to be the first to finish it, and they're not really into interacting with the other members of the group . . . they were just really concerned with getting it for their own benefit, rather than trying to work in the group. . . . I think they've got to learn to work in a group properly. (Jacqui)

This shows that Jacqui recognized and rejected the boys' competitive attitudes and placed responsibility for the lack of effective communication at their door. Some of her other comments indicated that being excluded from the discussion by these two boys had not in the long term affected her confidence in herself. I thought that the girls displayed considerable insight into the weaknesses of both groups, as Jacqui did in this example.

A few boys in the class appeared to belong to neither of the two groups described. One was a would-be Mate, not fully accepted by the group, but sharing many of their attitudes and behaviors, and associating with them when the opportunity arose. The remaining two were very quiet and did little to draw attention to themselves. They contributed in small-group discussions, but less than most other students. They did not volunteer to report on their group's work, nor did they say much in whole-class discussions. As they were not among the key informants interviewed, I did not get to know so much about them.

MASCULINITIES AND POWER

Masculinity is associated with power, and different forms of masculinity are related to different forms of power:

> Social power in terms of access to higher education, entry to professions, command of communication, is being delivered by the school system to boys who are academic "successes." The reaction of the "failed" is likely to be a claim to other sources of power, even other definitions of masculinity. Sporting prowess, physical aggression, sexual conquest may do. (Connell, 1989, p. 295)

Connell describes the resulting "contest for hegemony between rival versions of masculinity" as not a matter of individual choice, but "something that happens at

the level of the institution and in the organization of peer-group relationships"
(1989, p. 295).

Within the achievement-oriented culture of an independent school such as the
one in this study, and in particular within this class, selected because of the students'
previous success in mathematics, we might expect to find fewer differences between groups than in comprehensive secondary schools such as those studied by
Walker (1988) and Mac an Ghaill (1994). In particular, no differences based on social class were observable among the students, although undoubtedly the families
were not all equally prosperous and some may have struggled to pay the school
fees. Nevertheless, conflicting versions of masculinity could be discerned, and
each made claim to some form of power. As Rob and Pam Gilbert explain:

> While the physical dominance of the macho boys may place them in a powerful posi-
> tion in the peer culture, all the groups present themselves as powerful and superior in
> terms of some criterion, be it intellectual hardness, coolness and style, or pragmatic
> careerism. All these qualities can be a source of strength and toughness. (Gilbert &
> Gilbert, 1998, p. 142)

The Mates

The masculinity of the Mates was based in part on sporting prowess, and the ku-
dos which that brought within this school. Up to a point, it was very physical—the
Mates made use of body posture, movement, gestures, and tones of voice to draw
attention to themselves and maintain a dominant position in the classroom. However, intelligence, quick thinking, and verbal wit also played a part. They had not
only established a degree of dominance over other students, but also from time to
time attempted to test the authority of the teacher. Their behavior brings strongly to
mind the description of masculinity as performance (Johnson, 1997). Here, the performance seemed to be primarily for the benefit of the others in their group, and
only secondly for the teacher and the rest of the class. It was their means of establishing and maintaining group membership.

Although there was considerable variability within the group, these boys tended
to be extroverts, to seek or even demand attention, and to enjoy being in the lime-
light. Lynn Davies (1984) has given a definition of power as applied specifically to
school students that provides some insight into this attention-seeking behavior:

> Power has to be more than the ability to make others do what you want, or allow you to
> do what you want.... Power is not the same as status, though status may be an alterna-
> tive to power.... In its broadest sense, power is the ability to alter the course of events,
> to create a happening, *whether or not a particular end is in view*. (Davies, 1984, p. 3;
> italics in original)

Generally the Mates had good opinions of themselves, although one admitted pri-
vately to a lack of confidence. Appearing "cool" seemed to be paramount: they
projected the attitude that life, and school work, were not to be taken too seriously.
The pose of not taking work seriously, and not putting in too much effort, can be seen

as a defense against failure: if they did not try too hard, they could not be said to have failed, and could always claim that if they had tried they would have succeeded brilliantly.

All of the Mates were thinking about careers that would eventually place them in positions of authority, and their approach to school appeared to be a (probably unconscious) preparation for this. The wide range of activities in which they were involved was helping them to build networks of contacts. In group discussions, they liked to be in control and tended to lose interest if they were not.

These boys represent hegemonic masculinity as expressed within the culture of this school. This differs significantly from the form of hegemonic masculinity described, for example, by Mac an Ghaill as the "Macho Lads" or by Walker as the "footballers." Like these groups, sport played a significant role for the Mates, but unlike them, the Mates were neither underachieving nor antischool, but able and ambitious. They established their sense of identity through the school, by identifying strongly with the values of the school, and engaging in a wide variety of school-related activities.

The Technophiles

The Technophiles displayed a more rational form of masculinity. It was associated with ideas and the acquisition of knowledge—but not with the sharing of the ideas and knowledge with others. They were impressed by the power of mathematics to explain the physical world, and its usefulness in science and other practical applications.

This group shares some of the characteristics of Mac an Ghaill's "New Enterprisers," especially their interest in technology. In contrast to the overt, but joking, boastfulness of the Mates, the Technophiles kept their thoughts to themselves, but in private considered themselves superior thinkers and looked down a little on those whom they saw as less bright. One described the other two as "very, very intelligent . . . very smart" and himself as "catching on to things extremely quickly." They seemed a little resentful that the rest of the class did not acknowledge their ability. Although they knew that they had the respect of others in their group, they would also have liked wider recognition.

They were introspective, and appeared to value ideas more than relationships. They took mathematics seriously, and this may not have been seen as "cool" by the other students. As a result they tended to be marginalized, both by the Mates and by the girls, who saw them as "a bit weird." Although some of the girls also took mathematics seriously, the Technophiles distanced themselves from them by their unwillingness or inability to communicate. Marginalized to a greater or lesser extent by others in the class, they maintained their belief in themselves, and their sense of superiority, by competing to be the first to solve a problem, and by acknowledging one another's ability. Their status in the class was established through the mediation of the teacher, who encouraged them to explain their ideas to the class and praised them when they showed insight or developed "good" solutions to problems. It is unfortunate that their attitudes and values did not always facilitate their productive participation in small-group discussions.

Conflicting Discourses

This classroom was situated at the intersection of a number of conflicting discourses. As previously explained, the students generally adopted and supported the teacher's discourse on the value of learning by collaborative investigation. Interviews conducted a year after the initial period of research revealed that in retrospect they appreciated even more strongly the value they had derived from learning in this way.

Some students, however, attempted to mobilize other discourses in opposition to the teacher and in support of their own ends, such as avoiding effort or livening up lessons. At times students appealed to the discourse of traditional mathematics teaching to dispute the teacher's agenda, questioning, for example, whether work they were doing was going to be assessed. At other times, they appealed to the school's discourse on the importance of sport and other extra-curricular activities, explaining that it was not their fault when they missed lessons—these other activities made it necessary. And at times other class members supported the Mates' discourse about not taking work too seriously, by joining in the talk and the joking, and even accepting a certain degree of mockery with only minimal protest.

The cases of two students illustrate these conflicts clearly. Mike managed a delicate balancing act, taking part in all of the fun and banter of the Mates, but still managing to maintain a high standard of work and comply with everything the teacher asked. As a result, he was subjected to occasional teasing by the other Mates. In this case, there appears to have been a conflict between the values of hard work and achievement supported by his family, and the values and practices of the Mates. Mike resolved this by joining in the talk and joking in class, but working very hard at home to catch up with his work, bring notes up to date, and practice techniques and problems.

Robert, one of the Technophiles, was strongly influenced by his admiration for John. He allowed himself at times to be positioned as John's assistant and appeared to accept many of John's values instead of the values of collaborative learning promoted by the teacher. As a result, he tended to concentrate on trying to keep up with John, to the neglect of some of his own abilities. Robert was more reflective than John and had more skill with words. He might have gained much more from the collaborative work and contributed more to others' learning if he had been less keen to keep up with John, and more willing to listen to others, share his ideas with them, and explore the possibilities inherent in open-ended problems instead of rushing toward closure.

POSSIBLE CONSEQUENCES OF THE OBSERVED BEHAVIORS

Effects on the Students' Own Learning

In their desire to appear "cool," to have fun, and to guard against the appearance of failure, the Mates did not put as much effort into their work as they might have done and, hence, did not achieve as thorough an understanding of the mathematical concepts as they could have. The teacher reported that written work they handed in was often superficial. She said they did not "do themselves justice," and they made the same admission themselves in interviews, possibly echoing the words of teachers or parents.

By focussing on their own ways of solving problems, and disregarding alternative approaches, the Technophiles failed to gain as much as they might otherwise have done from the exchange of ideas. They undervalued the improved understanding that most students derive from explaining their ideas to others. Their poor written communication skills had a detrimental effect on their assessments in mathematics. Unless this improved, it would very likely seriously hinder their progress in future mathematics courses that were important for their career goals. Again, they could be described as not doing themselves justice—in this case because the ideas and insight they displayed in class discussions were not translated into assessable written work.

Effects on Other Students

The Mates tended to distract other students with their talk and fooling around and may have caused some, especially shyer students, to hesitate to put forward their ideas for fear of ridicule. Students who were deterred in this way from taking part in discussions would be disadvantaged by being deprived of opportunities to try out and develop their ideas. The off-task talk initiated by the Mates was more frequent than that of other students, male or female, and more disruptive. This slowed the progress of the whole class on occasions. In one documented incident, a group spent 2 minutes talking about betting at the races. As a result, when the teacher asked the class to stop work for a reporting-back session, they had not completed everything expected of them, forcing the teacher to change her plans and switch to discussing a different problem.

The Technophiles tended to pay less attention to ways of thinking that were different from their own. Consequently, a reduced range of points of view was represented in some of the small-group discussions, which were less rich and less productive than might have been the case. As a result, the others did not benefit as much as might have been possible from the interchange of ideas. The teacher countered this as far as possible by drawing out a range of ideas in class discussions.

IMPLICATIONS FOR TEACHING

As I observed it in action in this classroom, the overall success of the collaborative inquiry approach was evident. Further evidence not presented here indicated that this approach to learning resulted in a deep understanding of the subject matter. When student-student and student-teacher interactions during collaborative inquiry lessons were compared with interactions during whole-class lessons involving the same class and teacher, it was clear that there was a substantial reduction in the disadvantage to girls and the less assertive boys. More opportunities were available to them to express and develop their ideas, as well as to ask questions and receive explanations. Students who had been in this class were observed the following year to be more open to challenge and better able to think for themselves than other students, including some who had been judged by the school to be more mathematically able. Although this chapter has focused on some situations in which the outcomes of collaboration were less than optimal, this should not be allowed to detract from the overall effectiveness of this teaching approach.

No teacher can be aware of everything that goes on in a classroom while he or she is circulating around the groups and guiding their discussions. However, students who share a culture similar to that of the Mates need to be monitored carefully. To minimize potentially disruptive behavior, it may help to avoid having several of these students in the same group, as the teacher in this study did whenever possible. Teachers may find it necessary to check that all students have fully participated in the working out of the group's solution and have not left the details to one or two. There needs to be a very strong emphasis on accountability, on listening to others' ideas, and on every group member being able to explain all details of the group's solution. When the teacher joins a group to check progress, the tendency of students like the Mates to appropriate other students' work can be guarded against by directing questions to others and not allowing one student to become the main spokesperson. Students in a group who have said nothing in the discussion with the teacher need to be explicitly invited to contribute.

Students such as the Technophiles need to be convinced of the importance of both written and oral communication skills and given assistance in improving them. Establishing a supportive environment in which everyone is valued and no one is ever disparaged or made fun of will aid oral communication. The importance of listening to others also needs to be stressed to all students, but especially this group. As with the Mates, avoiding, if possible, placing two of these students in the same group will help. Because they take careers and higher education seriously, visitors holding scientific or technical jobs, or university students of science or technology, could be invited to visit the class to tell something about their work, including the important role of communication in their working lives—written reports and papers, oral presentations at conferences or meetings, grant applications, and so on. It may also help to stress the importance of keeping clear records of what they have done, to which they can return much later to help them recall what they did. David Clarke has described an assessment exercise (Clarke, 1996) in which a class is presented with several sample student reports of variable quality, and students are asked to study and compare them and work out for themselves what constitutes an excellent report. Such an exercise would benefit all students, but might be of particular help in convincing students such as the Technophiles of the importance of learning how to communicate mathematics.

CONCLUSION

Most studies of collaborative learning in mathematics have treated boys as a homogeneous group, whereas studies of the construction of masculinities have focused on schooling generally rather than specific subject areas. The results reported here provide a better understanding of factors influencing classroom interactions in the context where a teacher in a prosperous, independent school implements collaborative learning in mathematics. The observations emphasize the importance of taking into account socially constructed versions of masculinity and femininity when studying students' behavior in the mathematics classroom.

Comparison of student behavior during collaborative group work with the behaviors of the same students in a whole-class teaching context suggests that teachers may be able to decrease the influence of dominant groups of males by adopting a collaborative inquiry approach. However, the results also emphasize the need to monitor carefully and control the behavior of certain groups of males.

Some issues remain unresolved and will be the focus of further investigations. One of these is the extent to which the observations may be generalized beyond the particular class and school in which the research was carried out. The role of the culture of the school in determining which forms of masculinity are endorsed and which are marginalized needs to be considered. In this context, however, it is worth noting that when the behavior of the Mates and the Technophiles was described to a group of teachers from other schools, several acknowledged that they recognized the types of boys described. One said, "I have boys like these in my class," and others agreed.

Another question requiring more study is what forms of femininity may be found in the class, and in which ways the girls' behaviors and values influence, and are influenced by, the collaborative learning environment and the different forms of masculinity. Further research is also needed to investigate the constructions of masculinity and femininity likely to be found in schools such as rural schools and metropolitan schools catering to students of lower socioeconomic background, whose student populations differ in important ways from the school in this study. The effectiveness of the recommended strategies for teachers also remains untested.

As a guard against stereotyping students by gender, ethnicity, social class, or any other category, teachers frequently claim that they treat each child as an individual. But emphasizing students' individual characteristics may cause teachers to focus on psychological traits at the expense of the social context and social relationships within the classroom, and to avoid interrogating their own behaviors, attitudes, and values. This chapter has drawn attention to the importance of looking at subgroups of students within a class and, in particular, the specific discourses of masculinity operating within some such subgroups. These discourses intersect with students' direct experience of collaborative learning in mathematics and help to construct the cultural climate of the class as a whole.

ACKNOWLEDGMENTS

I thank Chris Brew, Leone Burton, David Clarke, Sue Helme, Gaell Hildebrand, and Gaye Williams for their helpful comments on earlier versions of this chapter. I would also like to thank the teacher and students of the class in the study for their willing and friendly cooperation.

REFERENCES

Australian Education Council. (1991). *A national statement on mathematics for Australian schools*. Carlton, Victoria, Australia: Curriculum Corporation.

Beynon, J. (1989). "A school for men": An ethnographic case study of routine violence in schooling. In S. Walker & L. Barton (Eds.), *Politics and the processes of schooling* (pp. 191–217). Milton Keynes, UK: Open University Press.

Boaler, J. (1997a). Equity, empowerment and different ways of knowing. *Mathematics Education Research Journal, 9*, 325–342.

Boaler, J. (1997b). *Experiencing school mathematics: Teaching styles, sex and setting*. Buckingham, UK: Open University Press.

Boaler, J. (1997c). Reclaiming school mathematics: The girls fight back. *Gender and Education, 9*, 285–305.

Clarke, D. J. (1996). Quality mathematics: How can we tell? In D. V. Lambdin, P. E. Kehle, & R. V. Preston (Eds.), *Emphasis on assessment: Readings from NCTM's school-based journals* (pp. 70–72). Reston, VA: National Council of Teachers of Mathematics.

Cobb, P., & Bauersfeld, H. (1995). *The emergence of mathematical meaning: Interaction in classroom cultures*. Hillsdale, NJ: Erlbaum.

Connell, R. W. (1987). *Gender and power*. Sydney, Australia: Allen & Unwin.

Connell, R. W. (1989). Cool guys, swots and wimps: The interplay of masculinity and education. *Oxford Review of Education, 15*, 291–303.

Connell, R. W., Ashenden, D. J., Kessler, S. J., & Dowsett, G. W. (1982). *Making the difference: Schools, families and social division*. Sydney, Australia: Allen & Unwin.

Cordeau, A. (1995). Empowering young women in mathematics: Two important considerations. In B. Grevholm & G. Hanna (Eds.), *Gender and mathematics education: An ICMI study in Stiftsgården Åkersberg, Höör, Sweden 1993* (pp. 121–128). Lund, Sweden: Lund University Press.

Davidson, N., & Kroll, D. L. (1991). An overview of research on cooperative learning related to mathematics. *Journal for Research in Mathematics Education, 22*, 362–365.

Davies, B. (1989). The discursive production of the male/female dualism in school settings. *Oxford Review of Education, 15*, 229–241.

Davies, B. (1994). *Poststructuralist theory and classroom practice*. Geelong, Victoria, Australia: Deakin University Press.

Davies, L. (1984). *Pupil power: Deviance and gender in school*. London: Falmer.

Eckert, P. (1989). *Jocks and burnouts*. New York: Teachers College Press.

Edwards, D., & Mercer, N. (1987). *Common knowledge: The development of understanding in the classroom*. London: Methuen.

Gilbert, R., & Gilbert, P. (1998). *Masculinity goes to school*. Sydney, Australia: Allen & Unwin.

Howe, C. (1997). *Gender and classroom interaction*. Edinburgh, Scotland: Scottish Council for Research in Education.

Jacobs, J. E. (1994). Feminist pedagogy and mathematics. *Zentralblatt für Didaktik der Mathematik, 26*(1), 12–17.

Johnson, S. (1997). Theorizing language and masculinity: A feminist perspective. In S. Johnson & U. H. Meinhof (Eds.), *Language and masculinity* (pp. 8–26). Oxford, UK: Blackwell.

Jones, A. (1993). Becoming a "girl": Post-structuralist suggestions for educational research. *Gender and Education, 5,* 157–167.

Koehler, M. S. (1990). Classrooms, teachers, and gender differences in mathematics learning. In E. Fennema & G. C. Leder (Eds.), *Mathematics and gender* (pp. 128–148). New York: Teachers College Press.

Leder, G. C. (1990). Teacher/student interactions in the mathematics classroom: A different perspective. In E. Fennema & G. C. Leder (Eds.), *Mathematics and gender* (pp. 149–168). New York: Teachers College Press.

Mac an Ghaill, M. (1994). *The making of men.* Buckingham, UK: Open University Press.

Mac an Ghaill, M., & Haywood, C. (1998). Gendered relations beyond the curriculum: Peer groups, family and work. In A. Clark & E. Millard (Eds.), *Gender in the secondary curriculum* (pp. 213–225). London: Routledge.

Morrow, C., & Morrow, J. (1996, March). *Connecting girls and women with mathematics: A sampling of strategies.* Paper presented at the ATMiM and Mathwest conference, Worcester, MA.

National Council of Teachers of Mathematics. (1989). *Curriculum and evaluation standards for school mathematics.* Reston, VA: Author.

Solar, C. (1995). From a feminist to an inclusive pedagogy in mathematics. In B. Grevholm & G. Hanna (Eds.), *Gender and mathematics education: An ICMI study in Stiftsgården Åkersberg, Höör, Sweden 1993* (pp. 327–336). Lund, Sweden: Lund University Press.

Walker, J. C. (1988). *Louts and legends: Male youth culture in an inner-city school.* Sydney, Australia: Allen & Unwin.

Walkerdine, V. (1986). Post-structuralist theory and everyday social practices: The family and the school. In S. Wilkinson (Ed.), *Feminist social psychology: Developing theory and practice* (pp. 57–76). Milton Keynes, UK: Open University Press.

Weedon, C. (1987). *Feminist practice and poststructuralist theory.* Oxford, UK: Blackwell.

Weiner, G. (1994). *Feminisms in education.* Buckingham, UK: Open University Press.

Weis, L. (1989). The 1980s: De-industrialization and change in white working class male and female cultural forms. In S. Walker & L. Barton (Eds.), *Politics and the processes of schooling* (pp. 126–165). Milton Keynes, UK: Open University Press.

Willis, P. (1977). *Learning to labour: How working class kids get working class jobs.* Farnborough, UK: Saxon House.

7

Identity, Agency, and Knowing in Mathematics Worlds

Jo Boaler and James G. Greeno

INTRODUCTION

The number of people who choose to pursue mathematics within or beyond university is small. In the United States, as well as other countries across the globe, declining proportions of students are majoring in mathematics, with particularly small numbers of women and non-Asian minorities entering the discipline (Anderson, 1997; Gutierrez, 2000). These facts are assumed by many, particularly those in mathematics departments, to be owing to the cognitive challenge of the subject. Mathematics is regarded as difficult and attainable only by some. We will present new data in this chapter that challenges this view through a representation of learning as a process of identity formation in "figured worlds" (Holland, Lachicotte, Skinner, & Cain, 1998). The figured worlds of many mathematics classrooms, particularly those at higher levels, are unusually narrow and ritualistic, leading able students to reject the discipline at a sensitive stage of their identity development. Traditional pedagogies and procedural views of mathematics combine to produce environments in which most students must surrender agency and thought in order to follow predetermined routines (Boaler, 1997a; Doyle, 1988; Schoenfeld, 1988). Many students are capable of such practices, but reject them, as they run counter to their developing identification as responsible, thinking agents (Wenger, 1998). The application of thought and the development of agency (Holland et al., 1998) should be an intrinsic part of any learning environment, yet there is evidence that such practices are dismally represented for students in many mathematics classrooms (Boaler, 1997a; Cheek & Castle, 1981; Stigler & Hiebert, 1999).

Learning mathematics has traditionally been regarded as an individual, cognitive activity. Educators have focused on the knowledge and understanding that students develop, as a product both of individual student resources and the practices in which students engage. A supporter of traditional teaching methods, for example, may argue that a student's knowledge would be enhanced by working through a textbook, while a reform-oriented teacher may argue that a student's knowledge would be enhanced through the act of mathematical discussion. Both of these educators regard the activity of learning mathematics as a vehicle for acquiring mathematics knowledge, but essentially distinct from the knowledge that is eventually developed. More recent theories of mathematical knowledge (e.g., Kitcher, 1983; Tymoczko, 1986) and learning (Greeno & MMAP, 1998; Lave, 1988, 1993; Lave & Wenger, 1991) challenge this distinction, claiming that the *practices* of learning mathematics define the knowledge that is produced. Such theories are supported by Boaler's finding (1997a, 1998, 2000a) that students of mathematics who had predominantly worked through textbooks found it difficult to use their mathematics in new and varied situations that required a different set of practices. Students who had engaged in practices of negotiation and interpretation in the mathematics classroom were more able to use mathematics in different situations that required such practices. Both sets of students had learned how to form and solve equations, for example, but, consistent with sociocultural (Rogoff, 1990) or situative (Greeno & MMAP, 1998; Lave, 1988, 1993; Lave & Wenger, 1991) theories of learning, students from the different learning environments had qualitatively different forms of knowledge, mediated by the beliefs that students developed about mathematics and learning in response to different teaching methods. Their knowledge was co-constituted by the practices of their learning and therefore differentially useful in real world situations (Boaler, 1997a). But situated theories do not only illuminate the discontinuity of mathematical practice that is recorded between sites in different research studies (Lave, 1988). Their focus on the patterns of participation that constitute learning gives insights into the nature and extent of identification and belonging that students develop as they learn to *be* mathematics learners (Dowling, 1996; Wenger, 1998).

We propose in this chapter that broadened perspectives of mathematics learning provide considerable insight both into students' mathematical understanding, as well as the choices they make about life and work. We consider knowing and understanding mathematics as aspects of participation in social practices, particularly discourse practices, in which people engage in sense-making and problem solving using mathematical representations, concepts, and methods as resources. Calling these "social practices" does not exclude activities of individuals who work alone, using and developing mathematical representations, concepts, and methods that they have encountered by participating in classrooms or by reading texts. An important implication of this idea is that students' learning of mathematics can be considered as a *trajectory of participation* in the practices of mathematical discourse and thinking. This view goes beyond recognizing that social practices provide a context for learning mathematics—instead, according to this view, participation in social practices is what learning mathematics is. The social practices of a community provide an environment in which students can participate, and their ways of participating are adaptations to the constraints and affordances of the environment (Greeno & MMAP, 1998).

In this chapter, we make use of a practice-based interpretation of mathematics learning in our analysis of interviews with 48 high school students of calculus. We interpret the results of these interviews using a concept of *ecologies of participation*. We find it useful to consider ecologies of participation in terms developed by Holland and associates (1998). This group of anthropologists discussed social systems in terms of *figured worlds, positioning,* and *authoring.* Figured worlds (Holland et al., 1998, p. 52) are places where agents come together to construct joint meanings and activities. A mathematics learning environment could be regarded as a particular figured world because students and teachers construct interpretations of actions that routinely take place there. Figured worlds are socially and culturally constructed realms "of interpretation in which particular characters and actors are recognized, significance is assigned to certain acts, and particular outcomes are valued over others" (1998, p. 52). The importance of this label for researchers of mathematics education resides in the characterization of a mathematics classroom as an interpretable realm, in which people fashion their senses of self. Figured worlds draw attention to interpretations by actors—students and teachers, for example—and to the rituals of practice. The mathematics classroom may be thought of as a particular social setting—that is, a figured world—in which children and teachers take on certain roles that help define who they are.

Holland and associates (1998) use the term "positional identity" to refer to the way in which people comprehend and enact their positions in the worlds in which they live. This builds on their theory that identities develop in and through social practice. They acknowledge that identities are centrally related to structural features of society such as ethnicity or gender but draw attention to the specific practices and activities situated in "worlds" such as academia, romance, or local politics. "Positional identities have to do with the day-to-day and on-the-ground relations of power, deference, and entitlement, social affiliation and distance—with the social-interactional, social-relational structures of the lived world" (Holland et al., 1998, pp. 127–128). Another aspect of identity they describe is the "space of authoring," which is encapsulated by the notion that "the world must be answered—authorship is not a choice" (1998, p. 272). This idea is concerned with the responses individuals give, with human agency, and with improvisation. The possibility and forms of authoring that are created in different mathematics environments, among learners who are often conceived as "receivers" of education (Corbett & Wilson, 1995), is an important question that will be pursued in this chapter.

We consider students' talk about their mathematics learning in their interviews with us as reports of their perceptions and understandings of the figured social worlds of mathematics education in which they participated as learners. The students' descriptions may also be taken to indicate their positionings in the ecologies of participation in practices of mathematics education and reflections of their authoring of identities as learners and performers of mathematics. The figured worlds of mathematics learning environments are not all alike, and our results illustrate two kinds of figured world that differ in an important way. In interpreting differences between the two kinds of learning environments these students described, we use concepts developed by Belenky, Clinchy, Goldberger, and Tarule (1986), and extended by Clinchy (1996) and Tarule (1996). Based on interviews with individuals about their beliefs and understandings of knowing and learning, these researchers developed distinctions that they referred to as *ways of knowing*. The typology that these researchers developed included the following:

- *Received knowing*, in which the individual considers her knowledge as primarily dependent on and derivative from an authoritative source other than herself
- *Subjective knowing,* in which the individual considers her knowledge as primarily a result of her affective reactions to information and ideas
- *Separate knowing,* in which the individual considers her knowledge as primarily being constructed to comply with rules that establish validity and to be defensible against challenges based on rules for validating knowledge
- *Connected knowing,* in which the individual considers her knowledge as primarily being constructed in interaction with other people (either directly, in conversation, or indirectly, through interacting with texts or other representations of others' knowledge and thinking), in a process that depends on understanding others' experiences, perspectives, and reasoning, and incorporates this understanding into the individual's knowing and understanding[1]

Belenky and associates' (1986) interviews were concerned with quite general aspects of knowing and learning, and they used their ways of knowing to characterize individuals. Our interviews dealt more specifically with students' experiences and beliefs regarding their learning of mathematics, and we consider that the different ways of knowing are characteristics of students' adaptations to their mathematics learning environments. Indeed, the interviews we report include considerable evidence of the different ways of knowing that students are required to accept, negotiate, or oppose in mathematics classrooms, compared with other school subjects.

RESEARCH METHODS

As part of a research project investigating the nature of mathematical confidence, researchers[2] interviewed 8 students from each of 6 Northern Californian high schools, 48 students in total. The students were all attending advanced placement (AP) calculus classes. The six schools are all part of the public system and serve diverse populations of students. The proportion of nonwhite students at the schools ranges from 37 to 61 percent, while the proportion of students classified as being eligible for free school meals ranges from 4 to 13 percent. The schools are located in a relatively affluent part of the United States, and they all include high proportions of middle and upper-middle class students. All six schools are popular with parents and contain large numbers of college-bound students. Researchers interviewed two girls and two boys that the teacher of AP calculus identified as mathematically confident, and two girls and two boys that the teacher identified as lacking confidence, in each of the six classes. The eight students in each school were interviewed in single-sex pairs. The teachers of the six classes, half of whom are female, are experienced and well respected in their departments. As the students were taken from AP calculus classes, they may all be regarded as successful students of mathematics, having all chosen to take mathematics into a fourth year, at an advanced level. Indeed, the success of the students and their self-selection into an advanced mathematics class meant that the students we interviewed were well placed to choose mathematics as a field of study. All of the interviews were coded using a system of open coding (Miles & Huberman, 1994). The different themes that emerged were then combined into broader categories, which are reported in this chapter. The interviews were semistructured, enabling the interviewer to pursue directions raised by the students. Students were asked to describe mathematics lessons; they were asked about lessons they particularly liked and disliked, the extent of discussion in mathematics, and the nature of mathematical confidence. In this chapter, we will consider the students' representation of their mathematics classroom environments and their subsequent beliefs about mathematics. In discussion, we will consider the implications of these different experiences and beliefs for the nature of mathematics knowing, identification, and participation.

RESEARCH RESULTS

We present our results in three sections. First, we describe students' reports of their perceptions of the mathematics classroom environments in which they worked and the characteristics of mathematics learning that they believed. These findings provide a picture of the figured social worlds of mathematics learning that the students experienced. Second, we describe students' reports of their beliefs about their places in the figured worlds of mathematics learning, their understandings of their positioning in these learning ecologies. Third, we present students' reports about their affective reactions and identifications toward their participation in mathematics learning, in the present and future. This provides information about the identities they authored regarding knowing and learning mathematics. Implications of the students' views for their future as mathematics learners and the future of mathematics education will be discussed.

The Figured Worlds of the Mathematics Classroom

All 48 of the students we interviewed were asked to describe their AP-calculus mathematics lessons, and interviewers engaged students in conversation about the different features they described. The students all described teachers reviewing homework, explaining methods at the board, and assigning questions to be completed. However, the descriptions of lessons at two of the schools differed in an important way. Teachers at two of the high schools, both women, encouraged students to work on questions collaboratively. When teachers explained methods to students, they encouraged student discussion, and when students worked on problems, they did so in groups. Students of the other four teachers described mathematics classes as individual environments in which their role was to practice and repeat the procedures teachers demonstrated. The nature of the different classroom environments will be explored briefly in the pages that follow.

Ecologies of Didactic Teaching

The pedagogical practices students reported in the four individualistic environments, which we call Apple, Cherry, Lemon, and Lime schools, were remarkably consistent, with student after student portraying an image of mathematics teaching that afforded received knowing. The teachers presented procedures that students were supposed to learn to perform. The students' characterizations of these classroom practices are illustrated by the following remarks:

> Basically, throughout my experience, we go to class and the teachers lecture, go over the material and show us exactly how to do the problems, cover the subjects that they're teaching and after the teacher's finished teaching if we ask questions and sort of like clear up anything that we don't know and then homework will be assigned to us that day, then we go home and do it. (Brad, Cherry school)

Students from these schools reported that mathematics classes always followed the same pattern—of reviewing homework and then working through exercises—and that even the questions in the exercises were similar:

> It's calculus! Everything is the same. It's all derivatives, and somehow you gotta use it somehow. I never liked derivatives or integrals, but the whole book so far has been the same thing, derivatives. (Khir, Apple school)

The students seemed to accept the lack of variety they reported in mathematics lessons, not because they enjoyed the lessons, but because they thought that was the way mathematics *had to be*. Few of the students had experienced anything different:

> K: I'm just not interested in, just, you give me a formula, I'm supposed to memorize the answer, apply it and that's it.
>
> Int: Does math have to be like that?
>
> B: I've just kind of learned it that way. I don't know if there's any other way.
>
> K: At the point I am right now, that's all I know. (Kristina and Betsy, Apple school)

The mathematics textbooks that the schools used all presented the fundamental theorem of calculus, expanded on the different concepts underlying the domain, and demonstrated procedures that could be used to solve problems. The books then introduced a series of questions that required students to practice the different procedures. Students reported that they worked through their textbooks every lesson, and they were encouraged to attend carefully to the words and practices of their teacher. Students were not expected nor encouraged to discuss the mathematics they were learning:

> There isn't much between students because you can't spend the time, like talking, if you want to pay attention and listen to what they're explaining. So unless like, when somebody next to me has a question, then I'll lean over because it's a little thing I can ask, I think it's more with the teacher. (Janet, Lemon school)

One of the students laughed for a long time when we asked him whether he and other students were encouraged to interact or talk to each other in mathematics lessons. He then gave the following response:

> Unless Mr. Bond says the marvelous sentence, "you have the period to yourself," we will *never* interact with each other directly. We go (whispering) "pass me your book"—we will never interact directly, not even with Mr. Bond because it's like our little cubicle, we have to do it. (Chris, Cherry school)

The figured worlds that these students portray, and that will be given more depth in the next section, are highly ritualized. Students come to class, watch the teachers demonstrate procedures, and then practice the procedures—alone. The ways in which students position themselves in such a world and form relationships with mathematics and each other is the focus of the next section. First, we offer a similarly brief characterization of the two other mathematics classes in which students were required to play a different role.

Ecologies of Discussion-based Teaching

Students from Grape and Orange schools painted a markedly different picture of mathematics lessons. The students talked about the time they spent discussing the different questions, as a class, and in student groups. They described being positioned as active agents in their classes, and their role involved contributing to the shared understanding of ideas that developed among the class. Their classroom practices afforded growth of connected knowing, with development of mathematical understanding that the students constructed and shared. The students from Grape and Orange schools were generally more positive about their experiences of calculus than students in the other schools, which they attributed to the relaxed nature of lessons, the positive relationships they formed with the teacher and other students, and the chance to derive meaning through discussion. When the students described their mathematics lessons, they gave discussion a central role and they talked about the increased access to understanding that collaboration provided:

V: Classes are social.

J: We work in groups most of the time.

V: Ms. Green works really hard on making it social and not just by yourself.

J: I think the groups are the best situation just because you can talk to the kids in your group and see if they can figure out the problem too. (Veena and Jazz, Orange school).

J: The teacher gives us something and has us work on a work sheet and then work with people in our group on the work sheet, because if I understand something, then I can explain it to the group members or if I don't understand it the group members may explain it to me. Whereas if she teaches the lesson and sends us home with it, I'm not really that confident because I haven't put like things together. (Jacob, Orange school)

The students appreciated the opportunity to discuss their work, partly because their discussions gave them deeper insights into the mathematics they met, but also because their discussions changed the nature of the classroom environment. When the students talked about AP calculus, they emphasized relationships—between the different aspects of mathematics as well as the people in the class. Their figured worlds did not center around individualized procedure repetition, but rather around collaboration of ideas within a community of learners (Lave & Wenger, 1991):

D: Yeah, this is my favorite class this year because the environment is so like family and you can just go there and talk about math or any problems you have.

B: She gives you time when she's not teaching, she lets you work on the problems, so she kind of walks around the room and it could be like socializing if you want. So it's like even when we socialize we still get math.

D: Yeah we always socialize about math. Weird but it happens.

B: I've definitely done better in this class than any other math class.

D: I think it's the relationships you have with other people in the class and with the teacher. (Debbie and Becky, Grape school)

In discussion-oriented figured worlds, connections between learners are emphasized as students are positioned as relational agents who are mutually committed and accountable to each other for constructing understanding in their discourse (Mclaughlin & Talbert, 1999; Wood, 1999). Students are expected to be co-authors, with their teachers, of their understanding of mathematical principles and procedures.

This brief section has presented a summary of the students' presentations of figured worlds. One group of students presented their worlds as structured, individualized, and ritualized, the other group as relational, communicative, and connected. The difference between the students' reported experiences in classrooms that did and did not encourage discussion was unexpected, as we knew little about the classrooms before we went in to interview the students. But it became clear to us, through our discussions with the students, that such differences had a significant impact on the students' positioning as learners in the two versions of figured worlds, as we shall now explore.

Students' Places in the Figured Worlds of Mathematics Learning

Positioning within Didactic Teaching

In order to consider students' roles as learners in their figured worlds, we engaged them in conversation about the nature of the knowledge they encountered and their roles as interpreters of that knowledge. We were interested to know whether students in the more traditional classes played an *active* role considering and interpreting the meaning of the procedures they encountered, which may have led to a broad, conceptual understanding of mathematics, or a *passive* role as receivers of predetermined knowledge that appeared unavailable for discussion or negotiation. Through conversation with the students from the more didactic classrooms, it became clear that their role in the mathematics classroom was narrowly defined:

> There's only one right answer and you can, it's not subject to your own interpretation or anything it's always in the back of the book right there. If you can't get it you're stuck. (Susan, Cherry school)

Some students believed that mathematics lessons did not require them to think in the way that other subject lessons did because of the closed nature of the problems they encountered:

> There's definitely a right answer to it. The other subjects like English and stuff that really have no right answer so I have to think about it. (Kim, Apple school)

Some of the students regarded thinking practices to be an unnecessary part of their mathematical experiences, in a similar way to the students' taught in traditional classes in Boaler's previous study (1997a), as one of the students from that study reported:

> L: In maths you have to remember; in other subjects you can think about it. (Louise, Year 11, set 1) (Boaler, 1997a, p. 36)

The idea that learning mathematics requires no or little thought, as students are only required to reproduce procedures, suggests that students are engaging in ritualistic acts of knowledge reproduction rather than thinking about the nature of the procedures and the reasons why and when they may be applied. That thinking practices are limited, even at such advanced levels of mathematics, seems both incredible and worrying. Further evidence for the limited role of thinking was provided by the students' answers to the following question, posed to them in the interviews: Is mathematics more about understanding concepts or memorizing procedures? Students from three of the four schools give these answers:

> G: I think it's very procedural. Different chapters they have this blue section, theorems, just memorize theorems. (Greg, Apple school)

K: Procedures. Because you have to learn this to learn this to understand this. I think of it like that. (Karen, Cherry school)

L: It's all about the formulas. If you know how to use it then you've got it made. Even if you don't quite understand the concept, if you're able to figure out all the parts of the formula, if you have the formula then you can do it. (Lori, Lime school)

P: I'd say it's a little of both. I don't think it's conceptual. Like, there are big concepts, and it's derivative and everything, things like that. But you have to remember all the little tricks and rules you have to follow. (Paul, Lime school)

This student suggests that though he appreciates that "big concepts" underlie the mathematics he is learning, the "little tricks and rules" dominate his perception. Other student reflections supported the idea that the practice of working through multiple procedures reduced the opportunity for a broader understanding:

A: If we actually went into detail about certain, like the stronger concepts that we'll maybe use later, I think we would remember more than just bombarding us with all these different things on a weekly basis. It gets to the point where you're doing so much you don't see the relationship, you're just doing so many problems. (Anthony, Lime school).

A: Concepts I think are second priority and I'll spend more time trying to learn the procedure.

B: The book does the worst job of explaining it. You might as well just get those notes down. Who knows how to use them, but somehow learn the procedure. (Arnetha and Barbara, Lime school).

Students of both sexes, different confidence levels, and various levels of attainment in the didactic classes told us that mathematics was a closed, rule-bound subject. The students related breadth and openness with thought. In contrast, mathematics questions requiring one answer, which could be achieved by following a standard procedure, required little thought. Despite the range of initiatives aimed at reforming school mathematics in the United States (Fennema & Nelson, 1997; National Council for Teachers of Mathematics, 1989), there is evidence that traditional pedagogies dominate mathematics classrooms, particularly at higher levels (Boaler, 1997c; Rogers 1995). Thus, teachers of mathematics frequently expect students to spend the majority of their time in mathematics lessons working through exercises practicing procedures (Schoenfeld, 1988). The aim of such work, presumably, is that students will become conversant in the use of the different procedures and be able to use them in a range of mathematical situations. However, the act of practicing procedures appears to become sufficiently dominant for many students that it obscures the meaning of the subject, and takes students' thoughts away from the concepts that are intended to be exemplified by the procedures (Mason, 1989; Perry, 1991). Many students described the act of working through procedures as oppositional to understanding the big ideas in the domain:

C: I see it more as procedures and solving one problem at a time. It's hard for me to see how it relates to everyday things, so I don't really get the big picture a lot of the time. (Cathy, Lemon school)

The students suggested that the procedural presentation of mathematics they encountered forced them to become passive receivers of knowledge—with a narrowly defined role that was one of memorization:

K: This is AP so it's definitely going to be harder, but I feel as long as I can memorize the formulas and memorize the derivatives and things like that, then I should be pretty well off. (Kim, Apple school)

V: You have to memorize these little steps, there's always an equation to solve something and you have to memorize stuff in the equation to get the answer and there's like a lot of different procedures. (Vicky, Lime school)

In the four schools in which students worked through calculus books alone, the students appeared to view the domain of mathematics as a collection of conceptually opaque procedures. The majority of students interviewed from the traditional classes reported that the goal of their learning activity was for them to memorize the different procedures they met. Such a figured world of didactic teaching and learning rests on an epistemology of received knowing. In this kind of figured world, mathematical knowledge is transmitted to students, who learn by attending carefully to teachers' and textbook demonstrations. Ball and Bass (2000) offer supporting evidence when they reflect that "students often receive mathematical knowledge in school that is justified by little else than the textbook's or the teacher's assertion. By default the book has epistemic authority: Teachers explain assignments to pupils by saying, 'This is what *they* want you to do here,' and the right answers are found in the answer key" (Ball & Bass, 2000). Students' positioning in this kind of ecology is that of receiving and absorbing knowledge from the teacher and textbook. This knowledge consists of the ability to select and perform procedures of symbol manipulation, thereby producing sequences of symbols that are correct, according to specifications taken from authoritative mathematics (Povey, Burton, Angier, & Boylan, 1999). The students' responses to their positioning as received knowers in this highly ritualized figured world will be the focus of our final section. First, we will explore the students' positioning in the discussion-oriented classes.

Positioning within Discussion-based Teaching

The students in Grape and Orange schools used the same, or similar, textbooks as students in the other four schools, but they did not work through the exercises producing answers that were supported or invalidated by the teacher or textbook. Instead, they were asked to discuss the different questions and consider the meaning of possible solutions with each other, thus engaging in the process of validation alongside the teacher. The students at Grape and Orange schools engaged in acts of negotiation and interpretation that appeared to lead to their distinctly more progressive views of mathematics as a discipline. The students did not describe mathematics as an abstract, closed, and procedural domain, but as a field of inquiry that they could discuss and explore. Concomitantly, they regarded themselves as active learners whose role went well beyond memorization:

> L: I can get more into it, not just like "oh this kind of problem" but "why is this the way you do it?"
>
> M: Yeah you want to figure out the problem, you want to understand the concept. (Lori and Melissa, Grape school)

Some of the students in Grape and Orange schools contrasted mathematics with English, as the students in some of the other schools had done, but they did so to illustrate the depth of thinking required in mathematics, rather than the procedural nature of the subject:

> M: I don't know, it just seems like math is more important. In my English class, I can just kind of flow, and whatever's going on, write an essay about whatever, it's not a lot, well, in my case, it's not a lot of deep thinking. Not a lot under the surface.
>
> Int: Is there in math—deep thinking?
>
> M: Yeah. Yeah because the thing, being conceptual, and that's a lot harder than just like memorizing formulas, definitely. (Melissa, Grape school)
>
> T: I guess I've liked math overall because it's a lot better than English or social studies, just because I don't like to memorize just a bunch of stuff. It's a lot of solving the problems, not like looking over past stuff, it's a lot of new stuff you're covering. (Tom, Orange school)

The students in the discussion-oriented classes regarded their role to be learning and understanding mathematical relationships, they did not perceive mathematics classes to be a ritual of procedure reproduction. When the students described their figured worlds, they centralized relationships between people. Debbie and Becky, cited earlier, described their mathematics class as a family environment; Angier and Povey (1999) received similar responses from students they interviewed who engaged in mathematical discussions in class. Such descriptions suggest that the relationships students form in their classes are central to the learning that takes place (McLaughlin & Talbert, 1999), rather than a casual by-product of a change in pedagogy. The following student relates the attainment of conceptual understanding to the relationships that are formed with teachers and classmates:

> D: I don't know, I guess there's a feeling of more, it's kind of more laid back, I mean we get a lot of work done, we have people get 100 percent on the tests and things like that. We have people who don't understand it, they still get a grasp of the general concept and it's not like we're sitting there with our hands on our desk, like. We're allowed to make, we're allowed to make jokes, to be out of whack sometimes. We have fun with the teacher, and when we get to work we get to work. With Mr. Cain, and our other teachers, it's kind of like, there's not that relationship. (David, Grape school)

In interviews at Grape and Orange schools, the students were extremely positive about the discussions of mathematics that took place in class, which they related, among other things, to the opportunities to learn through student language, the accessibility of other students' ideas, and the formation of strong, personal relationships that enhanced their learning. One of the students who was in one of the more didactic environments reflected on the discussions he had with friends when he was completing homework, concluding that discussions were helpful as they helped him consider mathematics from another person's perspective:

> S: You can't always understand every problem. Like if you go through a test or home-work or an assignment, like it's hard. Sometimes your mind doesn't always click on what you have to do for this certain problem, you have to approach it in a differ-ent way so you have to kind of get everyone's point of view. You have to get every-body's take on how to do it. So it helps if someone else could be looking at it in a different way, then they would have seen something a little bit different. That defi-nitely helps. (Seth, Lime school)

This student's reflection seems to encapsulate the spirit of connected knowing, with discussions of mathematics offering him the occasion to consider other people's representations of knowledge. He valued the opportunities that homework discussions provided for such insights, whereas the students at Grape and Orange schools were afforded occasions for connected knowing on a daily basis, the implications of which will be considered now.

Students' Authored Identities in Their Different Mathematics Worlds

Didactic Teaching and Received Knowing

For the students in Lemon, Lime, Apple, and Cherry schools, mathematics was presented as a series of procedures that needed to be learned, as the students have described. For students to be successful in such classes, they needed to both assume the role of a received knower and develop identities that were compatible with a procedure-driven figured world. We assert that compatibility with forms of know-ing, and identification with pedagogical practices, are both crucial aspects of math-ematical success and we expand on both of these points next. It is critical to our analysis that when we interviewed students in the didactic classes about the nature of success in mathematics classrooms, they did not prioritize "ability," the cogni-tive demand of the discipline, or even effort. Instead they prioritized students' will-ingness to accept a particular form of knowing and to build identities that give human agency a minimal role.

The following students, from three of the four didactic classes, were asked what it takes to be successful in mathematics. The interviewers of these students ex-pected to hear about interest, effort, or even talent, and were surprised by the stu-dents' replies:

A: Patience.

Int: Patience?

V: Yeh motivation and just wanting to do it. Perseverance. Wanting to do it over and over again. (Vicky and Amy, Lime school)

A: Obedience.

Int: Obedience?

A: Obedient. I've known these people like 4 years of my life and long enough to know that no matter, even if they didn't like what they're doing you would feel like what we're doing is completely ridiculous, they're not going to raise a fuss about it, they're not going to speak their mind about it. They'll just do it because it's required and that's what the teacher wants. The teacher would rather you do it and not hear your thoughts on the thing, than have you contest what you're doing and like—"I don't understand this." . . . I can't sit there for hours, just, I just can't follow directions when I see people doing something completely irrational. Or like if I don't agree with like the question that he wants us to answer or whatever. (Anthony, Lime school)

T: You have to be willing to accept that sometimes things don't look like—they don't seem that you should do them. Like they have a point. But you have to accept them. (Tom, Lemon school)

R: I guess it depends on how you take frustration. (Rick, Apple school)

These students suggest that success in their calculus classes required a form of received knowing, in which obedience, compliance, perseverance, and frustration played a central role. There seemed to be considerable consensus for this perspective among the students in the didactic classes, even though the students were divided in their responses to the form of knowing with which they apparently needed to comply. We asked all 32 of the students in the didactic classes whether they enjoyed mathematics; 18 said that they did (56 percent). Thirty of the students were asked whether they intended to take any other mathematics classes; 14 said that they did (47 percent). Those who disliked mathematics and had decided to cease their study of mathematics (generally the same students) were not unsuccessful in class; indeed, some of them were extremely able mathematics students. But the students resented the lack of opportunities they received to develop a deep, relational, and connected understanding of mathematics, as this student describes:

K: We knew HOW to do it. But we didn't know WHY we were doing it and we didn't know how we got around to doing it. Especially with limits, we knew what the answer was, but we didn't know WHY or how we went around doing it. We just plugged into it. And I think that's what I really struggled with is—I can get the answer, I just don't understand why. (Kate, Lime school)

That such responses were unrelated to "ability" is not surprising. In Boaler's previous study of students working in traditional classrooms (1997b, 1997c), the students who became most alienated, and ultimately unsuccessful, were at one time the highest attaining mathematics students in the school; their attainment progressively deteriorated as their mathematics teaching became more procedural. The alienated students in that study—most of whom were girls—were capable of practicing the procedures they were given and gaining success in the classroom and on tests, but they desired a more connected understanding that included consideration of "why" the procedures they used were effective. The alienated students in this study seemed to be rejecting mathematics for the same reasons. With a remarkable degree of consistency, the students who stated that they liked mathematics (11 of the 18 were boys) gave reflections that suggested they did so precisely because they wanted to be received knowers, with minimal requirement to interpret knowledge or think about connections within and across the mathematical domain:

Int: Why do you like math?

S: Because I think with so many of the other classes—what they teach and how they teach it, they're opinionated and political and it all depends, it's never the same, you can never depend on it. But with math, it's pretty constant. (Seth, Lime school)

R: For me, it's one of my strongest subjects and for me it's something I'm happy about and feel good in. Again, it's that methodology of mathematics that leads to the one answer that you can get, that there's no answer other than that. (Rich, Cherry school)

J: I always like subjects where there is a definite right or wrong answer. That's why I'm not a very inclined or good English student. Because I don't really think about how or why something is the way it is. I just like math because it is or it isn't. (Jerry, Lemon school)

It seems striking that the students in didactic classes who liked mathematics did so because there were only right and wrong answers, and because they did not have to consider different opinions or ideas, or use creativity or expression. Jerry states that he likes mathematics because he does not have to "think about how or why," the implications of which will be pursued in the conclusion to this chapter.

Belencky and associates describe "received knowers" in the following way: "For those who adhere to the perspective of received knowledge, there are no gradations of the truth—no gray areas. Paradox is inconceivable because received knowers believe several contradictory ideas are never simultaneously in accordance with fact. Because they see only blacks and whites but never shades of grey" (1986, p. 4). The three students quoted previously appear to exemplify this position. Seth describes other classes as "opinionated and political and it all depends," which to him was the anathema of the knowing he wanted. The following student reflects on the students who liked mathematics in his class, with a description that is strikingly similar to that of Belencky and associates' (1986) received knowers:

T: There's definitely a certain type of person who's better at math. Generally, if you're better at English they seem to be more social. And the math people. I don't know, they're just as social, but in a different way. They express themselves differently, they like to see things in black and white. They don't see the colors and greys between. (Tom, Lemon school)

Tom suggests that a certain type of person is attracted to mathematics and a certain type rejected. The differences align, not with capability, but with the ideas of knowing available.

Another striking aspect of the students' reflections on their response to mathematics, concerned the primacy they gave to their developing identities. A large proportion of the students interviewed appeared to reject mathematics because the pedagogical practices with which they had to engage were incompatible with their conceptions of self. Unlike the people Belenky and associates (1986) characterized as received knowers, for whom received knowing was a general pattern in their lives, these students considered themselves as constructive knowers in other school subjects. They understood themselves as received knowers in the limited circumstances of the mathematics classes in which the learning practices available to them required that they acquire specified procedures with no opportunity that they perceived to be thoughtful or creative about what they needed to learn to do. The students' descriptions particularly centered around the need they perceived for occasions to be creative, use language, and make decisions, for example:

Int: Why wouldn't you major in math?

C: I think I'm a more creative person, I can do it and I can understand it but it's not something I could do for the rest of my life and I think if I had a job I'd like one that let me be a little more creative.

Int: Math isn't creative . . . ?

C: No. (Cathy, Lemon school)

S: Well it's not that I don't understand it, when I understand concepts I like doing it because it's fun. I'm more of a language/history person, kind of. And also there's only one right answer and you can, it's not subject to your own interpretation or anything. (Susan, Cherry school)

Int: Do you like math?

V: No, I hate it.

Int: Why do you hate it?

V: It's just too, I'm into the history, English. . . . It's like too logical for me, it always has to be one answer, you can't get anything else BUT that answer. (Vicky, Lime school)

One of our calculus students suggested that women, in particular, needed to identify with subjects that allowed them to explore rather than receive knowledge:

I think women, being that they're more emotional, are more emotionally involved and math is more like concrete, it's so "it's that and that's it." Women are more, they want to explore stuff and that's life kind of like and I think that's why I like English and science, I'm more interested in like phenomena and nature and animals and I'm just not interested in just you give me a formula, I'm supposed to memorize the answer, apply it and that's it. (Kristina, Apple school)

A range of studies support the idea that girls and women are particularly likely to reject subjects that preclude deep, connected understanding (Becker, 1995; Burton, 1995). This suggests that the procedural presentations of knowledge that dominate within many higher level mathematics classes are likely to be a major factor in the under-representation of women at high levels. This seems partly to be due to the desire for connected understanding that is evident among many girls and women (Becker, 1995; Boaler, 1997c), and partly due to the need to pursue subjects that fit with developing identities. For many girls, mathematics appears too alien, other-worldly, and "weird" to be a major part of their lives:

> B: I used to love math, but now I think, it's like I'm going to make sure that I don't major in math or anything because it's starting to be like too much competition, it's so weird. When it came to calculus and precalculus, I just kind of lost interest. I care more about science and English, stuff that makes sense to me where I think I'm learning morals and lessons from this, where I can apply it to something. (Betsy, Apple school)

> L: I think that math is the lowest priority in my life. I don't have a favorite subject but math is the least important to me. It's OK and if I don't understand something I'm not going to die, I just don't think it's that applicable to what I want to do in life, and I don't even know what that is. (Lori, Lime school).

When students talked about their rejection of mathematics, their reasons went beyond cognitive likes and dislikes, to the establishment of their identities. They talked not about their inability to do the mathematics, but about the kinds of person (Schwab, 1969) they wanted to be—creative, verbal, and humane. Unfortunately for the students, there was a distinct inconsistency between the identities that were taking form in the ebb and flow of their lives and the requirements of AP-calculus classrooms. The students did not want to be told what to do and do it—when it was "completely irrational" (Anthony, Lime school); they were not prepared to give up the agency that they enjoyed in other aspects of their lives, or the opportunities to be creative, use language, exercise thought, or make decisions. The disaffected students we interviewed were being turned away from mathematics because of pedagogical practices that are unrelated to the nature of mathematics (Burton, 1999a, 1999b). Most of the students who had rejected mathematics in the four didactic classrooms—nine girls and five boys, all successful mathematics students—did so because they wanted to pursue subjects that offered opportunities for expression, interpretation, and agency.

Discussion Based Teaching and Connected Knowing

At Grape and Orange schools, 15 of the 16 students said that they enjoyed mathematics (94 percent), and 8 out of the 10 students asked (80 percent) stated that they planned to continue with other mathematics courses. Two of the girls interviewed stated that they planned to major in mathematics. Veena, cited in the following passage, was one of them:

> Sometimes you sit there and go "it's fun!" I'm a very verbal person and I'll just ask a question and even if I sound like a total idiot and it's a stupid question I'm just not seeing it, but usually for me it clicks pretty easily and then I can go on and work on it. But at first sometimes you just sit there and ask—"what is she teaching us?" "what am I learning?" but then it clicks, there's this certain point when it just connects and you see the connection and you get it. (Veena, Orange school)

One of the interesting aspects of Veena's statement is her description of herself as a "verbal person," which was one of the common reasons students gave for rejecting mathematics in the four didactic classes. Indeed, it seems worrying, but likely, that Veena may have rejected mathematics if she had been working in one of the four other classrooms in which the discussions and connections she valued were under-represented. It seems clear from Veena's statement that she valued both connected understanding as well as the opportunities she received to express her thinking, and that both of these were part of her mathematics world.

At Lemon, Lime, Apple, and Cherry schools, almost half of the students reported negative identifications with mathematics, in some cases contrasting this with their more positive identifications with other subjects, such as English, where they could be thoughtful or creative. Many of those students who reported positive identifications did so because mathematics allowed them to passively receive knowledge. Students at Grape and Orange schools, in contrast, identified more positively with mathematics and many of them did so because they were able to be thoughtful and to develop connected, relational understanding.

DISCUSSION AND CONCLUSION

In California, as well as other parts of the world, important decisions about mathematics education are being made by university mathematicians (Becker & Jacob, 2000). The majority of the mathematicians who involve themselves in matters of K-12 education appear to be outspoken opponents of nontraditional teaching methods. Mathematicians frequently argue that students in schools should be taught abstract mathematical procedures through repeated practice of the procedures, in order that they reach university conversant in the range of methods that they will need to use and apply there. But their assumptions about the importance of procedure repetition contain two important flaws. First, it is assumed that by practicing procedures out of context, students will be able to use and apply procedures in the future—a number of studies provide evidence that this is often not the case (Boaler, 1997a; Lave, 1988). Second, they overlook the fact that students do not just learn mathematics in school classrooms, they learn to *be,* and many students develop identities that give negative value to the passive reception of abstract knowledge. It is probable that many able students who could become world-class mathematicians leave mathematics because they do not want to author their identities as passive receivers of knowledge. This has been the subject of this chapter.

We have found it useful to consider mathematics classrooms in terms of "figured worlds" in which people are not only regarded as mathematics learners, assuming the cognitive order of the discipline, but people negotiating a sense of self. Figured worlds seem to extend Bourdieu's (1986) notion of habitus, which includes the norms and practices of a place, to the interpretations that people make and the significance that is attached to certain acts. Thus, what actually happens in mathematics classrooms matters less within representations of figured worlds than the teachers' or students' perceptions of what happens. This has been useful in this chapter in helping us understand students' responses to didactic pedagogy in which memorization and procedure repetition are central practices. Corbett and Wilson talk about the exclusion of students from conversations about reform, with adults dictating to students the "conditions of their participation" (1995, p. 15). In didactic mathematics classrooms, students' participation is defined by textbooks, rules, and procedures—they are excluded from the negotiation or development of procedures; they are restricted in their application of selves; and their ideas, inventiveness, and general agency do not appear to be valued. Becker (1995) has proposed that "connected teaching," in which teachers share the process of mathematical problem solving with students rather than presenting neatly solved problems and procedures, would enable connected knowing, making mathematics more equitably accessible, and also encouraging larger numbers of students to pursue mathematics as a career. She asserts that "mathematics needs to be taught as a process, not as a universal truth handed down by some disembodied, non-human force" (Becker, 1995, p. 168). Stephen Ball (1993) also talks about the "curriculum of the dead," describing the inclination of right-wing politicians to support curriculum that are composed of remote facts, in which students have no role to play other than receivers of those facts. Becker and Ball both highlight the nonhuman or nonliving characteristic of traditional curricula. Data from this study suggest that many students find the narrowly defined roles they are required to play within such curricula incompatible with their developing identities.

The type of participation that is required of students who study in discussion-oriented mathematics classrooms is different. Students are asked to contribute to the judgment of validity, and to generate questions and ideas. Students in this study described their involvement within such environments in terms of community participation and family relationships. The students in the discussion-based environments were not only required to contribute different aspects of their selves, they were required to contribute *more* of their selves. In the discussion-based classrooms students were, quite simply, given more agency. To be a successful participant of a traditional classroom, students need to give up their choice and decision making, which is reflected in the students' comments about obedience and compliance. The act of surrendering their thoughts and ideas is difficult for many students, including those who could make significant contributions to the discipline of mathematics.

Belencky and associates (1986) have presented different characterizations of "knowers," suggesting that some people need to make connections as they learn, either directly through interactions with people, or indirectly through interactions with texts and other representations of knowledge. Others prefer to receive knowledge that is derived solely from a separate authoritative source. For the students studying calculus in the four didactic classes, there appeared to be few, if any, opportunities for connections, and students were forced to become received knowers. We do not regard the categories that Belencky and associates offer as stable characteristics of the students we interviewed, as these learners seemed able to move in and out of different "forms of knowing" in different circumstances. Indeed, some learners enjoy the chance to receive knowledge in some circumstances as a change from others in which they are thinking and making connections. Nevertheless, it seemed clear that the mathematics environments at Lemon, Lime, Apple, and Cherry schools encouraged a particularly passive and received form of knowing that alienated many learners.

We have analyzed interviews with 48 high-attaining students in this chapter, 32 of whom were taught in traditional classes, 16 in discussion-oriented classes. Seventeen of the 48 students reported that they hated or disliked mathematics, 16 of these students (94 percent) were taught in the traditional classes. These are small numbers of students, but the students' reflections in interviews give meaning to this percentage. The students who were planning to leave the discipline wanted the opportunity to think, negotiate, and understand the procedures they encountered. When mathematicians oppose nontraditional pedagogies, they argue that they do not want the discipline to be "watered down" and they want standard procedures to be available for those students who choose to major in mathematics. But by emphasizing the drill and practice of procedures, they create a rite of passage that is attractive only for received knowers. This reduces the numbers of students who want to study mathematics at advanced levels to a critical minimum (at Stanford University, for example, approximately seven students per year choose to major in mathematics); it also eliminates creative, divergent thinkers from the discipline. The elimination of such learners may be extremely damaging for mathematics and out of place with our time (Noss, 1991). In years gone by, students may not have expected to challenge or negotiate ideas in school and procedural mathematics practices were less distinctive. Now students are offered choices, they expect to have their ideas valued, they enjoy being treated as responsible young adults, and many do not choose mathematics.

Burton (1999a, 1999b) conducted an important study, one of the first to give us insight into the practices of university mathematicians. She interviewed 70 research mathematicians to find out about the nature of their work, as well as their understanding of knowing. She found that the mathematicians emphasized the importance of intuition, uncertainty, and connectivity. Not surprisingly, they did not talk about the procedural nature of mathematics, but rather about the creativity of the enterprise with which they were engaged. They spoke about the euphoria they experienced when solving problems and the fun and excitement of mathematics, thus offering a sharp contrast to the views of many of the students interviewed in this study. Even those students we interviewed who enjoyed mathematics in didactic classes did not relate their enjoyment to the pleasure of problem solving, but to the structure and limits of the discipline as they experienced it. While the mathematicians Burton interviewed emphasized the uncertainty of their explorations, the students in didactic classes who liked mathematics emphasized the certainty of their work. This suggests that narrow mathematical practices within school are problematic, not only because they disenfranchise many students, but because they encourage forms of knowing and ways of working that are inconsistent with the discipline. Thus, school mathematics, as noted by Burton (1999a) and others, is unlike the mathematics encountered in life or university (Boaler 1997a; Noss, 1991).

Burton's results remind us that that the excitement of mathematical inquiry and discovery is not always experienced as a product of social interaction. Indeed, the prevailing image of mathematical work is that of an individual struggling, like Rodin's *The Thinker,* to find coherence in a deep conceptual problem, and experiencing near ecstasy if s/he is able to achieve an elegant solution. In our discussion here, we have opposed an individualistic version of received knowing of procedures with socially connected knowing that has conceptual depth. Those are the kinds of knowing that were reported by the students whom we interviewed, but we acknowledge that the coupling of social and conceptual aspects is not necessary or universal. Skills that are mainly procedural can be learned in socially cooperative environments (consider learning the steps of a traditional Gaelic dance in Britain or a square dance in the United States), and individuals can and do explore conceptual issues beyond the boundaries of the current understandings that members of their community support (consider the familiar examples of Galois and Ramanujan in the history of mathematics). We acknowledge that in mathematics classrooms, activities can be organized so the students engage in enjoyable social interaction without achieving significant mathematical learning—either conceptual or procedural. And there are some students who perceive even quite productive class discussions as "clutter" that distracts them from the concentrated individual attention to mathematical concepts and methods that they prefer. The conceptual framework that we have used to interpret the data of our interviews would need to be extended to accommodate examples of engaged conceptual knowing that is only weakly supported by discourse interactions in the individual's immediate learning community. We believe that such an extension could be quite important for mathematics education. It could involve hypothesizing a form of connected knowing that emphasizes the knower's being connected with the contents of a subject-matter domain.

We believe that the distinction between separate and connected knowing, discussed by Belenky and associates (1986) and Clinchy (1996) mainly in relation to other people, can also be used to understand different ways in which learners can relate to the things, ideas, and representations of a subject matter. Belenky and associates used Elbow's (1973) phrases, "the doubting game" and "the believing game," to convey an important difference between learners' ways of considering other people's experience and opinions in their distinction between separate and connected knowing. We consider these phrases as distinguishing between attitudes that can be directed toward things, texts, and ideas that a person studies, as well as toward other people with whom one communicates. One way that this distinction applies is in the relation of scientists to the things or people that they study. For example, many ethnographers have made the point that their main task is to understand the people they study in their own terms, the so-called "emic" stance. To take this ethnographic stance toward the people being studied is a version of "the believing game," in which the researcher assumes that the practices of other people are sensible, and the ways in which they are sensible can be learned by the researcher if he or she succeeds in their study. To succeed, the researcher needs to incorporate the ways of sense-making of the studied people into her or his ways of understanding. We consider this a profound kind of connected knowing, in which the knower-researcher has come to know the people he or she studied through an openness to their ways of knowing and understanding.

The attitude of openness—of understanding things on their own terms—also is expressed by scientists whose subject matter is not human social activity. A famous example is Barbara McClintock's attitude toward the plants she studied, expressed in the title of her biography, *A Feeling for the Organism* (Keller, 1983). Keller's characterization of McClintock's work and thinking includes phrases that identify her openness to learning by interacting sympathetically with the plants that she attended to so carefully. "McClintock's feeling for the organism is not simply a longing to behold the 'reason revealed in this world.' It is a longing to embrace the world in its very being, through reason and beyond" (Keller, 1983, p. 199). "Over the years, a special kind of sympathetic understanding grew in McClintock, heightening her powers of discernment, until finally, the objects of her study have become subjects in their own right; they claim from her a kind of attention that most of us experience only in relation to other persons" (Keller, 1983, p. 200).

We also contend that "the believing game" characterizes some people's learning relationship with conceptual domains. Indeed, the kind of study and knowing that characterized McClintock's scientific work is not just intimate and sympathetic incorporation of the subject's character into the scientist's way of understanding the world. It also includes finding an orderly and coherent explanatory account in the conceptual resources of the scientific discipline. Learning these conceptual resources can be approached either in the "believing" or the "doubting" game. More accurately, any conceptual learning includes a mixture of these attitudes, but we believe that people—including students—differ in their basic expectations regarding the prospects of a subject matter to provide productive sense-making resources in return for the effort of incorporating them into one's understanding. Engaging in "the believing game" with the concepts and methods of a subject-matter domain is relational, involving positive expectations both about the subject matter and about one's self as a learner of that subject.

The connection of a successful scientist with both the phenomena and the explanatory concepts of the subject-matter domain supports her or his expectation that there is order to be discovered in the phenomena and that the conceptual resources of the discipline can provide a way of representing that order and thereby explaining the phenomena. The moments of drama that scientists report often involve situations in which the scientist was faced with phenomena that he or she hoped or expected to be able to explain with the resources of her or his discipline, but seemed unable to; then achieved the understanding that was needed. An example in McClintock's biography occurred during a visit to Stanford as a relatively young, albeit quite well-established scientist, where she had been invited in the hope that she could solve a problem of working out the cytology of mutations and enzyme deficiencies in the bread mold *Neurospora*. At first, things did not go well. In Keller's telling:

> By her own account, her confidence had begun to fail even before setting out. "I was really quite petrified that maybe I was taking on more than I could really do." She went, set up the microscope, and proceeded to work, but after about three days, found she wasn't getting anywhere. "I got very discouraged, and realized that there was something wrong—something quite seriously wrong. I wasn't seeing things, I wasn't integrating. I wasn't getting things right at all. I was lost." Realizing she had to "do something" with herself, she set out for a walk.
>
> A long winding driveway on the Stanford campus is framed by two rows of giant eucalyptus trees. Beneath these trees, she found a bench where she could sit and think. She sat for half an hour. "Suddenly I jumped up, I couldn't wait to get back to the laboratory. I knew I was going to solve it—everything was going to be all right."
>
> She doesn't know quite what she did as she sat under those trees. She remembers she "let the tears roll a little," but mainly, "I must have done this very intense, subconscious thinking. And suddenly I knew everything was going to be just fine." It was. In five days, she had everything solved. (Keller, 1983, p. 115)

We interpret this as an example of reasoning that depended on McClintock's knowing of biological concepts, which supported her intuitive confidence in the potential validity of an explanatory scheme that she then went back and worked out.

We recognize that mathematics is unlike empirical sciences in that it lacks a domain of empirical phenomena that concepts and principles are used to explain. However, the natural histories of mathematical discoveries contain the same kinds of drama as they do in other domains. Here is an example, from Aczel's recounting of the proof of Fermat's Last Theorem. The situation was subsequent to Andrew Wiles's presentation of his analysis, which he believed to be a proof, at Cambridge and the discovery by others that his argument was flawed.

> When more than a year passed since his short-lived triumph in Cambridge, Andrew Wiles was about to give up all hope and to forget his crippled proof.
>
> On Monday morning, September 19, 1994, Wiles was sitting at his desk at Princeton University, piles of paper strewn all around him. He decided he would take one last look at his proof before chucking it all and abandoning all hope to prove Fermat's Last Theorem. He wanted to see exactly what it was that was preventing him from constructing the Euler System. He wanted to know—just for his own satisfaction—why he had failed. Why was there no Euler System?—he wanted to be able to pinpoint pre-

cisely which technical fact was making the whole thing fail. If he was going to give up, he felt, then at least he was owed an answer to why he had been wrong.

Wiles studied the papers in front of him, concentrating very hard for about twenty minutes. And then he saw exactly why he was unable to make the system work. Finally, he understood what was wrong. "It was the most important moment in my entire working life," he later described the feeling. "Suddenly, totally unexpectedly, I had this incredible revelation. Nothing I'll ever do again will . . . " at that moment tears welled up and Wiles was choking with emotion. What Wiles realized at that fateful moment was "so indescribably beautiful, it was so simple and so elegant . . . and I just stared in disbelief." Wiles realized that exactly what was making the Euler System fail is what would make the Horizontal Iwasawa Theory approach he had abandoned three years earlier *work*. Wiles stared at his paper for a long time. He must be dreaming, he thought, this was just too good to be true. But later he said it was simply too good to be *false*. The discovery was so powerful, so beautiful, that it *had* to be true. (Aczel, 1996, pp. 132–133)

And it was, as the mathematics community soon verified when Wiles circulated copies of his new argument to several close colleagues and successfully submitted his paper, co-authored by Richard Taylor, as a correction to the paper that Wiles had presented at Cambridge.

When mathematicians decide that a proof is "true," their judgment does not rest on empirical observations of the kind that biologists or physicists use. Instead, their verification depends on the outcome of applying accepted procedures of proof and computation. Pickering's (1995) analysis of agency in mathematical and scientific work provides a helpful framework for considering this.[3] In Pickering's terms, an advance in mathematics involves three processes, called *bridging, transcription,* and *filling.* Bridging involves a proposal for making some extension of a base model—that is, a set of accepted concepts and methods (establishing a "bridgehead"). Transcription involves transferring components of the base model analogically to the bridgehead—that is, attempting to treat the contents of the new topic with methods that are previously accepted. Filling involves providing additional definitions of terms in the new domain or modifying (preferably by generalization) methods from the base model. In the process of transcription, the mathematician performs procedures that he or she is not free to vary; Pickering refers to this as *agency of the discipline.*[4]

It is in bridging and filling that the agency of mathematical work resides with the human mathematical thinkers. In Pickering's words,

As I conceive them, bridging and filling are activities in which scientists display choice and discretion, the classic attributes of human agency. . . . Bridging and filling are free moves, as I shall say. In contrast, transcription is where discipline asserts itself, where the disciplinary agency just discussed carries scientists along, where scientists become passive in the fact of their training and established procedures. Transcriptions, in this sense, are disciplined forced moves. Conceptual practice therefore has, in fact, the familiar form of a dance of agency, in which the partners are alternately the classic human agent and disciplinary agency. (1995, p. 116)

Interpreting the example of Fermat's Last Theorem in these terms, Wiles's initial bridgehead was a proposal to prove the theorem by constructing an Euler System, and he believed that he had accomplished that transcription successfully, but his colleagues discovered that he had not. He revised the bridgehead to use the Horizontal Iwasawa Theory. When he said, in recollection, "The discovery was so powerful, so beautiful, that it *had* to be true," he expressed his conviction that the methods of that theory could be transcribed successfully for the proof of Fermat's Last Theorem. And this conviction proved correct.

We find Pickering's distinctions helpful in understanding differences like those between the four didactically procedure-oriented classrooms and the two more discussion- and conceptually oriented classrooms of the students interviewed for this study. We consider that learning mathematics is like doing mathematics in at least one important respect. At any stage of learning mathematics, learners have some concepts and methods that they already know and understand. Their next learning extends what they already know. We can think of a learning episode, then, as one that includes bridging and transcribing, and possibly filling, so that some new topic is included in, and integrated with, some of their previous mathematical knowledge. In didactic, procedure-driven learning, students are shown constituents of the mathematical discipline to absorb so they can apply them. In learning that focuses more on conceptual discussion, they can participate in bridging and filling, and experience the functional significance of transcription. In other words, by including students in processes of meaning-making, they can experience and learn those aspects of mathematical thinking—bridging and filling—in which human agency is significant. If their opportunities for learning are limited to acquiring procedures, then their understanding and perception of mathematics can easily be limited to the aspects of mathematical thinking in which the human agent is relatively passive.

As we know, a few students develop identities of significant mathematical agency even in didactic learning environments that mainly present the parts of mathematical practice that are performed passively. In our conceptual framework, the explanation for these exceptional students probably arises from their authoring of identities that overcome deficiencies of the environment. Holland and associates (1998) described some women in the southern American colleges they studied who resisted the general pressure to adopt mainly passive positions in their figured social worlds that were primarily concerned with romantic attractiveness. These women authored identities with significant social and intellectual agency that departed from the norms that most women complied with. It is not surprising, then, that there are some students in figured social worlds of didactic mathematics teaching who author identities of individual agency in which they construct meaningful understanding and capabilities to formulate questions, conjectures, and arguments that provide satisfying conceptual coherence in their practices of mathematical knowing.

We believe that careful study of mathematical learning environments could provide important understanding of the development of learning identities with significant agency. We hypothesize that many didactic classrooms are organized to promote as "gifted" one or two students whose relation to the subject matter of mathematics is extraordinarily agentive. We expect that teachers and students in these classrooms probably attribute these students' lack of conformity to some combination of mathematical "talent" and "interest" that both motivates and supports their unusual participation in learning practices. It may also include being at least slightly "weird" (Boaler, 2000b). We also expect that identification of students to fill the few available "gifted" slots involves interesting interactions in which parents and others play significant roles, and support for these slots probably is biased in favor of boys from relatively affluent families.Our data support the conjecture that when mathematics learning practices place students in positions with more significant conceptual agency, it is much easier for many of them to author their identities as learners with that kind of agency. The positional identities that students in the discussion-oriented classrooms expressed had agency that did not require them to resist the prevailing expectations and become identified as especially "gifted."

Mathematicians often complain about the dependency of undergraduate students, and one of Burton's research subjects characterized the common concern: "One of the things I find about students, undergraduates in particular, is that they seem to have very little intuition. They are dependent upon being spoon-fed" (cited in Burton, 1999b, p. 37). But whereas many mathematicians who are critical of school practices link such problems with the "reform movement," this study suggests that lack of intuition and over dependency are more likely to be a product of narrow pedagogical practices in traditional classrooms. The students who like mathematics because they believe it is abstract and definitive, with only one correct answer, are engaging in a distressingly limited version of the discipline of mathematics (Schoenfeld, 1988). The certainty they have come to enjoy, and on which they will make decisions about future subjects, appears to be inconsistent with the mathematics with which they would engage at the highest mathematical levels. Students who choose mathematics as their main field of study, based upon the idea that the subject is structured, certain, and nonnegotiable, may encounter significant problems as the mathematics they learn at university becomes more advanced. Those who rise to the top of their undergraduate classes and eventually become mathematicians must surely be those who have a deep, conceptual understanding of the material, and students such as Jerry, cited earlier, who do not like to think about "how or why something is the way it is" may be limited in the understanding that they develop. It is unusual for undergraduates who excel in mathematics to become school teachers of mathematics, which means that the mathematics majors who choose teaching are sometimes those who have preferences for "received knowing" that were developed in school and that have limited their attainment. Thus, we perpetuate a cycle of received knowers, teaching received forms of knowing. This is a highly speculative interpretation that we nevertheless offer as a hypothesis to help explain the recurrence of traditional mathematical practices in schools (Cohen, 1990; Fennema & Nelson, 1997).

There is evidence that knowledge presented in an abstract, decontextualized way is more alienating for girls than boys (Becker, 1995; Belencky et al., 1986; Boaler, 1997c)—and for non-Western than Western students (Banks, 1993). This suggests that traditional pedagogical practices will maintain inequality in the attainment and representation of mathematics students, particularly at the highest levels, even as stereotypical societal expectations diminish. University mathematics will continue to be a white, male preserve and large numbers of girls and students from particular minority groups will be excluded from a subject at which they could excel. By giving the final word to equity, we hope to communicate our commitment to a different world in which classroom mathematical practices support the development of thinking, responsible agents and mathematical identification and knowing becomes a possibility for a broader, more diverse group of students.

ACKNOWLEDGMENTS

Our thanks go to Megan Staples, who conducted the interviews with Jo, and to Alan Schoenfeld, who gave helpful comments on an earlier version of the chapter.

NOTES

1. Belenky and associates (1986) also characterized *silent knowing,* in which the individual considers herself powerless to know, and *constructed knowing,* which combines the stances of separate and connected knowing and emphasizes the knower's agency in the process of achieving and legitimizing knowledge. We use the term *constructive knowing* to refer to separate knowing, connected knowing, and constructed knowing. We depart, therefore, from Belenky and associates' use of the term *procedural knowing* for separate and connected knowing, mainly because "procedural" is a term that the community of mathematics education research uses to refer to a specific form of knowledge, consisting mainly of knowing how to perform procedures.

2. The interviews were conducted by Jo Boaler and Megan Staples.

3. Pickering developed these distinctions for mathematics with the example of Hamilton's construction of quaternions. He also discussed an example from physics, in which he analyzed agency as being divided by scientists and material systems; one example was Davis's development of the bubble chamber, and he attributed *material agency* to the functioning of apparatus that interacts with the agency of humans who construct apparatus in the hope that the material will behave in ways that support the construction of scientific findings related to theoretical issues.

4. To quote Pickering: "Think of an established concdptual practice—elementary algebra, say. To know algebra is to recognize a set of characteristic symbols *and how to use them. . . .* Such uses are [what I call] detached disciplines. . . . they are machinelike actions, in Harry Collins's terminology. Just as in arithmetic one completes '3 + 4 = ' by writing '7' without hesitation, so in algebra one authomatically multiplies out '$a(b + c)$' and '$ab + ac.$' Conceptual systems, then, hang together with specific disciplined patterns of human agency, particular routinized ways of connecting marks and symbols with one another. Such disciplines—acquired in training and refined in use—carry human conceptual practices along, as it were, independently of individual wishes and intents. The scientist is, in

this sense, passive in disciplines conceptual practice. . . . I want to redescribe this human passivity in terms of a notion of disciplinary agency. It is, I shall say, the agency of a discipline—elementary algebra, for example—that leads us through a series of manipulations withing an established conceptual system.

The notion of discipline as a pereformative agent might seem odd to those accustomed to thinking of discipline as a constraint upon human agency, but I want (like Foucault) to recognize that discipline is productive. There could be no conceptual practice without the kind of discipline at issue; there could be only marks on paper" (Pickering, 1995, p. 115).

REFERENCES

Aczel, A. D. (1996). *Fermat's last theorem: Unlocking the secret of an ancient mathematical problem.* New York: Dell.

Anderson, S. E. (1997). Worldmath curriculum: Fighting Eurocentrism in mathematics. In A. Powell & M. Frankenstein (Eds.), *Ethnomathematics:Challenging Eurocentrism in mathematics education* (pp. 291–306). Albany: State University of New York Press.

Angier, C., & Povey, H. (1999). One teacher and a class of school students: Their perception of the culture of their mathematics classroom and its construction. *Educational Review, 51*(2).

Ball, S. J. (1993). Education, majorism and the "curriculum of the dead." *Curriculum Studies, 1*(2), 195–214.

Ball, D. L., & Bass, H. (2000). Making believe: The collective construction of public mathematical knowledge in the elementary classroom. In D. Phillips (Ed.), *Yearbook of the National Society for the Study of Education: Constructivism in Education.* Chicago: Chicago University Press.

Banks, J. A. (1993). The canon debate, knowledge construction and multicultural education. *Educational Researcher*, 4–14.

Becker, J. R. (1995). Women's ways of knowing in mathematics. In P. Rogers & G. Kaiser (Eds.), *Equity in mathematics education: Influences of feminism and culture* (pp. 163–174). London: Falmer.

Becker, J., & Jacob, B. (2000). California school mathematics politics: The anti-reform of 1997—1999. *Phi Delta Kappan.*

Belencky, M. F., Clinchy, B. M., Goldberger, N. R., & Tarule, J. M. (1986). *Women's ways of knowing: The development of self, voice and mind.* New York: Basic Books.

Boaler, J. (1997a). *Experiencing school mathematics: Teaching styles, sex and setting.* Buckingham, UK: Open University Press.

Boaler, J. (1997b). Reclaiming school mathematics: The girls fight back. *Gender and Education, 9*(3), 285–306.

Boaler, J. (1997c). When even the winners are losers: Evaluating the experiences of "top set" students. *Journal of Curriculum Studies, 29*(2), 165–182.

Boaler, J. (1998). Open and closed mathematics: Student experiences and understandings. *Journal for Research in Mathematics Education, 29*(1), 41–62.

Boaler, J. (2000a). Exploring situated insights into research and learning. *Journal for Research in Mathematics Education.*

Boaler, J. (2000b). Mathematics from another world: Traditional communities and the alienation of learners. *Journal of Mathematical Behavior, 18*(4).

Bourdieu, P. (1986). The forms of capital. In J. Richardson (Ed.), *Handbook of theory and research for the sociology of education* (pp. 241–258). New York: Greenwood Press.

Burton, L. (1995). Moving towards a feminist epistemology of mathematics. In P. Rogers & G. Kaiser (Eds.), *Equity in mathematics education: Influences of feminism and culture* (pp. 209–226). London: Falmer.

Burton, L. (1999a). Exploring and reporting upon the content and diversity of mathematicians' views and practices. *For the Learning of Mathematics, 19*(2), 36–38.

Burton, L. (1999b). The practices of mathematicians: What do they tell us about coming to know mathematics? *Educational Studies in Mathematics, 37*, 121–143.

Clinchy, B. McV. (1996). Connected and separate knowing: Toward a marriage of two minds. In N. R. Goldberger, J. M. Tarule, B. McV. Clinchy, & M. F. Belenky (Eds.), *Knowledge, difference and power: Essays inspired by women's ways of knowing* (pp. 205–247). New York: Basic Books.

Cohen, D. (1990). A revolution in one classroom: The case of Mrs Oublier. *Educational Evaluation and Policy Analysis, 12*(3), 327–345.

Corbett, D., & Wilson, B. (1995). Make a difference with, not for, students: A plea to researchers and reformers. *Educational Researcher, 24*(5), 12–17.

Dowling, P. (1996). A sociological analysis of school mathematics texts. *Educational Studies in Mathematics, 31*, 389–415.

Doyle, W. (1988). Work in mathematics classes: The context of students' thinking during instruction. *Educational Psychologist, 23*(2), 167–180.

Elbow, P. (1973). *Writing without teachers*. London: Oxford University Press.

Fennema, E., & Nelson, B. S. (Eds.). (1997). *Mathematics teachers in transition*. Mahwah, NJ: Erlbaum.

Greeno, J. G., & MMAP. (1998). The situativity of knowing, learning and research. *American Psychologist, 53*(1), 5–26.

Gutierrez, R. (2000). Is the multiculturalization of mathematics doing use more harm than good? In R. Malalingham & C. McCarthy (Eds.), *Multicultural curriculum: New directions for social theory, practice and policy*. New York: Routledge.

Holland, D., Lachicotte, W., Skinner, D., & Cain, C. (1998). *Identity and agency in cultural worlds*. Cambridge MA: Harvard University Press.

Keller, E. F. (1983). *A feeling for the organism: The life and work of Barbara McClintock*. New York: Freeman.

Kitcher, P. (1983). *The nature of mathematical knowledge*. Oxford, UK: Oxford University Press.

Lave, J. (1988). *Cognition in practice*. Cambridge, UK: Cambridge University Press.

Lave, J., & Wenger, E. (1991). *Situated learning: Legitimate peripheral participation*. New York: Cambridge University Press.

Lave, J. (1993). Situating learning in communities of practice. In L. Resnick, J. Levine, & T. Teasley (Eds.), *Perspectives on socially shared cognition* (pp. 63–85). Washington, DC: American Psychological Association.

Mason, J. (1989). Mathematical abstraction as the result of a delicate shift in attention. *For the Learning of Mathematics, 9*(2), 2–9.

McLaughlin, M., & Talbert, J. (1999). *High school teaching in context*. Stanford, CA: Center for Research on the Context of Teaching.

Miles, M., & Huberman, M. (1994). *Qualitative data analysis: An expanded sourcebook*. Thousand Oaks, CA: Sage.

National Council for Teachers of Mathematics (NCTM). (1989). *Curriculum and education standards for school mathematics*. Virginia: NCTM.

Noss, R. (1991). The social shaping of computing in mathematics education. In D. Pimm & E. Love (Eds.), *Teaching and learning school mathematics* (pp. 205–219). London: Hodder & Stoughton.

Perry, M. (1991). Learning and transfer: Instructional conditions and conceptual change. *Cognitive Development, 6*(4), 449–468.

Pickering, A. (1995). *The mangle of practice: Time, agency, and science*. Chicago: University of Chicago Press.

Povey, H., Burton, L., Angier, C., & Boylan, M. (1999). Learners as authors in the mathematics classroom. In L. Burton (Ed.), *Learning mathematics: From hierarchies to networks* (pp. 232–245). London: Falmer.

Rogers, P. (1995). Putting theory into practice. In P. Rogers & G. Kaiser (Eds.), *Equity in mathematics education: Influences of feminism and culture* (pp. 175–185). London: Falmer Press.

Rogers, P., & Kaiser, G. (Eds.). (1995). *Equity in mathematics education: Influences of feminism and culture*. London: Falmer.

Rogoff, B. (1990). *Apprenticeship in thinking: Cognitive development in social context*. Oxford, UK: Oxford University Press.

Schoenfeld, A. H. (1988). When good teaching leads to bad results: The disasters of "well-taught" mathematics courses. *Educational Psychologist, 23*(2), 145–166.

Schoenfeld, A. (1998). *Notes on the preparation of educational researchers*. Paper prepared for the National Academy of Education's Commission for Improving Educational Research.

Schwab, J. J. (1969). *College curriculum and student protest*. Chicago: University of Chicago Press.

Stigler, J., & Hiebert, J. (1999). *The teaching gap: What teachers can learn from the world's best teachers*. New York: Free Press.

Tarule, J. M. (1996). Voices in dialogue: Collaborative ways of knowing. In N. R. Goldberger, J. M. Tarule, B. McV. Clinchy, & M. F. Belenky (Eds.), *Knowledge, difference and power: Essays inspired by women's ways of knowing* (pp. 274–304). New York: Basic Books.

Tymoczko, T. (Ed.). (1986). *New directions in the philosophy of mathematics*. Boston, Kirkhäuser.

Wenger, E. (1998). *Communities of practice: Learning, meaning and identity*. Cambridge, UK: Cambridge University Press.

Wood, T. (1999). Creating a context for argument in mathematics class. *Journal for Research in Mathematics Education, 30*(2), 171–191.

8

"Cracking the Code" of Mathematics Classrooms: School Success As a Function of Linguistic, Social, and Cultural Background

Robyn Zevenbergen

INTRODUCTION

The role of language in the teaching and learning of mathematics has been given increasing recognition over recent years. Much of this attention has been inspired by constructivist epistemologies that have placed aspects of language central to the learning process. These literatures have shown how language is inextricably bound to learning. It provides the medium through which communication of ideas is made possible, and negotiation of ideas and concepts is delivered. These literatures has alerted educators to the mismatch of language between experts (teachers) and novices (students) and suggested that a more appropriate level of language and communication is made possible through dialogue among the students. This chapter extends this work by drawing attention to the political nature of the language used in classrooms. Drawing on Bourdieu's notion of cultural capital, or more particularly, linguistic capital, it is argued that some students will have greater or lesser access to the modes of communication in a classroom, and hence have more or less access to the mathematics inherent in such communications.

Three common communicative strategies found in mathematics classrooms form the basis of this chapter. The first is the type of questions commonly found in texts and tests. These represent the register of mathematics that I argue is very structured and that students must come to learn in order to be able to participate in a productive and effective manner. The second communicative strategy is that of classroom talk, which has its own internal rules that are not made explicit to students but form the basis for communication in the classroom. The third and final example is that of what comes to constitute legitimate knowledge in the classroom, and this is bound to the contexts used to embed mathematical tasks.

The attempts made to make mathematics "real" come to be a veneer, which serves to include or marginalize students (Boaler, 1993).

In order to become a legitimate participant in a community, one must learn its language. Increasingly, mathematics educators are recognizing that mathematics is a language (Ellerton & Clements, 1991). Although it may be based in the language of instruction, such as English or French, it has its own internal logic and relationships between words and structure (grammar). In this light, it is most productive to consider it as a register, and as such, certain aspects of that language need to be considered. These range from specialized vocabulary to syntax and lexical density. Students must come to learn this register if they are to become effective speakers, listeners, and communicators in mathematics classrooms. Yet, in many cases, the teaching and learning of mathematics is seen to be a process of learning the mathematics as devoid of the language. In this chapter, I argue that students must come to learn mathematics as a language equally as a discipline of knowledge.

Bourdieu's notions of habitus and field are particularly useful in theorizing how social differences are manifested and legitimated through school mathematics. For Bourdieu, habitus is the embodiment of culture, and it provides the lens through which the world is interpreted. Through his detailed work with patterns of consumption and work, Bourdieu (1979) has shown how different social classes have distinctive preferences toward food, sport, leisure, housing, and so forth. For students who have been socialized within particular familial contexts, distinctive patterns are observable of which language use is one of the key differences across diverse groups. As students come to hear and use particular forms of language, this language becomes embodied to constitute a linguistic habitus. When students enter mathematics classrooms, they have accepted the language of their home environment, the consistency of which will vary with respect to formal school language. Where there is greater continuity between the home and school, there is greater chance of success in school mathematics (Bourdieu, Passeron, & de saint Martin, 1994).

When considering the differences between home and school, a number of studies have shown a disjunction between some homes and the school. In her studies of students from different backgrounds, Brice-Heath (Heath, 1982, 1983) has shown that students from economically disadvantaged backgrounds are more likely to be exposed to declarative statements when they are expected to undertake tasks, whereas students from economically advantaged homes are more likely to receive pseudo-questions from parents or guardians requesting their children to undertake tasks. Similarly, in their studies of mothers and daughters, Walkerdine and Lucey (1989) reported similar differences in interactions between social classes. From these familial interactions, children are more likely to embody different patterns of interaction, which will be differentially used and recognized within the formal school context. When the students enter the school context, their out-of-school language practices, which have become embodied in their habitus, provide a lens for interpreting and acting within the school context. Accordingly, when the teacher asks, "Could you get out your math books?," it is interpreted quite differently depending on children's previous experiences. When students are able to recognize the question as a pseudo-question that demands that they take out their math books and begin work, there is a greater chance of effective participation in that classroom. In contrast, when students interpret the question as one in which they are given an option as to whether or not they would like to take out their books, they are more likely to be constructed as deviant, and hence be positioned as marginal in the classroom.

This is not to suggest a deterministic reading of social background (as is commonly made of Bourdieu's works) but rather to recognize that differences exist between home and school languages and these have an impact on a students' performance in the classroom. Harker (1984) argues persuasively that the primary habitus can be reconstituted. In his view, for students whose habitus is different from that of the formal school context, there is potential for it to be brought closer to that which is legitimated through school practices, thus suggesting a transformative component of pedagogy rather than a deterministic reading. However, such reconstitution must be undertaken with considerable effort. According to this interpretation the linguistic background of the student can be converted to success, or restriction thereof, within the school context. The language background of the student can therefore be converted to academic rewards and become a form of capital, namely, linguistic capital.

Within this framework, linguistic capital gains its value by the social context within which it is located. Language, by itself, does not convey status or power, but rather practices within the school, classroom, or wider society serve to legitimate some forms of language over others. Different contexts confer different status on the language used. For example, the language used by members of a particular gang will convey different status on the street than when used in the context of the classroom. For this chapter, this implies that it is necessary to consider the context of the mathematics classroom, or more broadly, the formal school setting, within which the language is being used in order to understand how power is conveyed to students who display the desired patterns of language use.

Within the context of schools and classrooms, practices such as the use of an appropriate mathematics register or decoding of teacher-talk are seen to be valuable aspects of language use. Students who display or assimilate those socially legitimated linguistic practices within their own repertoire of behaviors are positioned more favorably. However, the skills seen to hold status and power within the field of school mathematics may be very different from those of another context. This is borne out in studies of ethnomathematics where students who display street-talk and skills within street selling may be positioned as marginal within the field of education. For these students, the dispositions that have become embodied within their habitus and that predispose them to be effective in bartering because of the structuring practices of the marketplace are positioned less favorably within mathematics education, where the structuring practices do not legitimate the practices of the marketplace. The practices within these two divergent fields differentially convey power on the participants. Mathematics education, as a field, values and conveys power and status on those who display the characteristics, attributes, and dispositions seen as desirable within the field at any given point in time. What conveys status may be different at different points in time, so it must be recognized that as a field, mathematics education is transitory. Further, students are rarely taught in an explicit manner regarding the differences in what is valued (Corbett & Wilson, 1995).

LANGUAGE AS A FORM OF CAPITAL

Linguistic competence—or incompetence—in mathematics reveals itself through daily exchanges. Within the mathematics classrooms, legitimate participation is acquired and achieved through a competence with written or spoken texts, or both. To be constructed as an effective learner of mathematics, students must be able to display a competence with these forms of texts. This frequently demands that students be able to render visible the social and political differences embedded within such texts. Bourdieu argues that:

> Linguistic competence is not a simple technical ability, but a statutory ability. . . . what goes in verbal communication, even the content of the message itself, remains unintelligible as long as one does not take into account the totality of the structure of the power positions that is present, yet invisible, in the exchange. (Bourdieu & Wacquant, 1992, p. 146)

When students are able to deconstruct texts for the underlying meaning, they are better positioned within the field. In most instances, this requires a familiarity with the language of representation—in this instance, the mathematics register when considering written texts, and interactional competence when considering oral language.

The linguistic habitus of students will have substantial impact on their capacity to make sense of the discursive practices of the mathematics classroom and, hence, their subsequent capacity to gain access to legitimate mathematical knowledge along with the power and status associated with that knowledge. The processes through which the schooling procedures are able to value one language and devalue others must be systematically understood. Through this process, we can better understand how mathematical pedagogy both inculcates mathematical knowledge and imposes domination.

In the following section, I explore the notion of mathematics being a particular register that students must come to learn in order that they may be able to "crack the code" of the mathematics classroom. Just as with other languages, mathematics has a particular form and the newcomer must be able to decipher that language. In much the same way as a tourist can make minimal sense of languages in foreign countries, the learning of mathematics is similar for students. Where a student gains competency in the intricacies of the mathematics register, he or she will be better able to decipher the subtle but precise meaning of mathematical expressions.

MATHEMATICS AS A REGISTER

In considering mathematics as a register, three components will be considered: the specialized vocabulary of mathematics, the semantic structure, and the lexical density of mathematics. These aspects of a mathematics register constitute a form of language for the discipline. To provide an example of how register influences students' performance in mathematics, a series of tasks are taken from a statewide testing scheme, "The 1997 Year 6 Test" (Education Queensland, Australia, 1997), which is implemented in the sixth year of formal schooling.

Specialized Vocabulary

Mathematics has a very particularized vocabulary to which students need access in order to be constructed as effective learners of mathematics. Many of the words used in mathematics are ambiguous for students in that they have very different meanings in the nonschool context versus the formal mathematics context. For example, words such as ruler, face, prime, odd, mean, right, rational, root, and mass have very different meanings depending on the context in which they are being used or intended. Learning mathematics is, in part, learning the unique correspondence between the signifiers (words) and signifieds (concepts) within a mathematics context with some words having different meanings depending on the strand[1] of the curriculum. Even these names can be considered arbitrary and will be determined by the national contexts. For example, base and square have very different meanings for students when used in the context of space and number. Similar difficulties are posed for students when words that sound similar are used. These include homophones such as sum/some and whole/hole along with words that are slightly different in sound such as off/of, sixty/sixteen, and tens/tenths, which demand careful attention. When a student is unable to decipher the specificity of the mathematics signifier, they are at risk of calling up a very different discourse than that intended by the teacher. For example, in a recent lesson on fractions that I observed, the teacher was using doughnuts to talk about two halves and then later how the two halves, when combined, made a whole. Unfortunately, the doughnut was one with a hole in the middle so many students were very confused as to how two halves could make a whole (rather than a hole!). However, their experiences in mathematics positioned them to accept the teacher's comments as truths. For this group of students the relationships of signification became a source of confusion, particularly for those who did not understand the concept or language to begin with.

A further variation on the theme of specialized vocabulary is the highly technical vocabulary of mathematics. These words are specific to mathematics and often unfamiliar to students. Such words would include tessellations, numerator, and denominator. The lack of specificity in meaning can be problematic. When dealing with common fractions, it is a common perception that numerator is the top number and denominator is the bottom number. However, this simplistic translation cannot be transferred to subtraction equations where the denominator (the bottom number) can be subtracted from the numerator (the top number). It also refers to the specific use of prepositions in mathematics. McGregor (1991, p. 7) has noted that the prepositions used in mathematics are a cause for difficulty in understanding tasks. She notes the use of prepositions in the following manner: The temperature fell *to* 10 degrees . . . *by* 10 degrees . . . *from* 10 degrees; and the effect of omitting the preposition: the temperature fell 10 degrees.

Trigger words, often embedded within word problems, need to be interpreted correctly if students are to perform the task contained within the problem. For example, in many word problems, trigger words such as more, less, got, or took away provide cues for the students as to what operation needs to be performed (Schoenfeld, 1988). In part, this is due to the ways mathematics is most frequently taught. This is a common strategy for students who do not have access to the richness and specificity of mathematics language. For example, deaf students tend to rely on this strategy significantly owing to their difficulty in comprehending the changes in meaning caused by order and other contextual words (Barham & Bishop, 1991; Hyde, Power, & Zevenbergen, 1999).

Semantic Structure

Mathematics language needs to be expanded to include the semantic structure used within problems. In considering the word problems identified as change, combine, and compare problems (De Corte & Verschaffel, 1991; Lean, Clements, & Del Campo, 1990) that are commonly found in the mathematics classroom, it is recognized that the problems are simple insofar as arithmetic is concerned, but semantically complex. Depending on the order of the problems and what operations need to be undertaken, the complexity of the tasks increases. For example, in an additive change problem where the unknown is the solution and the form of the equation is 3 + 2 = x, the task is relatively easy for the student. A question of this form may be: "John has 3 cars. Jenny gave him 2 more. How many did he have altogether?" In contrast, when the unknown is the first variable and, for example, the form of the equation is $x + 2 = 5$, the question could be of the form: "John had some cars. Jenny gave him 2 more so that he now has 5 cars. How many cars did John have to start with?" In this instance the complexity is much greater for the students and fewer students are able to respond (De Corte & Verschaffel, 1991; Lean et al., 1990). Research focused on changing the semantic structure so that it is more in line with the language used by students rather than the formal expression of the problems, increases students' capacity to solve the tasks (Carpenter, 1985, cited in De Corte & Verschaffel, 1991). However, while changing the semantic structure of the question may make the question more accessible and help the students find an answer, it does not help them "crack the code" of the mathematics register.

Lexical Density

Halliday (1975) points out that the lexical density found in mathematical and scientific registers is somewhat denser than that found in spoken or written language. He sums up the notion of lexical density as being "the number of lexical items as a ratio of the number of clauses" (1988, p. 67). Halliday suggests that lexical density contributes to the complexity of written problems in mathematics and may be a further barrier to learning. Mathematical tasks are often characterized by their conciseness and preciseness, where there are few redundant words and where all words have highly specific meaning. As noted previously, that specificity of meaning may not be the same as in the nonmathematics contexts. To translate a mathematical task into a more accessible form would require, in most cases, a more convoluted and lengthy description. As a consequence, the lexical density results in a high level of complexity in the translation of the problem. Dawe and Mulligan (1997, pp. 9–10) compared an example of a task where students had to estimate the volume of a phone box and then select from four options. The task contained a picture of a person and a phone box with the accompanying text reading: "The volume of a phone box is about 0.1 cubic metres, 2 cubic metres, 5 cubic metres, 10 cubic metres." They contrasted this with the question: "Trish's model boat is 8 cm long. It is fifty times shorter than the real boat. How long is the real boat? 4 m, 6.2 m, 40 m, 50 m." Clearly there are substantial differences in the vocabulary used including the use of comparative terms along with differences in the mathematical demands of the two tasks. However, the complexity of the task is compounded by the lexical density.

ANALYSIS OF A TESTING SCHEME

In this section, I seek to embed the theoretical issues discussed in the preceding section into a practical framework. The examples are taken from the 1997 Year 6 Test, which is implemented across all Queensland state schools and other schools wanting to participate in the testing scheme. The examples provided below yielded consistent results across the state of Queensland (Education Queensland, 1997). The test was chosen because it represents commonly occurring testing schedules in primary schooling rather than for other features unique to this particular test. One could critically evaluate the questions, but this is not the point of the exercise. Rather, it is my intention to show how the register of mathematics affects students' capacity to answer the questions posed. The overriding pattern of results was that in all questions, indigenous students performed significantly below nonindigenous students. Rather than interpreting these results from within a deficit framework, it is productive to analyze their linguistic features. This provides a lens through which it becomes possible to highlight aspects of language that hinder access to mathematics. For students whose language is not the dominant one of school or curriculum, in this case indigenous students, the chance of accessing the task is restricted.There was only one task in which the results for indigenous and nonindigenous students were similar. This task is shown in Figure 1.

This task required the students to place a piece of string (which was provided for the students, attached to the test papers) along a curved line and then measure it against the options. In spite of the words in the task, the provision of a length of

Figure 1.

Q6	Here is a piece of string.

Which line is about the same length as the piece of string
a) _____
b) _____
c) _____
d) _____

Source: 1997 Queensland Year 6 Test (Education Queensland, 1997)

string provided a cue for the students who could then assume that the task was to overlay the string along the lines and nominate the line of similar length. The equivalent performance of indigenous and nonindigenous students on this item suggests similar mathematical competence among the students, not accessed through the other test items. All other 39 items produced significant differences in performances. Some of the tasks are analyzed for aspects of a mathematical register that can be seen to create difficulty for students for whom the language of representation is different from their spoken language.

Comparison Word Problems

The syntax of the mathematics register often found in comparison word problems can be difficult for students to decipher. In the task shown in Figure 2, comparisons are made between two sets—namely, Anna and Maria—requiring a subtractive operation along with the conversion of length to a single form that has to be identified by the students.

The comprehension of task requirements is complex. The student must be able to identify that two different units are being used in the work problem. This in itself demands a recognition of the symbolism (m = meters, km = kilometers) and the conversion between the two units. The student then must be able to recognize that the term "further" actually refers to the comparison between the two walkers rather than some additional distance. The comparison is not made explicit but is to be understood by the term. The operation to be undertaken must be determined by the student. Although the term "further" suggests growth and hence addition, the student is required to undertake a subtraction of the distance traveled by Anna from the distance traveled by Maria. Students must also take into consideration the different

Figure 2.

Q8	Two friends walk to school. Anna travels 0.3 kms. Maria travels 760 m.

Which statement is correct?

a) Anna walks further by 300m   b) Maria walks further by 460 m

c) Anna walks further by 1.06 km   d) Maria walks further by 0.73 km

Source: 1997 Queensland Year 6 Test (Education Queensland, 1997)

units of measurement in order to determine the appropriate unit in which to make the comparisons.

Signifiers and Symbolism

The problems associated with symbolism and language used in mathematics become apparent in questions where the protocol for representation is embedded in the task. Students must be able to decode not only the linguistic form of the question but also the symbolism used in the mathematical practices. Often this symbolism is compounded by the lexical density of the question asked and the mathematics involved. This is further compounded when there is an overlaying context within which the task is embedded.

The space strand of mathematics is probably the most rich in terms of its linguistic complexity and its relationships of signification. Often this language specificity is seen to be the cause of many of the difficulties for learning this area of mathematics. If one considers the language of angles—even at the most simple level—words such as reflex, acute, obtuse, complimentary, and adjacent illustrate the complexity of demand. The difficulties of learning this area of mathematics are compounded by the complex symbolization of the strand. The protocols for representation must be learned and, if one considers the ways in which students come to represent cubes, this symbolization becomes obvious. In the example shown in Figure 3, students must recognize the protocol for representing 3D shapes whereby the hidden edges and vertices are drawn using dotted lines.

The student must not only access the symbolism of mathematics to effectively answer the question, but also the specific signifiers must be known. The complexity of terms such as pentagonal, prism, and vertices must be accessible in order for them to "crack the code" of the question. Being able to read and comprehend the question is critical to the capacity to answer it. To do this, the student must have access to the specific language embedded in the question as well as the formal symbolism of the diagrammatic representation.

Figure 3.

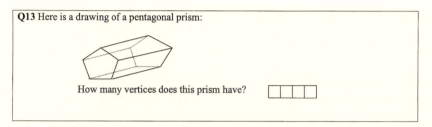

Q13 Here is a drawing of a pentagonal prism:

How many vertices does this prism have?

Source: 1997 Queensland Year 6 Test (Education Queensland, 1997)

In the task shown in Figure 4, the language is very limited yet this task was performed poorly by all students, but in particular, by indigenous students. The specificity of the symbols appears to create the difficulty for students. In this question, the students must be able to make sense at a number of very different levels. The first is to understand the complexity of the mathematical signifiers—both linguistic and symbolic. The linguistic signifiers of "whole number" and "number sentence" are keys to the task. A student must know what is meant by these terms. In terms of symbolic signifiers, the student must be able to make sense of the symbols in the equation: $120 \times 5 > 60 \; - - - -$.

At the second level is the complexity in the sentence structure. Even if the student is aware of the individual meanings for each signifier, these must then be linked in a way that makes the question and the equation make sense. At the third level, the student must be able to make sense of the question mathematically and link the elements into something coherent. Regardless of the strategies used to solve the equation (calculator, logic, etc.), the student must be able to link it all into a coherent form. If both sides of the equation were to be made equal, they would need to make 600 and the solution of the equation would be 10, but as the signifier is "greater than," the right-hand side must be less than or equal to the left. In this situation, experience with and understanding of the symbols $>$ and $\geq$ is needed if a correct answer is to be offered. Students who offer a 10 in this case will be incorrect as the correct answer is any number less than 10, but restricted interpretation of the symbolization is very common. When this task was given to a group of 150 first-year preservice teachers, 12 percent of the teachers answered incorrectly, with most mistaken answers failing to recognize the lack of inequality in the symbolization. The teachers either created an equal equation or misrecognized the direction of the $>$ sign so that the equation was greater than it should have been. When students in primary schools are given this task, their interpretation of the sign is likely to be hindered by less experience with the symbols. Furthermore, when students encounter the abstract nature of such symbolization, particularly when that symbolization is not common or relevant to their culture, as is the case with many indigenous students, then the chances of success in interpreting such abstractions is further restricted.

Figure 4.

Q 9   Write a whole number to make the number sentence true.
120 x 5 > 60 x [ ] [ ] [ ] [ ]

Source: 1997 Queensland Year 6 Test (Education Queensland, 1997)

A further complexity of the problem is the provision of the four boxes. Students must be able to understand the significance of the boxes and ascertain whether or not they provide relevant or redundant information.

Clearly, the specificity of the mathematics language creates difficulties for students whose first language is not English. However, it is equally necessary to be cognizant of those students whose command of the very particularized English used in mathematics classrooms is not strong. There is a growing literature that recognizes the language used by some students whose first language is English is not of the same form as others—in particular, students from working-class backgrounds. The research in language education (see, for example, Freebody, Ludwig, & Gunn, 1995) has produced some highly relevant and important work in the area (Lubienski, 1997; Secada, 1992). The role of the register of mathematics is critical in understanding how students make sense, or fail to make sense, of the questions posed in the classroom or on tests. In the preceding sections, aspects of register have been highlighted. This may be related to the contextualization of mathematical tasks. The movement in mathematics education to embed mathematical tasks into word problems with the intention of making them more meaningful (and supposedly more accessible) has not met with the success that was hoped for. Cooper and Dunne (1998) have found that students from different socioeconomic groups perform equally well on decontextualized tasks but differ when the tasks become contextualized. They contend that the language-richness of the contextualized tasks makes readability and comprehension difficult for working-class students. More centrally, they argue that the "correct" degree of engagement that is needed with real world contexts is a particular from of capital that is not equally accessible for working-class and middle-class students.

The previous section has highlighted the more formal aspects of mathematical language, particularly as it relates to written texts. A central aspect of mathematical language and success is oral and played out within classroom interactions. These aspects are discussed in the next section.

CLASSROOM INTERACTIONS

Studies of classroom interactions have demonstrated a regularity in the interactions that become *taken-for-granted* in a mathematics culture. The culture of the mathematics classroom has been well documented and has often been described by teachers and students within restricted frameworks. Many teachers hold beliefs about mathematics teaching that can be seen to be largely behaviorist in their foundations. Such approaches engender a narrow set of practices that are frequently recalled by students. Most often these are described as teacher directed, students undertaking routine exercises that are assessed using pencil-and-paper testing procedures (Leder & Forgasz, 1992). With a greater emphasis on inquiry modes of pedagogy such as those advocated by the National Council for Teachers of Mathematics (1989), mathematics classrooms that have adopted these new forms of pedagogy have provided fertile ground for research (see, for example, Bauersfeld, Krummheuer, & Voigt, 1988; and Wood 1994, for discussion of the ways in which changed interactional patterns brought about by changes in pedagogy can facilitate improved learning outcomes).

Bernstein (1990) has developed the notion of "relay" to describe the elusive ways in which cultural norms and knowledge are transmitted. Successful interaction patterns are rarely taught explicitly to our students; they must come to learn them covertly. In the following sections, I draw on the work of ethnomethodology that seeks to identify the micro interactions of classrooms that become a component of the culture of classrooms.

Micro Interactions

Within interactions between two or more people, there are particularized patterns. I refer to these as "micro interactions" as it connotes the minute detail of analysis that can be undertaken of the interactions. One of the most documented patterns of interaction in the classroom is that of "triadic dialogue" (Lemke, 1990). It has been found across all curriculum areas and all sectors of formal schooling. The phrase "triadic dialogue" as coined by Lemke is the one I use in this chapter, although others have described the same interaction patterns in different terms. Triadic dialogue consists of three key parts: the teacher initiates a question to which the students usually know the answer; a student responds; and the teacher then evaluates the student's response (Mehan, 1982; Sinclair & Coulthard, 1975). The extract below is taken from a classroom in which I was conducting research:

1. Teacher: Here is a diagram of a 3D shape—who can tell me what it is?
2. Student: A rectangular shape.
3. Teacher: Mmm, almost. John?
4. Student: A rectangular cube?
5. Teacher: Nearly, you are half right. Margaret?
6. Student: A rectangular prism.
7. Teacher: Good, that's it. A rectangular prism. Funny word, isn't it.

The first three lines show the nature of the three-phase interaction. When the response is not the desired one, the teacher leads the students into a more acceptable response while still retaining the three-part interaction. This structure is common across many Western countries (Stigler & Hiebert, 1999).

Triadic interactions serve the purpose of controlling student behavior while also prescribing the content of lessons. Lemke (1990) argues that rules for interacting are not explicitly taught and students have to learn them through participation in the interactions. However, Lemke also notes that the patterns of interaction are not consistent across the three phases of a lesson. Triadic dialogue is common in the introductory phase of a lesson where the teacher attempts to keep tight control of the content and students. Hence, a significant amount of power resides with the teacher. Similar observations are made of the concluding phase of the lesson. However, during the "work" phase of the lesson, the patterns of power are somewhat more equal and students can express their lack of understanding. The role of teachers' questions are critical in controlling the interactions with classrooms. As Lemke (1990) has shown through triadic dialogue, questions are used to control the flow of the lesson, the content to be covered, and the behavior of students, and to provide progressive evaluation of student learning and lesson implementation.

Acceptable classroom responses are rarely taught to students explicitly so students must learn them through participation. This is made easier if there is some continuity between the school and home. The contribution made by the studies cited previously (Heath, 1982, 1983; Walkerdine, 1990) shows that the transition from the home to the school is more difficult for working-class students or students whose cultural patterns of interaction are different from those within the formal school context, than for others. This transition is encapsulated in a comment offered by a mother when talking about the difficulties faced by socially different students in the school context: "My kid, he too scared to talk, 'cause nobody play by the rules he know. At home, I cain't shut him up" (cited in Heath 1982, p. 107).

In a 1–year, ethnographic study of three schools (an independent elite school serving a middle- to upper-class clientele, a government school serving a predominantly middle-class clientele, and a government school serving a predominantly working-class clientele), two classrooms were observed and mathematics lessons video recorded throughout the year. Interviews were conducted with students and participating teachers. These data were used to examine the practices within the schools in order to identify the ways in which social differences were being realized in and through the practices of mathematics. From the analysis of classroom interactions in middle-class settings, it was noted that there was a strong compliance with triadic dialogue in mathematics lessons. Students and teachers used this model of interaction effectively and efficiently to convey information and maintain control of the lesson and students. In contrast, in both classrooms at the school where the students were predominantly from working-class backgrounds, there were many challenges to the triadic dialogue and, hence, its use by the teachers was thwarted by the actions of the students. This made control of the content and students less effective (Zevenbergen, 1994, 1998). Freebody and associates' (Freebody, Ludwig, & Gunn, 1995) research in literacy classrooms has found similar patterns of interactions with students from disadvantaged backgrounds. In these studies of mathematics and literacy classrooms, it was found that students from working-class backgrounds were likely to transgress the unspoken rules of classroom interactions and disrupt the flow of lessons, thus making it more difficult for the teacher to "teach" the content of the lesson and ultimately cover the content identified through formal syllabus or statutory documents.

In a classroom in the sixth year of primary schooling at a working-class school in which I was observing, the teacher was undertaking a lesson on the construction of 3D shapes from nets. In the following extract from the orientating or introductory phase of the lesson, the teacher had been progressively leading the students through the various shape names and was seeking to elicit the word "prism" from the students. In the preceding discussion, he had been asking the students about various 2D shapes and linking them to 3D solids (e.g., squares to cubes). In the following extract, he has arrived at the point of naming a rectangular prism with the first mention of the signifier "prism":

1. Student: A rectangular oblong.
2. Teacher: The word we're looking for is "prism."
3. Student: Yeah, I said that.
4. Teacher: Say the word please [to the whole class].
5. Students: Prism.
6. Teacher: Not like go to jail prison, that's "prison."

This sequence indicates how the three-phase interaction controls student behavior. In the third line the student violates a classroom norm by calling out. This response is ignored indicating to students that this is not an appropriate nor valued comment. In other cases, the teacher may be more overt in chastising the students. The effect is that the teacher is able to control the flow of the lesson such that responses that are not wanted are either ignored or rejected whereas comments that are sought can be expanded or praised so that the students become aware of what is the "correct" response. Through this process, teachers are able to control behavior and content. However, Lemke is quick to point out that the level of questioning is often low and is aimed at keeping the lesson moving at a brisk pace to keep students motivated while introducing and covering the content that is the focus of the lesson.

The flow of interactions was far more consistent and smooth in the middle-class contexts than in the working-class contexts. In the following extract from a working-class classroom, the teacher is working with the students in the construction of nets.

1. T: Before we start, what shape do you think this one for example [cube net] is going to make when you fold it up and we'll pass the sticky tape around. Now there's only two rolls so it may take a while before you get it. You can actually stick it to make it together. What shape, Rebecca?
2. G: A cube.
3. T: Any other answers?

4. Cs: A cube.

5. T: A cube, good. It will have squares on it. What shape do you think this will make? [a triangular prism] Excuse me, are you concentrating? What shape do you think it will be?

6. G: [no answer].

7. G: A square.

8. T: It will certainly have squares on it.

9. B: A rectangle.

10. T: A rectangular. . . .

11. B: Prism?

12. T: What shape will it make?

13. C: It won't! [student stands up and calls out]

14. :T You may not have your chair if you don't use your manners.

15. B: What's it called? A triangle.

16. T: A triangle is part of it. Who can continue on, a triangle is part of it.

17. G:A right angle triangle.

18. T: Yes it would have a right angle triangle in it. This is the right angle triangle shape here. [calling out] Put your hand up if you're going to give an answer. Sit down David. Stop. Excuse me. Listen to us. We're asking for a name, do you have a name?

19. B: No.

20. B: A triangular prism.

21. B: I was going to say that. He stole my brain.

22. B: What brain?

23. C: The one inside my head.

24. [chatter]

25. T: OK, hand these out to each person [photocopied sheets with nets]. Could the hand-out monitors also hand out a pair of scissors between two people. If you have any in your tub, get them out please. You can get out your rules and see if you can start on these.

The interactions within this working-class classroom, appear substantially different to those in many middle-class classrooms. At line 13, a student challenges the teacher's authority and the remainder of the interactions appear to be more confrontational than compliant. These challenges to the teacher result in the teacher changing his approach to the lesson and moving to a work phase, where the students would be engaged in the active construction of nets. Although this approach would be expected in most classrooms, what is important to note is that the previous introduction was only a very short period of time (just under 2 minutes), thus suggesting that the students did not comply with the expected social norms of classroom interactions. This makes it very difficult for the teacher to continue with such modes of teaching and compels him to move to different strategies. It is noteworthy that such challenges were not observed in the middle-class classrooms in my study. In the middle-class classroom, there was a strong compliance with the triadic dialogue thus permitting the teacher to proceed through the lesson in a way that was congruous with her aims, enabling the students to cover the content necessary for the lesson.

These studies indicate that students from disadvantaged backgrounds may be excluded from significant mathematical knowledge through their noncompliance with the unspoken rules of classroom interactions.

LEGITIMATE CONTEXTS

The final section of this chapter is concerned with what is regarded as legitimate knowledge in mathematics. Two aspects need to be considered in concert with each other: the first is the language of the task, and the second is the biases represented by the contextualizing of the task itself. In considering the contexts in which school mathematics become embedded, the role of language is a key consideration. In the first instance, the role of language is essential for conveying ideas so that the contextualizing of tasks is achieved through linguistic turns. As Cooper and Dunne (1998) have demonstrated, working-class students are considerably disadvantaged by the embedding of tasks in a pseudo-mathematical context. In part, this is owing to the increasing complexity of demands of the task. Newman (Ellerton & Clements, 1992) has noted that several cognitive steps are needed in deconstructing and responding appropriately to a word problem: reading the problem, comprehending the problem, translating the problem into a mathematical task, undertaking the mathematics necessary for the task, and, finally, interpreting what the answer means. Students are able to make mistakes at any of these steps and hence produce incorrect responses. This is then further compounded by the language differences between that which is represented in and through the mathematics curriculum—as evident in the mathematics register—and the language of the students. Where there is greater synergy between the language of the mathematics problem and that of the student, there is greater potential for success. In contrast, where there is significant difference between the two registers, the chances of success are reduced.

Although the knowledge represented in and through the curriculum is seen to be important and worthwhile, there is a need to be critical about *whose* knowledge is actually being represented and with what effects. Over the past two decades, there has been an increasing international recognition that the mathematics embedded in the curriculum is culturally and socially biased. Historical studies have shown that there is very strong Eurocentric bias in the knowledge (Joseph, 1991; Joseph, 1987) wherein other cultures may have been working with mathematical ideas before Westerners, but this has not been recognized, thereby perpetuating a belief in the superiority of Western mathematics. Similarly, studies in the broad area of ethnomathematics have been active in drawing out the mathematics undertaken by particular social and cultural groups who have been perceived to be mathematically inferior. For example, studies of Mozambican basket weavers (Gerdes, 1988) have shown that quite complex mathematics is needed to weave strong baskets. Within the Australian context, Harris (1992) has argued that Indigenous Australian art shows strong mathematical concepts. There are criticisms of this type of work in that it is Eurocentric in its translation of those activities and subjugates the indigenous activity to a Western mathematics frame of reference (Dowling, 1998).

Other studies concerned with situated cognition and learning have drawn attention to the mismatch between school mathematics and out-of-school mathematics. Studies of street vendors (Carraher, 1988; Carraher, Carraher, & Schliemann, 1985; Saxe, 1988); shoppers (Lave, Murtaugh, & de la Rocha, 1984), and workplace mathematics (Kanes, 1996; Zevenbergen, 1997) have shown that the context of the activity provides a very strong support for effective performance. Often the performance undertaken in this context does not resemble the formal mathematics of school. When asked to transfer school mathematics to these contexts, participants are often not as confident with their work and produce more incorrect responses. Indeed, the context provides a high degree of motivation for the participants to the point where, in many cases, school mathematics is redundant or inappropriate, or both.

These studies draw attention to the need to question whose knowledge is being represented in the teaching and learning of mathematics that is being undertaken in our classrooms. When the culture, and hence in many cases, knowledge, of the students in many classrooms is different from that represented in the curriculum, then there is likely to be a greater mismatch between what is seen as relevant and meaningful. In many cases, this is blatantly obvious; for instance, where there is a big mismatch in cultures. Where there is less of a mismatch between the classroom and school, there is greater opportunity for seeing the activities as being relevant to all students.

One of the most common strategies used in mathematics teaching is to embed the mathematical concepts currently being taught into a context in an attempt to make the mathematics appear useful and purposeful. Typical tasks asked of students require them to apply curricula concepts and processes to a task that appears to have these elements occurring in it "naturally." For example, a task from a Year 9 textbook (Brodie & Swift, 1998, pp. 426–427) asked students to undertake an investigation into car purchasing through a loan process. The picture enclosed with the project was a Mitsubishi with a price tag of $9,999. A set of assumptions are built into the task including the "car will cover 16,000 km in the year, . . . will use petrol at a rate of approximately 9 km/L; . . . use approximately 1 L of oil for every 5,000 km, . . . service the car every 5,000 km, new tires at $120 each and a battery cost about $80 and lasts about 2 years" (p. 426). Other information about insurance, financing, registration, on-road costs, servicing and petrol should be sought from the RACQ (regional motoring club). It is assumed that the student has a deposit of $5,000. There are numerous examples such as this in school textbooks, often guided by the intention that they provide a real context in which students can make sense of the mathematics they have been studying and begin to see the relevance of the mathematics in the world beyond the classroom. Often, where there is some criticism of the tasks, there is the potential to suggest that students should still be able to encounter the applications as they prepare for activities that they may encounter in the world beyond school. From a more critical perspective, Boaler (1993) has argued that this process may indeed make the task more inaccessible for students. Furthermore, Cooper and Dunne (1998) have shown that the embedding of mathematics in contextualized tasks decreases the performance on tests for working-class students, whereas Boaler has shown that girls may similarly be disadvantaged by some "real world" contexts (Boaler, 1994).

I would support and extend these positions by arguing that it is necessary to consider the examples from a sociological as well as a linguistic and mathematical perspective. In many cases, the activities work on a mathematical assumption that students will need to be able to apply the mathematics in contexts that they are likely to encounter in their lives beyond school. It is seen to be the task of school mathematics to empower students to make the "right" choices in their adult lives, with mathematics being regarded as a key tool for making such informed decisions. From a school perspective, such tasks conform with the demands placed on teachers by syllabus and curriculum documents that are often mandated by statutory authorities. For many teachers, the activities in the books are ones that they encounter in their daily lives, and so the tasks have a veneer of authenticity and relevance to the teachers. However, projects such as the one cited previously are also ridden with considerable assumptions about what is seen as usual purchasing patterns, many of which are the antithesis of what disadvantaged students are likely to encounter when (or if) they come to purchase a car. Questions need to be asked that will deconstruct the assumptions underpinning the question in order that we can ascertain whose culture is being valued and, hence, whose is being devalued or even ignored. Some of these would include first asking whether the question has relevance to the students. Once this has been ascertained, then other questions need to be considered including the following:

- Is the context of the question relevant to the students? In this example, how could the task be best contextualized for a cohort of students? Would students consider the purchase of a car of this value? How could the task be best suited for the needs of students so that they can see the relevance of mathematics to their everyday lives? (If indeed there is any.) In some places, the purchase of a car would not even be contemplated.

- What are the usual patterns of purchase for a group of students? For many, this could be purchasing a friend's car and coming to some sort of arrangement with him or her insofar as repayments, or borrowing from parents or family rather than financial institutions.

- Deposits—What would be a deposit within the local community? It may be of a cash value, but may be something else (such as a stereo or the like). What savings schedules may be necessary prior to purchase of the car in order to have a deposit? Do the students have savings schedules?

- What are the constraints that they would be encountering when maintaining the car? Servicing—Would it be done as a friendship activity on the weekend with labor (and learning) occurring in a social situation? What sort of maintenance would be undertaken? What types of purchases would be made (second-hand parts, retreads for tires, etc.)? Mileage rates may not even be a consideration as purchase price determines what can be purchased; and so forth.

The implicit assumptions embedded in these types of questions needs to be questioned in relation to the real lives of the students. Simply embedding mathematics into contexts does not make it relevant and worthwhile. For students living in remote areas, the constraints that they would encounter when purchasing a car would be substantially different from those of their peers in inner city areas. These factors must be considered; if not, there is a tendency to recognize a particular cultural form over others and in so doing implicitly value that cultural form. Indeed, this process of recognizing the dominant forms of knowledge and contexts may compound the alienation of many students through the imposition of a particular value system on them that is of little or no relevance or meaning to them.

Within this context, not only must the links with the local community be explored and articulated, but also the language used by students. It is very likely that the language used by this group of students is different from the formal language of the tasks and should also be explored. In order that students be able to solve contextualized tasks, they need to be able to deconstruct the tasks mathematically, linguistically, and contextually. Where the language and context are different from their lived experiences, this creates greater cognitive demands for some students than others, thereby restricting their access to the tasks and subsequent resolution. This seems to correlate more closely with economic advantage than with potential or mathematical understanding.

CONCLUSION

By considering the teaching of mathematics as a cultural event, we can see that there are aspects of pedagogy and curriculum that can exclude some students. By understanding how the patterns of language, work, and power are implicated in the construction of mathematics, it become possible to understand how we can change our practices in order that they become more accessible and equitable for our students. This is not to suggest that the mathematics be watered down. Rather, we should consider the practices within which mathematics is embedded—linguistic, social, and contextual—in order that it becomes more accessible to more students. In this chapter, I have made explicit some of the ways in which the practices of mathematics can be exclusory for some students, particularly for those whose language is not that of the formal mathematics found within schools and classrooms. This is not to suggest a deficit in the language of the students, but to strongly advocate that there are differences between the language and experiences of the students and common school practices. It is now widely recognized that language is inextricably bound to world views. Wittgenstein and advocates (Watson, 1989; Wittgenstein, 1953, 1967) have argued persuasively that the ways in which people see and read the world are shaped through language which comes to construct forms of life that are the subjective realities for participants in the language games. For students coming into mathematics classrooms, there are particular language games they come to learn, with which they have some familiarity because of similarities with their home environments. For these students, the language games of the classroom—the registers, the interactions, the contexts—are familiar enough that they are able to participate more effectively and more efficiently and be seen as mathematically able students. For these students, their familiarity with the language games becomes a quality they can use or trade for success in classrooms. Accordingly, such familiarity is a form of capital that can be traded for educational rewards. If the language games of students are not part of their social or cultural backgrounds, then subsequent constructions of their success are far more elusive. Without substantial reconstruction of their familial habitus, effective participation in the mathematics classroom is transitory and intangible, making access to mathematics and success difficult to achieve.

NOTE

1. The term "strand" is used here to denote the different branches of the mathematics curriculum. These branches are arbitrary and vary across state and national contexts, but for the purposes of this chapter can be considered to be main divisions of the mathematics curriculum such as number study, chance and data, algebra, measurement, and space.

REFERENCES

Barham, J., & Bishop, A. J. (1991). Mathematics and the deaf child. In K. Durkin & B. Shire (Eds.), *Language in mathematical education* (pp. 179–187). Milton Keynes, UK: Open University Press.

Bauersfeld, H., Krummheuer, G., & Voigt, J. (1988). Interactional theory of learning and teaching mathematics and related microethnical studies. In H. G. Steiner & A. Vermandel (Eds.), *Foundations and methodology of the discipline of mathematics education* (pp. 174–188). Antwerp, Belgium: Proceedings of the TME Conference.

Bernstein, B. (1990). *Class, codes and control, vol. 4.* London: Routledge and Kegan Paul.

Boaler, J. (1993). The role of contexts in the mathematics classroom: Do they make mathematics more "real?" *For the Learning of Mathematics, 13*(2), 12–17.

Boaler, J. (1994). When do girls prefer football to fashion? An analysis of female underachievement in relation to "realistic" mathematics contexts. *British Educational Research Journal 20*(5), 551–564.

Bourdieu, P. (1979). *Distinction: A social critique of the judgement of taste* (1984 ed.). Cambridge, MA: Harvard University Press.

Bourdieu, P., & Wacquant, L. (1992). *An invitation to reflexive sociology.* Cambridge, UK: Polity.

Bourdieu, P., Passeron J.C., & de Saint Martin, M. (1994). *Academic discourse Linguistic misunderstanding and professorial power.* Stanford: Stanford University Press.

Brodie, R., & Swift, S. (1998). *SMQ 9: Secondary maths for Queensland.* Melbourne, Australia: Moreton Bay Publishing.

Carraher, T. N. (1988). Street mathematics and school mathematics. In A. Borbas (Ed.), *Proceeding of the twelfth PME conference* (Vol. 1, pp. 1–23). Veszprem, Hungary: International Group for the Psychology of Mathematics Education.

Carraher, T. N., Carraher, D. W., & Schliemann, A. D. (1985). Mathematics in the streets and in schools. *British Journal of Developmental Psychology, 3*, 21–29.

Corbett, D., & Wilson, B. (1995). Make a difference with, not for, students: A plea to researchers and reformers. *Educational Researcher 24*(5), 12–17.

Cooper, B., & Dunne, M. (1998, January). Anyone for tennis? Social class differences in children's responses to national curriculum mathematics testing. *The Sociological Review,* 115–148.

Dawe, L., & Mulligan, J. (1997). Classroom views of language in mathematics. In B. Doig & J. Lokan (Eds.), *Learning from children: Mathematics from a classroom perspective* (pp. 7–35). Melbourne, Australia: Australian Council for Educational Research.

De Corte, E., & Verschaffel, L. (1991). Some factors influencing the solution of addition and subtraction word problems. In K. Durkin & B. Shire (Eds.), *Language in mathematical education: Research and practice* (pp. 117–130). Milton Keyes, UK: Open University Press.

Dowling, P. (1998). *The sociology of mathematics education: Mathematical myths/pedagogical texts* (Vol. 7). London: Falmer.

Education Queensland. (1997). *The Year 6 Test*. Brisbane, Australia: GoPrint.

Ellerton, N. F., & Clements, M. A. (1991). *The mathematics of language: A review of language factors in school mathematics*. Geelong, Australia: Deakin University Press.

Ellerton, N. F., & Clements, M. A. (1992). Implications of Newman research for the issue of "What is basic in school mathematics?" In B. Southwell, B. Perry, & K. Owens (Eds.), *Space: The first and final frontier* (pp. 276–284). Sydney, Australia: Mathematics Education Research Group of Australasia.

Freebody, P., Ludwig, C., & Gunn, S. (1995). *Everyday literacy practice in and out of schools in low socio-economic urban communities*. Brisbane, Australia: Griffith University—Centre for Literacy Education Research.

Gerdes, P. (1988). On culture, geometric thinking and mathematics education. *Educational Studies in Mathematics, 19*(2), 137–162.

Halliday, M. A. K. (1975). Some aspects of sociolinguistics. In, *Interactions between linguistics and mathematical education* (pp. 64–73). Copenhagen, Denmark: UNESCO.

Halliday. M. A. K. (1988). *Spoken and written language*. Geelong, Australia: Deakin University Press.

Harris, P. (1992). Australian space: Pushing back frontiers. In B. Southwell, B. Perry, & K. Owens (Eds.), *Space: The first and final frontier* (pp. 55–72). Sydney, Australia: Mathematics Education Research Group of Australasia.

Heath, S. B. (1982). Questioning at home and at school: A comparative study. In G. D. Spindler (Ed.), *Doing the ethnography of schooling*. New York: Holt, Rinehart & Winston.

Heath, S. B. (1983). *Ways with words: Language, life and work in communities and classrooms* (1989 ed.). Cambridge, UK: University of Cambridge.

Horker, R. K. (1984). On reproduction, habitus and education. *British Journal of Sociology of Education*, 5(2), 117–127.

Hyde, M., Power, D., & Zevenbergen, R. (1999). Deaf students' solving of arithmetic word problems. In J. Truran & K. Truran (Eds.), *Making the difference* (pp.275–282). Adelaide, Australia: Mathematics Education Research Group of Australasia.

Joseph, G. G. (1991). *The crest of the peacock: Non-European roots of mathematics*. London: Tauris.

Joseph, G. J. (1987). Foundations of Eurocentrism in mathematics. *Race & Class, 28*(3), 13–28.

Kanes, C. (1996). Investigating the use of language and mathematics in the workplace setting. In P. Clarkson (Ed.), *Technology in mathematics education* (pp. 314–321). Melbourne, Australia: Mathematics Education Research Group of Australasia.

Lave, J., Murtaugh, M., & de la Rocha, O. (1984). The dialectic of arithmetic in grocery shopping. In B. Rogoff & J. Lave (Eds.), *Everyday cognition: Its development in social context.* (pp. 67–94). Cambridge, UK: Cambridge University Press.

Lean, G. A., Clements, M. A., & Del Campo, G. (1990). Linguistic and pedagogical factors affecting children's understanding of arithmetic word problems: A comparative study. *Educational Studies in Mathematics, 21*, 165–191.

Leder, G. H., & Forgasz, H. J. (1992). Perspectives on learning, teaching and assessment. In G. H. Leder (Ed.), *Assessment and learning of mathematics* (pp. 1–23). Melbourne, Australia: Australian Council for Educational Research.

Lemke, J. L. (1990). *Talking science: Language, learning and values.* Norwood, NJ: Ablex.

Lubienski, S.T. (1997). Class matters: A preliminary excursion. In J. Trentacosta & M.J. Kearney (Eds). *Multicultural and gender equity in ther mathematics classroom: The gift of diversity* (pp. 46–59). Reston VA: NCTM.

McGregor, M. (1991). Language, culture and mathematics learning. In M. McGregor & R. Moore (Eds.), *Teaching mathematics in the multicultural classroom: A resource for teachers and teacher educators* (pp. 5–25). Melbourne, Australia: University of Melbourne, School of Mathematics and Science Education.

Mehan, H. (1982). The structure of classroom events and their consequences for student performance. In P. G. Glatthorn & & A. A. Glatthorn (Eds.), *Children in and out of school: Ethnography and education* (pp. 59–87). Washington, DC: Center for Applied Linguistics.

National Council for Teachers of Mathematics. (1989*). Curriculum and evaluation standards for school mathematics*. Reston, VA: Author.

Saxe, G. B. (1988). Candy selling and math learning. *Educational Researcher, 17*(6), 14–21.

Schoenfeld, A. H. (1988). When good teaching leads to bad results: The disasters of "well-taught" mathematics courses. *Educational Psychologist, 23*(2), 145–166.

Seccda, W. G. (1992). Race ethnicity, social class, language and achievement in mathematics. In D.A. Grouws (Ed.) *Handbook of research on mathematics teaching and learning* (pp. 623–660). New York: Macmillan Publishing Company.

Sinclair, J., & Coulthard, M. (1975). *Towards a analysis of discourse*. Oxford, UK: Blackwell.

Stigler, J. W. & Hiebert, J. (1999). *The teaching gap: Best ideas from the world's teachers for improving education in the classroom*. New York: The Free Press.

Walkerdine, V. (1989). *Counting girls out*. London: Virago.

Walkerdine, V., & Lucey, H. (1989). *Democracy in the kitchen: Regulating mothers and socialising daughters*. London: Virago.

Watson, H. (1989). A Wittgensteinian view of mathematics: Implications for teachers of mathematics. In N. F. Ellerton & M. A. Clements (Eds.), *School mathematics: The challenge to change* (pp. 18–30). Geelong, Australia: Deakin University Press.

Wittgenstein, L. (1953). *Philosophical investigations* (Anscombe, G.E.M., Trans.) (1974 ed.). Oxford, UK: Basil Blackwell.

Wittgenstein, L. (1967). *Remarks on the foundations of mathematics*. London: Basil Backwell.

Wood, T. (1994). patterns of interaction and the culture of mathematics classrooms. In S. Lerman (Ed.), *Cultural perspectives on the mathematics classroom* (Vol. 14, pp. 149–168). Dordrecht, Holland: Kluwer.

Zevenbergen, R. (1994). *The construction of educational inequality: A critique of dominant discourses in mathematics education*. Geelong, Australia: Deakin University Press.

Zevenbergen, R. (1997). Situated numeracy: A case study of pool builders. In N. Scott & H. Hollingsworth (Eds.), *Mathematics: Creating the future* (pp. 89–94). Melbourne, Australia: Australian Association of Mathematics Teachers.

Zevenbergen, R. (1998). Language, mathematics and social disadvantage: A Bourdieuian analysis of cultural capital in mathematics education. In C. Kanes, M. Goos, & E. Warren (Eds.), *Teaching mathematics in new times* (Vol. 2, pp. 716–722). Gold Coast, Australia: Mathematics Education Research Group of Australasia.

9

Better Assessment in Mathematics Education? A Social Perspective

Candia Morgan

INTRODUCTION

Assessment of school mathematics has an important impact both on individual students and teachers and on groups within society. Its summative forms have traditionally been used in many countries as a primary means of discriminating between individuals in order to allocate scarce resources (often in the form of further educational and employment opportunities). It may be used to compare different groups within a population and thus has potential power as a tool of systematic discrimination, for example, using the results of tests to make and justify policy decisions about the forms of education that should be made available to various groups within a society. At various times and places, the results achieved by their students have also influenced teachers' pay and possibilities for advancement. Even at the classroom level, the day-to-day judgments of teachers about individual pupils inevitably affect future interactions, judgments, and hence opportunities. The act of assessment takes place in interaction between individual students, teachers, and social contexts, and its results have far-reaching social consequences, yet research within mathematics education that acknowledges the importance of a social perspective has overwhelmingly focused on curriculum and classrooms rather than on assessment.

The vast majority of existing research related to assessment within mathematics education has been done within two main traditions that I shall characterize as "psychological" and "curriculum reform." Although there is a body of research that addresses assessment from a sociological perspective, this has not yet substantially informed research within the mathematics education community. In this chapter, I intend to critique the "mainstream" mathematics assessment research and to discuss what might be meant by a social perspective on research into assessment in mathematics education. I shall also discuss some of the issues that arise, referring to examples of research that have taken or begun to take such a perspective. In conclusion, I shall suggest a number of questions that may be used to interrogate existing research on assessment in mathematics education and to guide future efforts.

MAINSTREAM TRADITIONS OF MATHEMATICS ASSESSMENT RESEARCH

There are three basic assumptions underpinning mainstream thinking on assessment. First, it is assumed that individuals possess attributes (such as knowledge, understanding, skill, ability, etc.) that are discoverable and measurable. Second, the primary purpose of assessment is to discover and measure these attributes. Finally, the assessment process and its outcomes are assumed to be fundamentally benign or even beneficial (although unfortunate side effects may be recognized and attempts made to ameliorate them). The benefits that "good" assessment is claimed to bring include the following: increased understanding of students' mathematical thinking, both collectively and individually; possibilities for improved teaching, with the design of schemes of work that match what is known about students; and opportunities to influence teachers' practice, bringing it in line with the ideals of those designing the assessment.

It is clear that these assumptions are rooted in a strongly positivist tradition. That is, they are predicated on the belief that there is an underlying truth to be assessed and that it is theoretically possible to get as close as one might wish to this underlying truth. This positivist tradition is perhaps even stronger in mathematics than in other subject areas, as many believe that there are only right or wrong answers; people either know the right answer or they do not. Uncertainty and nonexcluded middles in mathematical contexts are deeply uncomfortable for many people, even for those who might find them less surprising in other disciplines. Situated theories of learning challenge both the idea that there is some absolute "truth" about students' understanding of mathematics and the idea that any instrument could observe and measure such a state. Yet such epistemological concerns have had little impact on thinking about assessment (Galbraith, 1993).

The Psychological Tradition

Research related to assessment that is reported in the Proceedings of PME[1] (the International Group for the Psychology of Mathematics Education) has two main concerns. One is the development and use of assessment instruments to form improved (more valid) characterizations of the attributes of individual students. (See, for example, Hunter & Monaghan, 1996; Jaime & Gutiérrez, 1994; Karsenty & Vinner, 1996; Lawrie, 1998; Leung, 1994; Rickards & Fisher, 1997.) The second is the construction of models of the general characteristics of knowledge and understanding in a given area of mathematical activity (e.g., Garcia-Cruz & Martinón, 1997, 1998; Orton & Orton, 1996). The aspects of mathematics involved include both "traditional" areas of study, such as geometry, and areas associated with current curriculum reform movements, such as problem solving. Some of the studies reported appear to be "pure" research whereas others aim to provide tools for teachers to use or to influence teachers' practice, often linked to the "reform" tradition (see later discussion). Although there are substantial differences in the aims, content, and theoretical framing of these studies, they all share the three assumptions outlined earlier. In particular, they strive toward validity in order to discover the truth about students' knowledge—a completely appropriate aim for research in a cognitive psychological paradigm.

In recent years, learning has increasingly come to be seen as a social rather than solely individual process. Björkqvist (1997) has argued that this means mathematics education assessment research needs to take more account of social psychological frameworks. However, this does not yet seem to have had a significant influence. Moreover, Björkvist's primary concern, like that of others within the psychological tradition, is still with the search for validity. There is little room for considering either the social effects of the assessment process or the possibility that validity might be an illusory goal.

The Curriculum Reform Tradition

The field of mathematics education has witnessed many arguments about both the nature of the curriculum and the nature of its assessment. The link between curriculum and assessment is now explicitly seen as a two-way relationship and there has been increasing recognition of the role that assessment structures play in influencing what happens in classrooms, either hampering or "leading" efforts at curriculum reform (Burkhardt, 1988; Ridgway & Schoenfeld, 1994). The function of assessment that is of primary importance for curriculum reformers is the power to influence the curriculum, with accompanying concern that this influence should "match" the intentions of the reform. The focus of the curriculum reform tradition in relation to assessment has thus been twofold. First, researchers in this tradition have critiqued existing forms of assessment, considering both their effects on the curriculum and their effectiveness in producing valid measures of those aspects of students' mathematical thinking that are valued by the proposed curriculum. Second, they have proposed, developed, and trialled alternative forms of assessment intended to match more closely the aims of the reform curriculum, both in producing the desired effects in schools and classrooms, and in measuring that which the reform values.

In particular, there has been increasing interest in the idea of "authentic" assessment, in mathematics as in other subject areas (Torrance, 1995). The term "authentic" has a number of connotations, not all of which are made explicit in debates about assessment reform. Authentic tasks may have some "realistic" aspect; their assessment procedures may match more closely the aims, content, and breadth of the curriculum; and the results of the assessment may be a more genuine measure of students' achievement. There has been considerable international interest in discussing the characteristics of more "authentic" means of assessment as well as attempts to design and implement new forms of assessment in the context of curriculum reform (Leder, 1992; Lesh & Lamon, 1992; Niss, 1993a, 1993b; Romberg, 1995).

Concern for social issues, in particular for "equity" in relation to gender and minority ethnic groups, has been one of the motivations of recent curriculum reform movements, and this has been reflected in some of the principles underpinning parallel assessment reforms. In the United States, for example, the Assessment Standards produced by the National Council of Teachers of Mathematics include the principle that assessment should "promote equity" (NCTM, 1995, p.15). The dissatisfaction with traditional forms of assessment, in particular with timed tests demanding predetermined short answers to closed questions, has arisen in part from a growing awareness of cultural bias in even (or perhaps especially) the most "objective" of tests.

The power of assessment to influence the curriculum is, however, a double-edged sword. It is necessary to ask who is controlling the reform and in whose interests they act. In recent years in the United Kingdom, we have seen a change in the relationships between teachers, curriculum reforms, and assessment practices. In the 1970s and early 1980s, the official examination system allowed some possibilities for teachers to develop alternative practices. Although regional examination boards controlled the setting and marking of high-stakes examinations for students aged 16+ years, schools and groups of schools were able to apply for validation of their own syllabuses and examinations, while independent curriculum developers such as SMP, SMILE,[2] and the Association of Teachers of Mathematics were successful in developing alternative syllabuses and assessment regimens that could be adopted by schools. During this period, reformers who wished to see greater diversity in the curriculum and opportunities for wider groups of students to participate in mathematics made use of innovative assessment methods to encourage the teaching of problem solving and the use of mathematical investigation in the classroom (see, for example, Love, 1981). In 1988, with the introduction of a new national system of examination for England and Wales, some of these practices were officially endorsed and, eventually, made compulsory. As I have argued elsewhere (Morgan, 1998b), this use of assessment to instigate universal reform actually acted in some cases to distort and impoverish the types of rich mathematical activity it was intended to encourage. Since the late 1980s, assessment has increasingly been used as a tool in the move toward centralized control of the curriculum. Teachers have lost most of their opportunities to innovate and to have their innovations validated through the official assessment system. Both the content and the method of teaching have been deliberately engineered through the introduction and shaping of national tests for political as much as educational purposes. As Galbraith argues, the generally accepted idea that external assessment requirements should be used to influence the curriculum is "ultimately disempowering to teachers in impeding the growth of full professional responsibility, and to students in making their choices and interests irrelevant" (Galbraith, 1993, p. 82).

Critique of the Mainstream Traditions

Both psychological and curriculum reform traditions of assessment research have as their principle aim the search for validity, in the narrow sense of accuracy of measurement (of whatever is being measured) and in the broader senses of curricular and content validity. Their efforts are thus directed to the development of new and better assessment instruments. Critiques of traditional methods of assessment still tend to lie within the same positivist paradigm. For example, in the recent ICMI study on "Mathematics Education as a Research Domain," Ellerton and Clements (1998) identify "Questioning the Basis for Assessing Achievement in Mathematics" (p. 168) as one of 10 major concerns for mathematics education research. Yet their "questioning" leads primarily to the claim that "Closer research scrutiny needs to be given to the issue of how achievement is best measured in mathematics" (p. 169). Their point is illustrated by reference to research by Thongtawat that "found that students who scored poorly on a [multiple-choice] test could sometimes have a good conceptual grasp of the material which the items covered" (p. 169). This critique assumes that some (unspecified) alternative method of assessment can provide a more valid picture of students' "conceptual grasp." Even Galbraith's (1993) critique of the inconsistency of those who simultaneously espouse constructivist epistemologies and cling to positivist conceptions of assessment is not consistent. He, too, appears to argue that at least "local" forms of assessment that take into account cultural and contextual features could provide valid knowledge of students' understanding. He rejects the positivist principles of reliability and objectivity but still relies on the idea that it is possible to seek validity.

Although it is generally recognized that students interpret what teachers say in multiple ways, this insight into the contingent nature of meaning making is rarely extended to how teachers interpret what students say or write. Mainstream thinking about assessment is still based on a "commonsense" or naive transmission view of the nature of communication in which meaning resides within the text, independent of the reader, carrying the author's intentions exactly. The assessor's role is thus to "extract the meaning" from the text produced by the student. Obvious failures to communicate—where different modes of communication (for example, a written test and a teacher observation of a child working) provide different messages about the "same" student competence or where the teacher/assessor is unable to make sense of a written or spoken text produced by a student—are often seen to be a "language problem" for the student. But on what basis do we assume that, when teachers and other assessors do succeed in making sense of a student's text, they then know what the student intended to communicate? A more consistent epistemology would suggest that there is no necessary simple correspondence between a piece of text and the meanings its various readers construct. Rather, the meanings constructed will depend on the resources brought to bear on the text by individual readers. These resources will vary according to the discourse within which the text is read and the positions adopted by a particular reader within that discourse as well as the reader's previous experience (Kress, 1989). There can never be a guarantee that the interpretations made by the assessor are exactly those intended by the student. Indeed, studies of teacher/assessors demonstrate how different assessors can construct entirely different interpretations from the same text (Morgan, 1996; Watson and Morgan, 2000).

TOWARD A SOCIAL PERSPECTIVE ON ASSESSMENT IN MATHEMATICS EDUCATION

I have argued above that the aim of mainstream research related to assessment in mathematics education has generally been to develop and validate more "accurate" and "authentic" means of assessing student learning. I have also argued that this aim is an illusory one—that the first two assumptions on which both psychological and curriculum reform traditions are based are unfounded and inconsistent with epistemological stances that take into account the socially situated and contingent nature of knowledge and of communication. I now turn to the third assumption of the mainstream traditions—the assumption that assessment is fundamentally benign. In making this assumption, it is clear that mainstream research neglects the crucial functions that assessment performs within society.

What Is a "Social Perspective?"

What might constitute research with a "social perspective" on assessment in mathematics education? The term "social" can have reference at a number of different levels from interactions between two individuals to national and international structures and systems. But whatever aspect of the "social" is the object of study, I would argue that such a perspective must involve some consideration of values and consequences. Thus, it must involve asking the questions:

- Who benefits and who is disadvantaged?
- How do assessment processes and systems act to benefit or disadvantage individuals and groups?

In each case, the scope of the questions may vary from the level of an individual classroom to large-scale assessment systems, both national and international. Examples of questions at each of those levels could be:

- Who within this classroom is disadvantaged by the assessment that takes place?
- How does the form of these national examinations serve to disadvantage working-class children?
- How are the opportunities for learning in this country influenced by the government's desire to demonstrate international comparability of qualifications or to raise the country's standing in international comparisons such as the third International Mathematics and Science Study?

Unlike the mainstream tradition of assessment research discussed earlier, the object of research on assessment taking a social perspective cannot be the development of "more valid" assessment instruments, though lack of validity may be one aspect of the critique of existing instruments.

Assessment as Discrimination

Although I have argued that the mainstream tradition assumes that the primary purpose of assessment in mathematics is to discover and measure the mathematical attributes of individuals, it is, of course, generally acknowledged that the results may be used to serve a wide variety of functions, ranging from the design of individual learning programs, to determining students' future educational or occupational opportunities, to evaluating teachers. All these functions, however, are predicated on the belief that knowing the "truth" about an individual's state of knowledge or understanding is a proper basis for making such decisions. As Broadfoot (1996) points out, this belief is a relatively modern development, reflecting the dominance in modern society of individualism and of rational (rather than coercive) authority as the basis for hierarchical control. It is no longer acceptable, as it once was, to say that a certain type of education is not suitable for a particular group of children because their parents are peasants or factory workers. It is similarly unacceptable to say that this person is the right person to become a doctor or a lawyer or a priest because she or he comes from the appropriate social group. However, the dominant modern ideology allows arguments of the form: this child should be taught in this way because of his own talents or difficulties; this person should be trained to be a lawyer because she has demonstrated that she has the necessary intellectual and personal attributes (including the desire to become a lawyer). Whether rational authority and the resulting "meritocracy" is superior (ethically or practically) to other bases of discriminating between people in order to organize the division of labor and distribution of resources within society is not an issue I wish to address here. The point is that this ideology is a means of legitimating divisions and control within society.

Rather than seeing assessment as the attempt to discover the truth of a student's state of understanding, it is thus useful to look at it as the process by which a student may gain or be denied access to particular forms of privilege or power. We know that mathematics qualifications serve in many societies around the world as a means of discriminating between individuals when allocating educational and occupational opportunities, even where knowledge of mathematics itself may be irrelevant to the future performance of the individual. As Noss claimed in his critique of the U.K. National Curriculum, the purpose of assessing ability to perform long division is to "divide and rule" (Noss, 1990).

There is a tension for mathematics educators in taking such a perspective on their activity as most have entered the field with a major interest in mathematics and in students' learning. If schooling and assessment are regarded as a means of discriminating between individuals, then the mathematics and the learning become unimportant by-products. Vinner (1997) takes a moral stance against the pursuit (by teachers and students) of "pseudo-knowledge" (that is, knowledge that enables acceptable answers to be given to school mathematics questions but does not represent "true" mathematical understanding) as a means of gaining "credit" within the system. He claims that the "intention" of the educational system is "to give credit for true knowledge and not for pseudo-knowledge" (p. 68) and that to gain credit for pseudo-knowledge is a form of "cheating." It is not clear to me how a system can have "intentions," though individuals and groups within it can. What is clear is that the system functions to discriminate and select on the basis of the credits gained rather than the quality of the knowledge acquired.[3]

What is it that assessment gives credit for? I would agree with Vinner that it is not "knowledge," because this is not directly observable, but the extent to which the student is able to participate in the form of discourse that is valued within the particular classroom or assessment regime. "Knowledge" itself will not be given credit unless it somehow manifests itself in ways that are recognized within that discourse. A teacher makes judgments about a student's mathematical knowledge by interpreting oral and written texts and other behavior produced by the student. The teacher's interpretation of these texts as evidence of knowledge or lack of knowledge depends on the extent to which their form matches the teacher's expectations of mathematical texts—expectations shaped by his or her own knowledge and experience of discourses of mathematics and mathematics education. To be successful in gaining credit, therefore, the student must learn to produce texts that will be judged to be legitimate texts (Bernstein, 1996) within the practices of the mathematics classroom.

It can be argued that learning to participate in mathematical discourse is learning mathematics. I would also argue that the discourse of mathematics classrooms is mathematical—not because it necessarily matches up to some ideal of "real" mathematical thinking (as defined by mathematicians or mathematics educators), but because it happens in mathematics classrooms (see Morgan, 1998a, for a fuller discussion of what may be labeled "mathematical"). Thus, all those who participate to any extent are learning mathematics, even if much of it might be classified by Vinner as pseudo-mathematics. The problem is that much discourse in mathematics classrooms consists of forms of mathematics that are of low status and lack power to enable students either to gain valued credit within the existing society or to take action to transform that society. Dowling's (1998) analysis of the discourse of a scheme of mathematics textbooks demonstrates how these act to construct and confirm students in their class positions, allowing the "high attainers" access to high-status esoteric domain mathematics that could serve to apprentice them as mathematicians as well as leading to valued qualifications, whereas the texts for "low attainers" position them as manual workers and induct them into a narrow and low status form of "real world" mathematical activity. Dowling does not address assessment directly, but his work provides some insight into how division and disadvantage may be constructed in classrooms. The form of the public examination system in the United Kingdom legitimates and necessitates this division. Different groups of students are only allowed to enter one of several "tiers" of examination, usually determined by their teachers. Only those entered for the highest tier have access to the highest grades, whereas those entered for the lowest tier may achieve a maximum grade of "D"—largely considered to be a failing grade and carrying little value as a qualification for employment or further education opportunities (see Boaler, 1997, for students' responses to this).

Existing Research with a Social Perspective

I turn now to consider the research into assessment of mathematics that has addressed the two questions (who benefits/is disadvantaged and how) suggested earlier as central to a social perspective. There are three main types of issues that have been addressed:

- Differential access to 'high-stakes' assessment and qualifications
- Differential performance on various types of assessment tasks
- Potential inequity in judgments formed by assessors

I do not aim to present a full review in this chapter but to illustrate some of the ways in which these issues have been addressed and to discuss some of the questions and methodological issues that remain. Most of the research I shall discuss is based within the education system of England and Wales. Although I would suggest that the three issues identified here are also likely to be of importance in other education systems, there may well be other issues that arise elsewhere, particularly in so-called developing nations.

Differential Access to High-Stakes Assessment

One obvious way in which individuals and groups can be disadvantaged by an assessment system is through being excluded from access to those forms of assessment that lead to benefits (in the form of high-status qualifications or opportunities to progress within the school). As I have described earlier, the mathematics examination system in England and Wales at age 16+ years is structured so that only those considered by their teachers to be "suitable" may be entered for the tier of examination that allows access to the highest grades; others must make do with second- or third-rate qualifications. (This is not the case in all subject areas; in English, for example, all students are entered for the same papers.) Stobart, Elwood, and Quinlan's (1992) study showed that girls are entered in disproportionate numbers for the "intermediate" tier of examination. Although success in this examination allows students to achieve the "C" grade that is a requirement for many further courses and employment, it is not usually accepted as an adequate basis for advanced study in mathematics. The researchers suggest that the decision to enter some girls for the intermediate rather than the higher examination may be the result of a perception shared by both teachers and pupils that girls lack confidence in mathematics. (See also discussion of similar decisions about entry to high- and low-status examination by Walden & Walkerdine, 1985.) Dunne's (1998) study of entries for National Curriculum tests at Key Stage 3 (age 14) also shows that different schools use different bases for making decisions about the level test for which pupils are to be entered. Thus, a pupil might be entered for the highest tier in one school, but the middle or lowest tier in another.

The use of results of examinations to evaluate and rank schools encourages schools, departments, and teachers to "play safe" in the decisions they make about entries to maximize the appearance of the results of the school as a whole. In the United Kingdom, the principle measure used to compare schools is the number of A to C grades achieved in the GCSE examination.[4] As a grade C can be achieved in the intermediate level examination, there is substantial anecdotal evidence to suggest that schools are making more entries at intermediate level because it is perceived that it is easier to gain a C by that route. The interests of the school but not necessarily the interests of the individual student may be served by such a decision. Moreover, it seems that some schools target scarce resources on students who are borderline between C and D grades, providing extra lessons and support for these students—the motivation being to maximize the school's achievement rather than that of the students (Gillborn & Youdell, 1999).

The provision of differentiated examinations is often justified by suggesting that it allows all candidates to attempt tasks at a level with which they can cope and achieve some measure of success (Cockcroft, 1982). As soon as decisions must be made about entry levels, however, it becomes clear that some students or groups of students may be disadvantaged by variation in the way the decisions are made and applied to them. The way in which teachers arrive at the assessments on which such decisions are based forms another area of research and is discussed next.

Differential Performance on Various Types of Assessment Tasks

Because of the prominent place of mathematics in the curriculum and the high status attached to qualifications in mathematics, the subject has often been included as an example within more general studies of bias in testing and examinations. Studies of responses to different forms of assessment tasks have shown that differences between the performance of girls and boys vary between multiple-choice tests, "free response" questions, and extended "coursework" tasks (Anderson, 1989; Stobart et al., 1992). These studies and others addressing the idea of "bias" (see Gipps & Murphy, 1994, for a much fuller discussion), tend to rest on an assumption that it is theoretically possible to make use of the knowledge about differences that they have identified in order to construct assessment instruments that are not biased—thus working with the mainstream assumptions I have critiqued earlier.

Within mathematics education, the "context" within which assessment tasks are presented has been seen to be an important variable in making the tasks easier or more difficult for various groups of students. In some cases, this has been based on rather simplistic models of the way in which such bias might operate. For example, a subcommittee of the Mathematical Association (MA) entitled "Monitoring GCSE Papers for Bias" defined its task to be to examine the contexts of examination questions for their "cultural diversity," reporting in 1990 that:

> ... some papers contain an imbalance in mentions of male/female, and traditional stereotypical roles for girls and women. ... There is a little use of "Asian" names, and a very inappropriate drawing of black children which offends, but no signs at all that any paper acknowledges, yet alone promotes, multiculturalism. (Mathematical Association, 1990)

Although the MA report bases its investigation on general principles about a "multicultural" approach to mathematics education rather than specific claims about the effects of such "bias" on students' performance in the examinations, it also cites extracts from the policy statements of examination boards which suggest that their concern is underpinned by the assumption that the cultural context does have such effects:

> The Board will be alert to the need to be fair to its candidates by developing schemes of examination whose components do not bias against particular ethnic groups. The culture free examination is an unrealistic aim and would, in any case, lead to dull examinations. (London Examinations and Assessment Group, cited in Mathematical Association, 1990)

This is a rather naive approach to issues of cultural disadvantage. Where the effects of context on students' mathematical problem-solving behavior and success have been studied, it is apparent that the simplistic equation "culturally familiar/sympathetic context = easier" does not work. Indeed, there are indications that familiar contexts can make problems more difficult for some groups of students (Boaler, 1993, 1994; Cooper, 1998; Cooper & Dunne, 1998).

A more theoretically informed approach is taken by Cooper and Dunne in their studies of students' approaches to and performance on assessment tasks (taken from national tests for 11– and 14–year-olds) set in "everyday" contexts. In comparing the performance of 11–year-old students from working-class and professional families, they show that working-class children, already achieving at a lower level overall, were even less successful on "realistic" questions (Cooper & Dunne, 1998). Whereas the rules for answering traditional "esoteric" mathematics questions are clear-cut, in order to answer such contextualized questions successfully, students have to judge very finely exactly how much everyday "realistic" knowledge to use. The relatively poor performance of working-class children on such contextualized tasks appears to be related to their use of inappropriate "everyday" modes of response when they would need to draw on more formal mathematical methods in order to achieve the answers expected by the test setters (Cooper, 1998). The researchers draw on the work of Bourdieu (1990) and Bernstein (1996) to explain differences in competence on these tasks between students from different social groups.

Potential Inequity in Judgments Formed by Assessors

In rejecting so-called objective multiple-choice tests as invalid in relation to the curriculum and inequitable in the opportunities they provide for different groups to display competence, the question of how assessors interpret and form judgments about student responses to assessment tasks becomes crucial. Moreover, teachers' judgments about their students not only may contribute to summative assessments (including the decisions about access to qualifications discussed earlier) but also influence their day-to-day interactions and the opportunities they provide their students for learning. (A more detailed discussion of the sources of inequity in teacher assessment may be found in Watson and Morgan, 2000.) It has long been established that teacher expectations and teacher stereotyping of student characteristics can lead to differential treatment of students, to differences in student performance, and to differences in the ways in which student behavior is interpreted and evaluated. At the same time, however, it must be acknowledged that, in most cases, such inequity does not arise from any deliberate discrimination on the part of the teacher/assessor. It is, therefore, important to ask how it does arise and whether, through understanding its nature and sources, it can be challenged.

Studies of teacher assessment in mathematics have suggested that much assessment of students makes use of general constructs of "ability" or "level" (see, for example, Gill, 1993; Ruthven, 1987) and that teachers have confidence in the "implicit and largely unarticulated process" (Dunne, 1998, p. 153) by which they reach their judgments about student "ability." Dunne (1998) points out that these judgments are likely to be influenced by the presence or absence of "cultural affinity" between teacher and students. Studies of the detail of teacher/assessor interpretation of texts produced by students (in the form of observable behavior, spoken or written production; see Morgan, 1996, 1998b; Watson, 1997, 1998) reveal the extent to which different teachers may attend to different aspects and construct very different meanings from the same student text.

The implicit nature of the assessment process identified by Dunne in relation to general judgments of "ability" also applies to what might appear to be much more concrete cases of assessment of particular incidents or examples of student texts. When studying teachers evaluating student reports of mathematical investigations, I found that, whereas the teachers were able to rank student texts without difficulty and were able to point to some of those aspects of the texts that they approved or disapproved, they were unable to articulate the evaluation criteria they were using in a way specific enough to help students to produce acceptable texts (Morgan, 1998b). For example, whereas a teacher might provide general advice to his or her students to make use of diagrams in their reports, when the same teacher was actually reading a text with diagrams in it, only some kinds of diagrams were valued while others were condemned as "a waste of time" or apparently taken as a sign of a limited level of mathematical thinking.

The challenge for the student, then, is not to acquire knowledge and understanding of mathematics but to acquire knowledge of the characteristics of the forms of behavior that will allow her to be seen to know and understand, together with the skills necessary to display the appropriate behavior. In Bernstein's terms, the student needs to acquire the recognition rules that "regulate what meanings are relevant" and the realization rules that "regulate how the meanings are to be put together to create the legitimate text" (Bernstein, 1996, p. 32). The ideals of "reform" mathematics curricula, unfortunately, increase this challenge for the student. By weakening the framing of the pedagogical discourse—valuing creativity rather than industry, student empowerment rather than rule following—the criteria by which students are to be evaluated become increasingly implicit and invisible. This does not mean that assessment criteria are any less determinate, merely that it is more difficult to determine what they are. Lerman and Tsatsaroni (1998) have argued that, just as traditional (strongly framed) forms of pedagogical discourse are inaccessible to working-class students, these same students may be further disadvantaged by the discourse of "reform" curricula and evaluation practices. The implicit evaluation "rules" are likely to be most accessible to those groups of students whose cultural and linguistic backgrounds are closest to that of the school.

CONCLUSION

In this chapter, I have called into question the assumptions underlying mainstream research into assessment in mathematics education, in particular the search for "validity," recognizing that assessment is an interpersonal interpretative practice, not a scientific measurement, and challenging the assumption that assessment is fundamentally benign. Assessment takes place and acts at a number of different levels: in everyday interactions between individual teachers and students; within classes, departments, and schools; in national and international systems. In particular, it functions to discriminate between individuals and groups at all these levels. This discriminatory function needs to be recognized and examined.

Mainstream mathematics education research has taken as its major aim the search for "better" assessment instruments. The issues that have been discussed in this chapter suggest that this search needs to be interrogated from a social perspective, asking the questions:

- Which students are identified as high and low attainers by these instruments?

- What are the criteria by which students' responses are to be judged and to what extent are the students both aware of the criteria and in command of the resources needed to demonstrate that they have met them?

- Is access to this awareness and command of resources differentially distributed among various social groups?

- How will use of the assessment instruments differentially affect the future of high and low attainers (considering issues of immediate curricular opportunities and access as well as qualifications for longer term education and employment)?

- What effects may implementation of these instruments have on teachers (considering issues of teachers' professionalism, control of the curriculum, and their immediate objectives as well as effects on the ways in which they interact with their students)?

Rather than attempting to find "better" ways of assessing, a major aim of research into assessment in mathematics education that takes a social perspective must first be to understand how assessment works in mathematics classrooms and more broadly in education systems, and to understand what its consequences are for individuals and for groups within society. Understanding the ways in which assessment works and the consequences of assessment for both teachers and students must entail understanding the complex relationships between individual teachers and students and the broader structures of the societies within which they act. It is only with such understanding of assessment as a social practice that the discriminatory effects of assessment practices can be recognized and challenged.

NOTES

1. I believe I am justified in taking the research reported in PME to be representative of the psychological tradition in mathematics education research. There are, of course, other places where work in this tradition is published. My purpose here is not, however, to review the field but to characterize it.

2. SMP (School Mathematics Project) involved academics and teachers (initially largely from independent schools) in developing textbooks. The materials are very widely used in schools throughout England. SMILE (Secondary Mathematics Individualised Learning Experiment—later changed to "Experience") was developed by groups of teachers, mainly within London, who produced materials that allowed students to work on individually designed programs. Teacher involvement in developing materials continues, though recent years have seen a decline in the number of schools adopting the individualized way of working.

3. Baldino (1998) proposes a solution to the mismatch in the mathematics classroom between discourse (which claims to value learning) and action (directed toward gaining credit) that leads to what he terms "cynical consciousness." He suggests that hard work (always a hidden criterion for success) should be made an explicit criterion. Indeed, he has gone so far as to suggest that it should be the only criterion for awarding credit (personal communication). Although this might be a possible approach for individual teachers in education systems that allow them substantial autonomy in deciding how to assess their students, it is not a practical proposition for those teachers who are themselves subject to surveillance and evaluation.

4. General Certificate of Secondary Education is an examination taken by nearly all students in the United Kingdom at the age of 16+ years.

REFERENCES

Anderson, J. (1989). Sex-related differences on objective tests among undergraduates. *Educational Studies in Mathematics, 20*, 165–177.

Baldino, R. R. (1998). School and surplus-value: Contribution from a third-world country. In P. Gates (Ed.), *Proceedings of the First International Mathematics Education and Society Conference* (pp. 74–81). Nottingham, UK: Centre for the Study of Mathematics Education, Nottingham University.

Bernstein, B. (1996). *Pedagogy, symbolic control and identity: Theory, research, critique.* London: Taylor & Francis.

Björkqvist, O. (1997). Some psychological issues in the assessment of mathematical performance. In E. Pehkonen (Ed.), *Proceedings of the 21st conference of the International Group for the Psychology of Mathematics Education* (Vol. 1, pp. 3–17). Lahti, Finland: University of Helsinki.

Boaler, J. (1993). The role of contexts in the mathematics classroom: Do they make mathematics more "real?" *For the Learning of Mathematics, 13*(2), 12–17.

Boaler, J. (1994). When do girls prefer football to fashion? An analysis of female underachievement in relation to "realistic" mathematics contexts. *British Educational Research Journal, 20*(5), 551–564.

Boaler, J. (1997). *Experiencing school mathematics: Teaching styles, sex and setting.* Buckingham, UK: Open University Press.

Bourdieu, P. (1990). *The logic of practice.* Oxford, UK: Blackwell.

Broadfoot, P. M. (1996). *Education, assessment and society.* Buckingham, UK: Open University Press.

Burkhardt, H. (1988). National testing—liability or asset. *Mathematics Teaching, 122,* 33–35.

Cockcroft, W. H. (1982). *Mathematics counts.* London: HMSO.

Cooper, B. (1998). Assessing National Curriculum mathematics in England: Exploring children's interpretation of Key Stage 2 tests in clinical interviews. *Educational Studies in Mathematics, 35*(1), 19–49.

Cooper, B., & Dunne, M. (1998). Social class, gender, equity and National Curriculum tests in mathematics. In P. Gates (Ed.), *Proceedings of the First International Mathematics Education and Society Conference* (pp. 132–147). Nottingham, UK: Centre for the Study of Mathematics Education, Nottingham University.

Dowling, P. (1998). *The sociology of mathematics education: Mathematical myths/pedagogic texts.* London: Falmer.

Dunne, M. (1998). Pupil entry for Nathional Curriculum Mathematics tests: The public and private life of teacher assessment. In P. Gates (Ed.), *Proceedings of the First International Mathematics Education and Society Conference* (pp. 148–157). Nottingham, UK: Centre for the Study of Mathematics Education, Nottingham University.

Ellerton, N. F., & Clements, M. A. K. (1998). Transforming the international mathematics education agenda. In A. Sierpinska & J. Kilpatrick (Eds.), *Mathematics education as a research domain: A search for identity—an ICMI study* (Vol. 1; pp. 153–175). Dordrecht, Holland: Kluwer.

Galbraith, P. (1993). Paradigms, problems and assessment: some ideological implications. In M. Niss (Ed.), *Investigations into assessment in mathematics education: An ICMI study* (pp. 73–86). Dordrecht, Holland: Kluwer.

Garcia-Cruz, J. A., & Martinón, A. (1997). Actions and invariant schemata in linear generalising problems. In E. Pehkonen (Ed.), *Proceedings of the 21st conference of the International Group for the Psychology of Mathematics Education* (Vol. 2, pp. 289–296). Lahti, Finland: University of Helsinki.

Garcia-Cruz, J. A., & Martinón, A. (1998). Levels of generalisation in linear patterns. In A. Olivier & K. Newstead (Eds.), *Proceedings of the 22nd conference of the International Group for the Psychology of Mathematics Education* (Vol. 2, pp. 329–336). Stellenbosch, South Africa: University of Stellenbosch.

Gill, P. (1993). Using the construct of "levelness" in assessing open work in the National Curriculum. *British Journal of Curriculum and Assessment, 3*(3), 17–18.

Gillborn, D., & Youdell, D. (1999, November 26). Weakest not at the table. *Times Educational Supplement,* 13.

Gipps, C., & Murphy, P. (1994). *A fair test? Assessment, achievement and equity.* Buckingham, UK: Open University Press.

Hunter, M., & Monaghan, J. (1996). Some issues in assessing proceptual understanding. In L. Puig & A. Gutiérrez (Eds.), *Proceedings of the 20th conference of the International Group for the Psychology of Mathematics Education* (Vol. 3, pp. 97–104). Valencia, Spain: University of Valencia.

Jaime, A., & Gutiérrez, A. (1994). A model of test design to assess the van Hiele levels. In J. P. da Ponte & J. F. Matos (Eds.), *Proceedings of the 18th International Conference for the Psychology of Mathematics Education* (Vol. 3, pp. 41–48). Lisbon, Portugal: University of Lisbon.

Karsenty, R., & Vinner, S. (1996). To have or not to have mathematical ability, and what is the question. In L. Puig & A. Gutiérrez (Eds.), *Proceedings of the 20th conference of the International Group for the Psychology of Mathematics Education* (Vol. 3, pp. 177–184). Valencia, Spain: University of Valencia.

Kress, G. (1989). *Linguistic processes in sociocultural practice.* (2nd ed.). Oxford, UK: Oxford University Press.

Lawrie, C. (1998). An alternative assessment: The Gutierrez, Jaime and Fortuny technique. In A. Olivier & K. Newstead (Eds.), *Proceedings of the 22nd conference of the International Group for the Psychology of Mathematics Education* (Vol. 3, pp. 174–182). Stellenbosch, South Africa: University of Stellenbosch.

Leder, G. (Ed.). (1992). *Assessment and learning of mathematics.* Victoria, Australia: Australian Council for Educational Research.

Lerman, S., & Tsatsaroni, A. (1998). Why children fail and what the field of mathematics education can do about it: The role of sociology. In P. Gates (Ed.), *Proceedings of the First International Mathematics Education and Society Conference* (pp. 26–33). Nottingham, UK: Centre for the Study of Mathematics Education, Nottingham University.

Lesh, R., & Lamon, S. J. (Eds.). (1992). *Assessment of authentic performance in school mathematics.* Washington DC: American Association for the Advancement of Science.

Leung, S. S. (1994). On analyzing problem-posing processes: A study of prospective elementary teachers differing in mathematics knowledge. In J. P. da Ponte & J. F. Matos (Eds.), *Proceedings of the 18th International Conference for the Psychology of Mathematics Education* (Vol. 3, pp. 168–175). Lisbon, Portugal: University of Lisbon.

Love, E. (1981). Examinations at 16–plus. *Mathematics Teaching, 96,* 42–46.

Mathematical Association. (1990). *Cultural diversity and bias: Does GCSE mathematics meet the criteria—A report on the 1990 papers.* Leicester, UK: The Mathematical Association.

Morgan, C. (1996). Teacher as examiner: The case of mathematics coursework. *Assessment in Education, 3*(3), 353–375.

Morgan, C. (1998a). Assessment of mathematical behaviour: A social perspective. In P. Gates (Ed.), *Proceedings of the First International Mathematics Education and Society Conference* (pp. 277–283). Nottingham, UK: Centre for the Study of Mathematics Education, Nottingham University.

Morgan, C. (1998b). *Writing mathematically: The discourse of investigation.* London: Falmer.

National Council of Teachers of Mathematics (NCTM). (1995). *Assessment standards for school mathematics.* Reston VA: Author.

Niss, M. (Ed.). (1993a). *Cases of assessment in mathematics education: An ICMI study.* Dordrecht, Holland: Kluwer.

Niss, M. (Ed.). (1993b). *Investigations into assessment in mathematics Education: An ICMI study.* Dordrecht, Holland: Kluwer.

Noss, R. (1990). The National Curriculum and mathematics: A case of divide and rule? In P. Dowling & R. Noss (Eds.), *Mathematics versus the National Curriculum* (pp. 13–32). Basingstoke, UK: Falmer.

Orton, J., & Orton, A. (1996). Making sense of children's patterning. In L. Puig & A. Gutiérrez (Eds.), *Proceedings of the 20th conference of the International Group for the Psychology of Mathematics Education* (Vol. 4, pp. 83–90). Valencia, Spain: University of Valencia.

Rickards, T., & Fisher, D. (1997). Assessment of teacher-student interpersonal behaviour: A seed for change. In E. Pehkonen (Ed.), *Proceedings of the 21st conference of the International Group for the Psychology of Mathematics Education* (Vol. 4, pp. 56–63). Lahti, Finland: University of Helsinki.

Ridgway, J., & Schoenfeld, A. (1994). *Balanced assessment: Designing assessment schemes to promote desirable change in mathematics education.* Paper presented at the EARI Email Conference on Assessment.

Romberg, T. A. (Ed.). (1995). *Reform in school mathematics and authentic assessment.* New York: SUNY Press.

Ruthven, K. (1987). Ability stereotyping in mathematics. *Educational Studies in Mathematics, 18,* 243–253.

Stobart, G., Elwood, J., & Quinlan, M. (1992). Gender bias in examinations: How equal are the opportunities? *British Educational Research Journal, 18*(3), 261–176.

Torrance, H. (Ed.). (1995). *Evaluating authentic assessment.* Buckingham, UK: Open University Press.

Vinner, S. (1997). From intuition to inhibition—mathematics, education and other endangered species. In E. Pehkonen (Ed.), *Proceedings of the 21st conference of the International Group for the Psychology of Mathematics Education* (Vol. 1, pp. 63–78). Lahti, Finland: University of Helsinki.

Walden, R., & Walkerdine, V. (1985). *Girls and mathematics: From primary to secondary schooling.* Bedford Way Papers 24. London: Heinemann.

Watson, A. (1997). Coming to know pupils: A study of informal teacher assessment of mathematics. In E. Pehkonen (Ed.), *Proceedings of the 21st conference of the In-*

ternational Group for the Psychology of Mathematics Education (Vol. 4, pp. 270–277). Lahti, Finland: University of Helsinki.

Watson, A. (1998). What makes a mathematical performance noteworthy in informal teacher assessment? In A. Olivier & K. Newstead (Eds.), *Proceedings of the 22nd conference of the International Group for the Psychology of Mathematics Education* (Vol. 4, pp. 169–176). Stellenbosch, South Africa: University of Stellenbosch.

Watson, A. and Morgan, C. (2000). Teacher-assessment and equity. In J.F. Matos and M. Santos (Eds.), *Proceedings of the Second International Mathematics Education and Society Conference* (pp. 404–414). Lisbon, Portugal: University of Lisbon.

10

Mathematics Reform Through Conservative Modernization? Standards, Markets, and Inequality in Education

Michael W. Apple

THINKING RELATIONALLY

It is unfortunate but true that there is not a long tradition within the mainstream of mathematics education of both critically and rigorously examining the connections between mathematics as an area of study and the larger relations of unequal economic, political, and cultural power. A number of scholars and activists throughout the world have attempted to build such a tradition of critical work in mathematics education (see, for example, Boaler, 1997; Borba & Skovsmose, 1997; Frankenstein, 1990; Mellin-Olsen, 1987; Skovsmose, 1994; Valero, 1999). Although I have written elsewhere about some of the ways in which recent "reforms" in mathematics education may result in increasing inequalities (see, e.g., Apple, 1995, 1999), I want to contribute to the development of such critical work by focussing on the larger context in which mathematics education operates. I want to critically examine the current context of educational "reforms," a context that is structured by neoliberal and neoconservative movements. Without an examination of these movements and the ideological tendencies that characterize them, I do not believe that we will be able to adequately understand the limits and possibilities of a more democratic and critical education. In an essay of this length, I can only outline the tendencies that are currently structuring the terrain on which we operate. But, I want to give a picture of the social movements and ideological mobilizations that unfortunately are gaining even more power in education and the larger society in general now than has been true in the past. As something of an outsider to mathematics education, I hope that this examination of this larger picture provides sufficient detail for you to make the connections to specific movements, debates, and tensions within mathematics education in particular.

RIGHT TURN

In his influential history of curriculum debates, Herbert Kliebard has documented that educational issues have consistently involved major conflicts and compromises among groups with competing visions of "legitimate" knowledge, what counts as "good" teaching and learning, and what is a "just" society (Kliebard, 1986). Although I believe neither that these competing visions have ever had equal holds on the imagination of educators or the general citizenry nor that they have ever had equal power to effect their visions, it is still clear that no analysis of education can be fully serious without placing at its very core a sensitivity to the ongoing struggles that constantly shape the terrain on which the curriculum operates.

Today is no different than in the past. A "new" set of compromises, new alliance, and new power bloc has been formed that has increasing influence in education and all things social. This power bloc combines multiple fractions of capital who are committed to neoliberal marketized solutions to educational problems, neoconservative intellectuals who want a "return" to higher standards and a "common culture," authoritarian populist religious fundamentalists who are deeply worried about secularity and the preservation of their own traditions, and particular fractions of the professionally oriented new middle-class who are committed to the ideology and techniques of accountability, measurement, and "management." Although there are clear tensions and conflicts within this alliance, in general its overall aims are in providing the educational conditions believed necessary both for increasing international competitiveness, profit, and discipline and for returning us to a romanticized past of the "ideal" home, family, and school (Apple, 1996, 2000).

In essence, the new alliance—what I have elsewhere called "conservative modernization" (Apple, 1996)—has integrated education into a wider set of ideological commitments. The objectives in education are the same as those that guide its economic and social welfare goals. They include the dramatic expansion of that eloquent fiction, the free market; the drastic reduction of government responsibility for social needs; the reinforcement of intensely competitive structures of mobility both inside and outside the school; the lowering of people's expectations for economic security; the "disciplining" of culture and the body; and the popularization of what is clearly a form of social Darwinist thinking, as the popularity only a few years ago of *The Bell Curve* (Herrnstein & Murray, 1994), with its claim that people of color, poor people, and women are genetically deficient, so obviously and distressingly indicates.

The seemingly contradictory discourse of competition, markets, and choice on the one hand and accountability, performance objectives, standards, national testing, and national curriculum have created such a din that it is hard to hear anything else. As I have shown in *Cultural Politics and Education* (Apple, 1996), these tendencies oddly reinforce each other and help cement conservative educational positions into our daily lives. Although lamentable, the changes that are occurring present an exceptional opportunity for critical investigations. Here, I am not speaking of merely the accumulation of studies to promote the academic careers of researchers, although the accumulation of serious studies is not unimportant. Rather,

I am suggesting that in a time of radical social and educational change it is crucial to document the processes and effects of the various and sometimes contradictory elements of the forces of conservative modernization and of the ways in which they are mediated, compromised with, accepted, used in different ways by different groups for their own purposes, and/or struggled over in the policies and practices of people's daily educational lives (Ranson, 1995, p. 427). I shall want to give a sense of how this might be happening in current "reforms" such as marketization and national curricula and national testing in this essay.

NEW MARKETS, OLD TRADITIONS

Behind a good deal of the New Right's emerging discursive ensemble is a position that emphasizes "a culturalist construction of the nation as a (threatened) haven for white (Christian) traditions and values" (Gillborn, 1997a, p. 2). This involves the construction of an imagined national past that is at least partly mythologized, and employed to castigate the present. Gary McCulloch argues that the nature of the historical images of schooling has changed. Dominant imagery of education as being "safe, domesticated, and progressive" (that is, as leading toward progress and social/personal improvement) has shifted to become "threatening, estranged, and regressive" (McCulloch, 1997, p. 80). The past is no longer used as a source of stability, but a mark of relative failure, disappointment, and loss. This is seen most vividly in the attacks on the "progressive orthodoxy" that supposedly now reigns supreme in classrooms in many nations.

For example, in England—though much the same is echoed in the United States, Australia, and elsewhere—Michael Jones, the political editor of *The Sunday Times,* recalls the primary school of his day.

> Primary school was a happy time for me. About 40 of us sat at fixed wooden desks with ink wells and moved from them only with grudging permission. Teacher sat in a higher desk in front of us and moved only to the blackboard. She smelled of scent and inspired awe. (Quoted in McCulloch, 1997, p. 78)

The mix of metaphors invoking discipline, scent (visceral and almost "natural"), and awe is fascinating. But he goes on, lamenting the past 30 years of "reform" that transformed primary schools. Speaking of his own children's experience, Jones says:

> My children spent their primary years in a showplace school where they were allowed to wander around at will, develop their real individuality and dodge the 3Rs. It was all for the best, we were assured. But it was not. (Quoted in McCulloch, 1997, p. 78).

For Jones, the "dogmatic orthodoxy" of progressive education "had led directly to educational and social decline." Only the rightist reforms instituted in the 1990s could halt and then reverse this decline (McCulloch, 1997, p. 78). Only then could the imagined past return.

Much the same is being said on my own side of the Atlantic. These sentiments are echoed in the public pronouncements of such figures as William Bennett, E. D. Hirsch Jr., and others, all of whom seem to believe that progressivism is now in the dominant position in educational policy and practice and has destroyed a valued past. All of them believe that only by tightening control over curriculum and teaching (and students, of course), restoring "our" lost traditions, making education more disciplined and competitive as they are certain it was in the past—only then can we have effective schools. These figures are joined by others who have similar criticisms, but instead turn to a different past for a different future. Their past is less that of scent and awe and authority, but one of market "freedom." For them, nothing can be accomplished—even the restoration of awe and authority—without setting the market loose on schools so as to ensure that only "good" ones survive.

We should understand that these policies are radical transformations. If they had come from the other side of the political spectrum, they would have been ridiculed in many ways, given the ideological tendencies in our nations. Further, not only are these policies based on a romanticized pastoral past, these reforms have not been notable for their grounding in research findings. Indeed, when research has been used, it has often either served as a rhetoric of justification for preconceived beliefs about the supposed efficacy of markets or regimes of tight accountability or they have been based—as in the case of Chubb and Moe's much publicized work on the benefits of marketization in education (Chubb & Moe, 1990)—on quite flawed research (see, e.g., Whitty, 1997).

Yet, no matter how radical some of these proposed "reforms" are and no matter how weak the empirical basis of their support, they have now redefined the terrain of debate of all things educational. After years of conservative attacks and mobilizations, it has become clear that "ideas that were once deemed fanciful, unworkable—or just plain extreme" are now increasingly being seen as commonsense (Gillborn, 1997b, p. 357).

Tactically, the reconstruction of commonsense that has been accomplished has proven to be extremely effective. For example, there are clear discursive strategies being employed here, ones that are characterized by "plain speaking" and speaking in a language that "everyone can understand." (I do not wish to be wholly negative about this. The importance of these things is something many "progressive" educators have yet to understand.) These strategies also involve not only presenting one's own position as "commonsense," but tacitly implying that there is something of a conspiracy among one's opponents to deny the truth or to say only that which is "fashionable" (Gillborn, 1997b, p. 353). As Gillborn notes,

> This is a powerful technique. First, it assumes that there are no *genuine* arguments against the chosen position; any opposing views are thereby positioned as false, insincere or self-serving. Second, the technique presents the speaker as someone brave or honest enough to speak the (previously) unspeakable. Hence, the moral high ground is assumed and opponents are further denigrated. (Gillborn, 1997b, p. 353)

It is hard to miss these characteristics in some of the conservative literature such as Herrnstein and Murray's (1994) publicizing of the unthinkable "truth" about genetics and intelligence or E. D. Hirsch's (1996) latest "tough" discussion of the destruction of "serious" schooling by progressive educators.

MARKETS AND PERFORMANCE

Let us take as an example of the ways in which all this operates one element of the conservative restoration—the neoliberal claim that the invisible hand of the market will inexorably lead to better schools. As Roger Dale reminds us, "the market" acts as a metaphor rather than an explicit guide for action. It is not denotative, but connotative. Thus, it must itself be "marketed" to those who will exist in it and live with its effects (Roger Dale, quoted in Menter, Muschamp, Nicholls, Ozga, & Pollard, 1997, p. 27). Markets are marketed, are made legitimate, by a depoliticizing strategy. They are said to be natural and neutral, and governed by effort and merit. And those opposed to them are by definition, hence, also opposed to effort and merit. Markets, as well, are supposedly less subject to political interference and the weight of bureaucratic procedures. Plus, they are grounded in the rational choices of individual actors (Menter et al., 1997, p.27). Thus, markets and the guarantee of rewards for effort and merit are to be coupled together to produce "neutral," yet positive, results. Mechanisms, hence, must be put into place that give evidence of entrepreneurial efficiency and effectiveness. This coupling of markets and mechanisms for the generation of evidence of performance is exactly what has occurred. Whether it works is open to question.

In what is perhaps the most comprehensive critical review of all of the evidence on marketization, Geoff Whitty cautions us not to mistake rhetoric for reality. After examining research from a number of countries, Whitty argues that whereas advocates of marketized "choice" plans assume that competition will enhance the efficiency and responsiveness of schools, as well as give disadvantaged children opportunities that they currently do not have, this may be a false hope (Whitty, 1997, p. 58). These hopes are not now being realized and are unlikely to be realized in the future "in the context of broader policies that do nothing to challenge deeper social and cultural inequalities" (Whitty, 1997, p. 58). As he goes on to say, "Atomized decision-making in a highly stratified society may appear to give everyone equal opportunities, but transforming responsibility for decision-making from the public to the private sphere can actually reduce the scope of collective action to improve the quality of education for all" (p. 58). When this is connected to the fact that, as I shall show shortly, in practice neoliberal policies involving market "solutions" may actually serve to reproduce—not subvert—traditional hierarchies of class and race, this should give us reason to pause (Apple, 1996; Whitty, 1997; Whitty, Edwards, & Gewirtz, 1993; Whitty, Power, & Halpin, 1998).

Thus, rather than taking neoliberal claims at face value, we should want to ask about their hidden effects that are too often invisible in the rhetoric and metaphors of their proponents. Given the limitations of what one can say in an essay of this length, I shall select a few issues that have been given less attention than they deserve, but on which there is now significant research.

The English experience is useful here, especially as Chubb and Moe (1990) rely so heavily on it. In England, the 1993 Education Act documents the state's commitment to marketization. Governing bodies of local educational authority (LEA) schools were mandated to formally consider going "grant maintained" (GM) each year (that is, opting out of the local school system's control, being funded directly by the state, and entering into the competitive market) (Power, Halpin, & Fitz, 1994, p. 27). Thus, the weight of the state stands behind the press toward neoliberal reforms there.[1] Yet, rather than leading to curriculum responsiveness and diversification, the competitive market has not created much that is different from the traditional models so firmly entrenched in schools today (Power et al., 1994, p. 39). Nor has it radically altered the relations of inequality that characterize schooling.

In their own extensive analyses of the effects of marketized reforms "on the ground," Ball and his colleagues point to some of the reasons why we need to be quite cautious here. As they document, in these situations educational principles and values are often compromised such that commercial issues become more important in curriculum design and resource allocation (Ball, Bowe, & Gewirtz, 1994, p. 19). For instance, the coupling of markets with the demand for and publication of performance indicators such as "examination league tables" in England has meant that schools are increasingly looking for ways to attract "motivated" parents with "able" children. In this way, schools are able to enhance their relative position in local systems of competition. This represents a subtle, but crucial shift in emphasis—one that is not openly discussed as often as it should be—from student needs to student performance and from what the school does for the student to what the student does for the school. This is also accompanied too uncomfortably often by a shift of resources away from students who are labeled as having special needs or learning difficulties, with some of these needed resources now being shifted to marketing and public relations. "Special needs" students are expensive (although schools are given additional resources for those students who are formally classified), and they deflate test scores on those all important league tables.[2]

Not only does this make it difficult to "manage public impressions," but it also makes it difficult to attract the "best" and most academically talented teachers (Ball et al, 1994, pp. 17–19). The entire enterprise does, however, establish a new metric and a new set of goals based on a constant striving to win the market game. What this means is of considerable import, not only in terms of its effects on daily school life but in the ways it signifies a transformation of what counts as a good society and a responsible citizen. Let me say something about this generally.

Drawing on Kliebard's significant historical work, I noted earlier that behind all educational proposals are visions of a just society and a good student. The neoliberal reforms I have been discussing construct this in a particular way. Although the defining characteristic of neoliberalism is largely based on the central tenets of classical liberalism, in particular classic economic liberalism, there are crucial differences between classical liberalism and neoliberalism. These differences are absolutely essential in understanding the politics of education and the transformations education is currently undergoing. Mark Olssen clearly details these differences in the following passage. It is worth quoting in its entirety.

> Whereas classical liberalism represents a negative conception of state power in that the individual was to be taken as an object to be freed from the interventions of the state, neo-liberalism has come to represent a positive conception of the state's role in creating the appropriate market by providing the conditions, laws and institutions necessary for its operation. In classical liberalism, the individual is characterized as having an autonomous human nature and can practice freedom. In neo-liberalism the state seeks to create an individual who is an enterprising and competitive entrepreneur. In the classical model the theoretical aim of the state was to limit and minimize its role based on postulates which included universal egoism (the self-interested individual); invisible hand theory which dictated that the interests of the individual were also the interests of the society as a whole; and the political maxim of laissez-faire. In the shift from classical liberalism to neo-liberalism, then, there is a further element added, for such a shift involves a change in subject position from "homo economicus," who naturally behaves out of self-interest and is relatively detached from the state, to "manipulatable man," who is created by the state and who is continually encouraged to be "perpetually responsive." It is not that the conception of the self-interested subject is replaced or done away with by the new ideals of "neo-liberalism," but that in an age of universal welfare, the perceived possibilities of slothful indolence create necessities for new forms of vigilance, surveillance, "performance appraisal" and of forms of control generally. In this model the state has taken it upon itself to keep us all up to the mark. The state will see to it that each one makes a "continual enterprise of ourselves" . . . in what seems to be a process of "governing without governing." (Olssen, 1996, p. 340)

The results of Ball and colleagues' research (Gewirtz, Ball, & Bowe, 1995) document how the state does indeed do this, enhancing that odd combination of marketized individualism and control through constant and comparative public assessment. Widely publicized league tables determine one's relative value in the educational marketplace. Only those schools with good results, irrespective of attainment upon entry, are worthy. And only those students who can "make a continual enterprise of themselves" can keep such schools going in the "correct" direction. Yet, although these issues are important, they fail to fully illuminate some of the other mechanisms through which *differential* effects are produced by neoliberal reforms. Here, class issues come to the fore in ways that Ball and his colleagues (1994) make clear.

Middle-class parents are clearly the most advantaged in this kind of cultural assemblage, and not only as we saw because the principals of schools seek them out. Middle-class parents have become quite skilled, in general, in exploiting market mechanisms in education and in bringing their social, economic, and cultural capital to bear upon them. "Middle class parents are more likely to have the knowledge, skills and contacts to decode and manipulate what are increasingly complex and deregulated systems of choice and recruitment. The more deregulation, the more possibility of informal procedures being employed. The middle class also, on the whole, are more able to move their children around the system" (Ball et al., 1994, p. 19). That class and race intersect and interact in complex ways means that—even though we need to be clear that marketized systems in education often *expressly* have their conscious and unconscious raison d'etre in a fear of "the other" and often express a racialization of educational policy—the differential results will "naturally" be decidedly raced as well as classed.[3]

Economic and social capital can be converted into cultural capital in various ways. In marketized plans, more affluent parents often have more flexible hours and can visit multiple schools. They have cars—often more than one—and can *afford* to drive their children across town to attend a "better" school. They can also fund the hidden cultural resources such as camps and after-school programs (dance, music, computer classes, etc.) that give their children an "ease," a "style," that seems "natural" and acts as a set of cultural resources. Their previous stock of social capital—who they know, their "comfort" in social encounters with educational officials—is an unseen but powerful storehouse of resources. Thus, more affluent parents are more likely to have the informal knowledge and skill—what Bourdieu would call the habitus (Bourdieu, 1984)—to be able to decode and use marketized forms to their own benefit. This sense of what might be called "confidence"—which is itself the result of past choices that tacitly but no less powerfully depend on the economic resources to have had the ability to make economic choices—is the unseen capital that underpins their ability to negotiate marketized forms and "work the system" through sets of informal cultural rules (Ball et al., 1994, pp. 20–22).

Of course, it needs to be said that working-class, poor, or immigrant parents are not skill-less in this regard, by any means. (After all, it requires an immense amount of skill, courage, and social and cultural resources to survive under exploitative and depressing material conditions. Thus, collective bonds, informal networks and contacts, and an ability to work the system are developed in quite nuanced, intelligent, and often impressive ways here.) However, the match between the historically grounded habitus expected in schools and in its actors and those of more affluent parents, combined with the material resources available to more affluent parents, usually leads to a successful conversion of economic and social capital into cultural capital (see Bourdieu, 1996). And this is exactly what is happening in England, the United States, and elsewhere (see, e.g., Gewirtz et al., 1995; Lauder & Hughes, 1999).

These empirical findings can be placed in their larger context by employing Pierre Bourdieu's analysis of the relative weight given to cultural capital as part of mobility strategies today (Bourdieu, 1996). The rise in importance of cultural capital infiltrates all institutions in such a way that there is a relative movement away from the *direct* reproduction of class privilege (where power is transmitted largely within families through economic property) to *school-mediated* forms of class privilege. Here, "the bequeathal of privilege is simultaneously effectuated and transfigured by the intercession of educational institutions" (Wacquant, 1996, p.

xiii). This is *not* a conspiracy; it is not "conscious" in the ways we normally use that concept. Rather it is the result of a long chain of relatively autonomous connections between differentially accumulated economic, social, and cultural capital operating at the level of daily events as we make our respective ways in the world, including as we saw in the world of school choice.

Thus, while not taking an unyieldingly determinist position, Bourdieu argues that a class habitus tends to reproduce the conditions of its own reproduction "unconsciously." It does this by producing a relatively coherent and systematically *characteristic* set of seemingly natural and unconscious strategies—in essence, ways of understanding and acting on the world that act as forms of cultural capital that can be and are employed to protect and enhance one's status in a social field of power. He aptly compares this similarity of habitus across class actors to handwriting.

> Just as the acquired disposition we call "handwriting," that is a particular way of forming letters, always produces the same "writing"—that is, graphic lines that despite differences in size, matter, and color related to writing surface (sheet of paper or blackboard) and implement (pencil, pen, or chalk), that is despite differences in vehicles for the action, have an immediately recognizable affinity of style or a family resemblance—the practices of a single agent, or, more broadly, the practices of all agents endowed with similar habitus, owe the affinity of style that makes each a metaphor for the others to the fact that they are the products of the implementation in different fields of the same schemata of perception, thought, and action. (Bourdieu, 1996, p. 273)

This very connection of habitus across fields of power—the ease of bringing one's economic, social, and cultural resources to bear on "markets"—enables a comfort between markets and self that characterizes the middle-class actor here. This constantly *produces* differential effects. These effects are not neutral, no matter what the advocates of neoliberalism suggest. Rather, they are themselves the results of a particular kind of morality. Unlike the conditions of what might best be called "thick morality" where principles of the common good are the ethical basis for adjudicating policies and practices, markets are grounded in aggregative principles. They are constituted out of the sum of individual goods and choices. "Founded on individual and property rights that enable citizens to address problems of interdependence via exchange," they offer a prime example of "thin morality" by generating both hierarchy and division based on competitive individualism (Ball et al., 1994, p. 24). And in this competition, the general outline of the winners and losers *has* been identified empirically.

NATIONAL CURRICULUM AND NATIONAL TESTING

I showed in the previous section that there are connections between at least two dynamics operating in neoliberal reforms, "free" markets and increased surveillance. This can be seen in the fact that in many contexts, marketization has been accompanied by a set of particular policies for "producers," for those professionals working within education. These policies have been strongly regulatory. As in the case of the linkage between national tests and performance indicators published as league tables, they have been organized around a concern for external supervision, regulation, and external judgement of performance (Menter et al., 1997, p. 8). This concern for external supervision and regulation is not only connected with a strong mistrust of "producers" (e.g., teachers) and to the need for ensuring that people continually make enterprises out of themselves. It is also clearly linked both to the neoconservative sense of a need to "return" to a lost past of high standards, discipline, awe, and "real" knowledge and to the professional middle class's own ability to carve out a sphere of authority within the state for its own commitment to management techniques and efficiency.

There has been a shift in the relationship between the state and "professionals." In essence, the move toward a small strong state that is increasingly guided by market needs seems inevitably to bring with it reduced professional power and status (Menter et al., 1997, p. 57). Managerialism takes center stage here.

Managerialism is largely charged with "bringing about the cultural transformation that shifts professional identities in order to make them more responsive to client demand and external judgement" (Menter et al., 1997, p. 9). It aims to justify and to have people internalize fundamental alterations in professional practices. It both harnesses energy and discourages dissent (Menter et al., 1997, p. 9).

There is no necessary contradiction between a general set of marketizing and deregulating interests and processes, such as voucher and choice plans, and a set of enhanced regulatory processes, such as plans for national curricula and national testing. "The regulatory form permits the state to maintain 'steerage' over the aims and processes of education from within the market mechanism" (Menter et al., 1997, p. 24). Such steerage has often been vested in such things as national standards, national curricula, and national testing. Forms of all of these are being pushed for in the United States currently and are the subject of considerable controversy, some of which cuts across ideological lines and shows some of the tensions within the different elements contained under the umbrella of the conservative restoration.

I have argued elsewhere that national curriculum and especially national testing programs are paradoxically the first and most essential steps toward increased marketization. They actually provide the mechanisms for comparative data that "consumers" need to make markets work as markets (Apple, 1996). Without these mechanisms, there is no comparative base of information for "choice." Yet, we do not have to argue about these regulatory forms in a vacuum. Like the neoliberal markets I discussed in the previous section, they too have been instituted in England; and, once again, there is important research available that can and must make us duly cautious in going down this path.

One might want to claim that a set of national standards, national curricula, and national tests would provide the conditions for "thick morality." After all, such regulatory reforms are supposedly based on shared values and common sentiments that also create social spaces in which common issues of concern can be debated and made subject to moral interrogation (Ball et al., 1994, p. 23). Yet, what counts as the "common," and how and by whom it is actually determined, is rather more thin than thick.

It is the case that whereas the national curriculum now so solidly in place in England and Wales is clearly prescriptive, it has not always proven to be the kind of straitjacket it has often been made out to be. As a number of researchers have documented, it is not only possible that policies and legislative mandates are interpreted and adapted, but it seems inevitable. Thus, the national curriculum is "not so much being 'implemented' in schools as being 'recreated,' not so much 'reproduced,' as 'produced'" (Power et al., 1994, p. 38).

In general, it is nearly a truism that there is no simplistic linear model of policy formation, distribution, and implementation. There are always complex mediations at each level of the process. There is a complex politics that goes on within each group and between these groups and external forces in the formulation of policy, in its being written up as a legislative mandate, in its distribution, and in its reception at the level of practice (Ranson, 1995, p. 436). Thus, the state may legislate changes in curriculum, evaluation, or policy (which is itself produced through conflict, compromise, and political maneuvering), but policy writers and curriculum writers may be unable to control the meanings and implementations of their texts. All texts are "leaky" documents. They are subject to "recontextualization" at every stage of the process (Ranson, 1995, p. 436).

However, this general principle may be just a bit too romantic. None of this occurs on a level playing field. As with market plans, there are very real differences in power in one's ability to influence, mediate, transform, or reject a policy or a regulatory process. Granted, it is important to recognize that a "state control model"—with its assumption of top-down linearity—is much too simplistic and that the possibility of human agency and influence is always there. However, having said this, this should not imply that such agency and influence will be powerful (Ranson, 1995, p. 437).

The case of national curriculum and national testing in England and Wales documents the tensions in these two accounts. It was the case that the national curriculum that was first legislated and then imposed there was indeed struggled over. It was originally too detailed and too specific, and, hence, was subject to major transformations at the national, community, school, and then classroom levels. However, even though the national curriculum was subject to conflict, mediation, and some transformation of its content, organization, and its invasive and immensely time-consuming forms of evaluation, its utter power is demonstrated in its radical reconfiguration of the very process of knowledge selection, organization, and assessment. It changed the entire terrain of education radically. Its subject divisions "provide more constraint than scope for discretion." The accompanying national curriculum tests that have been mandated cement these constraints into the institution. "The imposition of national testing locks the national curriculum in place as the dominant framework of teachers' work whatever opportunities teachers may take to evade or reshape it" (Richard Hatcher and Barry Troyna quoted in Ranson, 1995, p. 438).

Thus, it is not sufficient to state that the world of education is complex and has multiple influences. The purpose of any serious analysis is to go beyond such overly broad conclusions. Rather, we need to "discriminate degrees of influence in the world," to weigh the relative efficacy of the factors involved. Hence, although it is clear that while the national curriculum and national tests that now exist in England and Wales have come about because of a complex interplay of forces and influences, it is equally clear that "state control has the upper hand" (Ranson, 1995, p. 438).

The national curricula and national tests *did* generate conflict about issues. They did partly lead to the creation of social spaces for moral questions to be asked. (Of course, these moral questions had been asked all along by dispossessed groups.) Thus, it was clear to many people that the creation of mandatory and reductive tests that emphasized memory and decontextualized abstraction pulled the national curriculum in a particular direction—that of encouraging a selective educational market in which elite students and elite schools with a wide range of resources would be well (if narrowly) served (O'Hear, 1994, p. 66). Diverse groups of people argued that such reductive, detailed, and simplistic paper and pencil tests "had the potential to do enormous damage," a situation that was made even worse because the tests were so onerous in terms of time and record keeping (O'Hear, 1994, pp. 55–56). Teachers had a good deal of support when as a group they decided to boycott the administration of the test in a remarkable act of public protest. This also led to serious questioning of the arbitrary, inflexible, and overly prescriptive national curriculum. Although the curriculum is still inherently problematic and the assessment system still contains numerous dangerous and onerous elements, organized activity against them did have an impact (O'Hear, 1994, pp. 56–57).

Yet, unfortunately, the story does not end there. By the mid-1990s, even with the government's partial retreat on such regulatory forms as its program of constant and reductive testing, it had become clearer by the year that the development of testing and the specification of content had been "hijacked" by those who were ideologically committed to traditional pedagogies and to the idea of more rigorous selection (O'Hear, 1994, p. 68). The residual effects are both material and ideological. They include a continuing emphasis on trying to provide the "rigor [that is] missing in the practice of most teachers . . . judging progress solely by what is testable in tests of this kind" and the development of a "very hostile view of the accountability of teachers" that was seen as "part of a wider thrust of policy to take away professional control of public services and establish so called consumer control through a market structure" (O'Hear, 1994, pp. 65–66).

The authors of an extremely thorough review of recent assessment programs instituted in England and Wales provide a summary of what has happened. Gipps and Murphy argue that it has become increasingly obvious that the national assessment program attached to the national curriculum is more and more dominated by traditional models of testing and the assumptions about teaching and learning that lie behind them. At the same time, equity issues are becoming much less visible (Gipps & Murphy, 1994, p. 209). In the calculus of values now in place in the regulatory state, efficiency, speed, and cost control replace more substantive concerns about social and educational justice. The pressure to get tests in place rapidly has meant that "the speed of test development is so great, and the curriculum and assessment changes so regular, that [there is] little time to carry out detailed analyses and trialing to ensure that the tests are as fair as possible to all groups" (Gipps & Murphy, 1994, p. 209). The conditions for "thin morality"—in which the competitive individual of the market dominates and social justice will somehow take care of itself—are reproduced here. The combination of the neoliberal market and the regulatory state, then, does indeed "work." However, it works in ways in which the metaphors of free market, merit, and effort hide the differential reality that is produced.

Basil Bernstein's discussion of the general principles by which knowledge and policies ("texts") move from one arena to another is useful in understanding this. As Bernstein reminds us (and as Lerman discusses in this volume), when talking about educational change there are three fields with which we must be concerned. Each field has its own rules of access, regulation, privilege, and special interests: (1) the field of "production" where new knowledge is constructed; (2) the field of "reproduction" where pedagogy and curriculum are actually enacted in schools; and, between these other two, (3) the "recontextualizing" field where discourses from the field of production are appropriated and then transformed into pedagogical discourse and recommendations (Bernstein, 1990, 1996). This appropriation and recontextualization of knowledge for educational purposes is itself governed by two sets of principles. The first—de-location—implies that there is always a *selective* appropriation of knowledge and discourse from the field of production. The second—re-location—points to the fact that when knowledge and discourse from the field of production is pulled within the recontextualizing field, it is subject to ideological transformations as a result of the various specialized or political interests whose conflicts structure the recontextualizing field (Evans & Penney, 1995).

A good example of this, one that confirms Gipps and Murphy's analysis of the dynamics of national curricula and national testing during their more recent iterations, is found in the process by which the content and organization of the mandated national curriculum in physical education was struggled over and ultimately formed in England. In this instance, a working group of academics both within and outside the field of physical education, headmasters of private and state-supported schools, well known athletes, and business leaders (but *no* teachers) was formed.

The original curriculum policies that arose from the groups were relatively mixed educationally and ideologically, taking account of the field of production of knowledge within physical education. That is, they contained both progressive elements and elements of the conservative restoration, as well as academic perspectives within the specialized fields from the university. However, as these made their way from report to recommendations and then from recommendations to action, they steadily came closer to restorational principles. An emphasis on efficiency, basic skills, and performance testing; on the social control of the body; and on competitive norms ultimately won out. Like the middle class capturing of the market discussed earlier, this too was not a conspiracy. Rather, it was the result of a process of "overdetermination." That is, it was not owing to an imposition of these norms, but to a combination of interests in the recontextualizing field—an economic context in which public spending was under severe scrutiny and cost savings had to be sought everywhere; government officials who were opposed to "frills" and consistently intervened to institute only a selection of the recommendations (conservative ones that did *not* come from "professional academics" preferably); ideological attacks on critical, progressive, or child-centered approaches to physical education; and a predominant discourse of "being pragmatic." These came together in the recontextualizing field and helped ensure in practice that conservative principles would be reinscribed in policies and mandates, and that critical forms were seen as too ideological, too costly, or too impractical (Evans & Penney, 1995, pp. 41–42). "Standards" were upheld; critical voices were heard, but ultimately to little effect; the norms of competitive performance were made central and employed as regulatory devices. Regulatory devices served to privilege specific groups in much the same way as did markets. Thus goes democracy in education.

CONCLUSION

In this relatively brief essay, I have been rather ambitious. I have raised serious questions about current educational "reform" efforts now underway in a number of nations, in large part because I believe that reforms in mathematics education must not be seen as isolated from larger educational, social, and ideological movements, reforms, and conflicts. I have used research on the English experience(s) to document some of the hidden differential effects of two connected strategies—neoliberal-inspired market proposals and neoliberal-, neoconservative-, and middle-class managerial—inspired regulatory proposals. Taking a key from Herbert Kliebard's powerful historical analyses, I have described how different interests with different educational and social visions compete for dominion in the social field of power surrounding educational policy and practice. In the process, I have documented some of the complexities and imbalances in this field of power. These complexities and imbalances result in "thin" rather than "thick" morality and in the reproduction of both dominant pedagogical and curricular forms and ideologies and the social privileges that accompany them.

Having said this, however, I want to point to a hidden paradox in what I have done. Even though much of my own and others' research recently has been on the conservative restoration, there are dangers in such a focus of which we should be aware. Research on the history, politics, and practices of rightist social and educational movements and "reforms" has enabled us to show the contradictions and unequal effects of such policies and practices. It has enabled the rearticulation of claims to social justice on the basis of solid evidence. This is all to the good. However, in the process, one of the latent effects has been the gradual framing of educational issues largely in terms of the conservative agenda. The very categories themselves—markets, choice, national curricula, national testing, standards—bring the debate onto the terrain established by neoliberals and neoconservatives. The analysis of "what is" has led to a neglect of "what might be." Thus, there has been a withering of substantive, large-scale discussions of feasible alternatives to neoliberal and neoconservative visions, policies, and practices, especially alternatives that would move well beyond such conservative positions (Seddon, 1997, pp. 165–166).

Because of this, at least part of our task may be politically and conceptually complex, but it can be said simply. In the long term, we need to "develop a political project that is both local yet generalizable, systematic without making Eurocentric, masculinist claims to essential and universal truths about human subjects" (Luke, 1995, pp. vi-vii). Another part of our task, though, must be and is more proximate, more appropriately educational. Defensible, articulate, and fully fleshed out alternative progressive policies and practices in curriculum, teaching, and evaluation need to be developed and made widely available.

Although, in *Democratic Schools,* James Beane and I have brought together a number of such examples for a larger educational audience (Apple & Beane, 1995, 1999), so much more needs to done. Of course, we are not starting anew in any of this. The history of democratically and critically oriented educational reforms in mathematics education and elsewhere in all of our nations is filled with examples, with resources of hope. Sometimes we can go forward by looking back, by recapturing what the criticisms of past iterations of current rhetorical "reforms" have been, and by rediscovering a valued set of traditions of educational criticism and educational action that have always tried to keep the vast river of democracy flowing. We will not find all of the answers by looking at our past, but we will reconnect with and stand on the shoulders of educators whose lives were spent in struggle against some of the very same ideological forces we face today.

Although crucial, it is then not enough, as I have done in this essay, to deconstruct the policies of conservative modernization in education. Neoliberals and neoconservatives have shown how important changes in commonsense are in the struggle for education. It is our task to collectively help rebuild it by reestablishing a sense that "thick" morality, and a "thick" democracy, are truly possible today. There is political and practical work that needs to be done. If we do not do it, who will?

NOTES

1. Whether there have been changes in this given the victory by "New Labour" over the Conservatives a number of years ago remains to be seen, although the outlook is not necessarily good in many ways. Certain aspects of neoliberal and neoconservative policies have been accepted by Labour, such as the acceptance of stringent cost controls put in place by the previous Conservative government and an aggressive focus on "raising standards" in association with strict performance indicators. See, for example, Jones (1999) and Gillborn and Youdell (2000).

2. This is a complex situation. Many schools engage in a process of cost-benefit analysis, because extra money does come from the state for such students. Further, because of the increased emphasis in individual schools on getting their students to have more "passes" on national tests, more attention is paid to those students on the borderline between passing and failing. Less attention is given to those students who are predicted to fail. These latter students tend to be poor or students of color, or both. See Gillborn and Youdell (2000).

3. See the discussion of the racial state in Omi and Winant (1994) and the analyses of race and representation in McCarthy and Crichlow (1994).

REFERENCES

Apple, M. W. (1995). Taking power seriously. In W. Secada, E. Fennema, & L. B. Adajian (Eds.), *New directions for equity in mathematics education*. New York: Cambridge University Press.

Apple, M. W. (1996). *Cultural politics and education*. New York: Teachers College Press.

Apple, M. W. (1999). *Power, meaning, and identity*. New York: Peter Lang.

Apple, M. W. (2000). *Official knowledge* (2nd ed.). New York: Routledge

Apple, M. W., & Beane, J. A. (1995). *Democratic schools*. Washington, DC: Association for Supervision and Curriculum Development.

Apple, M. W., & Beane, J. A. (1999). *Democratic schools: Lessons from the chalk face*. Buckingham, UK: Open University Press.

Ball, S., Bowe, R., & Gewirtz, S. (1994). Market forces and parental choice. In S. Tomlinson (Ed.), *Educational reform and its consequences* (pp. 13–25). London: IPPR/Rivers Oram Press.

Bernstein, B. (1990). *The structuring of pedagogic discourse*. New York: Routledge.

Bernstein, B. (1996). *Pedagogy, symbolic control, and identity*. Bristol, PA: Taylor and Francis.

Boaler, J. (1997). *Experiencing school mathematics*. Philadelphia: Open University Press.

Borba, M., & Skovsmose, O. (1997). The ideology of certainty in mathematics education. *For the Learning of Mathematics, 17*(3), 17–23.

Bourdieu, P. (1994). *Distinction*. Cambridge, MA: Harvard University Press.

Bourdieu, P. (1996). *The state nobility*. Stanford, CA: Stanford University Press.

Chubb, J., & Moe, T. (1990). *Politics, markets, and America's schools*. Washington, DC: Brookings Institution.

Evans, J., & Penney, D. (1995). The politics of pedagogy. *Journal of Education Policy, 10*, 27–44.

Frankenstein, M. (1990). Incorporating race, gender, and class issues into a critical mathematical literacy curriculum. *Journal of Negro Education, 59*(3), 336–347.

Gewirtz, S., Ball, S., & Bowe, R. (1995). *Markets, choice and equity in education*. Buckingham, UK: Open University Press.

Gillborn, D. (1997a). *Race, nation, and education*. Unpublished paper, Institute of Education, University of London.

Gillborn, D. (1997b). Racism and reform. *British Educational Research Journal, 23*, 345–360

Gillborn, D., & Youdell, D. (2000). *Rationing education*. Philadelphia: Open University Press.

Gipps, C., & Murphy, P. (1994). *A fair test?* Philadelphia: Open University Press.

Herrnstein, R., & Murray, C. (1994). *The bell curve.* New York: Free Press.

Hirsch, E. D. Jr. (1996). *The schools we want and why we don't have them.* New York: Doubleday.

Jones, K. (1999). In the shadow of the centre-left: Post-conservative politics and rethinking educational change. *Discourse, 20,* 235–247.

Kliebard, H. (1986). *The struggle for the American curriculum.* New York: Routledge.

Lauder, H., & Hughes, D. (1999). *Trading in places.* Buckingham, UK: Open University Press.

Luke, A. (1995). Series editor's introduction. In J. L. Lemke, *Textual politics* (pp. iv–ix). Bristol, PA: Taylor and Francis.

McCarthy, C., & Crichlow, W. (1994). *Race, identity, and representation in education.* New York: Routledge.

McCulloch, G. (1997). Privatizing the past? *British Journal of Educational Studies, 45,* 69–82.

Mellin-Olsen, S. (1987). *The politics of mathematics education* (Vol. 4). Dordrecht, Holland: Kluwer.

Menter, I., Muschamp, P., Nicholls, P., Ozga, J., & Pollard, A. (1997). *Work and identity in the primary school.* Philadelphia: Open University Press.

O'Hear, P. (1994). An alternative national curriculum. In S. Tomlinson (Ed.), *Educational reform and its consequences* (pp. 52–72). London: IPPR/Rivers Oram Press.

Olssen, M. (1996). In defence of the welfare state and publicly provided education. *Journal of Education Policy, 11,* 337–362.

Omi, M., & Winant, H. (1994). *Racial formation in the United States.* New York: Routledge.

Power, S., Halpin, D., & Fitz, J. (1994). Underpinning choice and diversity? In S. Tomlinson (Ed.), *Educational reform and its consequences* (pp. 26–40). London: IPPR/Rivers Oram Press.

Ranson, S. (1995). Theorizing educational policy. *Journal of Education Policy, 10,* 427–448.

Seddon, T. (1997). Markets and the English. *British Journal of Sociology of Education, 18,* 165–185.

Skovsmose, O. (1994). *Towards a philosophy of critical mathematics education.* Dordrecht, Holland: Kluwer.

Valero, P. (1999). Deliberative mathematics education for social democratization in Latin America. *Zentralblatt fur Didaktik der Mathematik, 98*(6), 20–26.

Wacquant, L. (1996). Foreword. In P. Bourdieu, *The state nobility* (pp. ix–xxii). Stanford, CA: Stanford University Press.

Whitty, G. (1997). Creating quasi-markets in education. In M. W. Apple (Ed.), *Review of research in education* (Vol. 22) pp. 3–47). Washington, DC: American Educational Research Association.

Whitty, G., Edwards, T., & Gewirtz, S. (1993). *Specialization and choice in urban education.* New York: Routledge.

Whitty, G., Power, S., & Halpin, D. (1998). *Devolution and choice in education.* Buckingham, UK: Open University Press.

Author Index

Subject Index

About the Editors and Contributors

MICHAEL W. APPLE is the John Bascom Professor of Curriculum and Instruction and Educational Policy Studies at the University of Wisconsin, Madison. A former elementary and secondary school teacher and past-president of a teachers union, he has worked with educators, governments, unions, and dissident groups throughout the world to democratize educational research, policy, and practice. Among his many books are *Ideology and Curriculum, Education and Power, Teachers and Texts, Official Knowledge, Cultural Politics and Education, and Power, Meaning and Identity.*

DEBORAH LOEWENBERG BALL is Arthur F. Thurnau Professor of Mathematics Education and Teacher Education at the University of Michigan. Ball's work focuses on studies of instruction and of the processes of learning to teach. She also investigates efforts to improve teaching through policy, reform initiatives, and teacher education. Ball's publications include articles on teacher learning and teacher education; the role of subject matter knowledge in teaching and learning to teach; endemic challenges of teaching; and the relations of policy and practice in instructional improvement.

MARY BARNES, formerly Director of the Mathematics Learning Centre at the University of Sydney, is now a free-lance mathematics education consultant and a doctoral student at the University of Melbourne. Her interests in mathematics education include gender equity, calculus teaching, assessment, and applications of technology. She is the author of *Investigating change*: *An introduction to calculus for Australian schools* (a series of units on calculus for senior secondary students, designed to be gender-inclusive) and joint author of *Girls count in maths and science*. Her current research is on students' experiences of collaborative learning in secondary classrooms. This includes looking at power relationships within collaborative groups, and the social construction of both gender and mathematical competence.

HYMAN BASS is the Roger Lyndon Collegiate Professor of Mathematics and Professor of Mathematics Education at the University of Michigan. His mathematical research publications cover broad areas of algebra, with connections to geometry, topology and number theory. During the past four years he has been collaborating with Deborah Ball and her research group at the University of Michigan on the nature of mathematical knowledge required for teaching. He is interested in the challenge of building bridges between diverse professional communities and stakeholders involved in mathematics education, both here and abroad.

JO BOALER is an assistant professor of mathematics education at Stanford University. She is a former secondary school teacher of mathematics. She taught in diverse, inner London comprehensive schools, across the 11-18 age range. She has also worked as the deputy director of a national assessment project in the UK, researching and developing assessments for students across the country. She is author of the book *Experiencing School Mathematics*, which was published by the Open University Press in 1997 and won the Outstanding Book of the Year award in education in Britain. Her research interests include mathematics teaching approaches, assessment and equity. She is currently the PI of a NSF project investigating the relationship between mathematics teaching, learning and curriculum approach.

LEONE BURTON is Emeritus Professor of Education (Mathematics and Science) at The University of Birmingham, Visiting Professor of Mathematics Education, King's College, London, 2000-2003, and Jubilee Professor in the Department of Mathematics, Chalmers University, Gothenburg, Sweden for the year 2000. Her most recent work has been on the epistemologies of practicing research mathematicians and their implications for teaching and learning mathematics. This work has also involved her in researching the learning experiences of university mathematics undergraduates and students specializing in mathematics for their university entrance examinations. Her publications include a number of edited collections on the theme of gender and mathematics, books on the use of problem-solving in teaching and learning mathematics, and many journal articles on assessment. Her last publication was an edited collection, published in 1999 by Falmer Press, called *Learning Mathematics: from Hierarchies to Networks*.

PAUL COBB is a Professor of Mathematics Education at Vanderbilt University. His overarching research interests focus on students' mathematical learning as it occurs in the social context of the classroom. To this end, he conducts classroom design experiments in the course of which he investigates innovative instructional approaches in inquiry-based classrooms. Classroom-based work of this nature brings together issues concerning students' learning, teachers' activity, classroom interactions, and the nature of instructional activities. Further, the mathematics classroom can be viewed as the site in which issues of cultural diversity and equity play out in face-to-face interaction. Cobb also views the classrooms in which he works as settings in which to address these issues.

JAMES G. GREENO is the Margaret Jacks Professor of Education at Stanford University. His research examines processes of learning, reasoning, and understanding, especially involving mathematical concepts. In his current research, he is working toward a theory that treats conceptual understanding as an aspect of discourse and treats conceptual learning as change in discourse that occurs as students participate in activities of inquiry. He collaborated with Shelley Goldman, Ray McDermott, Jennifer Knudsen and others in the Middle-school Mathematics through Applications Project, which developed and studied a 6-8 grade mathematics curriculum centered on students' participation in design activities. Previously, he developed cognitive computer-simulation models of knowledge and strategies used by students in solving textbook problems in elementary-school arithmetic and secondary-school geometry. He hopes to be able to analyze learning, reasoning, and understanding in a way that represents both its cognitive-informational aspects and its social-interactional aspects coherently.

STEPHEN LERMAN taught mathematics in secondary schools in England and in Israel before becoming a researcher, then lecturer in mathematics education at the Institute of Education, University of London. He is now Professor of Mathematics Education at South Bank University in London and Head of Educational Research. He was President of the International Group for the Psychology of Mathematics Education from 1995 to 1998 and Chair of the British Society for Research into Learning Mathematics from 1994 to 1996. His research interests include: philosophy of mathematics; teacher education; equity issues; learning theories; and socio-cultural analyses of mathematics teaching and learning.

CANDIA MORGAN is a senior lecturer in mathematics education at the Institute for Education, University of London. She spent a number of years teaching mathematics and acting as an advisory teacher for mathematics in London secondary schools and, before moving to the Institute of Education, taught mathematics and mathematics education at South Bank University. Her current research interests include language in mathematics and mathematics education, teacher assessment, and the use of critical discourse analytic approaches in the study of mathematics education.

REED STEVENS is currently an Assistant Professor of Cognition & Technology at the University of Washington in Seattle. He earned his Ph.D. from the Cognition and Development program in the Graduate School of Education at the University of California, Berkeley. He is a former mathematics teacher and has a BA in mathematics from Pomona College. His research and teaching focus on naturalistic studies of cognition and learning across diverse social settings. His research program is broadly comparative and has included studies of classrooms, scientific workplaces, architecture and engineering firms, and science museums. His main interests are the comparative development of mathematical practices in and out of school and the analysis of discourse and interaction as vehicles for learning and teaching. He is currently a co-principal investigator on a NSF funded design experiment that compares student and teacher discourse across the subject matter disciplines of science and history in elementary school.

ROBYN ZEVENBERGEN is a senior lecturer at Griffith University, Australia. She is based at the Gold Coast Campus where she works in the area of mathematics education. She completed her doctoral studies at Deakin University. Most of her work is concentrated in the elementary years of schooling. Her interests are in the area of equity and social justice. She is particularly interested in issues of social class and indigenous education, where she takes a socially critical perspective to understanding the construction of inequity in and through mathematics. Currently she is working on projects related to the language of mathematics; in reform in mathematics pedagogy; and the construction of mathematical identity (among adolescent students).